The Complete Plays of John Galsworthy

VOLUME 1

The Complete Plays of John Galsworthy

VOLUME 1

John Galsworthy

THE COMPLETE PLAYS OF JOHN GALSWORTHY
VOLUME 1

Published in the United States by IndyPublish.com
Boston, Massachusetts

ISBN 1-4043-0087-2 (paperback)

CONTENTS

First Series:

The Silver Box
Joy
Strife

THE SILVER BOX

A COMEDY IN THREE ACTS

PERSONS OF THE PLAY

JOHN BARTHWICK, M.P., a wealthy Liberal
MRS. BARTHWICK, his wife
JACK BARTHWICK, their son
ROPER, their solicitor
MRS. JONES, their charwoman
MARLOW, their manservant
WHEELER, their maidservant
JONES, the stranger within their gates
MRS. SEDDON, a landlady
SNOW, a detective
A POLICE MAGISTRATE
AN UNKNOWN LADY, from beyond
TWO LITTLE GIRLS, homeless
LIVENS, their father
A RELIEVING OFFICER
A MAGISTRATE'S CLERK
AN USHER
POLICEMEN, CLERKS, AND OTHERS

TIME: The present. The action of the first two Acts takes place on Easter Tuesday; the action of the third on Easter Wednesday week.

ACT I

SCENE I

The curtain rises on the BARTHWICK'S dining-room, large, modern, and well furnished; the window curtains drawn. Electric light is burning. On the large round dining-table is set out a tray with whisky, a syphon, and a silver cigarette-box. It is past midnight.

A fumbling is heard outside the door. It is opened suddenly; JACK BARTH-WICK seems to fall into the room. He stands holding by the door knob, staring before him, with a beatific smile. He is in evening dress and opera hat, and carries in his hand a sky-blue velvet lady's reticule. His boyish face is freshly coloured and clean-shaven. An overcoat is hanging on his arm.

JACK. Hello! I've got home all ri——[Defiantly.] Who says I sh 'd never 've opened th' door without 'sistance. [He staggers in, fumbling with the reticule. A lady's handkerchief and purse of crimson silk fall out.] Serve her joll' well right—everything droppin' out. Th' cat. I 've scored her off— I 've got her bag. [He swings the reticule.] Serves her joly' well right. [He takes a cigarette out of the silver box and puts it in his mouth.] Never gave tha' fellow anything! [He hunts through all his pockets and pulls a shilling out; it drops and rolls away. He looks for it.] Beastly shilling! [He looks again.] Base ingratitude! Absolutely nothing. [He laughs.] Mus' tell him I've got absolutely nothing.

[He lurches through the door and down a corridor, and presently returns, followed by JONES, who is advanced in liquor. JONES, about thirty years of age, has hollow cheeks, black circles round his eyes, and rusty clothes: He looks as though he might be unemployed, and enters in a hang-dog manner.]

JACK. Sh! sh! sh! Don't you make a noise, whatever you do. Shu' the door, an' have a drink. [Very solemnly.] You helped me to open the door—I 've got nothin, for you. This is my house. My father's name's Barthwick; he's Member of Parliament—Liberal Member of Parliament: I've told you that before. Have a drink! [He pours out whisky and drinks it up.] I'm not drunk [Subsiding on a sofa.] Tha's all right. Wha's your name? My name's Barthwick, so's my father's; I'm a Liberal too—wha're you?

JONES. [In a thick, sardonic voice.] I'm a bloomin' Conservative. My name's Jones! My wife works 'ere; she's the char; she works 'ere.

JACK. Jones? [He laughs.] There's 'nother Jones at College with me. I'm not a Socialist myself; I'm a Liberal—there's ve—lill difference, because of the principles of the Lib—Liberal Party. We're all equal before the law—tha's rot, tha's silly. [Laughs.] Wha' was I about to say? Give me some whisky.

[JONES gives him the whisky he desires, together with a squirt of syphon.]

Wha' I was goin' tell you was—I 've had a row with her. [He waves the reticule.] Have a drink, Jonessh 'd never have got in without you—tha 's why I 'm giving you a drink. Don' care who knows I've scored her off. Th' cat! [He throws his feet up on the sofa.] Don' you make a noise, whatever you do. You pour out a drink—you make yourself good long, long drink—you take cigarette—you take anything you like. Sh'd never have got in without you. [Closing his eyes.] You're a Tory—you're a Tory Socialist. I'm Liberal myself—have a drink—I 'm an excel'nt chap.

[His head drops back. He, smiling, falls asleep, and JONES stands looking at him; then, snatching up JACK's glass, he drinks it off. He picks the reticule from off JACK'S shirt-front, holds it to the light, and smells at it.]

JONES. Been on the tiles and brought 'ome some of yer cat's fur. [He stuffs it into JACK's breast pocket.]

JACK. [Murmuring.] I 've scored you off! You cat!

[JONES looks around him furtively; he pours out whisky and drinks it. From the silver box he takes a cigarette, puffs at it, and drinks more whisky. There is no sobriety left in him.]

JONES.   Fat lot o' things they've got 'ere! [He sees the crimson purse lying on
        the floor.] More cat's fur. Puss, puss! [He fingers it, drops it on the tray,
        and looks at JACK.] Calf! Fat calf! [He sees his own presentment in a
        mirror. Lifting his hands, with fingers spread, he stares at it; then looks
        again at JACK, clenching his fist as if to batter in his sleeping, smiling
        face. Suddenly he tilts the rest o f the whisky into the glass and drinks it.
        With cunning glee he takes the silver box and purse and pockets them.]
        I 'll score you off too, that 's wot I 'll do!

[He gives a little snarling laugh and lurches to the door. His shoulder rubs against the switch; the light goes out. There is a sound as of a closing outer door.]

The curtain falls.

The curtain rises again at once.

SCENE II

In the BARTHWICK'S dining-room. JACK is still asleep; the morning light is coming through the curtains. The time is half-past eight. WHEELER, brisk person enters with a dust-pan, and MRS. JONES more slowly with a scuttle.

WHEELER.   [Drawing the curtains.] That precious husband of yours was round
        for you after you'd gone yesterday, Mrs. Jones. Wanted your money
        for drink, I suppose. He hangs about the corner here half the time.
        I saw him outside the "Goat and Bells" when I went to the post last
        night. If I were you I would n't live with him. I would n't live with
        a man that raised his hand to me. I wouldn't put up with it. Why
        don't you take your children and leave him? If you put up with 'im
        it'll only make him worse. I never can see why, because a man's
        married you, he should knock you about.

MRS. JONES.   [Slim, dark-eyed, and dark-haired; oval-faced, and with a smooth,
        soft, even voice; her manner patient, her way of talking quite

impersonal; she wears a blue linen dress, and boots with holes.]
It was nearly two last night before he come home, and he wasn't
himself. He made me get up, and he knocked me about; he did-
n't seem to know what he was saying or doing. Of course I would
leave him, but I'm really afraid of what he'd do to me. He 's such
a violent man when he's not himself.

WHEELER. Why don't you get him locked up? You'll never have any peace until
you get him locked up. If I were you I'd go to the police court
tomorrow. That's what I would do.

MRS. JONES. Of course I ought to go, because he does treat me so badly when
he's not himself. But you see, Bettina, he has a very hard time—
he 's been out of work two months, and it preys upon his mind.
When he's in work he behaves himself much better. It's when he's
out of work that he's so violent.

WHEELER. Well, if you won't take any steps you 'll never get rid of him.

MRS. JONES. Of course it's very wearing to me; I don't get my sleep at nights.
And it 's not as if I were getting help from him, because I have to
do for the children and all of us. And he throws such dreadful
things up at me, talks of my having men to follow me about.
Such a thing never happens; no man ever speaks to me. And of
course, it's just the other way. It's what he does that's wrong and
makes me so unhappy. And then he 's always threatenin' to cut
my throat if I leave him. It's all the drink, and things preying on
his mind; he 's not a bad man really. Sometimes he'll speak quite
kind to me, but I've stood so much from him, I don't feel it in me
to speak kind back, but just keep myself to myself. And he's all
right with the children too, except when he's not himself.

WHEELER. You mean when he's drunk, the beauty.

MRS. JONES. Yes. [Without change of voice] There's the young gentleman
asleep on the sofa.

[They both look silently at Jack.]

MRS. JONES. [At last, in her soft voice.] He does n't look quite himself.

WHEELER. He's a young limb, that's what he is. It 's my belief he was tipsy last night, like your husband. It 's another kind of bein' out of work that sets him to drink. I 'll go and tell Marlow. This is his job.

[She goes.]

[Mrs. Jones, upon her knees, begins a gentle sweeping.]

JACK. [Waking.] Who's there? What is it?

MRS. JONES. It's me, sir, Mrs. Jones.

JACK. [Sitting up and looking round.] Where is it—what—what time is it?

MRS. JONES. It's getting on for nine o'clock, sir.

JACK. For nine! Why—what! [Rising, and loosening his tongue; putting hands to his head, and staring hard at Mrs. Jones.] Look here, you, Mrs.—— Mrs. Jones—don't you say you caught me asleep here.

MRS. JONES. No, sir, of course I won't sir.

JACK. It's quite an accident; I don't know how it happened. I must have forgotten to go to bed. It's a queer thing. I 've got a most beastly headache. Mind you don't say anything, Mrs. Jones.

[Goes out and passes MARLOW in the doorway. MARLOW is young and quiet; he is cleanshaven, and his hair is brushed high from his forehead in a coxcomb. Incidentally a butler, he is first a man. He looks at MRS. JONES, and smiles a private smile.]

MARLOW. Not the first time, and won't be the last. Looked a bit dicky, eh, Mrs. Jones?

MRS. JONES. He did n't look quite himself. Of course I did n't take notice.

MARLOW. You're used to them. How's your old man?

MRS. JONES. [Softly as throughout.] Well, he was very bad last night; he did n't seem to know what he was about. He was very late, and he was most abusive. But now, of course, he's asleep.

MARLOW. That's his way of finding a job, eh?

MRS. JONES. As a rule, Mr. Marlow, he goes out early every morning looking for work, and sometimes he comes in fit to drop—and of course I can't say he does n't try to get it, because he does. Trade's very bad. [She stands quite still, her fan and brush before her, at the beginning and the end of long vistas of experience, traversing them with her impersonal eye.] But he's not a good husband to me—last night he hit me, and he was so dreadfully abusive.

MARLOW. Bank 'oliday, eh! He 's too fond of the "Goat and Bells," that's what's the matter with him. I see him at the corner late every night. He hangs about.

MRS. JONES. He gets to feeling very low walking about all day after work, and being refused so often, and then when he gets a drop in him it goes to his head. But he shouldn't treat his wife as he treats me. Sometimes I 've had to go and walk about at night, when he wouldn't let me stay in the room; but he's sorry for it afterwards. And he hangs about after me, he waits for me in the street; and I don't think he ought to, because I 've always been a good wife to him. And I tell him Mrs. Barthwick wouldn't like him coming about the place. But that only makes him angry, and he says dreadful things about the gentry. Of course it was through me that he first lost his place, through his not treating me right; and that's made him bitter against the gentry. He had a very good place as groom in the country; but it made such a stir, because of course he did n't treat me right.

MARLOW. Got the sack?

MRS. JONES. Yes; his employer said he couldn't keep him, because there was a great deal of talk; and he said it was such a bad example. But it's very important for me to keep my work here; I have the three children, and I don't want him to come about after me in the streets, and make a disturbance as he sometimes does.

MARLOW. [Holding up the empty decanter.] Not a drain! Next time he hits you get a witness and go down to the court——

MRS. JONES. Yes, I think I 've made up my mind. I think I ought to.

MARLOW. That's right. Where's the ciga——?

[He searches for the silver box; he looks at MRS. JONES, who is sweeping on her hands and knees; he checks himself and stands reflecting. From the tray he picks two half-smoked cigarettes, and reads the name on them.]

Nestor—where the deuce——?

[With a meditative air he looks again at MRS. JONES, and, taking up JACK'S overcoat, he searches in the pockets. WHEELER, with a tray of breakfast things, comes in.]

MARLOW. [Aside to WHEELER.] Have you seen the cigarette-box?

WHEELER. No.

MARLOW. Well, it's gone. I put it on the tray last night. And he's been smoking. [Showing her the ends of cigarettes.] It's not in these pockets. He can't have taken it upstairs this morning! Have a good look in his room when he comes down. Who's been in here?

WHEELER. Only me and Mrs. Jones.

MRS. JONES. I 've finished here; shall I do the drawing-room now?

WHEELER. [Looking at her doubtfully.] Have you seen——Better do the boudwower first.

[MRS. JONES goes out with pan and brush. MARLOW and WHEELER look each other in the face.]

MARLOW. It'll turn up.

WHEELER. [Hesitating.] You don't think she—— [Nodding at the door.]

MARLOW. [Stoutly.] I don't——I never believes anything of anybody.

WHEELER. But the master'll have to be told.

MARLOW. You wait a bit, and see if it don't turn up. Suspicion's no business of ours. I set my mind against it.

The curtain falls.

The curtain rises again at once.

SCENE III

BARTHWICK and MRS. BARTHWICK are seated at the breakfast table. He is a man between fifty and sixty; quietly important, with a bald forehead, and pince-nez, and the "Times" in his hand. She is a lady of nearly fifty, well dressed, with greyish hair, good features, and a decided manner. They face each other.

BARTHWICK. [From behind his paper.] The Labour man has got in at the by-election for Barnside, my dear.

MRS. BARTHWICK. Another Labour? I can't think what on earth the country is about.

BARTHWICK. I predicted it. It's not a matter of vast importance.

MRS. BARTHWICK. Not? How can you take it so calmly, John? To me it's simply outrageous. And there you sit, you Liberals, and pretend to encourage these people!

BARTHWICK. [Frowning.] The representation of all parties is necessary for any proper reform, for any proper social policy.

MRS. BARTHWICK. I've no patience with your talk of reform—all that non-sense about social policy. We know perfectly well what it is they want; they want things for themselves. Those Socialists and Labour men are an absolutely selfish set of people. They have no sense of patriotism, like the upper classes; they simply want what we've got.

BARTHWICK. Want what we've got! [He stares into space.] My dear, what are you talking about? [With a contortion.] I 'm no alarmist.

MRS. BARTHWICK. Cream? Quite uneducated men! Wait until they begin to tax our investments. I 'm convinced that when they once get a chance they will tax everything—they 've no feeling for the country. You Liberals and Conservatives, you 're all alike; you don't see an inch before your noses. You've no imagination, not a scrap of imagination between you. You ought to join hands and nip it in the bud.

BARTHWICK. You 're talking nonsense! How is it possible for Liberals and Conservatives to join hands, as you call it? That shows how absurd it is for women——Why, the very essence of a Liberal is to trust in the people!

MRS. BARTHWICK. Now, John, eat your breakfast. As if there were any real difference between you and the Conservatives. All the upper classes have the same interests to protect, and the same principles. [Calmly.] Oh! you're sitting upon a volcano, John.

BARTHWICK. What!

MRS. BARTHWICK. I read a letter in the paper yesterday. I forget the man's name, but it made the whole thing perfectly clear. You don't look things in the face.

BARTHWICK. Indeed! [Heavily.] I am a Liberal! Drop the subject, please!

MRS. BARTHWICK. Toast? I quite agree with what this man says: Education is simply ruining the lower classes. It unsettles them, and that's the worst thing for us all. I see an enormous difference in the manner of servants.

BARTHWICK, [With suspicious emphasis.] I welcome any change that will lead to something better. [He opens a letter.] H'm! This is that affair of Master Jack's again. "High Street, Oxford. Sir, We have received Mr. John Barthwick, Senior's, draft for forty pounds!" Oh! the letter's to him! "We now enclose the cheque you cashed with us, which, as we stated in our previous letter, was not met on presentation at your bank. We are, Sir, yours obediently, Moss and Sons, Tailors." H 'm! [Staring at the

cheque.] A pretty business altogether! The boy might have
been prosecuted.

MRS. BARTHWICK.   Come, John, you know Jack did n't mean anything; he
                   only thought he was overdrawing. I still think his bank
                   ought to have cashed that cheque. They must know
                   your position.

BARTHWICK.   [Replacing in the envelope the letter and the cheque.] Much
             good that would have done him in a court of law.

[He stops as JACK comes in, fastening his waistcoat and staunching a razor cut
upon his chin.]

JACK.   [Sitting down between them, and speaking with an artificial joviality.]
        Sorry I 'm late. [He looks lugubriously at the dishes.] Tea, please, moth-
        er. Any letters for me? [BARTHWICK hands the letter to him.] But look
        here, I say, this has been opened! I do wish you would n't——

BARTHWICK.   [Touching the envelope.] I suppose I 'm entitled to this name.

JACK.   [Sulkily.] Well, I can't help having your name, father! [He reads the let-
        ter, and mutters.] Brutes!

BARTHWICK.   [Eyeing him.] You don't deserve to be so well out of that.

JACK.   Haven't you ragged me enough, dad?

MRS. BARTHWICK.   Yes, John, let Jack have his breakfast.

BARTHWICK.   If you hadn't had me to come to, where would you have been?
             It's the merest accident—suppose you had been the son of a
             poor man or a clerk. Obtaining money with a cheque you
             knew your bank could not meet. It might have ruined you for
             life. I can't see what's to become of you if these are your prin-
             ciples. I never did anything of the sort myself.

JACK.   I expect you always had lots of money. If you've got plenty of money, of
        course——

BARTHWICK.   On the contrary, I had not your advantages. My father kept me
             very short of money.

JACK. How much had you, dad?

BARTHWICK. It's not material. The question is, do you feel the gravity of what you did?

JACK. I don't know about the gravity. Of course, I 'm very sorry if you think it was wrong. Have n't I said so! I should never have done it at all if I had n't been so jolly hard up.

BARTHWICK. How much of that forty pounds have you got left, Jack?

JACK. [Hesitating.] I don't know—not much.

BARTHWICK. How much?

JACK. [Desperately.] I have n't got any.

BARTHWICK. What?

JACK. I know I 've got the most beastly headache.

[He leans his head on his hand.]

MRS. BARTHWICK. Headache? My dear boy! Can't you eat any breakfast?

JACK. [Drawing in his breath.] Too jolly bad!

MRS. BARTHWICK. I'm so sorry. Come with me; dear; I'll give you something that will take it away at once.

[They leave the room; and BARTHWICK, tearing up the letter, goes to the fireplace and puts the pieces in the fire. While he is doing this MARLOW comes in, and looking round him, is about quietly to withdraw.]

BARTHWICK. What's that? What d 'you want?

MARLOW. I was looking for Mr. John, sir.

BARTHWICK. What d' you want Mr. John for?

MARLOW. [With hesitation.] I thought I should find him here, sir.

BARTHWICK. [Suspiciously.] Yes, but what do you want him for?

MARLOW. [Offhandedly.] There's a lady called—asked to speak to him for a minute, sir.

BARTHWICK. A lady, at this time in the morning. What sort of a lady?

MARLOW. [Without expression in his voice.] I can't tell, sir; no particular sort. She might be after charity. She might be a Sister of Mercy, I should think, sir.

BARTHWICK. Is she dressed like one?

MARLOW. No, sir, she's in plain clothes, sir.

BARTHWICK. Did n't she say what she wanted?

MARLOW. No sir.

BARTHWICK. Where did you leave her?

MARLOW. In the hall, sir.

BARTHWICK. In the hall? How do you know she's not a thief—not got designs on the house?

MARLOW. No, sir, I don't fancy so, sir.

BARTHWICK. Well, show her in here; I'll see her myself.

[MARLOW goes out with a private gesture of dismay. He soon returns, ushering in a young pale lady with dark eyes and pretty figure, in a modish, black, but rather shabby dress, a black and white trimmed hat with a bunch of Parma violets wrongly placed, and fuzzy-spotted veil. At the Sight of MR. BARTHWICK she exhibits every sign of nervousness. MARLOW goes out.]

UNKNOWN LADY. Oh! but—I beg pardon there's some mistake—I [She turns to fly.]

BARTHWICK. Whom did you want to see, madam?

UNKNOWN. [Stopping and looking back.] It was Mr. John Barthwick I wanted to see.

BARTHWICK. I am John Barthwick, madam. What can I have the pleasure of
doing for you?

UNKNOWN. Oh! I—I don't [She drops her eyes. BARTHWICK scrutinis-
es her, and purses his lips.]

BARTHWICK. It was my son, perhaps, you wished to see?

UNKNOWN. [Quickly.] Yes, of course, it's your son.

BARTHWICK. May I ask whom I have the pleasure of speaking to?

UNKNOWN. [Appeal and hardiness upon her face.] My name is——oh! it
does n't matter—I don't want to make any fuss. I just want to
see your son for a minute. [Boldly.] In fact, I must see him.

BARTHWICK. [Controlling his uneasiness.] My son is not very well. If necessary, no doubt I could attend to the matter; be so kind as to let
me know——

UNKNOWN. Oh! but I must see him—I 've come on purpose—[She bursts
out nervously.] I don't want to make any fuss, but the fact is,
last—last night your son took away—he took away my [She
stops.]

BARTHWICK. [Severely.] Yes, madam, what?

UNKNOWN. He took away my—my reticule.

BARTHWICK. Your reti——?

UNKNOWN. I don't care about the reticule; it's not that I want—I 'm sure I
don't want to make any fuss—[her face is quivering]—but- -
but—all my money was in it!

BARTHWICK. In what—in what?

UNKNOWN. In my purse, in the reticule. It was a crimson silk purse. Really, I wouldn't have come—I don't want to make any fuss. But I must get my money back—mustn't I?

BARTHWICK. Do you tell me that my son——?

UNKNOWN. Oh! well, you see, he was n't quite I mean he was

[She smiles mesmerically.]

BARTHWICK. I beg your pardon.

UNKNOWN. [Stamping her foot.] Oh! don't you see—tipsy! We had a quarrel.

BARTHWICK. [Scandalised.] How? Where?

UNKNOWN. [Defiantly.] At my place. We'd had supper at the——and your son——

BARTHWICK. [Pressing the bell.] May I ask how you knew this house? Did he give you his name and address?

UNKNOWN. [Glancing sidelong.] I got it out of his overcoat.

BARTHWICK. [Sardonically.] Oh! you got it out of his overcoat. And may I ask if my son will know you by daylight?

UNKNOWN. Know me? I should jolly—I mean, of course he will! [MARLOW comes in.]

BARTHWICK. Ask Mr. John to come down.

[MARLOW goes out, and BARTHWICK walks uneasily about.]

And how long have you enjoyed his acquaintanceship?

UNKNOWN. Only since—only since Good Friday.

BARTHWICK. I am at a loss—I repeat I am at a——

[He glances at this unknown lady, who stands with eyes cast down, twisting her hands And suddenly Jack appears. He stops on seeing who is here, and the unknown lady hysterically giggles. There is a silence.]

BARTHWICK. [Portentously.] This young—er—lady says that last night—I think you said last night madam—you took away——

UNKNOWN. [Impulsively.] My reticule, and all my money was in a crimson silk purse.

JACK. Reticule. [Looking round for any chance to get away.] I don't know anything about it.

BARTHWICK. [Sharply.] Come, do you deny seeing this young lady last night?

JACK. Deny? No, of course. [Whispering.] Why did you give me away like this? What on earth did you come here for?

UNKNOWN. [Tearfully.] I'm sure I didn't want to—it's not likely, is it? You snatched it out of my hand—you know you did—and the purse had all my money in it. I did n't follow you last night because I did n't want to make a fuss and it was so late, and you were so——

BARTHWICK. Come, sir, don't turn your back on me—explain!

JACK. [Desperately.] I don't remember anything about it. [In a low voice to his friend.] Why on earth could n't you have written?

UNKNOWN. [Sullenly.] I want it now; I must have, it—I 've got to pay my rent to-day. [She looks at BARTHWICK.] They're only too glad to jump on people who are not—not well off.

JACK. I don't remember anything about it, really. I don't remember anything about last night at all. [He puts his hand up to his head.] It's all—cloudy, and I 've got such a beastly headache.

UNKNOWN. But you took it; you know you did. You said you'd score me off.

JACK. Well, then, it must be here. I remember now—I remember something. Why did I take the beastly thing?

BARTHWICK. Yes, why did you take the beastly——[He turns abruptly to the window.]

UNKNOWN. [With her mesmeric smile.] You were n't quite were you?

JACK. [Smiling pallidly.] I'm awfully sorry. If there's anything I can do——

BARTHWICK. Do? You can restore this property, I suppose.

JACK. I'll go and have a look, but I really don't think I 've got it.

[He goes out hurriedly. And BARTHWICK, placing a chair, motions to the visitor to sit; then, with pursed lips, he stands and eyes her fixedly. She sits, and steals a look at him; then turns away, and, drawing up her veil, stealthily wipes her eyes. And Jack comes back.]

JACK. [Ruefully holding out the empty reticule.] Is that the thing? I 've looked all over—I can't find the purse anywhere. Are you sure it was there?

UNKNOWN. [Tearfully.] Sure? Of course I'm sure. A crimson silk purse. It was all the money I had.

JACK. I really am awfully sorry—my head's so jolly bad. I 've asked the butler, but he has n't seen it.

UNKNOWN. I must have my money——

JACK. Oh! Of course—that'll be all right; I'll see that that's all right. How much?

UNKNOWN. [Sullenly.] Seven pounds-twelve—it's all I 've got in the world.

JACK. That'll be all right; I'll—send you a cheque.

UNKNOWN. [Eagerly.] No; now, please. Give me what was in my purse; I've got to pay my rent this morning. They won't' give me another day; I'm a fortnight behind already.

JACK. [Blankly.] I'm awfully sorry; I really have n't a penny in my pocket.

[He glances stealthily at BARTHWICK.]

UNKNOWN.   [Excitedly.] Come I say you must—it's my money, and you took it. I'm not going away without it. They 'll turn me out of my place.

JACK.   [Clasping his head.] But I can't give you what I have n't got. Don't I tell you I have n't a beastly cent.

UNKNOWN.   [Tearing at her handkerchief.] Oh! do give it me! [She puts her hands together in appeal; then, with sudden fierceness.] If you don't I'll summons you. It's stealing, that's what it is!

BARTHWICK.   [Uneasily.] One moment, please. As a matter of—-er- principle, I shall settle this claim. [He produces money.] Here is eight pounds; the extra will cover the value of the purse and your cab fares. I need make no comment—no thanks are necessary.

[Touching the bell, he holds the door ajar in silence. The unknown lady stores the money in her reticule, she looks from JACK to BARTHWICK, and her face is quivering faintly with a smile. She hides it with her hand, and steals away. Behind her BARTHWICK shuts the door.]

BARTHWICK.   [With solemnity.] H'm! This is nice thing to happen!

JACK.   [Impersonally.] What awful luck!

BARTHWICK.   So this is the way that forty pounds has gone! One thing after another! Once more I should like to know where you 'd have been if it had n't been for me! You don't seem to have any principles. You—you're one of those who are a nuisance to society; you—you're dangerous! What your mother would say I don't know. Your conduct, as far as I can see, is absolutely unjustifiable. It's—it's criminal. Why, a poor man who behaved as you've done—— d' you think he'd have any mercy shown him? What you want is a good lesson. You and your sort are—[he speaks with feeling]—a nuisance to the community. Don't ask me to help you next time. You're not fit to be helped.

JACK.   [Turning upon his sire, with unexpected fierceness.] All right, I won't then, and see how you like it. You would n't have helped me this time, I

know, if you had n't been scared the thing would get into the papers.
Where are the cigarettes?

BARTHWICK. [Regarding him uneasily.] Well I 'll say no more about it. [He
                rings the bell.] I 'll pass it over for this once, but—— [MAR-
                LOW Comes in.] You can clear away.

[He hides his face behind the "Times."]

JACK. [Brightening.] I say, Marlow, where are the cigarettes?

MARLOW. I put the box out with the whisky last night, sir, but this morning I
             can't find it anywhere.

JACK. Did you look in my room?

MARLOW. Yes, sir; I've looked all over the house. I found two Nestor ends in
             the tray this morning, so you must have been smokin' last night, sir.
             [Hesitating.] I 'm really afraid some one's purloined the box.

JACK. [Uneasily.] Stolen it!

BARTHWICK. What's that? The cigarette-box! Is anything else missing?

MARLOW. No, sir; I 've been through the plate.

BARTHWICK. Was the house all right this morning? None of the windows
             open?

MARLOW. No, sir. [Quietly to JACK.] You left your latch-key in the door last
             night, sir.

[He hands it back, unseen by BARTHWICK]

JACK. Tst!

BARTHWICK. Who's been in the room this morning?

MARLOW. Me and Wheeler, and Mrs. Jones is all, sir, as far as I know.

BARTHWICK. Have you asked Mrs. Barthwick?

[To JACK.] Go and ask your mother if she's had it; ask her to look and see if she's missed anything else.

[JACK goes upon this mission.]

Nothing is more disquieting than losing things like this.

MARLOW. No, sir.

BARTHWICK. Have you any suspicions?

MARLOW, No, sir.

BARTHWICK. This Mrs. Jones—how long has she been working here?

MARLOW. Only this last month, sir.

BARTHWICK. What sort of person?

MARLOW. I don't know much about her, sir; seems a very quiet, respectable woman.

BARTHWICK. Who did the room this morning?

MARLOW. Wheeler and Mrs. Jones, Sir.

BARTHWICK. [With his forefinger upraised.] Now, was this Mrs. Jones in the room alone at any time?

MARLOW. [Expressionless.] Yes, Sir.

BARTHWICK. How do you know that?

MARLOW. [Reluctantly.] I found her here, sir.

BARTHWICK. And has Wheeler been in the room alone?

MARLOW. No, sir, she's not, sir. I should say, sir, that Mrs. Jones seems a very honest——

BARTHWICK. [Holding up his hand.] I want to know this: Has this Mrs. Jones been here the whole morning?

MARLOW. Yes, sir—no, sir—she stepped over to the greengrocer's for cook.

BARTHWICK. H'm! Is she in the house now?

MARLOW. Yes, Sir.

BARTHWICK. Very good. I shall make a point of clearing this up. On principle I shall make a point of fixing the responsibility; it goes to the foundations of security. In all your interests——

MARLOW. Yes, Sir.

BARTHWICK. What sort of circumstances is this Mrs. Jones in? Is her husband in work?

MARLOW. I believe not, sir.

BARTHWICK. Very well. Say nothing about it to any one. Tell Wheeler not to speak of it, and ask Mrs. Jones to step up here.

MARLOW. Very good, sir.

[MARLOW goes out, his face concerned; and BARTHWICK stays, his face judicial and a little pleased, as befits a man conducting an inquiry. MRS. BARTHWICK and hey son come in.]

BARTHWICK. Well, my dear, you've not seen it, I suppose?

MRS. BARTHWICK. No. But what an extraordinary thing, John! Marlow, of course, is out of the question. I 'm certain none of the maids as for cook!

BARTHWICK. Oh, cook!

MRS. BARTHWICK. Of course! It's perfectly detestable to me to suspect anybody.

BARTHWICK. It is not a question of one's feelings. It's a question of justice. On principle——

MRS. BARTHWICK. I should n't be a bit surprised if the charwoman knew something about it. It was Laura who recommended her.

BARTHWICK. [Judicially.] I am going to have Mrs. Jones up. Leave it to me; and—er—remember that nobody is guilty until they're proved so. I shall be careful. I have no intention of frightening her; I shall give her every chance. I hear she's in poor circumstances. If we are not able to do much for them we are bound to have the greatest sympathy with the poor. [MRS. JONES comes in.] [Pleasantly.] Oh! good morning, Mrs. Jones.

MRS. JONES. [Soft, and even, unemphatic.] Good morning, sir! Good morning, ma'am!

BARTHWICK. About your husband—he's not in work, I hear?

MRS. JONES. No, sir; of course he's not in work just now.

BARTHWICK. Then I suppose he's earning nothing.

MRS. JONES. No, sir, he's not earning anything just now, sir.

BARTHWICK. And how many children have you?

MRS. JONES. Three children; but of course they don't eat very much sir. [A little silence.]

BARTHWICK. And how old is the eldest?

MRS. JONES. Nine years old, sir.

BARTHWICK. Do they go to school?

MRS. JONES, Yes, sir, they all three go to school every day.

BARTHWICK. [Severely.] And what about their food when you're out at work?

MRS. JONES. Well, Sir, I have to give them their dinner to take with them. Of course I 'm not always able to give them anything; sometimes I have to send them without; but my husband is very good about the children when he's in work. But when he's not in work of course he's a very difficult man.

BARTHWICK. He drinks, I suppose?

MRS. JONES. Yes, Sir. Of course I can't say he does n't drink, because he does.

BARTHWICK. And I suppose he takes all your money?

MRS. JONES. No, sir, he's very good about my money, except when he's not himself, and then, of course, he treats me very badly.

BARTHWICK. Now what is he—your husband?

MRS. JONES. By profession, sir, of course he's a groom.

BARTHWICK. A groom! How came he to lose his place?

MRS. JONES. He lost his place a long time ago, sir, and he's never had a very long job since; and now, of course, the motor-cars are against him.

BARTHWICK. When were you married to him, Mrs. Jones?

MRS. JONES. Eight years ago, sir that was in——

MRS. BARTHWICK. [Sharply.] Eight? You said the eldest child was nine.

MRS. JONES.   Yes, ma'am; of course that was why he lost his place. He did n't treat me rightly, and of course his employer said he couldn't keep him because of the example.

BARTHWICK. You mean he—ahem——

MRS. JONES. Yes, sir; and of course after he lost his place he married me.

MRS. BARTHWICK. You actually mean to say you—you were——

BARTHWICK. My dear——

MRS. BARTHWICK. [Indignantly.] How disgraceful!

BARTHWICK. [Hurriedly.] And where are you living now, Mrs. Jones?

MRS. JONES. We've not got a home, sir. Of course we've been obliged to put away most of our things.

BARTHWICK. Put your things away! You mean to—to—er—to pawn them?

MRS. JONES. Yes, sir, to put them away. We're living in Merthyr Street—that is close by here, sir—at No. 34. We just have the one room.

BARTHWICK. And what do you pay a week?

MRS. JONES. We pay six shillings a week, sir, for a furnished room.

BARTHWICK. And I suppose you're behind in the rent?

MRS. JONES. Yes, sir, we're a little behind in the rent.

BARTHWICK. But you're in good work, aren't you?

MRS. JONES. Well, Sir, I have a day in Stamford Place Thursdays. And Mondays and Wednesdays and Fridays I come here. But to-day, of course, is a half-day, because of yesterday's Bank Holiday.

BARTHWICK. I see; four days a week, and you get half a crown a day, is that it?

MRS. JONES. Yes, sir, and my dinner; but sometimes it's only half a day, and that's eighteen pence.

BARTHWICK. And when your husband earns anything he spends it in drink, I suppose?

MRS. JONES. Sometimes he does, sir, and sometimes he gives it to me for the children. Of course he would work if he could get it, sir, but it seems there are a great many people out of work.

BARTHWICK. Ah! Yes. We—er—won't go into that. [Sympathetically.] And how about your work here? Do you find it hard?

MRS. JONES.   Oh! no, sir, not very hard, sir; except of course, when I don't get my sleep at night.

BARTHWICK. Ah! And you help do all the rooms? And sometimes, I suppose, you go out for cook?

MRS. JONES. Yes, Sir.

BARTHWICK. And you 've been out this morning?

MRS. JONES. Yes, sir, of course I had to go to the greengrocer's.

BARTHWICK. Exactly. So your husband earns nothing? And he's a bad character.

MRS. JONES. No, Sir, I don't say that, sir. I think there's a great deal of good in him; though he does treat me very bad sometimes. And of course I don't like to leave him, but I think I ought to, because really I hardly know how to stay with him. He often raises his hand to me. Not long ago he gave me a blow here [touches her breast] and I can feel it now. So I think I ought to leave him, don't you, sir?

BARTHWICK. Ah! I can't help you there. It's a very serious thing to leave your husband. Very serious thing.

MRS. JONES. Yes, sir, of course I 'm afraid of what he might do to me if I were to leave him; he can be so very violent.

BARTHWICK. H'm! Well, that I can't pretend to say anything about. It's the bad principle I'm speaking of——

MRS. JONES. Yes, Sir; I know nobody can help me. I know I must decide for myself, and of course I know that he has a very hard life. And he's fond of the children, and its very hard for him to see them going without food.

BARTHWICK. [Hastily.] Well—er—thank you, I just wanted to hear about you. I don't think I need detain you any longer, Mrs. Jones.

MRS. JONES. No, sir, thank you, sir.

BARTHWICK. Good morning, then.

MRS. JONES. Good morning, sir; good morning, ma'am.

BARTHWICK. [Exchanging glances with his wife.] By the way, Mrs. Jones—I think it is only fair to tell you, a silver cigarette-box —er—is missing.

MRS. JONES. [Looking from one face to the other.] I am very sorry, sir.

BARTHWICK. Yes; you have not seen it, I suppose?

MRS. JONES. [Realising that suspicion is upon her; with an uneasy movement.] Where was it, sir; if you please, sir?

BARTHWICK. [Evasively.] Where did Marlow say? Er—in this room, yes, in this room.

MRS. JONES. No, Sir, I have n't seen it—of course if I 'd seen it I should have noticed it.

BARTHWICK. [Giving hey a rapid glance.] You—you are sure of that?

MRS. JONES. [Impassively.] Yes, Sir. [With a slow nodding of her head.] I have not seen it, and of course I don't know where it is.

[She turns and goes quietly out.]

BARTHWICK. H'm!

[The three BARTHWICKS avoid each other's glances.]

The curtain falls.

ACT II

SCENE I

The JONES's lodgings, Merthyr Street, at half-past two o'clock.

The bare room, with tattered oilcloth and damp, distempered walls, has an air of tidy wretchedness. On the bed lies JONES, half-dressed; his coat is thrown across his feet, and muddy boots are lying on the floor close by. He is asleep. The door is opened and MRS. JONES comes in, dressed in a pinched black jacket and old black sailor hat; she carries a parcel wrapped up in the "Times." She puts her parcel down, unwraps an apron, half a loaf, two onions, three potatoes, and a tiny piece of bacon. Taking a teapot from the cupboard, she rinses it, shakes into it some powdered tea out of a screw of paper, puts it on the hearth, and sitting in a wooden chair quietly begins to cry.

JONES. [Stirring and yawning.] That you? What's the time?

MRS. JONES. [Drying her eyes, and in her usual voice.] Half-past two.

JONES. What you back so soon for?

MRS. JONES. I only had the half day to-day, Jem.

JONES. [On his back, and in a drowsy voice.] Got anything for dinner?

MRS. JONES.   Mrs. BARTHWICK's cook gave me a little bit of bacon. I'm going to make a stew. [She prepares for cooking.] There's fourteen shillings owing for rent, James, and of course I 've only got two and fourpence. They'll be coming for it to-day.

JONES.   [Turning towards her on his elbow.] Let 'em come and find my surprise packet. I've had enough o' this tryin' for work. Why should I go round and round after a job like a bloomin' squirrel in a cage. "Give us a job, sir"—"Take a man on"—"Got a wife and three children." Sick of it I am! I 'd sooner lie here and rot. "Jones, you come and join the demonstration; come and 'old a flag, and listen to the ruddy orators, and go 'ome as empty as you came." There's some that seems to like that—the sheep! When I go seekin' for a job now, and see the brutes lookin' me up an' down, it's like a thousand serpents in me. I 'm not arskin' for any treat. A man wants to sweat hisself silly and not allowed that's a rum start, ain't it? A man wants to sweat his soul out to keep the breath in him and ain't allowed—that's justice that's freedom and all the rest of it! [He turns his face towards the wall.] You're so milky mild; you don't know what goes on inside o' me. I'm done with the silly game. If they want me, let 'em come for me!

[MRS. JONES stops cooking and stands unmoving at the table.]

I've tried and done with it, I tell you. I've never been afraid of what 's before me. You mark my words—if you think they've broke my spirit, you're mistook. I 'll lie and rot sooner than arsk 'em again. What makes you stand like that—you long-sufferin', Gawd- forsaken image—that's why I can't keep my hands off you. So now you know. Work! You can work, but you have n't the spirit of a louse!

MRS. JONES.   [Quietly.] You talk more wild sometimes when you're yourself, James, than when you 're not. If you don't get work, how are we to go on? They won't let us stay here; they're looking to their money to-day, I know.

JONES.   I see this BARTHWICK o' yours every day goin' down to Pawlyment snug and comfortable to talk his silly soul out; an' I see that young calf, his son, swellin' it about, and goin' on the razzle-dazzle. Wot 'ave they done that makes 'em any better than wot I am? They never did a day's work in their lives. I see 'em day after day.

MRS. JONES. And I wish you wouldn't come after me like that, and hang about
the house. You don't seem able to keep away at all, and whatever you do it for I can't think, because of course they notice it.

JONES. I suppose I may go where I like. Where may I go? The other day I went
to a place in the Edgware Road. "Gov'nor," I says to the boss, "take me
on," I says. "I 'aven't done a stroke o' work not these two months; it takes
the heart out of a man," I says; "I 'm one to work; I 'm not afraid of anything you can give me!" "My good man," 'e says, "I 've had thirty of you
here this morning. I took the first two," he says, "and that's all I want."
"Thank you, then rot the world!" I says. "Blasphemin'," he says, "is not
the way to get a job. Out you go, my lad!" [He laughs sardonically.]
Don't you raise your voice because you're starvin'; don't yer even think of
it; take it lyin' down! Take it like a sensible man, carn't you? And a little
way down the street a lady says to me: [Pinching his voice] "D' you want
to earn a few pence, my man?" and gives me her dog to 'old outside a
shop-fat as a butler 'e was—tons o' meat had gone to the makin' of him.
It did 'er good, it did, made 'er feel 'erself that charitable, but I see 'er
lookin' at the copper standin' alongside o' me, for fear I should make off
with 'er bloomin' fat dog. [He sits on the edge of the bed and puts a boot
on. Then looking up.] What's in that head o' yours? [Almost patheti-
cally.] Carn't you speak for once?

[There is a knock, and MRS. SEDDON, the landlady, appears, an anxious,
harassed, shabby woman in working clothes.]

MRS. SEDDON. I thought I 'eard you come in, Mrs. Jones. I 've spoke to my
'usband, but he says he really can't afford to wait another day.

JONES. [With scowling jocularity.] Never you mind what your 'usband says,
you go your own way like a proper independent woman. Here, jenny,
chuck her that.

[Producing a sovereign from his trousers pocket, he throws it to his wife, who
catches it in her apron with a gasp. JONES resumes the lacing of his boots.]

MRS. JONES. [Rubbing the sovereign stealthily.] I'm very sorry we're so late
with it, and of course it's fourteen shillings, so if you've got six
that will be right.

[MRS. SEDDON takes the sovereign and fumbles for the change.]

JONES. [With his eyes fixed on his boots.] Bit of a surprise for yer, ain't it?

MRS. SEDDON. Thank you, and I'm sure I'm very much obliged. [She does indeed appear surprised.] I 'll bring you the change.

JONES. [Mockingly.] Don't mention it.

MRS. SEDDON. Thank you, and I'm sure I'm very much obliged. [She slides away.]

[MRS. JONES gazes at JONES who is still lacing up his boots.]

JONES. I 've had a bit of luck. [Pulling out the crimson purse and some loose coins.] Picked up a purse—seven pound and more.

MRS. JONES. Oh, James!

JONES. Oh, James! What about Oh, James! I picked it up I tell you. This is lost property, this is!

MRS. JONES. But is n't there a name in it, or something?

JONES. Name? No, there ain't no name. This don't belong to such as 'ave vis- itin' cards. This belongs to a perfec' lidy. Tike an' smell it. [He pitches her the purse, which she puts gently to her nose.] Now, you tell me what I ought to have done. You tell me that. You can always tell me what I ought to ha' done, can't yer?

MRS. JONES. [Laying down the purse.] I can't say what you ought to have done, James. Of course the money was n't yours; you've taken somebody else's money.

JONES. Finding's keeping. I 'll take it as wages for the time I 've gone about the streets asking for what's my rights. I'll take it for what's overdue, d' ye hear? [With strange triumph.] I've got money in my pocket, my girl.

[MRS. JONES goes on again with the preparation of the meal, JONES looking at hser furtively.]

Money in my pocket! And I 'm not goin' to waste it. With this 'ere money I'm goin' to Canada. I'll let you have a pound.

[A silence.]

You've often talked of leavin' me. You 've often told me I treat you badly—well I 'ope you 'll be glad when I 'm gone.

MRS. JONES. [Impassively.] You have, treated me very badly, James, and of course I can't prevent your going; but I can't tell whether I shall be glad when you're gone.

JONES. It'll change my luck. I 've 'ad nothing but bad luck since I first took up with you. [More softly.] And you've 'ad no bloomin' picnic.

MRS. JONES. Of course it would have been better for us if we had never met. We were n't meant for each other. But you're set against me, that's what you are, and you have been for a long time. And you treat me so badly, James, going after that Rosie and all. You don't ever seem to think of the children that I 've had to bring into the world, and of all the trouble I 've had to keep them, and what 'll become of them when you're gone.

JONES. [Crossing the room gloomily.] If you think I want to leave the little beggars you're bloomin' well mistaken.

MRS. JONES. Of course I know you're fond of them.

JONES. [Fingering the purse, half angrily.] Well, then, you stow it, old girl. The kids 'll get along better with you than when I 'm here. If I 'd ha' known as much as I do now, I 'd never ha' had one o' them. What's the use o' bringin' 'em into a state o' things like this? It's a crime, that's what it is; but you find it out too late; that's what's the matter with this 'ere world.

[He puts the purse back in his pocket.]

MRS. JONES. Of course it would have been better for them, poor little things; but they're your own children, and I wonder at you talkin' like that. I should miss them dreadfully if I was to lose them.

JONES. [Sullenly.] An' you ain't the only one. If I make money out there— [Looking up, he sees her shaking out his coat—in a changed voice.] Leave that coat alone!

[The silver box drops from the pocket, scattering the cigarettes upon the bed. Taking up the box she stares at it; he rushes at her and snatches the box away.]

MRS. JONES. [Cowering back against the bed.] Oh, Jem! oh, Jem!

JONES. [Dropping the box onto the table.] You mind what you're sayin'! When I go out I 'll take and chuck it in the water along with that there purse. I 'ad it when I was in liquor, and for what you do when you 're in liquor you're not responsible-and that's Gawd's truth as you ought to know. I don't want the thing—I won't have it. I took it out o' spite. I 'm no thief, I tell you; and don't you call me one, or it'll be the worse for you.

MRS. JONES. [Twisting her apron strings.] It's Mr. Barthwick's! You've taken away my reputation. Oh, Jem, whatever made you?

JONES. What d' you mean?

MRS. JONES. It's been missed; they think it's me. Oh! whatever made you do it, Jem?

JONES. I tell you I was in liquor. I don't want it; what's the good of it to me? If I were to pawn it they'd only nab me. I 'm no thief. I 'm no worse than wot that young Barthwick is; he brought 'ome that purse that I picked up—a lady's purse—'ad it off 'er in a row, kept sayin' 'e 'd scored 'er off. Well, I scored 'im off. Tight as an owl 'e was! And d' you think anything'll happen to him?

MRS. JONES. [As though speaking to herself.] Oh, Jem! it's the bread out of our mouths!

JONES. Is it then? I'll make it hot for 'em yet. What about that purse? What about young BARTHWICK?

[MRS. JONES comes forward to the table and tries to take the box; JONES prevents her.] What do you want with that? You drop it, I say!

MRS. JONES. I 'll take it back and tell them all about it. [She attempts to wrest the box from him.]

JONES. Ah, would yer?

[He drops the box, and rushes on her with a snarl. She slips back past the bed. He follows; a chair is overturned. The door is opened; Snow comes in, a detective in plain clothes and bowler hat, with clipped moustaches. JONES drops his arms, MRS. JONES stands by the window gasping; SNOW, advancing swiftly to the table, puts his hand on the silver box.]

SNOW. Doin' a bit o' skylarkin'? Fancy this is what I 'm after. J. B., the very same. [He gets back to the door, scrutinising the crest and cypher on the box. To MRS. JONES.] I'm a police officer. Are you Mrs. Jones?

MRS. JONES. Yes, Sir.

SNOW. My instructions are to take you on a charge of stealing this box from J. BARTHWICK, Esquire, M.P., of 6, Rockingham Gate. Anything you say may be used against you. Well, Missis?

MRS. JONES. [In her quiet voice, still out of breath, her hand upon. her breast.] Of course I did not take it, sir. I never have taken anything that did n't belong to me; and of course I know nothing about it.

SNOW. You were at the house this morning; you did the room in which the box was left; you were alone in the room. I find the box 'ere. You say you did n't take it?

MRS. JONES. Yes, sir, of course I say I did not take it, because I did not.

SNOW. Then how does the box come to be here?

MRS. JONES. I would rather not say anything about it.

SNOW. Is this your husband?

MRS. JONES. Yes, sir, this is my husband, sir.

SNOW. Do you wish to say anything before I take her?

[JONES remains silent, with his head bend down.]

Well then, Missis. I 'll just trouble you to come along with me quietly.

MRS. JONES. [Twisting her hands.] Of course I would n't say I had n't taken
        it if I had—and I did n't take it, indeed I did n't. Of course I
        know appearances are against me, and I can't tell you what real-
        ly happened: But my children are at school, and they'll be com-
        ing home—and I don't know what they'll do without me.

SNOW. Your 'usband'll see to them, don't you worry. [He takes the woman gen-
        tly by the arm.]

JONES. You drop it—she's all right! [Sullenly.] I took the thing myself.

SNOW. [Eyeing him] There, there, it does you credit. Come along, Missis.

JONES. [Passionately.] Drop it, I say, you blooming teck. She's my wife; she 's
        a respectable woman. Take her if you dare!

SNOW. Now, now. What's the good of this? Keep a civil tongue, and it'll be the
        better for all of us.

[He puts his whistle in his mouth and draws the woman to the door.]

JONES. [With a rush.] Drop her, and put up your 'ands, or I 'll soon make yer.
        You leave her alone, will yer! Don't I tell yer, I took the thing myself.

SNOW. [Blowing his whistle.] Drop your hands, or I 'll take you too. Ah, would
        you?

[JONES, closing, deals him a blow. A Policeman in uniform appears; there is a
short struggle and JONES is overpowered. MRS. JONES raises her hands avid
drops her face on them.]

The curtain falls.

SCENE II

The BARTHWICKS' dining-room the same evening. The BARTHWICKS are
seated at dessert.

MRS. BARTHWICK. John! [A silence broken by the cracking of nuts.] John!

BARTHWICK. I wish you'd speak about the nuts they're uneatable. [He puts one in his mouth.]

MRS. BARTHWICK. It's not the season for them. I called on the Holyroods.

[BARTHWICK fills his glass with port.]

JACK. Crackers, please, Dad.

[BARTHWICK passes the crackers. His demeanour is reflective.]

MRS. BARTHWICK. Lady Holyrood has got very stout. I 've noticed it coming for a long time.

BARTHWICK. [Gloomily.] Stout? [He takes up the crackers—with transparent airiness.] The Holyroods had some trouble with their servants, had n't they?

JACK. Crackers, please, Dad.

BARTHWICK. [Passing the crackers.] It got into the papers. The cook, was n't it?

MRS. BARTHWICK. No, the lady's maid. I was talking it over with Lady Holyrood. The girl used to have her young man to see her.

BARTHWICK. [Uneasily.] I'm not sure they were wise——

MRS. BARTHWICK. My dear John, what are you talking about? How could there be any alternative? Think of the effect on the other servants!

BARTHWICK. Of course in principle—I wasn't thinking of that.

JACK. [Maliciously.] Crackers, please, Dad.

[BARTHWICK is compelled to pass the crackers.]

MRS. BARTHWICK. Lady Holyrood told me: "I had her up," she said; "I said to her, 'You'll leave my house at once; I think your conduct disgraceful. I can't tell, I don't know, and I don't wish to know, what you were doing. I send you away on principle; you need not come to me for a character.' And the girl said: 'If you don't give me my notice, my lady, I want a month's wages. I'm perfectly respectable. I've done nothing.'"—Done nothing!

BARTHWICK. H'm!

MRS. BARTHWICK. Servants have too much license. They hang together so terribly you never can tell what they're really thinking; it's as if they were all in a conspiracy to keep you in the dark. Even with Marlow, you feel that he never lets you know what's really in his mind. I hate that secretiveness; it destroys all confidence. I feel sometimes I should like to shake him.

JACK. Marlow's a most decent chap. It's simply beastly every one knowing your affairs.

BARTHWICK. The less you say about that the better!

MRS. BARTHWICK. It goes all through the lower classes. You can not tell when they are speaking the truth. To-day when I was shopping after leaving the Holyroods, one of these unemployed came up and spoke to me. I suppose I only had twenty yards or so to walk to the carnage, but he seemed to spring up in the street.

BARTHWICK. Ah! You must be very careful whom you speak to in these days.

MRS. BARTHWICK. I did n't answer him, of course. But I could see at once that he wasn't telling the truth.

BARTHWICK. [Cracking a nut.] There's one very good rule—look at their eyes.

JACK. Crackers, please, Dad.

BARTHWICK. [Passing the crackers.] If their eyes are straight- forward I some- times give them sixpence. It 's against my principles, but it's most difficult to refuse. If you see that they're desperate, and dull, and shifty-looking, as so many of them are, it's certain to mean drink, or crime, or something unsatisfactory.

MRS. BARTHWICK. This man had dreadful eyes. He looked as if he could commit a murder. "I 've 'ad nothing to eat to-day," he said. Just like that.

BARTHWICK. What was William about? He ought to have been waiting.

JACK. [Raising his wine-glass to his nose.] Is this the '63, Dad?

[BARTHWICK, holding his wine-glass to his eye, lowers it and passes it before his nose.]

MRS. BARTHWICK. I hate people that can't speak the truth. [Father and son exchange a look behind their port.] It 's just as easy to speak the truth as not. I've always found it easy enough. It makes it impossible to tell what is genuine; one feels as if one were continually being taken in.

BARTHWICK. [Sententiously.] The lower classes are their own enemies. If they would only trust us, they would get on so much better.

MRS. BARTHWICK. But even then it's so often their own fault. Look at that Mrs. Jones this morning.

BARTHWICK. I only want to do what's right in that matter. I had occasion to see Roper this afternoon. I mentioned it to him. He's coming in this evening. It all depends on what the detective says. I've had my doubts. I've been thinking it over.

MRS. BARTHWICK. The woman impressed me most unfavourably. She seemed to have no shame. That affair she was talking about—she and the man when they were young, so immoral! And before you and Jack! I could have put her out of the room!

BARTHWICK. Oh! I don't want to excuse them, but in looking at these matters one must consider——

MRS. BARTHWICK. Perhaps you'll say the man's employer was wrong in dismissing him?

BARTHWICK. Of course not. It's not there that I feel doubt. What I ask myself is——

JACK. Port, please, Dad.

BARTHWICK. [Circulating the decanter in religious imitation of the rising and setting of the sun.] I ask myself whether we are sufficiently careful in making inquiries about people before we engage them, especially as regards moral conduct.

JACK. Pass the-port, please, Mother!

MRS. BARTHWICK. [Passing it.] My dear boy, are n't you drinking too much?

[JACK fills his glass.]

MARLOW. [Entering.] Detective Snow to see you, Sir.

BARTHWICK. [Uneasily.] Ah! say I'll be with him in a minute.

MRS. BARTHWICK. [Without turning.] Let him come in here, Marlow.

[SNOW enters in an overcoat, his bowler hat in hand.]

BARTHWICK. [Half-rising.] Oh! Good evening!

SNOW. Good evening, sir; good evening, ma'am. I 've called round to report what I 've done, rather late, I 'm afraid—another case took me away. [He takes the silver box out o f his pocket, causing a sensation in the BARTHWICK family.] This is the identical article, I believe.

BARTHWICK. Certainly, certainly.

SNOW. Havin' your crest and cypher, as you described to me, sir, I 'd no hesitation in the matter.

BARTHWICK. Excellent. Will you have a glass of [he glances at the waning port]—er—sherry-[pours out sherry]. Jack, just give Mr. Snow this.

[JACK rises and gives the glass to SNOW; then, lolling in his chair, regards him indolently.]

SNOW. [Drinking off wine and putting down the glass.] After seeing you I went round to this woman's lodgings, sir. It's a low neighborhood, and I thought it as well to place a constable below— and not without 'e was wanted, as things turned out.

BARTHWICK. Indeed!

SNOW. Yes, Sir, I 'ad some trouble. I asked her to account for the presence of the article. She could give me no answer, except to deny the theft; so I took her into custody; then her husband came for me, so I was obliged to take him, too, for assault. He was very violent on the way to the station—very violent—threatened you and your son, and altogether he was a handful, I can till you.

MRS. BARTHWICK. What a ruffian he must be!

SNOW. Yes, ma'am, a rough customer.

JACK. [Sipping his mine, bemused.] Punch the beggar's head.

SNOW. Given to drink, as I understand, sir.

MRS. BARTHWICK. It's to be hoped he will get a severe punishment.

SNOW. The odd thing is, sir, that he persists in sayin' he took the box himself.

BARTHWICK. Took the box himself! [He smiles.] What does he think to gain by that?

SNOW. He says the young gentleman was intoxicated last night

[JACK stops the cracking of a nut, and looks at SNOW.]

[BARTHWICK, losing his smile, has put his wine-glass down; there is a silence— SNOW, looking from face to face, remarks]

—took him into the house and gave him whisky; and under the influence of an empty stomach the man says he took the box.

MRS. BARTHWICK. The impudent wretch!

BARTHWICK. D' you mean that he—er—intends to put this forward to-mor-row?

SNOW. That'll be his line, sir; but whether he's endeavouring to shield his wife, or whether [he looks at JACK] there's something in it, will be for the magistrate to say.

MRS. BARTHWICK. [Haughtily.] Something in what? I don't understand you. As if my son would bring a man like that into the house!

BARTHWICK. [From the fireplace, with an effort to be calm.] My son can speak for himself, no doubt. Well, Jack, what do you say?

MRS. BARTHWICK. [Sharply.] What does he say? Why, of course, he says the whole story's stuff!

JACK. [Embarrassed.] Well, of course, I—of course, I don't know anything about it.

MRS. BARTHWICK. I should think not, indeed! [To Snow.] The man is an audacious ruffian!

BARTHWICK. [Suppressing jumps.] But in view of my son's saying there's nothing in this—this fable—will it be necessary to proceed against the man under the circumstances?

SNOW. We shall have to charge him with the assault, sir. It would be as well for your son to come down to the Court. There'll be a remand, no doubt. The queer thing is there was quite a sum of money found on him, and a crimson silk purse.

[BARTHWICK starts; JACK rises and sits dozen again.]

I suppose the lady has n't missed her purse?

BARTHWICK. [Hastily.] Oh, no! Oh! No!

JACK. No!

MRS. BARTHWICK. [Dreamily.] No! [To SNOW.] I 've been inquiring of the servants. This man does hang about the house. I shall feel much safer if he gets a good long sentence; I do think we ought to be protected against such ruffians.

BARTHWICK. Yes, yes, of course, on principle but in this case we have a number of things to think of. [To SNOW.] I suppose, as you say, the man must be charged, eh?

SNOW. No question about that, sir.

BARTHWICK. [Staring gloomily at JACK.] This prosecution goes very much against the grain with me. I have great sympathy with the poor. In my position I 'm bound to recognise the distress there is amongst them. The condition of the people leaves much to be desired. D' you follow me? I wish I could see my way to drop it.

MRS. BARTHWICK. [Sharply.] John! it's simply not fair to other people. It's putting property at the mercy of any one who likes to take it.

BARTHWICK. [Trying to make signs to her aside.] I 'm not defending him, not at all. I'm trying to look at the matter broadly.

MRS. BARTHWICK. Nonsense, John, there's a time for everything.

SNOW. [Rather sardonically.] I might point out, sir, that to withdraw the charge of stealing would not make much difference, because the facts must come out [he looks significantly at JACK] in reference to the assault; and as I said that charge will have to go forward.

BARTHWICK. [Hastily.] Yes, oh! exactly! It's entirely on the woman's account—entirely a matter of my own private feelings.

SNOW. If I were you, sir, I should let things take their course. It's not likely there'll be much difficulty. These things are very quick settled.

BARTHWICK. [Doubtfully.] You think so—you think so?

JACK. [Rousing himself.] I say, what shall I have to swear to?

SNOW. That's best known to yourself, sir. [Retreating to the door.] Better employ a solicitor, sir, in case anything should arise. We shall have the butler to prove the loss of the article. You'll excuse me going, I 'm rather pressed to-night. The case may come on any time after eleven. Good evening, sir; good evening, ma'am. I shall have to produce the box in court to-morrow, so if you'll excuse me, sir, I may as well take it with me.

[He takes the silver box and leaves them with a little bow.]

[BARTHWICK makes a move to follow him, then dashing his hands beneath his coat tails, speaks with desperation.]

BARTHWICK. I do wish you'd leave me to manage things myself. You will put your nose into matters you know nothing of. A pretty mess you've made of this!

MRS. BARTHWICK. [Coldly.] I don't in the least know what you're talking about. If you can't stand up for your rights, I can. I 've no patience with your principles, it's such nonsense.

BARTHWICK. Principles! Good Heavens! What have principles to do with it for goodness sake? Don't you know that Jack was drunk last night!

JACK. Dad!

MRS. BARTHWICK. [In horror rising.] Jack!

JACK. Look here, Mother—I had supper. Everybody does. I mean to say—you know what I mean—it's absurd to call it being drunk. At Oxford everybody gets a bit "on" sometimes——

MRS. BARTHWICK. Well, I think it's most dreadful! If that is really what you do at Oxford?

JACK. [Angrily.] Well, why did you send me there? One must do as other fellows do. It's such nonsense, I mean, to call it being drunk. Of course I 'm awfully sorry. I 've had such a beastly headache all day.

BARTHWICK. Tcha! If you'd only had the common decency to remember what happened when you came in. Then we should know what truth there was in what this fellow says—as it is, it's all the most confounded darkness.

JACK. [Staring as though at half-formed visions.] I just get a— and then—it 's gone——

MRS. BARTHWICK. Oh, Jack! do you mean to say you were so tipsy you can't even remember——

JACK. Look here, Mother! Of course I remember I came—I must have come—

BARTHWICK. [Unguardedly, and walking up and down.] Tcha!—and that infernal purse! Good Heavens! It'll get into the papers. Who on earth could have foreseen a thing like this? Better to have lost a dozen cigarette-boxes, and said nothing about it. [To his wife.] It's all your doing. I told you so from the first. I wish to goodness Roper would come!

MRS. BARTHWICK. [Sharply.] I don't know what you're talking about, John.

BARTHWICK. [Turning on her.] No, you—you—you don't know anything! [Sharply.] Where the devil is Roper? If he can see a way out of this he's a better man than I take him for. I defy any one to see a way out of it. I can't.

JACK. Look here, don't excite Dad—I can simply say I was too beastly tired, and don't remember anything except that I came in and [in a dying voice] went to bed the same as usual.

BARTHWICK. Went to bed? Who knows where you went—I 've lost all confidence. For all I know you slept on the floor.

JACK. [Indignantly.] I did n't, I slept on the——

BARTHWICK. [Sitting on the sofa.] Who cares where you slept; what does it matter if he mentions the—the—a perfect disgrace?

MRS. BARTHWICK. What? [A silence.] I insist on knowing.

JACK. Oh! nothing.

MRS. BARTHWICK. Nothing? What do you mean by nothing, Jack? There's
        your father in such a state about it!

JACK. It's only my purse.

MRS. BARTHWICK. Your purse! You know perfectly well you have n't got one.

JACK. Well, it was somebody else's—it was all a joke—I did n't want the beast-
        ly thing.

MRS. BARTHWICK. Do you mean that you had another person's purse, and
        that this man took it too?

BARTHWICK. Tcha! Of course he took it too! A man like that Jones will make
        the most of it. It'll get into the papers.

MRS. BARTHWICK. I don't understand. What on earth is all the fuss about?
        [Bending over JACK, and softly.] Jack now, tell me dear!
        Don't be afraid. What is it? Come!

JACK. Oh, don't Mother!

MRS. BARTHWICK. But don't what, dear?

JACK. It was pure sport. I don't know how I got the thing. Of course I 'd had
        a bit of a row—I did n't know what I was doing—I was—I Was—well, you
        know—I suppose I must have pulled the bag out of her hand.

MRS. BARTHWICK. Out of her hand? Whose hand? What bag—whose bag?

JACK. Oh! I don't know—her bag—it belonged to—[in a desperate and rising
        voice] a woman.

MRS. BARTHWICK. A woman? Oh! Jack! No!

JACK. [Jumping up.] You would have it. I did n't want to tell you. It's not my
        fault.

[The door opens and MARLOW ushers in a man of middle age, inclined to cor-
pulence, in evening dress. He has a ruddy, thin moustache, and dark, quick-mov-
ing little eyes. His eyebrows aye Chinese.]

MARLOW. Mr. Roper, Sir. [He leaves the room.]

ROPER. [With a quick look round.] How do you do?

[But neither JACK nor MRS. BARTHWICK make a sign.]

BARTHWICK. [Hurrying.] Thank goodness you've come, Roper. You remem-
            ber what I told you this afternoon; we've just had the detective
            here.

ROPER. Got the box?

BARTHWICK. Yes, yes, but look here—it was n't the charwoman at all; her
            drunken loafer of a husband took the things—he says that fel-
            low there [he waves his hand at JACK, who with his shoulder
            raised, seems trying to ward off a blow] let him into the house
            last night. Can you imagine such a thing.

[Roper laughs.]

BARTHWICK. [With excited emphasis.]. It's no laughing matter, Roper. I told
            you about that business of Jack's too—don't you see the brute
            took both the things—took that infernal purse. It'll get into the
            papers.

ROPER. [Raising his eyebrows.] H'm! The purse! Depravity in high life! What
        does your son say?

BARTHWICK. He remembers nothing. D—n! Did you ever see such a mess?
            It 'll get into the papers.

MRS. BARTHWICK. [With her hand across hey eyes.] Oh! it's not that——

[BARTHWICK and ROPER turn and look at her.]

BARTHWICK. It's the idea of that woman—she's just heard——

[ROPER nods. And MRS. BARTHWICK, setting her lips, gives a slow look at
JACK, and sits down at the table.]

What on earth's to be done, Roper? A ruffian like this Jones will make all the capital he can out of that purse.

MRS. BARTHWICK. I don't believe that Jack took that purse.

BARTHWICK. What—when the woman came here for it this morning?

MRS. BARTHWICK. Here? She had the impudence? Why was n't I told?

[She looks round from face to face—no one answers hey, there is a pause.]

BARTHWICK. [Suddenly.] What's to be done, Roper?

ROPER. [Quietly to JACK.] I suppose you did n't leave your latch- key in the door?

JACK. [Sullenly.] Yes, I did.

BARTHWICK. Good heavens! What next?

MRS. BARTHWICK. I 'm certain you never let that man into the house, Jack, it's a wild invention. I'm sure there's not a word of truth in it, Mr. Roper.

ROPER. [Very suddenly.] Where did you sleep last night?

JACK. [Promptly.] On the sofa, there—[hesitating]—that is—I——

BARTHWICK. On the sofa? D' you mean to say you did n't go to bed?

JACK.[Sullenly.] No.

BARTHWICK. If you don't remember anything, how can you remember that?

JACK. Because I woke up there in the morning.

MRS. BARTHWICK. Oh, Jack!

BARTHWICK. Good Gracious!

JACK. And Mrs. Jones saw me. I wish you would n't bait me so.

ROPER. Do you remember giving any one a drink?

JACK. By Jove, I do seem to remember a fellow with—a fellow with [He looks at Roper.] I say, d' you want me——?

ROPER. [Quick as lightning.] With a dirty face?

JACK. [With illumination.] I do—I distinctly remember his——

[BARTHWICK moves abruptly; MRS. BARTHWICK looks at ROPER angrily, and touches her son's arm.]

MRS. BARTHWICK. You don't remember, it's ridiculous! I don't believe the man was ever here at all.

BARTHWICK. You must speak the truth, if it is the truth. But if you do remember such a dirty business, I shall wash my hands of you altogether.

JACK. [Glaring at them.] Well, what the devil——

MRS. BARTHWICK. Jack!

JACK. Well, Mother, I—I don't know what you do want.

MRS. BARTHWICK. We want you to speak the truth and say you never let this low man into the house.

BARTHWICK. Of course if you think that you really gave this man whisky in that disgraceful way, and let him see what you'd been doing, and were in such a disgusting condition that you don't remember a word of it——

ROPER. [Quick.] I've no memory myself—never had.

BARTHWICK. [Desperately.] I don't know what you're to say.

ROPER. [To JACK.] Say nothing at all! Don't put yourself in a false position. The man stole the things or the woman stole the things, you had nothing to do with it. You were asleep on the sofa.

MRS. BARTHWICK. Your leaving the latch-key in the door was quite bad enough, there's no need to mention anything else. [Touching his forehead softly.] My dear, how hot your head is!

JACK. But I want to know what I 'm to do. [Passionately.] I won't be badgered like this.

[MRS. BARTHWICK recoils from him.]

ROPER. [Very quickly.] You forget all about it. You were asleep.

JACK. Must I go down to the Court to-morrow?

ROPER. [Shaking his head.] No.

BARTHWICK. [In a relieved voice.] Is that so?

ROPER. Yes.

BARTHWICK. But you'll go, Roper.

ROPER. Yes.

JACK. [With wan cheerfulness.] Thanks, awfully! So long as I don't have to go. [Putting his hand up to his head.] I think if you'll excuse me—I've had a most beastly day. [He looks from his father to his mother.]

MRS. BARTHWICK. [Turning quickly.] Goodnight, my boy.

JACK. Good-night, Mother.

[He goes out. MRS. BARTHWICK heaves a sigh. There is a silence.]

BARTHWICK. He gets off too easily. But for my money that woman would have prosecuted him.

ROPER. You find money useful.

BARTHWICK. I've my doubts whether we ought to hide'the truth——

ROPER. There'll be a remand.

BARTHWICK. What! D' you mean he'll have to appear on the remand.

ROPER. Yes.

BARTHWICK. H'm, I thought you'd be able to——Look here, Roper, you must keep that purse out of the papers.

[ROPER fixes his little eyes on him and nods.]

MRS. BARTHWICK. Mr. Roper, don't you think the magistrate ought to be told what sort of people these Jones's are; I mean about their immorality before they were married. I don't know if John told you.

ROPER. Afraid it's not material.

MRS. BARTHWICK. Not material?

ROPER. Purely private life! May have happened to the magistrate.

BARTHWICK. [With a movement as if to shift a burden.] Then you'll take the thing into your hands?

ROPER. If the gods are kind. [He holds his hand out.]

BARTHWICK. [Shaking it dubiously.] Kind eh? What? You going?

ROPER. Yes. I've another case, something like yours—most unexpected.

[He bows to MRS. BARTHWICK, and goes out, followed by BARTHWICK, talking to the last. MRS. BARTHWICK at the table bursts into smothered sobs. BARTHWICK returns.]

BARTHWICK. [To himself.] There'll be a scandal!

MRS. BARTHWICK. [Disguising her grief at once.] I simply can't imagine what Roper means by making a joke of a thing like that!

BARTHWICK. [Staring strangely.] You! You can't imagine anything! You've no more imagination than a fly!

MRS. BARTHWICK. [Angrily.] You dare to tell me that I have no imagination.

BARTHWICK. [Flustered.] I—I 'm upset. From beginning to end, the whole thing has been utterly against my principles.

MRS. BARTHWICK. Rubbish! You have n't any! Your principles are nothing in the world but sheer fright!

BARTHWICK. [Walking to the window.] I've never been frightened in my life. You heard what Roper said. It's enough to upset one when a thing like this happens. Everything one says and does seems to turn in one's mouth—it's—it's uncanny. It's not the sort of thing I've been accustomed to. [As though stifling, he throws the window open. The faint sobbing of a child comes in.] What's that?

[They listen.]

MRS. BARTHWICK. [Sharply.] I can't stand that crying. I must send Marlow to stop it. My nerves are all on edge. [She rings the bell.]

BARTHWICK. I'll shut the window; you'll hear nothing. [He shuts the window. There is silence.]

MRS. BARTHWICK. [Sharply.] That's no good! It's on my nerves. Nothing upsets me like a child's crying.

[MARLOW comes in.]

What's that noise of crying, Marlow? It sounds like a child.

BARTHWICK. It is a child. I can see it against the railings.

MARLOW. [Opening the window, and looking out quietly.] It's Mrs. Jones's little boy, ma'am; he came here after his mother.

MRS. BARTHWICK. [Moving quickly to the window.] Poor little chap! John, we ought n't to go on with this!

BARTHWICK. [Sitting heavily in a chair.] Ah! but it's out of our hands!

[MRS. BARTHWICK turns her back to the window. There is an expression of distress on hey face. She stands motionless, compressing her lips. The crying begins again. BARTHWICK coveys his ears with his hands, and MARLOW shuts the window. The crying ceases.]

The curtain falls.

ACT III

Eight days have passed, and the scene is a London Police Court at one o'clock. A canopied seat of Justice is surmounted by the lion and unicorn. Before the fire a worn-looking MAGISTRATE is warming his coat-tails, and staring at two little girls in faded blue and orange rags, who are placed before the dock. Close to the witness-box is a RELIEVING OFFICER in an overcoat, and a short brown beard. Beside the little girls stands a bald POLICE CONSTABLE. On the front bench are sitting BARTHWICK and ROPER, and behind them JACK. In the railed enclosure are seedy-looking men and women. Some prosperous constables sit or stand about.

MAGISTRATE. [In his paternal and ferocious voice, hissing his s's.] Now let us dispose of these young ladies.

USHER. Theresa Livens, Maud Livens.

[The bald CONSTABLE indicates the little girls, who remain silent, disillusioned, inattentive.]

Relieving Officer!

[The RELIEVING OFFICER Steps into the witness-box.]

USHER. The evidence you give to the Court shall be the truth, the whole truth, and nothing but the truth, so help you God! Kiss the book!

[The book is kissed.]

RELIEVING OFFICER. [In a monotone, pausing slightly at each sentence end, that his evidence may be inscribed.] About ten o'clock this morning, your Worship, I found these two little girls in Blue Street, Fulham, crying outside a public-house. Asked where their home was, they said they had no home. Mother had gone away. Asked about their father. Their father had no work. Asked where they slept last night. At their aunt's. I 've made inquiries, your Worship. The wife has broken up the home and gone on the streets. The husband is out of work and living in common lodging-houses. The husband's sister has eight children of her own, and says she can't afford to keep these little girls any longer.

MAGISTRATE. [Returning to his seat beneath the canopy of justice.] Now, let me see. You say the mother is on the streets; what evidence have you of that?

RELIEVING OFFICER. I have the husband here, your Worship.

MAGISTRATE. Very well; then let us see him.

[There are cries of "LIVENS." The MAGISTRATE leans forward, and stares with hard compassion at the little girls. LIVENS comes in. He is quiet, with grizzled hair, and a muffler for a collar. He stands beside the witness-box.]

And you, are their father? Now, why don't you keep your little girls at home. How is it you leave them to wander about the streets like this?

LIVENS. I've got no home, your Worship. I'm living from 'and to mouth. I 've got no work; and nothin' to keep them on.

MAGISTRATE. How is that?

LIVENS. [Ashamedly.] My wife, she broke my 'ome up, and pawned the things.

MAGISTRATE. But what made you let her?

LEVINS. Your Worship, I'd no chance to stop 'er, she did it when I was out lookin' for work.

MAGISTRATE. Did you ill-treat her?

LIVENS. [Emphatically.] I never raised my 'and to her in my life, your Worship.

MAGISTRATE. Then what was it—did she drink?

LIVENS. Yes, your Worship.

MAGISTRATE. Was she loose in her behaviour?

LIVENS. [In a low voice.] Yes, your Worship.

MAGISTRATE. And where is she now?

LIVENS. I don't know your Worship. She went off with a man, and after that I—

MAGISTRATE. Yes, yes. Who knows anything of her? [To the bald CONSTABLE.] Is she known here?

RELIEVING OFFICER. Not in this district, your Worship; but I have ascertained that she is well known——

MAGISTRATE. Yes—yes; we'll stop at that. Now [To the Father] you say that she has broken up your home, and left these little girls. What provision can you make for them? You look a strong man.

LIVENS. So I am, your Worship. I'm willin' enough to work, but for the life of me I can't get anything to do.

MAGISTRATE. But have you tried?

LIVENS. I've tried everything, your Worship—I 've tried my 'ardest.

MAGISTRATE. Well, well——   [There is a silence.]

RELIEVING OFFICER. If your Worship thinks it's a case, my people are willing to take them.

MAGISTRATE. Yes, yes, I know; but I've no evidence that this man is not the proper guardian for his children.

[He rises oval goes back to the fire.]

RELIEVING OFFICER. The mother, your Worship, is able to get access to
      them.

MAGISTRATE. Yes, yes; the mother, of course, is an improper person to have
      anything to do with them. [To the Father.] Well, now what do
      you say?

LIVENS. Your Worship, I can only say that if I could get work I should be only
      too willing to provide for them. But what can I do, your Worship? Here
      I am obliged to live from 'and to mouth in these 'ere common lodging-
      houses. I 'm a strong man—I'm willing to work —I'm half as alive again
      as some of 'em—but you see, your Worship, my 'airs' turned a bit, owing
      to the fever—[Touches his hair]—and that's against me; and I don't seem
      to get a chance anyhow.

MAGISTRATE. Yes-yes. [Slowly.] Well, I think it 's a case. [Staring his hardest
      at the little girls.] Now, are you willing that these little girls
      should be sent to a home.

LIVENS. Yes, your Worship, I should be very willing.

MAGISTRATE. Well, I'll remand them for a week. Bring them again to-day
      week; if I see no reason against it then, I 'll make an order.

RELIEVING OFFICER. To-day week, your Worship.

[The bald CONSTABLE takes the little girls out by the shoulders. The father follows them. The MAGISTRATE, returning to his seat, bends over and talks to his
CLERK inaudibly.]

BARTHWICK. [Speaking behind his hand.] A painful case, Roper; very dis-
      tressing state of things.

ROPER. Hundreds like this in the Police Courts.

BARTHWICK. Most distressing! The more I see of it, the more important this
      question of the condition of the people seems to become. I
      shall certainly make a point of taking up the cudgels in the
      House. I shall move——

[The MAGISTRATE ceases talking to his CLERK.]

CLERK. Remands!

[BARTHWICK stops abruptly. There is a stir and MRS. JONES comes in by the public door; JONES, ushered by policemen, comes from the prisoner's door. They file into the dock.]

CLERK. James Jones, Jane Jones.

USHER. Jane Jones!

BARTHWICK. [In a whisper.] The purse—the purse must be kept out of it, Roper. Whatever happens you must keep that out of the papers.

[ROPER nods.]

BALD CONSTABLE. Hush!

[MRS. JONES, dressed in hey thin, black, wispy dress, and black straw hat, stands motionless with hands crossed on the front rail of the dock. JONES leans against the back rail of the dock, and keeps half turning, glancing defiantly about him. He is haggard and unshaven.]

CLERK. [Consulting with his papers.] This is the case remanded from last Wednesday, Sir. Theft of a silver cigarette-box and assault on the police; the two charges were taken together. Jane Jones! James Jones!

MAGISTRATE. [Staring.] Yes, yes; I remember.

CLERK. Jane Jones.

MRS. JONES. Yes, Sir.

CLERK. Do you admit stealing a silver cigarette-box valued at five pounds, ten shillings, from the house of John BARTHWICK, M.P., between the hours of 11 p.m. on Easter Monday and 8.45 a.m. on Easter Tuesday last? Yes, or no?

MRS. JONES. [In a logy voice.] No, Sir, I do not, sir.

CLERK. James Jones? Do you admit stealing a silver cigarette-box valued at five pounds, ten shillings, from the house of John BARTHWICK, M.P., between the hours of 11 p.m. on Easter Monday and 8.45 A.M. on Easter Tuesday last. And further making an assault on the police when in the execution of their duty at 3 p.m. on Easter Tuesday? Yes or no?

JONES. [Sullenly.] Yes, but I've got a lot to say about it.

MAGISTRATE. [To the CLERK.] Yes—yes. But how comes it that these two people are charged with the same offence? Are they husband and wife?

CLERK. Yes, Sir. You remember you ordered a remand for further evidence as to the story of the male prisoner.

MAGISTRATE. Have they been in custody since?

CLERK. You released the woman on her own recognisances, sir.

MAGISTRATE. Yes, yes, this is the case of the silver box; I remember now. Well?

CLERK. Thomas Marlow.

[The cry of "THOMAS MARLOW" is repeated MARLOW comes in, and steps into the witness-box.]

USHER. The evidence you give to the court shall be the truth, the whole truth, and nothing but the truth, so help you God. Kiss the book.

[The book is kissed. The silver box is handed up, and placed on the rail.]

CLERK. [Reading from his papers.] Your name is Thomas Marlow? Are you, butler to John BARTHWICK, M.P., of 6, Rockingham Gate?

MARLOW. Yes, Sir.

CLERK. Is that the box?

MARLOW. Yes Sir.

CLERK. And did you miss the same at 8.45 on the following morning, on going to remove the tray?

MARLOW. Yes, Sir.

CLERK. Is the female prisoner known to you?

[MARLOW nods.]

Is she the charwoman, employed at 6, Rockingham Gate?

[Again MARLOW nods.]

Did you at the time of your missing the box find her in the room alone?

MARLOW. Yes, Sir.

CLERK. Did you afterwards communicate the loss to your employer, and did he send you to the police station?

MARLOW. Yes, Sir.

CLERK. [To MRS. JONES.] Have you anything to ask him?

MRS. JONES. No, sir, nothing, thank you, sir.

CLERK. [To JONES.] James Jones, have you anything to ask this witness?

JONES. I don't know 'im.

MAGISTRATE. Are you sure you put the box in the place you say at the time you say?

MARLOW. Yes, your Worship.

MAGISTRATE. Very well; then now let us have the officer.

[MARLOW leaves the box, and Snow goes into it.]

USHER. The evidence you give to the court shall be the truth, the whole truth, and nothing but the truth, so help you God. [The book is kissed.]

CLERK. [Reading from his papers.] Your name is Robert Allow? You are a detective in the X. B. division of the Metropolitan police force? According to instructions received did you on Easter Tuesday last proceed to the prisoner's lodgings at 34, Merthyr Street, St. Soames's? And did you on entering see the box produced, lying on the table?

SNOW. Yes, Sir.

CLERK. Is that the box?

Snow. [Fingering the box.] Yes, Sir.

CLERK. And did you thereupon take possession of it, and charge the female prisoner with theft of the box from 6, Rockingham Gate? And did she deny the same?

SNOW. Yes, Sir.

CLERK. Did you take her into custody?

Snow. Yes, Sir.

MAGISTRATE. What was her behaviour?

SNOW. Perfectly quiet, your Worship. She persisted in the denial. That's all.

MAGISTRATE. DO you know her?

SNOW. No, your Worship.

MAGISTRATE. Is she known here?

BALD CONSTABLE. No, your Worship, they're neither of them known, we 've nothing against them at all.

CLERK. [To MRS. JONES.] Have you anything to ask the officer?

MRS. JONES. No, sir, thank you, I 've nothing to ask him.

MAGISTRATE. Very well then—go on.

CLERK. [Reading from his papers.] And while you were taking the female prisoner did the male prisoner interpose, and endeavour to hinder you in the execution of your duty, and did he strike you a blow?

SNOW. Yes, Sir.

CLERK. And did he say, "You, let her go, I took the box myself"?

SNOW. He did.

CLERK. And did you blow your whistle and obtain the assistance of another constable, and take him into custody?

SNOW. I did.

CLERK. Was he violent on the way to the station, and did he use bad language, and did he several times repeat that he had taken the box himself?

[Snow nods.]

Did you thereupon ask him in what manner he had stolen the box? And did you understand him to say he had entered the house at the invitation of young Mr. BARTHWICK

[BARTHWICK, turning in his seat, frowns at ROPER.]

after midnight on Easter Monday, and partaken of whisky, and that under the influence of the whisky he had taken the box?

SNOW. I did, sir.

CLERK. And was his demeanour throughout very violent?

SNOW. It was very violent.

JONES. [Breaking in.] Violent—of course it was! You put your 'ands on my wife when I kept tellin' you I took the thing myself.

MAGISTRATE. [Hissing, with protruded neck.] Now—you will have your chance of saying what you want to say presently. Have you anything to ask the officer?

JONES. [Sullenly.] No.

MAGISTRATE. Very well then. Now let us hear what the female prisoner has to say first.

MRS. JONES. Well, your Worship, of course I can only say what I 've said all along, that I did n't take the box.

MAGISTRATE. Yes, but did you know that it was taken?

MRS. JONES. No, your Worship. And, of course, to what my husband says, your Worship, I can't speak of my own knowledge. Of course, I know that he came home very late on the Monday night. It was past one o'clock when he came in, and he was not himself at all.

MAGISTRATE. Had he been drinking?

MRS. JONES. Yes, your Worship.

MAGISTRATE. And was he drunk?

MRS. JONES. Yes, your Worship, he was almost quite drunk.

MAGISTRATE. And did he say anything to you?

MRS. JONES. No, your Worship, only to call me names. And of course in the morning when I got up and went to work he was asleep. And I don't know anything more about it until I came home again. Except that Mr. BARTHWICK—that 's my employer, your Worship—told me the box was missing.

MAGISTRATE. Yes, yes.

MRS. JONES. But of course when I was shaking out my husband's coat the cigarette-box fell out and all the cigarettes were scattered on the bed.

MAGISTRATE. You say all the cigarettes were scattered on the bed? [To SNOW.] Did you see the cigarettes scattered on the bed?

SNOW. No, your Worship, I did not.

MAGISTRATE. You see he says he did n't see them.

JONES. Well, they were there for all that.

SNOW. I can't say, your Worship, that I had the opportunity of going round the room; I had all my work cut out with the male prisoner.

MAGISTRATE. [To MRS. JONES.] Well, what more have you to say?

MRS. JONES. Of course when I saw the box, your Worship, I was dreadfully upset, and I could n't think why he had done such a thing; when the officer came we were having words about it, because it is ruin to me, your Worship, in my profession, and I have three little children dependent on me.

MAGISTRATE. [Protruding his neck]. Yes—yes—but what did he say to you?

MRS. JONES. I asked him whatever came over him to do such a thing- and he said it was the drink. He said he had had too much to drink, and something came over him. And of course, your Worship, he had had very little to eat all day, and the drink does go to the head when you have not had enough to eat. Your Worship may not know, but it is the truth. And I would like to say that all through his married life, I have never known him to do such a thing before, though we have passed through great hardships and [speaking with soft emphasis] I am quite sure he would not have done it if he had been himself at the time.

MAGISTRATE. Yes, yes. But don't you know that that is no excuse?

MRS. JONES. Yes, your Worship. I know that it is no excuse.

[The MAGISTRATE leans over and parleys with his CLERK.]

JACK. [Leaning over from his seat behind.] I say, Dad——

BARTHWICK. Tsst! [Sheltering his mouth he speaks to ROPER.] Roper, you had better get up now and say that considering the circumstances and the poverty of the prisoners, we have no wish to proceed any further, and if the magistrate would deal with the case as one of disorder only on the part of——

BALD CONSTABLE. HSSShh!

[ROPER shakes his head.]

MAGISTRATE. Now, supposing what you say and what your husband says is true, what I have to consider is—how did he obtain access to this house, and were you in any way a party to his obtaining access? You are the charwoman employed at the house?

MRS. JONES. Yes, your Worship, and of course if I had let him into the house it would have been very wrong of me; and I have never done such a thing in any of the houses where I have been employed.

MAGISTRATE. Well—so you say. Now let us hear what story the male prisoner makes of it.

JONES. [Who leans with his arms on the dock behind, speaks in a slow, sullen voice.] Wot I say is wot my wife says. I 've never been 'ad up in a police court before, an' I can prove I took it when in liquor. I told her, and she can tell you the same, that I was goin' to throw the thing into the water sooner then 'ave it on my mind.

MAGISTRATE. But how did you get into the HOUSE?

JONES. I was passin'. I was goin' 'ome from the "Goat and Bells."

MAGISTRATE. The "Goat and Bells,"—what is that? A public-house?

JONES. Yes, at the corner. It was Bank 'oliday, an' I'd 'ad a drop to drink. I see this young Mr. BARTHWICK tryin' to find the keyhole on the wrong side of the door.

MAGISTRATE. Well?

JONES. [Slowly and with many pauses.] Well——I 'elped 'im to find it—drunk as a lord 'e was. He goes on, an' comes back again, and says, I 've got nothin' for you, 'e says, but come in an' 'ave a drink. So I went in just as you might 'ave done yourself. We 'ad a drink o' whisky just as you might have 'ad, 'nd young Mr. BARTHWICK says to me, "Take a drink 'nd a smoke. Take anything you like, 'e says." And then he went to sleep on the sofa. I 'ad some more whisky—an' I 'ad a smoke—and I 'ad some more whisky—an' I carn't tell yer what 'appened after that.

MAGISTRATE. Do you mean to say that you were so drunk that you can remember nothing?

JACK. [Softly to his father.] I say, that's exactly what——

BARTHWICK. TSSh!

JONES. That's what I do mean.

MAGISTRATE. And yet you say you stole the box?

JONES. I never stole the box. I took it.

MAGISTRATE. [Hissing with protruded neck.] You did not steal it— you took it. Did it belong to you—what is that but stealing?

JONES. I took it.

MAGISTRATE. You took it—you took it away from their house and you took it to your house——

JONES. [Sullenly breaking in.] I ain't got a house.

MAGISTRATE. Very well, let us hear what this young man Mr.—Mr. BARTH-WICK has to say to your story.

[SNOW leaves the witness-box. The BALD CONSTABLE beckons JACK, who, clutching his hat, goes into the witness-box. ROPER moves to the table set apart for his profession.]

SWEARING CLERK. The evidence you give to the court shall be the truth, the whole truth, and nothing but the truth, so help you God. Kiss the book.

[The book is kissed.]

ROPER. [Examining.] What is your name?

JACK. [In a low voice.] John BARTHWICK, Junior.

[The CLERK writes it down.]

ROPER. Where do you live?

JACK. At 6, Rockingham Gate.

[All his answers are recorded by the Clerk.]

ROPER. You are the son of the owner?

JACK. [In a very low voice.] Yes.

ROPER. Speak up, please. Do you know the prisoners?

JACK. [Looking at the JONESES, in a low voice.] I 've seen Mrs. Jones. I [in a loud voice] don't know the man.

JONES. Well, I know you!

BALD CONSTABLE. HSSh!

ROPER. Now, did you come in late on the night of Easter Monday?

JACK. Yes.

ROPER. And did you by mistake leave your latch key in the door?

JACK. Yes.

MAGISTRATE. Oh! You left your latch-key in the door?

ROPER. And is that all you can remember about your coming in?

JACK. [In a loud voice.] Yes, it is.

MAGISTRATE. Now, you have heard the male prisoner's story, what do you say to that?

JACK. [Turning to the MAGISTRATE, speaks suddenly in a confident, straight-forward voice.] The fact of the matter is, sir, that I 'd been out to the the-atre that night, and had supper afterwards, and I came in late.

MAGISTRATE. Do you remember this man being outside when you came in?

JACK. No, Sir. [He hesitates.] I don't think I do.

MAGISTRATE. [Somewhat puzzled.] Well, did he help you to open the door, as he says? Did any one help you to open the door?

JACK. No, sir—I don't think so, sir—I don't know.

MAGISTRATE. You don't know? But you must know. It is n't a usual thing for you to have the door opened for you, is it?

JACK. [With a shamefaced smile.] No.

MAGISTRATE. Very well, then——

JACK. [Desperately.] The fact of the matter is, sir, I'm afraid I'd had too much champagne that night.

MAGISTRATE. [Smiling.] Oh! you'd had too much champagne?

JONES. May I ask the gentleman a question?

MAGISTRATE. Yes—yes—you may ask him what questions you like.

JONES. Don't you remember you said you was a Liberal, same as your father, and you asked me wot I was?

JACK. [With his hand against his brow.] I seem to remember——

JONES. And I said to you, "I'm a bloomin' Conservative," I said; an' you said to me, "You look more like one of these 'ere Socialists. Take wotever you like," you said.

JACK. [With sudden resolution.] No, I don't. I don't remember anything of the sort.

JONES. Well, I do, an' my word's as good as yours. I 've never been had up in a police court before. Look 'ere, don't you remember you had a sky-blue bag in your 'and [BARTHWICK jumps.]

ROPER. I submit to your worship that these questions are hardly to the point, the prisoner having admitted that he himself does not remember anything. [There is a smile on the face of Justice.] It is a case of the blind leading the blind.

JONES. [Violently.] I've done no more than wot he 'as. I'm a poor man; I've got no money an' no friends—he 's a toff—he can do wot I can't.

MAGISTRATE: Now, now? All this won't help you—you must be quiet. You say you took this box? Now, what made you take it? Were you pressed for money?

JONES. I'm always pressed for money.

MAGISTRATE. Was that the reason you took it?

JONES. No.

MAGISTRATE. [To SNOW.] Was anything found on him?

SNOW. Yes, your worship. There was six pounds twelve shillin's found on him, and this purse.

[The red silk purse is handed to the MAGISTRATE. BARTHWICK rises his seat, but hastily sits down again.]

MAGISTRATE. [Staring at the purse.] Yes, yes—let me see [There is a silence.] No, no, I 've nothing before me as to the purse. How did you come by all that money?

JONES. [After a long pause, suddenly.] I declines to say.

MAGISTRATE. But if you had all that money, what made you take this box?

JONES. I took it out of spite.

MAGISTRATE. [Hissing, with protruded neck.] You took it out of spite? Well now, that's something! But do you imagine you can go about the town taking things out of spite?

JONES. If you had my life, if you'd been out of work——

MAGISTRATE. Yes, yes; I know—because you're out of work you think it's an excuse for everything.

JONES. [Pointing at JACK.] You ask 'im wot made 'im take the——

ROPER. [Quietly.] Does your Worship require this witness in the box any longer?

MAGISTRATE. [Ironically.] I think not; he is hardly profitable.

[JACK leaves the witness-box, and hanging his head, resumes his seat.]

JONES. You ask 'im wot made 'im take the lady's——

[But the BALD CONSTABLE catches him by the sleeve.]

BALD CONSTABLE. SSSh!

MAGISTRATE. [Emphatically.] Now listen to me.

I 've nothing to do with what he may or may not have taken. Why did you resist the police in the execution of their duty?

JONES. It war n't their duty to take my wife, a respectable woman, that 'ad n't done nothing.

MAGISTRATE. But I say it was. What made you strike the officer a blow?

JONES. Any man would a struck 'im a blow. I'd strike 'im again, I would.

MAGISTRATE. You are not making your case any better by violence. How do you suppose we could get on if everybody behaved like you?

JONES. [Leaning forward, earnestly.] Well, wot, about 'er; who's to make up to 'er for this? Who's to give 'er back 'er good name?

MRS. JONES.   Your Worship, it's the children that's preying on his mind, because of course I 've lost my work.   And I've had to find another room owing to the scandal.

MAGISTRATE.   Yes, yes, I know—but if he had n't acted like this nobody would have suffered.

JONES.   [Glaring round at JACK.]   I 've done no worse than wot 'e 'as.   Wot I want to know is wot 's goin' to be done to 'im.

[The BALD CONSTABLE again says "HSSh"]

ROPER.   Mr. BARTHWICK wishes it known, your Worship, that considering the poverty of the prisoners, he does not press the charge as to the box. Perhaps your Worship would deal with the case as one of disorder.

JONES.   I don't want it smothered up, I want it all dealt with fair- -I want my rights——

MAGISTRATE.   [Rapping his desk.]   Now you have said all you have to say, and you will be quiet.

[There is a silence; the MAGISTRATE bends over and parleys with his CLERK.]

Yes, I think I may discharge the woman.   [In a kindly voice he addresses MRS. JONES, who stands unmoving with her hands crossed on the rail.]   It is very unfortunate for you that this man has behaved as he has.   It is not the consequences to him but the consequences to you.   You have been brought here twice, you have lost your work— [He glares at JONES]—and this is what always happens.   Now you may go away, and I am very sorry it was necessary to bring you here at all.

MRS. JONES.   [Softly.]   Thank you very much, your Worship.

[She leaves the dock, and looking back at JONES, twists her fingers and is still.]

MAGISTRATE.   Yes, yes, but I can't pass it over.   Go away, there's a good woman.

[MRS. JONES stands back.   The MAGISTRATE leans his head on his hand; then raising it he speaks to JONES.]

Now, listen to me. Do you wish the case to be settled here, or do you wish it to go before a jury?

JONES. [Muttering.] I don't want no jury.

MAGISTRATE. Very well then, I will deal with it here. [After a pause.] You have pleaded guilty to stealing this box——

JONES. Not to stealin'——

BALD CONSTABLE. HSSShh!

MAGISTRATE. And to assaulting the police——

JONES. Any man as was a man——

MAGISTRATE. Your conduct here has been most improper. You give the excuse that you were drunk when you stole the box. I tell you that is no excuse. If you choose to get drunk and break the law afterwards you must take the consequences. And let me tell you that men like you, who get drunk and give way to your spite or whatever it is that's in you, are—are—a nuisance to the community.

JACK. [Leaning from his seat.] Dad! that's what you said to me!

BARTHWICK. TSSt!

[There is a silence, while the MAGISTRATE consults his CLERK; JONES leans forward waiting.]

MAGISTRATE. This is your first offence, and I am going to give you a light sentence. [Speaking sharply, but without expression.] One month with hard labour.

[He bends, and parleys with his CLERK. The BALD CONSTABLE and another help JONES from the dock.]

JONES. [Stopping and twisting round.] Call this justice? What about 'im? 'E got drunk! 'E took the purse—'e took the purse but [in a muffled shout] it's 'is money got 'im off—JUSTICE!

[The prisoner's door is shut on JONES, and from the seedy- looking men and women comes a hoarse and whispering groan.]

MAGISTRATE. We will now adjourn for lunch! [He rises from his seat.]

[The Court is in a stir. ROPER gets up and speaks to the reporter. JACK, throwing up his head, walks with a swagger to the corridor; BARTHWICK follows.]

MRS. JONES. [Turning to him zenith a humble gesture.] Oh! sir!

[BARTHWICK hesitates, then yielding to his nerves, he makes a shame-faced gesture of refusal, and hurries out of court. MRS. JONES stands looking after him.]

The curtain falls.

JOY

A PLAY ON THE LETTER "I" IN THREE ACTS

PERSONS OF THE PLAY

COLONEL HOPE, R.A., retired
MRS. HOPE, his wife
MISS BEECH, their old governess
LETTY, their daughter
ERNEST BLUNT, her husband
MRS. GWYN, their niece
JOY, her daughter
DICK MERTON, their young friend
HON. MAURICE LEVER, their guest
ROSE, their parlour-maid

TIME: The present. The action passes throughout midsummer day on the lawn of Colonel Hope's house, near the Thames above Oxford.

ACT I

The time is morning, and the scene a level lawn, beyond which the river is running amongst fields. A huge old beech tree overshadows everything, in the darkness of whose hollow many things are hidden. A rustic seat encircles it. A low wall clothed in creepers, with two openings, divides this lawn from the flowery approaches to the house. Close to the wall there is a swing. The sky is clear and sunny. COLONEL HOPE is seated in a garden-chair, reading a newspaper through pince-nez. He is fifty-five and bald, with drooping grey moustaches and a weather-darkened face. He wears a flannel suit and a hat from Panama; a tennis racquet leans against his chair. MRS. HOPE comes quickly through the opening of the wall, with roses in her hands. She is going grey; she wears tan gauntlets, and no hat. Her manner is decided, her voice emphatic, as though aware that there is no nonsense in its owner's composition. Screened from sight, MISS BEECH is seated behind the hollow tree; and JOY is perched on a lower branch hidden by foliage.

MRS. HOPE. I told Molly in my letter that she'd have to walk up, Tom.

COLONEL. Walk up in this heat? My dear, why didn't you order Benson's fly?

MRS. HOPE. Expense for nothing! Bob can bring up her things in the barrow. I've told Joy I won't have her going down to meet the train. She's so excited about her mother's coming there's no doing anything with her.

COLONEL. No wonder, after two months.

MRS. HOPE. Well, she's going home to-morrow; she must just keep herself fresh
                        for the dancing tonight. I'm not going to get people in to dance,
                        and have Joy worn out before they begin.

COLONEL. [Dropping his paper.] I don't like Molly's walking up.

MRS. HOPE. A great strong woman like Molly Gwyn! It isn't half a mile.

COLONEL. I don't like it, Nell; it's not hospitable.

MRS. HOPE. Rubbish! If you want to throw away money, you must just find
                        some better investment than those wretched 3 per cents. of yours.
                        The greenflies are in my roses already! Did you ever see anything
                        so disgusting? [They bend over the roses they have grown, and
                        lose all sense of everything.] Where's the syringe? I saw you
                        mooning about with it last night, Tom.

COLONEL. [Uneasily.] Mooning!

[He retires behind his paper. MRS. HOPE enters the hollow of the tree.]

There's an account of that West Australian swindle. Set of ruffians! Listen to this,
Nell! "It is understood that amongst the share- holders are large numbers of
women, clergymen, and Army officers." How people can be such fools!

[Becoming aware that his absorption is unobserved, he drops his glasses, and
reverses his chair towards the tree.]

MRS. HOPE. [Reappearing with a garden syringe. I simply won't have Dick
                        keep his fishing things in the tree; there's a whole potful of dis-
                        gusting worms. I can't touch them. You must go and take 'em
                        out, Tom.

[In his turn the COLONEL enters the hollow of the tree.]

MRS. HOPE. [Personally.] What on earth's the pleasure of it? I can't see! He
                        never catches anything worth eating.

[The COLONEL reappears with a paint pot full of worms; he holds them out abstractedly.]

MRS. HOPE. [Jumping.] Don't put them near me!

MISS BEECH. [From behind the tree.] Don't hurt the poor creatures.

COLONEL. [Turning.] Hallo, Peachey? What are you doing round there?

[He puts the worms down on the seat.]

MRS. HOPE. Tom, take the worms off that seat at once!

COLONEL. [Somewhat flurried.] Good gad! I don't know what to do with the beastly worms!

MRS. HOPE. It's not my business to look after Dick's worms. Don't put them on the ground. I won't have them anywhere where they can crawl about. [She flicks some greenflies off her roses.]

COLONEL. [Looking into the pot as though the worms could tell him where to put them.] Dash!

MISS BEECH. Give them to me.

MRS. HOPE. [Relieved.] Yes, give them to Peachey.

[There comes from round the tree Miss BEECH, old-fashioned, barrel-shaped, balloony in the skirts. She takes the paint pot, and sits beside it on the rustic seat.]

MISS BEECH. Poor creatures!

MRS. HOPE. Well, it's beyond me how you can make pets of worms- wriggling, crawling, horrible things!

[ROSE, who is young and comely, in a pale print frock, comes from the house and places letters before her on a silver salver.]

[Taking the letters.]

What about Miss joy's frock, Rose?

ROSE. Please, 'm, I can't get on with the back without Miss Joy.

MRS. HOPE. Well, then you must just find her. I don't know where she is.

ROSE. [In a slow, sidelong manner.] If you please, Mum, I think Miss Joy's up in the——

[She stops, seeing Miss BEECH signing to her with both hands.]

MRS. HOPE. [Sharply.] What is it, Peachey?

MISS BEECH. [Selecting a finger.] Pricked meself!

MRS. HOPE. Let's look!

[She bends to look, but Miss BEECH places the finger in her mouth.]

ROSE. [Glancing askance at the COLONEL.] If you please, Mum, it's below the waist; I think I can manage with the dummy.

MRS. HOPE. Well, you can try. [Opening her letter as ROSE retires.] Here's Molly about her train.

MISS BEECH. Is there a letter for me?

MRS. HOPE. No, Peachey.

MISS BEECH. There never is.

COLONEL. What's that? You got four by the first post.

MISS BEECH. Exceptions!

COLONEL. [Looking over his glasses.] Why! You know, you get 'em every day!

MRS. HOPE. Molly says she'll be down by the eleven thirty. [In an injured voice.] She'll be here in half an hour! [Reading with disapproval from the letter.] "MAURICE LEVER is coming down by the same train to see Mr. Henty about the Tocopala Gold Mine. Could you give him a bed for the night?"

[Silence, slight but ominous.]

COLONEL. [Calling into his aid his sacred hospitality.] Of course we must give him a bed!

MRS. HOPE. Just like a man! What room I should like to know!

COLONEL. Pink.

MRS. HOPE. As if Molly wouldn't have the pink!

COLONEL. [Ruefully.] I thought she'd have the blue!

MRS. HOPE. You know perfectly well it's full of earwigs, Tom. I killed ten there yesterday morning.

MISS BEECH. Poor creatures!

MRS. HOPE. I don't know that I approve of this Mr. Lever's dancing attendance. Molly's only thirty-six.

COLONEL. [In a high voice.] You can't refuse him a bed; I never heard of such a thing.

MRS. HOPE. [Reading from the letter.] "This gold mine seems to be a splendid chance. [She glances at the COLONEL.] I've put all my spare cash into it. They're issuing some Preference shares now; if Uncle Tom wants an investment"—[She pauses, then in a changed, decided voice]—Well, I suppose I shall have to screw him in somehow.

COLONEL. What's that about gold mines? Gambling nonsense! Molly ought to know my views.

MRS. HOPE. [Folding the letter away out of her consciousness.] Oh! your views! This may be a specially good chance.

MISS BEECH. Ahem! Special case!

MRS. HOPE. [Paying no attention.] I 'm sick of these 3 per cent. dividends. When you've only got so little money, to put it all into that India

Stock, when it might be earning 6 per cent. at least, quite safely! There are ever so many things I want.

COLONEL. There you go!

MRS. HOPE. As to Molly, I think it's high time her husband came home to look after her, instead of sticking out there in that hot place. In fact

[Miss BEECH looks up at the tree and exhibits cerebral excitement]

I don't know what Geoff's about; why doesn't he find something in England, where they could live together.

COLONEL. Don't say anything against Molly, Nell!

MRS. HOPE. Well, I don't believe in husband and wife being separated. That's not my idea of married life.

[The COLONEL whistles quizzically.]

Ah, yes, she's your niece, not mime! Molly's very——

MISS BEECH. Ouch! [She sucks her finger.]

MRS. HOPE. Well, if I couldn't sew at your age, Peachey, without pricking my fingers! Tom, if I have Mr. Lever here, you'll just attend to what I say and look into that mine!

COLONEL. Look into your grandmother! I have n't made a study of geology for nothing. For every ounce you take out of a gold mine, you put an ounce and a half in. Any fool knows that, eh, Peachey?

MISS BEECH. I hate your horrid mines, with all the poor creatures underground.

MRS. HOPE. Nonsense, Peachey! As if they'd go there if they did n't want to!

COLONEL. Why don't you read your paper, then you'd see what a lot of wildcat things there are about.

MRS. HOPE. [Abstractedly.] I can't put Ernest and Letty in the blue room, there's only the single bed. Suppose I put Mr. Lever there, and say nothing about the earwigs. I daresay he'll never notice.

COLONEL. Treat a guest like that!

MRS. HOPE. Then where am I to put him for goodness sake?

COLONEL. Put him in my dressing-room, I'll turn out.

MRS. HOPE. Rubbish, Tom, I won't have you turned out, that's flat. He can have Joy's room, and she can sleep with the earwigs.

JOY. [From her hiding-place upon a lower branch of the hollow tree.] I won't.

[MRS. HOPE and the COLONEL jump.]

COLONEL. God bless my soul!

MRS. HOPE. You wretched girl! I told you never to climb that tree again. Did you know, Peachey? [Miss BEECH smiles.] She's always up there, spoiling all her frocks. Come down now, Joy; there's a good child!

JOY. I don't want to sleep with earwigs, Aunt Nell.

MISS BEECH. I'll sleep with the poor creatures.

MRS. HOPE, [After a pause.] Well, it would be a mercy if you would for once, Peachey.

COLONEL. Nonsense, I won't have Peachey——

MRS. HOPE. Well, who is to sleep there then?

JOY. [Coaxingly.] Let me sleep with Mother, Aunt Nell, do!

MRS. HOPE. Litter her up with a great girl like you, as if we'd only one spare room! Tom, see that she comes down—I can't stay here, I must manage something. [She goes away towards the house.]

COLONEL. [Moving to the tree, and looking up.] You heard what your aunt said?

JOY. [Softly.] Oh, Uncle Tom!

COLONEL. I shall have to come up after you.

JOY. Oh, do, and Peachey too!

COLONEL. [Trying to restrain a smile.] Peachey, you talk to her. [Without waiting for MISS BEECH, however, he proceeds.] What'll your aunt say to me if I don't get you down?

MISS BEECH. Poor creature!

JOY. I don't want to be worried about my frock.

COLONEL. [Scratching his bald head.] Well, I shall catch it.

JOY. Oh, Uncle Tom, your head is so beautiful from here! [Leaning over, she fans it with a leafy twig.]

MISS BEECH. Disrespectful little toad!

COLONEL. [Quickly putting on his hat.] You'll fall out, and a pretty mess that'll make on—[he looks uneasily at the ground]—my lawn!

[A voice is heard calling "Colonel! Colonel!"]

JOY. There's Dick calling you, Uncle Tom.

[She disappears.]

DICK. [Appearing in the opening of the wall.] Ernie's waiting to play you that single, Colonel!

[He disappears.]

JOY. Quick, Uncle Tom! Oh! do go, before he finds I 'm up here.

MISS. BEECH. Secret little creature!

[The COLONEL picks up his racquet, shakes his fist, and goes away.]

JOY. [Calmly.] I'm coming down now, Peachey.

[Climbing down.]

Look out! I'm dropping on your head.

MISS BEECH. [Unmoved.] Don't hurt yourself!

[Joy drops on the rustic seat and rubs her shin. Told you so!]

[She hunts in a little bag for plaster.]

Let's see!

JOY. [Seeing the worms.] Ugh!

MISS BEECH. What's the matter with the poor creatures?

JOY. They're so wriggly!

[She backs away and sits down in the swing. She is just seventeen, light and slim, brown-haired, fresh-coloured, and grey-eyed; her white frock reaches to her ankles, she wears a sunbonnet.] Peachey, how long were you Mother's governess.

MISS BEECH. Five years.

JOY. Was she as bad to teach as me?

MISS BEECH. Worse!

[Joy claps her hands.]

She was the worst girl I ever taught.

JOY. Then you weren't fond of her?

MISS BEECH. Oh! yes, I was.

JOY. Fonder than of me?

MISS BEECH. Don't you ask such a lot of questions.

JOY. Peachey, duckie, what was Mother's worst fault?

MISS BEECH. Doing what she knew she oughtn't.

JOY. Was she ever sorry?

MISS BEECH. Yes, but she always went on doin' it.

JOY. I think being sorry 's stupid!

MISS BEECH. Oh, do you?

JOY. It isn't any good. Was Mother revengeful, like me?

MISS BEECH. Ah! Wasn't she?

JOY. And jealous?

MISS BEECH. The most jealous girl I ever saw.

JOY. [Nodding.] I like to be like her.

MISS BEECH. [Regarding her intently.] Yes! you've got all your troubles before
    you.

JOY. Mother was married at eighteen, wasn't she, Peachey? Was she— was she
    much in love with Father then?

MISS BEECH. [With a sniff.] About as much as usual. [She takes the paint pot,
    and walking round begins to release the worms.]

JOY. [Indifferently.] They don't get on now, you know.

MISS BEECH. What d'you mean by that, disrespectful little creature?

JOY. [In a hard voice.] They haven't ever since I've known them. MISS BEECH.
    [Looks at her, and turns away again.] Don't talk about such things.

JOY. I suppose you don't know Mr. Lever? [Bitterly.] He's such a cool beast. He never loses his temper.

MISS BEECH. Is that why you don't like him?

JOY. [Frowning.] No—yes—I don't know.

MISS BEECH. Oh! perhaps you do like him?

JOY. I don't; I hate him.

MISS BEECH. [Standing still.] Fie! Naughty Temper!

JOY. Well, so would you! He takes up all Mother's time.

MISS BEECH. [In a peculiar voice.] Oh! does he?

JOY. When he comes I might just as well go to bed. [Passionately.] And now he's chosen to-day to come down here, when I haven't seen her for two months! Why couldn't he come when Mother and I'd gone home. It's simply brutal!

MISS BEECH. But your mother likes him?

JOY. [Sullenly.] I don't want her to like him.

MISS BEECH. [With a long look at Joy.] I see!

JOY. What are you doing, Peachey?

MISS BEECH. [Releasing a worm.] Letting the poor creatures go.

JOY. If I tell Dick he'll never forgive you.

MISS BEECH. [Sidling behind the swing and plucking off Joy's sunbonnet. With devilry.] Ah-h-h! You've done your hair up; so that's why you wouldn't come down!

JOY. [Springing up, anal pouting.] I didn't want any one to see before Mother. You are a pig, Peachey!

MISS BEECH. I thought there was something!

JOY. [Twisting round.] How does it look?

MISS BEECH. I've seen better.

JOY. You tell any one before Mother comes, and see what I do!

MISS BEECH. Well, don't you tell about my worms, then!

JOY. Give me my hat! [Backing hastily towards the tree, and putting her finger
    to her lips.] Look out! Dick!

MISS BEECH. Oh! dear!

[She sits down on the swing, concealing the paint pot with her feet and skirts.]

JOY. [On the rustic seat, and in a violent whisper.] I hope the worms will crawl
    up your legs!

[DICK, in flannels and a hard straw hat comes in. He is a quiet and cheerful boy
of twenty. His eyes are always fixed on joy.]

DICK. [Grimacing.] The Colonel's getting licked. Hallo! Peachey, in the swing?

JOY. [Chuckling.] Swing her, Dick!

MISS BEECH. [Quivering with emotion.] Little creature!

JOY. Swing her!

[DICK takes the ropes.]

MISS BEECH. [Quietly.] It makes me sick, young man.

DICK. [Patting her gently on the back.] All right, Peachey.

MISS BEECH. [Maliciously.] Could you get me my sewing from the seat? Just
    behind Joy.

JOY. [Leaning her head against the tree.] If you do, I won't dance with you to-night.

[DICK stands paralysed. Miss BEECH gets off the swing, picks up the paint pot, and stands concealing it behind her.]

JOY. Look what she's got behind her, sly old thing!

MISS BEECH. Oh! dear!

JOY. Dance with her, Dick!

MISS BEECH. If he dare!

JOY. Dance with her, or I won't dance with you to-night. [She whistles a waltz.]

DICK. [Desperately.] Come on then, Peachey. We must.

JOY. Dance, dance!

[DICK seizes Miss BEECH by the waist. She drops the paint pot. They revolve.] [Convulsed.]

Oh, Peachey, Oh!

[Miss BEECH is dropped upon the rustic seat. DICK seizes joy's hands and drags her up.]

No, no! I won't!

MISS BEECH. [Panting.] Dance, dance with the poor young man! [She moves her hands.] La la-la-la la-la la la!

[DICK and JOY dance.]

DICK. By Jove, Joy! You've done your hair up. I say, how jolly! You do look—

JOY. [Throwing her hands up to her hair.] I did n't mean you to see!

DICK. [In a hurt voice.] Oh! didn't you? I'm awfully sorry!

JOY. [Flashing round.] Oh, you old Peachey!

[She looks at the ground, and then again at DICK.]

MISS BEECH. [Sidling round the tree.] Oh! dear!

JOY. [Whispering.] She's been letting out your worms. [Miss BEECH disappears from view.] Look!

DICK. [Quickly.] Hang the worms! Joy, promise me the second and fourth and sixth and eighth and tenth and supper, to-night. Promise! Do!

[Joy shakes her head.]

It's not much to ask.

JOY. I won't promise anything.

DICK. Why not?

JOY. Because Mother's coming. I won't make any arrangements.

DICK. [Tragically.] It's our last night.

JOY. [Scornfully.] You don't understand! [Dancing and clasping her hands.] Mother's coming, Mother's coming!

DICK. [Violently.] I wish——Promise, Joy!

JOY. [Looking over her shoulder.] Sly old thing! If you'll pay Peachey out, I'll promise you supper!

MISS BEECH. [From behind the tree.] I hear you.

JOY. [Whispering.] Pay her out, pay her out! She's let out all your worms!

DICK. [Looking moodily at the paint pot.] I say, is it true that Maurice Lever's coming with your mother? I've met him playing cricket, he's rather a good sort.

JOY. [Flashing out.] I hate him.

DICK. [Troubled.] Do you? Why? I thought—I didn't know—if I'd known of
    course, I'd have———

[He is going to say "hated him too!" But the voices of ERNEST BLUNT and the
COLONEL are heard approaching, in dispute.]

JOY. Oh! Dick, hide me, I don't want my hair seen till Mother comes.

[She springs into the hollow tree. The COLONEL and ERNEST appear in the
opening of the wall.]

ERNEST. The ball was out, Colonel.

COLONEL. Nothing of the sort.

ERNEST. A good foot out.

COLONEL. It was not, sir. I saw the chalk fly.

[ERNEST is twenty-eight, with a little moustache, and the positive cool voice of
a young man who knows that he knows everything. He is perfectly calm.]

ERNEST. I was nearer to it than you.

COLONEL. [In a high, hot voice.] I don't care where you were, I hate a fellow
    who can't keep cool.

MISS BEECH. [From behind the hollow tree.] Fie! Fie!

ERNEST. We're two to one, Letty says the ball was out.

COLONEL. Letty's your wife, she'd say anything.

ERNEST. Well, look here, Colonel, I'll show you the very place it pitched.

COLONEL. Gammon! You've lost your temper, you don't know what you're
    talking about.

ERNEST. [coolly.] I suppose you'll admit the rule that one umpires one's own
    court.

COLONEL. [Hotly.] Certainly not, in this case!

MISS BEECH. [From behind the hollow tree.] Special case!

ERNEST. [Moving chin in collar—very coolly.] Well, of course if you won't play the game!

COLONEL. [In a towering passion.] If you lose your temper like this, I 'll never play with you again.

[To LETTY, a pretty soul in a linen suit, approaching through the wall.]

Do you mean to say that ball was out, Letty?

LETTY. Of course it was, Father.

COLONEL. You say that because he's your husband. [He sits on the rustic seat.] If your mother'd been there she'd have backed me up!

LETTY. Mother wants Joy, Dick, about her frock.

DICK. I—I don't know where she is.

MISS BEECH. [From behind the hollow tree.] Ahem!

LETTY. What's the matter, Peachey?

MISS BEECH. Swallowed a fly. Poor creature!

ERNEST. [Returning to his point.] Why I know the ball was out, Colonel, was because it pitched in a line with that arbutus tree.

COLONEL. [Rising.] Arbutus tree! [To his daughter.] Where's your mother?

LETTY. In the blue room, Father.

ERNEST. The ball was a good foot out; at the height it was coming when it passed me.

COLONEL. [Staring at him.] You're a—you're aa theorist! From where you were you could n't see the ball at all. [To LETTY.] Where's your mother?

LETTY. [Emphatically.] In the blue room, Father!

[The COLONEL glares confusedly, and goes away towards the blue room.]

ERNEST. [In the swing, and with a smile.] Your old Dad'll never be a sports-man!

LETTY. [Indignantly.] I wish you wouldn't call Father old, Ernie! What time's Molly coming, Peachey?

[ROSE has come from the house, and stands waiting for a chance to speak.]

ERNEST. [Breaking in.] Your old Dad's only got one fault: he can't take an impersonal view of things.

MISS BEECH. Can you find me any one who can?

ERNEST. [With a smile.] Well, Peachey!

MISS BEECH. [Ironically.] Oh! of course, there's you!

ERNEST. I don't know about that! But——

ROSE. [To LETTY,] Please, Miss, the Missis says will you and Mr. Ernest please to move your things into Miss Peachey's room.

ERNEST. [Vexed.] Deuce of a nuisance havin' to turn out for this fellow Lever. What did Molly want to bring him for?

MISS BEECH. Course you've no personal feeling in the matter!

ROSE. [Speaking to Miss BEECH.] The Missis says you're to please move your things into the blue room, please Miss.

LETTY. Aha, Peachey! That settles you! Come on, Ernie!

[She goes towards the house. ERNEST, rising from the swing, turns to Miss BEECH, who follows.]

ERNEST. [Smiling, faintly superior.] Personal, not a bit! I only think while Molly 's out at grass, she oughtn't to——

MISS BEECH. [Sharply.] Oh! do you?

[She hustles ERNEST out through the wall, but his voice is heard faintly from the distance: "I think it's jolly thin."]

ROSE. [To DICK.] The Missis says you're to take all your worms and things, Sir, and put them where they won't be seen.

DICK. [Shortly.] Have n't got any!

ROSE. The Missis says she'll be very angry if you don't put your worms away; and would you come and help kill earwigs in the blue——?

DICK. Hang! [He goes, and ROSE is left alone.]

ROSE. [Looking straight before her.] Please, Miss Joy, the Missis says will you go to her about your frock.

[There is a little pause, then from the hollow tree joy's voice is heard.]

JOY. No-o!

ROSE. If you did n't come, I was to tell you she was going to put you in the blue.

[Joy looks out of the tree.]

[Immovable, but smiling.]

Oh, Miss joy, you've done your hair up! [Joy retires into the tree.] Please, Miss, what shall I tell the Missis?

JOY. [Joy's voice is heard.] Anything you like.

ROSE. [Over her shoulder.] I shall be drove to tell her a story, Miss.

JOY. All right! Tell it.

[ROSE goes away, and JOY comes out. She sits on the rustic seat and waits. DICK, coming softly from the house, approaches her.]

DICK. [Looking at her intently.] Joy! I wanted to say something

[Joy does not look at him, but twists her fingers.]

I shan't see you again you know after to-morrow till I come up for the 'Varsity match.

JOY. [Smiling.] But that's next week.

DICK. Must you go home to-morrow?

[Joy nods three times.]

[Coming closer.]

I shall miss you so awfully. You don't know how I——

[Joy shakes her head.]

Do look at me! [JOY steals a look.] Oh! Joy!

[Again joy shakes her head.]

JOY. [Suddenly.] Don't!

DICK. [Seizing her hand.] Oh, Joy! Can't you——

JOY. [Drawing the hand away.] Oh! don't.

DICK. [Bending his head.] It's—it's—so——

JOY. [Quietly.] Don't, Dick!

DICK. But I can't help it! It's too much for me, Joy, I must tell you——

[MRS. GWYN is seen approaching towards the house.]

JOY. [Spinning round.] It's Mother—oh, Mother! [She rushes at her.]

[MRS. GWYN is a handsome creature of thirty-six, dressed in a muslin frock. She twists her daughter round, and kisses her.]

MRS. GWYN.   How sweet you look with your hair up, Joy!   Who 's this? [Glancing with a smile at DICK.]

JOY. Dick Merton—in my letters you know.

[She looks at DICK as though she wished him gone.]

MRS. GWYN. How do you do?

DICK. [Shaking hands.] How d 'you do? I think if you'll excuse me —I'll go in.

[He goes uncertainly.

MRS. GWYN. What's the matter with him?

JOY. Oh, nothing! [Hugging her.] Mother! You do look such a duck. Why did you come by the towing-path, was n't it cooking?

MRS. GWYN. [Avoiding her eyes.] Mr. Lever wanted to go into Mr. Henty's.

[Her manner is rather artificially composed.]

JOY. [Dully.] Oh! Is he-is he really coming here, Mother?

MRS. GWYN. [Whose voice has hardened just a little.] If Aunt Nell's got a room for him—of course—why not?

JOY. [Digging her chin into her mother's shoulder.]

[Why couldn't he choose some day when we'd gone? I wanted you all to myself.]

MRS. GWYN. You are a quaint child—when I was your age——

JOY. [Suddenly looking up.] Oh! Mother, you must have been a chook!

MRS. GWYN. Well, I was about twice as old as you, I know that.

JOY. Had you any—any other offers before you were married, Mother?

MRS. GWYN. [Smilingly.] Heaps!

JOY. [Reflectively.] Oh!

MRS. GWYN. Why? Have you been having any?

JOY. [Glancing at MRS. GWYN, and then down.] N-o, of course not!

MRS. GWYN. Where are they all? Where's Peachey?

JOY. Fussing about somewhere; don't let's hurry! Oh! you duckie— duckie! Aren't there any letters from Dad?

MRS. GWYN. [In a harder voice.] Yes, one or two.

JOY. [Hesitating.] Can't I see?

MRS. GWYN. I didn't bring them. [Changing the subject obviously.] Help me to tidy—I'm so hot I don't know what to do.

[She takes out a powder-puff bag, with a tiny looking-glass.]

JOY. How lovely it'll be to-morrow-going home!

MRS. GWYN. [With an uneasy look.] London's dreadfully stuffy, Joy. You 'll only get knocked up again.

JOY. [With consternation.] Oh! but Mother, I must come.

MRS. GWYN. (Forcing a smile.) Oh, well, if you must, you must!

[Joy makes a dash at her.]

Don't rumple me again. Here's Uncle Tom.

JOY. [Quickly.] Mother, we're going to dance tonight; promise to dance with me—there are three more girls than men, at least—and don't dance too much with—with—you know—because I'm—[dropping her voice and very still]—jealous.

MRS. GWYN. [Forcing a laugh.] You are funny!

JOY. [Very quickly.] I haven't made any engagements because of you.

[The COLONEL approaches through the wall.]

MRS. GWYN. Well, Uncle Tom?

COLONEL. [Genially.] Why, Molly! [He kisses her.] What made you come by
the towing-path?

JOY. Because it's so much cooler, of course.

COLONEL. Hallo! What's the matter with you? Phew! you've got your hair
up! Go and tell your aunt your mother's on the lawn. Cut along!

[Joy goes, blowing a kiss.]

Cracked about you, Molly! Simply cracked! We shall miss her when you take her
off to-morrow. [He places a chair for her.] Sit down, sit down, you must be tired
in this heat. I 've sent Bob for your things with the wheelbarrow; what have you
got?—only a bag, I suppose.

MRS. GWYN. [Sitting, with a smile.] That's all, Uncle Tom, except— my trunk
and hat-box.

COLONEL. Phew! And what's-his-name brought a bag, I suppose?

MRS. GWYN. They're all together. I hope it's not too much, Uncle Tom.

COLONEL. [Dubiously.] Oh! Bob'll manage! I suppose you see a good deal
of—of—Lever. That's his brother in the Guards, isn't it?

MRS. GWYN. Yes.

COLONEL. Now what does this chap do?

MRS. GWYN. What should he do, Uncle Tom? He's a Director.

COLONEL. Guinea-pig! [Dubiously.] Your bringing him down was a good
idea.

[MRS. GWYN, looking at him sidelong, bites her lips.]

I should like to have a look at him. But, I say, you know, Molly— mines, mines! There are a lot of these chaps about, whose business is to cook their own dinners. Your aunt thinks——

MRS. GWYN. Oh! Uncle Tom, don't tell me what Aunt Nell thinks!

COLONEL. Well-well! Look here, old girl! It's my experience never to—what I mean is—never to trust too much to a man who has to do with mining. I've always refused to have anything to do with mines. If your husband were in England, of course, I'd say nothing.

MRS. GWYN. [Very still.] We'd better keep him out of the question, had n't we?

COLONEL. Of course, if you wish it, my dear.

MRS. GWYN. Unfortunately, I do.

COLONEL. [Nervously.] Ah! yes, I know; but look here, Molly, your aunt thinks you're in a very delicate position-in fact, she thinks you see too much of young Lever.

MRS. GWYN. [Stretching herself like an angry cat.] Does she? And what do you think?

COLONEL. I? I make a point of not thinking. I only know that here he is, and I don't want you to go burning your fingers, eh?

[MRS. GWYN sits with a vindictive smile.]

A gold mine's a gold mine. I don't mean he deliberately—but they take in women and parsons, and—and all sorts of fools. [Looking down.] And then, you know, I can't tell your feelings, my dear, and I don't want to; but a man about town 'll compromise a woman as soon as he'll look at her, and [softly shaking his head] I don't like that, Molly! It 's not the thing!

[MRS. GWYN sits unmoved, smiling the same smile, and the COLONEL gives her a nervous look.]

If—if you were any other woman I should n't care—and if—if you were a plain woman, damme, you might do what you liked! I know you and Geoff don't get on; but here's this child of yours, devoted to you, and—and don't you see, old girl? Eh?

MRS. GWYN. [With a little hard laugh.] Thanks! Perfectly! I suppose as you don't think, Uncle Tom, it never occurred to you that I have rather a lonely time of it.

COLONEL. [With compunction.] Oh! my dear, yes, of course I know it must be beastly.

MRS. GWYN. [Stonily.] It is.

COLONEL. Yes, yes! [Speaking in a surprised voice.] I don't know what I 'm talking like this for! It's your aunt! She goes on at me till she gets on my nerves. What d' you think she wants me to do now? Put money into this gold mine! Did you ever hear such folly?

MRS. GWYN. [Breaking into laughter.] Oh! Uncle Tom!

COLONEL. All very well for you to laugh, Molly!

MRS. GWYN. [Calmly.] And how much are you going to put in?

COLONEL. Not a farthing! Why, I've got nothing but my pension and three thousand India stock!

MRS. GWYN. Only ninety pounds a year, besides your pension! D' you mean to say that's all you've got, Uncle Tom? I never knew that before. What a shame!

COLONEL. [Feelingly.] It is a, d—d shame! I don't suppose there's another case in the army of a man being treated as I've been.

MRS. GWYN. But how on earth do you manage here on so little?

COLONEL. [Brooding.] Your aunt's very funny. She's a born manager. She 'd manage the hind leg off a donkey; but if I want five shillings for a charity or what not, I have to whistle for it. And then all of a sudden, Molly, she'll take it into her head to spend goodness knows what on some trumpery or other and come to me for the money. If I have n't got it to give her, out she flies about 3 per cent., and worries me to invest in some wild-cat or other, like your friend's thing, the Jaco what is it? I don't pay the slightest attention to her.

MRS. HOPE. [From the direction of the house.] Tom!

COLONEL. [Rising.] Yes, dear! [Then dropping his voice.] I say, Molly, don't you mind what I said about young Lever. I don't want you to imagine that I think harm of people—you know I don't—but so many women come to grief, and—[hotly]—I can't stand men about town; not that he of course——

MRS. HOPE, [Peremptorily.] Tom!

COLONEL. [In hasty confidence.] I find it best to let your aunt run on. If she says anything——

MRS. HOPE. To-om!

COLONEL. Yes, dear!

[He goes hastily. MRS. GWYN sits drawing circles on the ground with her charming parasol. Suddenly she springs to her feet, and stands waiting like an animal at bay. The COLONEL and MRS. HOPE approach her talking.]

MRS. HOPE. Well, how was I to know?

COLONEL. Did n't Joy come and tell you?

MRS. HOPE. I don't know what's the matter with that child? Well, Molly, so here you are. You're before your time—that train's always late.

MRS. GWYN. [With faint irony.] I'm sorry, Aunt Nell!

[They bob, seem to take fright, and kiss each other gingerly.]

MRS. HOPE. What have you done with Mr. Lever? I shall have to put him in Peachey's room. Tom's got no champagne.

COLONEL. They've a very decent brand down at the George, Molly, I'll send Bob over——

MRS. HOPE. Rubbish, Tom! He'll just have to put up with what he can get!

MRS. GWYN. Of course! He's not a snob! For goodness sake, Aunt Nell, don't put yourself out! I'm sorry I suggested his coming.

COLONEL. My dear, we ought to have champagne in the house—in case of accident.

MRS. GWYN. [Shaking him gently by the coat.] No, please, Uncle Tom!

MRS. HOPE. [Suddenly.] Now, I've told your uncle, Molly, that he's not to go in for this gold mine without making certain it's a good thing. Mind, I think you've been very rash. I'm going to give you a good talking to; and that's not all—you ought n't to go about like this with a young man; he's not at all bad looking. I remember him perfectly well at the Fleming's dance.

[On MRS. GWYN's lips there comes a little mocking smile.]

COLONEL. [Pulling his wife's sleeve.] Nell!

MRS. HOPE. No, Tom, I'm going to talk to Molly; she's old enough to know better.

MRS. GWYN. Yes?

MRS. HOPE. Yes, and you'll get yourself into a mess; I don't approve of it, and when I see a thing I don't approve of——

COLONEL. [Walking about, and pulling his moustache.] Nell, I won't have it, I simply won't have it.

MRS. HOPE. What rate of interest are these Preference shares to pay?

MRS. GWYN. [Still smiling.] Ten per cent.

MRS. HOPE. What did I tell you, Tom? And are they safe?

MRS. GWYN. You'd better ask Maurice.

MRS. HOPE. There, you see, you call him Maurice! Now supposing your uncle went in for some of them——

COLONEL. [Taking off his hat-in a high, hot voice] I'm not going in for anything of the sort.

MRS. HOPE. Don't swing your hat by the brim! Go and look if you can see him coming!

[The COLONEL goes.]

[In a lower voice.] Your uncle's getting very bald. I 've only shoulder of lamb for lunch, and a salad. It's lucky it's too hot to eat.

[MISS BEECH has appeared while she is speaking.]

Here she is, Peachey!

MISS BEECH. I see her. [She kisses MRS. GWYN, and looks at her intently.]

MRS. GWYN. [Shrugging her shoulders.] Well, Peachey! What d 'you make of me?

COLONEL. [Returning from his search.] There's a white hat crossing the second stile. Is that your friend, Molly?

[MRS. GWYN nods.]

MRS. HOPE. Oh! before I forget, Peachey—Letty and Ernest can move their things back again. I'm going to put Mr. Lever in your room. [Catching sight o f the paint pot on the ground.] There's that disgusting paint pot! Take it up at once, Tom, and put it in the tree.

[The COLONEL picks up the pot and bears it to the hollow tree followed by MRS. HOPE; he enters.]

MRS. HOPE. [Speaking into the tree.] Not there!

COLONEL. [From within.] Well, where then?

MRS. HOPE. Why—up—oh! gracious!

[MRS. GWYN, standing alone, is smiling. LEVER approaches from the towing-path. He is a man like a fencer's wrist, supple and steely. A man whose age is difficult to tell, with a quick, good-looking face, and a line between his brows; his darkish hair is flecked with grey. He gives the feeling that he has always had to spurt to keep pace with his own life.]

MRS. HOPE. [Also entering the hollow tree.] No-oh!

COLONEL. [From the depths, in a high voice.] Well, dash it then! What do you want?

MRS. GWYN. Peachey, may I introduce Mr. Lever to you? Miss Beech, my old governess.

[They shake each other by the hand.]

LEVER. How do you do? [His voice is pleasant, his manner easy.]

MISS BEECH. Pleased to meet you.

[Her manner is that of one who is not pleased. She watches.]

MRS. GWYN. [Pointing to the tree-maliciously.] This is my uncle and my aunt. They're taking exercise, I think.

[The COLONEL and MRS. HOPE emerge convulsively. They are very hot. LEVER and MRS. GWYN are very cool.]

MRS. HOPE. [Shaking hands with him.] So you 've got here! Are n't you very hot?—Tom!

COLONEL. Brought a splendid day with you! Splendid!

[As he speaks, Joy comes running with a bunch of roses; seeing LEVER, she stops and stands quite rigid.]

MISS BEECH. [Sitting in the swing.] Thunder!

COLONEL. Thunder? Nonsense, Peachey, you're always imagining something. Look at the sky!

MISS BEECH. Thunder!

[MRS. GWYN's smile has faded.]

MRS. HOPE. [Turning.] Joy, don't you see Mr. Lever?

[Joy, turning to her mother, gives her the roses. With a forced smile, LEVER advances, holding out his hand.]

LEVER. How are you, Joy? Have n't seen you for an age!

JOY. [Without expression.] I am very well, thank you.

[She raises her hand, and just touches his. MRS. GWYN'S eyes are fixed on her daughter. Miss BEECH is watching them intently. MRS. HOPE is buttoning the COLONEL'S coat.]

The curtain falls.

ACT II

It is afternoon, and at a garden-table placed beneath the hollow tree, the COLONEL is poring over plans. Astride of a garden- chair, LEVER is smoking cigarettes. DICK is hanging Chinese lanterns to the hollow tree.

LEVER. Of course, if this level [pointing with his cigarette] peters out to the West we shall be in a tightish place; you know what a mine is at this stage, Colonel Hope.

COLONEL. [Absently.] Yes, yes. [Tracing a line.] What is there to prevent its running out here to the East?

LEVER. Well, nothing, except that as a matter of fact it doesn't.

COLONEL. [With some excitement.] I'm very glad you showed me these papers, very glad! I say that it's a most astonishing thing if the ore suddenly stops there. [A gleam of humour visits LEVER'S face.] I'm not an expert, but you ought to prove that ground to the East more thoroughly.

LEVER. [Quizzically.] Of course, sir, if you advise that——

COLONEL. If it were mine, I'd no more sit down under the belief that the ore stopped there than I 'd——There's a harmony in these things.

NEVER. I can only tell you what our experts say.

COLONEL. Ah! Experts! No faith in them—never had! Miners, lawyers, theologians, cowardly lot—pays them to be cowardly. When they have n't their own axes to grind, they've got their theories; a theory's a dangerous thing. [He loses himself in contemplation of the papers.] Now my theory is, you 're in strata here of what we call the Triassic Age.

LEVER. [Smiling faintly.] Ah!

COLONEL. You've struck a fault, that's what's happened. The ore may be as much as thirty or forty yards out; but it 's there, depend on it.

LEVER. Would you back that opinion, sir?

COLONEL. [With dignity.] I never give an opinion that I'm not prepared to back. I want to get to the bottom of this. What's to prevent the gold going down indefinitely?

LEVER. Nothing, so far as I know.

COLONEL. [With suspicion.] Eh!

LEVER. All I can tell you is: This is as far as we've got, and we want more money before we can get any farther.

COLONEL. [Absently.] Yes, yes; that's very usual.

LEVER. If you ask my personal opinion I think it's very doubtful that the gold does go down.

COLONEL. [Smiling.] Oh! a personal opinion a matter of this sort!

LEVER. [As though about to take the papers.] Perhaps we'd better close the sitting, sir; sorry to have bored you.

COLONEL. Now, now! Don't be so touchy! If I'm to put money in, I'm bound to look at it all round.

LEVER. [With lifted brows.] Please don't imagine that I want you to put money in.

COLONEL. Confound it, sir! D 'you suppose I take you for a Company promoter?

LEVER. Thank you!

COLONEL. [Looking at him doubtfully.] You've got Irish blood in you—um? You're so hasty!

LEVER. If you 're really thinking of taking shares—my advice to you is, don't!

COLONEL. [Regretfully.] If this were an ordinary gold mine, I wouldn't dream of looking at it, I want you to understand that. Nobody has a greater objection to gold mines than I.

LEVER. [Looks down at his host with half-closed eyes.] But it is a gold mine, Colonel Hope.

COLONEL. I know, I know; but I 've been into it for myself; I've formed my opinion personally. Now, what 's the reason you don't want me to invest?

LEVER. Well, if it doesn't turn out as you expect, you'll say it's my doing. I know what investors are.

COLONEL. [Dubiously.] If it were a Westralian or a Kaffir I would n't touch it with a pair of tongs! It 's not as if I were going to put much in! [He suddenly bends above the papers as though magnetically attracted.] I like these Triassic formations!

[DICK, who has hung the last lantern, moodily departs.]

LEVER. [Looking after him.] That young man seems depressed.

COLONEL. [As though remembering his principles.] I don't like mines, never have! [Suddenly absorbed again.] I tell you what, Lever—this thing's got tremendous possibilities. You don't seem to believe in it enough. No mine's any good without faith; until I see for myself, however, I shan't commit myself beyond a thousand.

LEVER. Are you serious, sir?

COLONEL. Certainly! I've been thinking it over ever since you told me Henty had fought shy. I 've a poor opinion of Henty. He's one of those fellows that says one thing and does another. An opportunist!

LEVER. [Slowly.] I'm afraid we're all that, more or less. [He sits beneath the hollow tree.]

COLONEL. A man never knows what he is himself. There 's my wife. She thinks she 's——By the way, don't say anything to her about this, please. And, Lever [nervously], I don't think, you know, this is quite the sort of thing for my niece.

LEVER. [Quietly.] I agree. I mean to get her out of it.

COLONEL. [A little taken aback.] Ah! You know, she—she's in a very delicate position, living by herself in London. [LEVER looks at him ironically.] You [very nervously] see a good deal of her? If it had n't been for Joy growing so fast, we shouldn't have had the child down here. Her mother ought to have her with her. Eh! Don't you think so?

LEVER. [Forcing a smile.] Mrs. Gwyn always seems to me to get on all right.

COLONEL. [As though making a discovery.] You know, I've found that when a woman's living alone and unprotected, the very least thing will set a lot of hags and jackanapes talking. [Hotly.] The more unprotected and helpless a woman is, the more they revel in it. If there's anything I hate in this world, it's those wretched creatures who babble about their neighbours' affairs.

LEVER. I agree with you.

COLONEL. One ought to be very careful not to give them—that is—— [checks himself confused; then hurrying on]—I suppose you and Joy get on all right?

LEVER. [Coolly.] Pretty well, thanks. I'm not exactly in Joy's line; have n't seen very much of her, in fact.

[Miss BEECH and JOY have been approaching from the house. But seeing LEVER, JOY turns abruptly, hesitates a moment, and with an angry gesture goes away.]

COLONEL [Unconscious.] Wonderfully affectionate little thing! Well, she'll be going home to-morrow!

MISS BEECH. [Who has been gazing after JOY.] Talkin' business, poor creatures?

LEVER. Oh, no! If you'll excuse me, I'll wash my hands before tea.

[He glances at the COLONEL poring over papers, and, shrugging his shoulders, strolls away.]

MISS BEECH. [Sitting in the swing.] I see your horrid papers.

COLONEL. Be quiet, Peachey!

MISS BEECH. On a beautiful summer's day, too.

COLONEL. That'll do now.

MISS BEECH. [Unmoved.] For every ounce you take out of a gold mine you put two in.

COLONEL. Who told you that rubbish?

MISS BEECH. [With devilry.] You did!

COLONEL. This is n't an ordinary gold mine.

MISS BEECH. Oh! quite a special thing.

[COLONEL stares at her, but subsiding at hey impassivity, he pores again over the papers.]

[Rosy has approached with a tea cloth.]

ROSE. If you please, sir, the Missis told me to lay the tea.

COLONEL. Go away! Ten fives fifty. Ten 5 16ths, Peachey?

MISS BEECH. I hate your nasty sums!

[ROSE goes away. The COLONEL Writes. MRS. HOPE'S voice is heard, "Now then, bring those chairs, you two. Not that one, Ernest." ERNEST arid LETTY appear through the openings of the wall, each with a chair.]

COLONEL. [With dull exasperation.] What do you want?

LETTY. Tea, Father.

[She places her chair arid goes away.]

ERNEST. That Johnny-bird Lever is too cocksure for me, Colonel. Those South American things are no good at all. I know all about them from young Scrotton. There's not one that's worth a red cent. If you want a flutter——

COLONEL. [Explosively.] Flutter! I'm not a gambler, sir!

ERNEST. Well, Colonel [with a smile], I only don't want you to chuck your money away on a stiff 'un. If you want anything good you should go to Mexico.

COLONEL. [Jumping up and holding out the map.] Go to [He stops in time.] What d'you call that, eh? M-E-X——

ERNEST. [Not to be embarrassed.] It all depend on what part.

COLONEL. You think you know everything—you think nothing's right unless it's your own idea! Be good enough to keep your advice to yourself.

ERNEST. [Moving with his chair, and stopping with a smile.] If you ask me, I should say it wasn't playing the game to put Molly into a thing like that.

COLONEL. What do you mean, sir?

ERNEST. Any Juggins can see that she's a bit gone on our friend.

COLONEL. [Freezingly.] Indeed!

ERNEST. He's not at all the sort of Johnny that appeals to me.

COLONEL. Really?

ERNEST. [Unmoved.] If I were you, Colonel, I should tip her the wink. He was hanging about her at Ascot all the time. It 's a bit thick!

[MRS. HOPE followed by ROSE appears from the house.]

COLONEL. [Stammering with passion.] Jackanapes!

MRS. HOPE. Don't stand there, Tom; clear those papers, and let Rose lay the table. Now, Ernest, go and get another chair.

[The COLONEL looks wildly round and sits beneath the hollow tree, with his head held in his hands. ROSE lays the cloth.]

MRS. BEECH. [Sitting beside the COLONEL.] Poor creature!

ERNEST. [Carrying his chair about with him.] Ask any Johnny in the City, he 'll tell you Mexico's a very tricky country—the people are awful rotters

MRS. HOPE. Put that chair down, Ernest.

[ERNEST looks at the chair, puts it down, opens his mouth, and goes away. ROSE follows him.]

What's he been talking about? You oughtn't to get so excited, Tom; is your head bad, old man? Here, take these papers! [She hands the papers to the COLONEL.] Peachey, go in and tell them tea 'll be ready in a minute, there 's a good soul? Oh! and on my dressing table you'll find a bottle of Eau de Cologne.

MRS. BEECH. Don't let him get in a temper again. That 's three times to-day!

[She goes towards the house.]

COLONEL. Never met such a fellow in my life, the most opinionated, narrow-minded—thinks he knows everything. Whatever Letty could see in him I can't think. Pragmatical beggar!

MRS. HOPE. Now Tom! What have you been up to, to get into a state like this?

COLONEL. [Avoiding her eyes.] I shall lose my temper with him one of these days. He's got that confounded habit of thinking nobody can be right but himself.

MRS. HOPE. That's enough! I want to talk to you seriously! Dick's in love. I'm perfectly certain of it.

COLONEL. Love! Who's he in love with—Peachey?

MRS. HOPE. You can see it all over him. If I saw any signs of Joy's breaking out, I'd send them both away. I simply won't have it.

COLONEL. Why, she's a child!

MRS. HOPE. [Pursuing her own thoughts.] But she isn't—not yet. I've been watching her very carefully. She's more in love with her Mother than any one, follows her about like a dog! She's been quite rude to Mr. Lever.

COLONEL. [Pursuing his own thoughts.] I don't believe a word of it.

[He rises and walks about]

MRS. HOPE. Don't believe a word of what?

[The COLONEL is Silent.]

[Pursuing his thoughts with her own.]

If I thought there was anything between Molly and Mr. Lever, d 'you suppose I'd have him in the house?

[The COLONEL stops, and gives a sort of grunt.]

He's a very nice fellow; and I want you to pump him well, Tom, and see what there is in this mine.

COLONEL. [Uneasily.] Pump!

MRS. HOPE. [Looking at him curiously.] Yes, you 've been up to something! Now what is it?

COLONEL. Pump my own guest! I never heard of such a thing!

MRS. HOPE. There you are on your high horse! I do wish you had a little common-sense, Tom!

COLONEL. I'd as soon you asked me to sneak about eavesdropping! Pump!

MRS. HOPE. Well, what were you looking at these papers for? It does drive me so wild the way you throw away all the chances you have of making a little money. I've got you this opportunity, and you do nothing but rave up and down, and talk nonsense!

COLONEL. [In a high voice] Much you know about it! I 've taken a thousand shares in this mine

[He stops dead. There is a silence.]

MRS. HOPE. You 've—WHAT? Without consulting me? Well, then, you 'll just go and take them out again!

COLONEL. You want me to——?

MRS. HOPE. The idea! As if you could trust your judgment in a thing like that! You 'll just go at once and say there was a mistake; then we 'll talk it over calmly.

COLONEL. [Drawing himself up.] Go back on what I 've said? Not if I lose every penny! First you worry me to take the shares, and then you worry me not—I won't have it, Nell, I won't have it!

MRS. HOPE. Well, if I'd thought you'd have forgotten what you said this morning and turned about like this, d'you suppose I'd have spoken to you at all? Now, do you?

COLONEL. Rubbish! If you can't see that this is a special opportunity!

[He walks away followed by MRS. HOPE, who endeavors to make him see her point of view. ERNEST and LETTY are now returning from the house armed with a third chair.]

LETTY. What's the matter with everybody? Is it the heat?

ERNEST. [Preoccupied and sitting in the swing.] That sportsman, Lever, you know, ought to be warned off.

LETTY. [Signing t0 ERNEST.] Where's Miss Joy, Rose?

ROSE. Don't know, Miss.

[Putting down the tray, she goes.]

[ROSE, has followed with the tea tray.]

LETTY. Ernie, be careful, you never know where Joy is.

ERNEST. [Preoccupied with his reflections.] Your old Dad 's as mad as a hatter with me.

LETTY. Why?

ERNEST. Well, I merely said what I thought, that Molly ought to look out what's she's doing, and he dropped on me like a cartload of bricks.

LETTY. The Dad's very fond of Molly.

ERNEST. But look here, d'you mean to tell me that she and Lever are n't——

LETTY. Don't! Suppose they are! If joy were to hear it'd be simply awful. I like Molly. I 'm not going to believe anything against her. I don't see the use of it. If it is, it is, and if it is n't, it is n't.

ERNEST. Well, all I know is that when I told her the mine was probably a frost she went for me like steam.

LETTY. Well, so should I. She was only sticking up for her friends.

ERNEST. Ask the old Peachey-bird. She knows a thing or two. Look here, I don't mind a man's being a bit of a sportsman, but I think Molly's bringin' him down here is too thick. Your old Dad's got one of his notions that because this Josser's his guest, he must keep him in a glass case, and take shares in his mine, and all the rest of it.

LETTY. I do think people are horrible, always thinking things. It's not as if Molly were a stranger. She's my own cousin. I 'm not going to believe anything about my own cousin. I simply won't.

ERNEST. [Reluctantly realising the difference that this makes.] I suppose it does make a difference, her bein' your cousin.

LETTY. Of course it does! I only hope to goodness no one will make Joy suspect——

[She stops and buts her finger to her lips, for JOY is coming towards them, as the tea-bell sounds. She is followed by DICK and MISS BEECH with the Eau de Cologne. The COLONEL and MRS. HOPE are also coming back, discussing still each other's point of view.]

JOY. Where 's Mother? Isn't she here?

MRS. HOPE. Now Joy, come and sit down; your mother's been told tea's ready; if she lets it get cold it's her lookout.

DICK. [Producing a rug, and spreading it beneath the tree.] Plenty of room, Joy.

JOY. I don't believe Mother knows, Aunt Nell.

[MRS. GWYN and LEVER appear in the opening of the wall.]

LETTY. [Touching ERNEST's arm.] Look, Ernie! Four couples and Peachey—

ERNEST. [Preoccupied.] What couples?

JOY. Oh! Mums, here you are!

[Seizing her, she turns her back on LEVER. They sit in various seats, and MRS. HOPE pours out the tea.]

MRS. HOPE. Hand the sandwiches to Mr. Lever, Peachey. It's our own jam, Mr. Lever.

LEVER. Thanks. [He takes a bite.] It's splendid!

MRS. GWYN. [With forced gaiety.] It's the first time I've ever seen you eat jam.

LEVER. [Smiling a forced smile.] Really! But I love it.

MRS. GWYN. [With a little bow.] You always refuse mine.

JOY. [Who has been staring at her enemy, suddenly.] I'm all burnt up! Are n't you simply boiled, Mother?

[She touches her Mother's forehead.]

MRS. GWYN. Ugh! You're quite clammy, Joy.

JOY. It's enough to make any one clammy.

[Her eyes go back to LEVER'S face as though to stab him.]

ERNEST. [From the swing.] I say, you know, the glass is going down.

LEVER. [Suavely.] The glass in the hall's steady enough.

ERNEST. Oh, I never go by that; that's a rotten old glass.

COLONEL. Oh! is it?

ERNEST. [Paying no attention.] I've got a little ripper—never puts you in the cart. Bet you what you like we have thunder before tomorrow night.

MISS BEECH. [Removing her gaze from JOY to LEVER.] You don't think we shall have it before to-night, do you?

LEVER. [Suavely.] I beg your pardon; did you speak to me?

MISS BEECH. I said, you don't think we shall have the thunder before to-night, do you?

[She resumes her watch on joy.]

LEVER. [Blandly.] Really, I don't see any signs of it.

[Joy, crossing to the rug, flings herself down. And DICK sits cross-legged, with his eyes fast fixed on her.]

MISS BEECH. [Eating.] People don't often see what they don't want to, do they?

[LEVER only lifts his brows.]

MRS. GWYN. [Quickly breaking ivy.] What are you talking about? The weather's perfect.

MISS BEECH. Isn't it?

MRS. HOPE. You'd better make a good tea, Peachey; nobody'll get anything till eight, and then only cold shoulder. You must just put up with no hot dinner, Mr. Lever.

LEVER. [Bowing.] Whatever is good enough for Miss Beech is good enough for me.

MISS BEECH. [Sardonically-taking another sandwich.] So you think!

MRS. GWYN. [With forced gaiety.] Don't be so absurd, Peachey.

[MISS BEECH, grunts slightly.]

COLONEL. [Once more busy with his papers.] I see the name of your engineer is Rodriguez—Italian, eh?

LEVER. Portuguese.

COLONEL. Don't like that!

LEVER. I believe he was born in England.

COLONEL. [Reassured.] Oh, was he? Ah!

ERNEST. Awful rotters, those Portuguese!

COLONEL. There you go!

LETTY. Well, Father, Ernie only said what you said.

MRS. HOPE. Now I want to ask you, Mr. Lever, is this gold mine safe? If it isn't—I simply won't allow Tom to take these shares; he can't afford it.

LEVER. It rather depends on what you call safe, Mrs. Hope.

MRS. HOPE. I don't want anything extravagant, of course; if they're going to pay their 10 per cent, regularly, and Tom can have his money out at any time—[There is a faint whistle from the swing.] I only want to know that it's a thoroughly genuine thing.

MRS. GWYN. [Indignantly.] As if Maurice would be a Director if it was n't?

MRS. HOPE. Now Molly, I'm simply asking——

MRS. GWYN. Yes, you are!

COLONEL. [Rising.] I'll take two thousand of those shares, Lever. To have my wife talk like that—I 'm quite ashamed.

LEVER. Oh, come, sir, Mrs. Hope only meant——

[MRS. GWYN looks eagerly at LEVER.]

DICK. [Quietly.] Let's go on the river, Joy.

[JOY rises, and goes to her Mother's chair.]

MRS. HOPE. Of course! What rubbish, Tom! As if any one ever invested money without making sure!

LEVER. [Ironically.] It seems a little difficult to make sure in this case. There isn't the smallest necessity for Colonel Hope to take any shares, and it looks to me as if he'd better not.

[He lights a cigarette.]

MRS. HOPE. Now, Mr. Lever, don't be offended! I'm very anxious for Tom to take the shares if you say the thing's so good.

LEVER. I 'm afraid I must ask to be left out, please.

JOY. [Whispering.] Mother, if you've finished, do come, I want to show you my room.

MRS. HOPE. I would n't say a word, only Tom's so easily taken in.

MRS. GWYN. [Fiercely.] Aunt Nell, how can't you? [Joy gives a little savage laugh.]

LETTY. [Hastily.] Ernie, will you play Dick and me? Come on, Dick!

[All three go out towards the lawn.]

MRS. HOPE. You ought to know your Uncle by this time, Molly. He's just like a child. He'd be a pauper to-morrow if I did n't see to things.

COLONEL. Understand once for all that I shall take two thousand shares in this mine. I 'm—I 'm humiliated. [He turns and goes towards the house.]

MRS. HOPE. Well, what on earth have I said?

[She hurries after him.]

MRS. GWYN. [In a low voice as she passes.] You need n't insult my friends!

[LEVER, shrugging his shoulders, has strolled aside. JOY, with a passionate movement seen only by Miss BEECH, goes off towards the house. MISS BEECH and MRS. GWYN aye left alone beside the remnants of the feast.]

MISS BEECH. Molly!

[MRS. GWYN looks up startled.]

Take care, Molly, take care! The child! Can't you see? [Apostrophising LEVER.] Take care, Molly, take care!

LEVER. [Coming back.] Awfully hot, is n't it?

MISS BEECH. Ah! and it'll be hotter if we don't mind.

LEVER. [Suavely.] Do we control these things?

[MISS BEECH looking from face to face, nods her head repeatedly; then gathering her skirts she walks towards the house. MRS. GWYN sits motionless, staying before her.]

Extraordinary old lady! [He pitches away his cigarette.] What's the matter with her, Molly?

MRS. GWYN, [With an effort.] Oh! Peachey's a character!

LEVER. [Frowning.] So I see! [There is a silence.]

MRS. GWYN. Maurice!

LEVER. Yes.

MRS. GWYN. Aunt Nell's hopeless, you mustn't mind her.

LEVER. [In a dubious and ironic voice.] My dear girl, I 've too much to bother me to mind trifles like that.

MRS. GWYN. [Going to him suddenly.] Tell me, won't you?

[LEVER shrugs his shoulders.]

A month ago you'd have told me soon enough!

LEVER. Now, Molly!

MRS. GWYN. Ah! [With a bitter smile.] The Spring's soon over.

LEVER. It 's always Spring between us.

MRS. GWYN. Is it?

LEVER. You did n't tell me what you were thinking about just now when you sat there like stone.

MRS. GWYN. It does n't do for a woman to say too much.

LEVER. Have I been so bad to you that you need feel like that, Molly?

MRS. GWYN. [With a little warm squeeze of his arm.] Oh! my dear, it's only that I'm so——

[She stops.]

LEVER. [Gently]. So what?

MRS. GWYN. [In a low voice.] It's hateful here.

LEVER. I didn't want to come. I don't understand why you suggested it. [MRS. GWYN is silent.] It's been a mistake.

MRS. GWYN. [Her eyes fixed on the ground.] Joy comes home to- morrow. I thought if I brought you here—I should know——

LEVER. [Vexedly.] Um!

MRS. GWYN. [Losing her control.] Can't you SEE? It haunts me? How are we to go on? I must know—I must know!

LEVER. I don't see that my coming——

MRS. GWYN. I thought I should have more confidence; I thought I should be able to face it better in London, if you came down here open- ly—and now—I feel I must n't speak or look at you.

LEVER. You don't think your Aunt——

MRS. GWYN. [Scornfully.] She! It's only Joy I care about.

LEVER. [Frowning.] We must be more careful, that's all. We mustn't give our- selves away again, as we were doing just now.

MRS. GWYN. When any one says anything horrid to you, I can't help it.

[She puts her hand on the label of his coat.]

LEVER. My dear child, take care!

[MRS. GWYN drops her hand. She throws her head back, and her throat is seen to work as though she were gulping down a bitter draught. She moves away.]

[Following hastily.] Don't dear, don't! I only meant—Come, Molly, let's be sensible. I want to tell you something about the mine.

MRS. GWYN. [With a quavering smile.] Yes-let 's talk sensibly, and walk properly in this sensible, proper place.

[LEVER is seen trying to soothe her, and yet to walk properly. As they disappear, they are viewed by JOY, who, like the shadow parted from its figure, has come to join it again. She stands now, foiled, a carnation in her hand; then flings herself on a chair, and leans her elbows on the table.]

JOY. I hate him! Pig!

ROSE. [Who has come to clear the tea things.] Did you call, Miss?

JOY. Not you!

ROSE. [Motionless.] No, Miss!

JOY. [Leaning back and tearing the flower.] Oh! do hurry up, Rose!

ROSE. [Collects the tea things.] Mr. Dick's coming down the path! Aren't I going to get you to do your frock, Miss Joy?

JOY. No.

ROSE. What will the Missis say?

JOY. Oh, don't be so stuck, Rose!

[ROSE goes, but DICK has come.]

DICK. Come on the river, Joy, just for half an hour, as far as the kingfishers— do! [Joy shakes her head.] Why not? It 'll be so jolly and cool. I'm most awfully sorry if I worried you this morning. I didn't mean to. I won't again, I promise. [Joy slides a look at him, and from that look he gains a little courage.] Do come! It'll be the last time. I feel it awfully, Joy.

JOY. There's nothing to hurt you!

DICK. [Gloomily.] Isn't there—when you're like this?

JOY. [In a hard voice.] If you don't like me, why do you follow me about?

DICK. What is the matter?

JOY. [Looking up, as if for want of air.] Oh! Don't!

DICK. Oh, Joy, what is the matter? Is it the heat?

JOY. [With a little laugh.] Yes.

DICK. Have some Eau de Cologne. I 'll make you a bandage. [He takes the Eau de Cologne, and makes a bandage with his handkerchief.] It's quite clean.

JOY. Oh, Dick, you are so funny!

DICK. [Bandaging her forehead.] I can't bear you to feel bad; it puts me off completely. I mean I don't generally make a fuss about people, but when it 's you——

JOY. [Suddenly.] I'm all right.

DICK. Is that comfy?

JOY. [With her chin up, and her eyes fast closed.] Quite.

DICK. I'm not going to stay and worry you. You ought to rest. Only, Joy! Look here! If you want me to do anything for you, any time——

JOY. [Half opening her eyes.] Only to go away.

[DICK bites his lips and walks away.]

Dick—[softly]—Dick!

[DICK stops.]

I didn't mean that; will you get me some water-irises for this evening?

DICK. Won't I? [He goes to the hollow tree and from its darkness takes a bucket and a boat-hook.] I know where there are some rippers!

[JOY stays unmoving with her eyes half closed.]

Are you sure you 're all right. Joy? You 'll just rest here in the shade, won't you, till I come back?—it 'll do you no end of good. I shan't be twenty minutes.

[He goes, but cannot help returning softly, to make sure.]

You're quite sure you 're all right?

[JOY nods. He goes away towards the river. But there is no rest for JOY. The voices of MRS. GWYN and LEVER are heard returning.]

JOY. [With a gesture of anger.] Hateful! Hateful!

[She runs away.]

[MRS. GWYN and LEVER are seen approaching; they pass the tree, in conversation.]

MRS. GWYN. But I don't see why, Maurice.

LEVER. We mean to sell the mine; we must do some more work on it, and for that we must have money.

MRS. GWYN. If you only want a little, I should have thought you could have got it in a minute in the City.

LEVER. [Shaking his head.] No, no; we must get it privately.

MRS. GWYN. [Doubtfully.] Oh! [She slowly adds.] Then it isn't such a good thing!

[And she does not look at him.]

LEVER. Well, we mean to sell it.

MRS. GWYN. What about the people who buy?

LEVER. [Dubiously regarding her.] My dear girl, they've just as much chance as we had. It 's not my business to think of them. There's YOUR thousand pounds——

MRS. GWYN. [Softly.] Don't bother about my money, Maurice. I don't want you to do anything not quite——

LEVER. [Evasively.] Oh! There's my brother's and my sister's too. I 'm not going to let any of you run any risk. When we all went in for it the thing looked splendid; it 's only the last month that we 've had doubts. What bothers me now is your Uncle. I don't want him to take these shares. It looks as if I'd come here on purpose.

MRS. GWYN. Oh! he mustn't take them!

LEVER. That 's all very well; but it 's not so simple.

MRS. GWYN. [Shyly.] But, Maurice, have you told him about the selling?

LEVER. [Gloomily, under the hollow tree.] It 's a Board secret. I'd no business to tell even you.

MRS. GWYN. But he thinks he's taking shares in a good—a permanent thing.

LEVER. You can't go into a mining venture without some risk.

MRS. GWYN. Oh yes, I know—but—but Uncle Tom is such a dear!

LEVER. [Stubbornly.] I can't help his being the sort of man he is. I did n't want him to take these shares; I told him so in so many words. Put yourself in my place, Molly: how can I go to him and say, "This thing may turn out rotten," when he knows I got you to put your money into it?

[But JOY, the lost shadow, has come back. She moves forward resolutely. They are divided from her by the hollow tree; she is unseen. She stops.]

MRS. GWYN. I think he ought to be told about the selling; it 's not fair.

LEVER. What on earth made him rush at the thing like that? I don't understand
    that kind of man.

MRS. GWYN. [Impulsively.] I must tell him, Maurice; I can't let him take the
    shares without——

[She puts her hand on his arm.]

[Joy turns, as if to go back whence she came, but stops once more.]

LEVER. [Slowly and very quietly.] I did n't think you'd give me away, Molly.

MRS. GWYN. I don't think I quite understand.

LEVER. If you tell the Colonel about this sale the poor old chap will think me
    a man that you ought to have nothing to do with. Do you want that?

[MRS. GWYN, giving her lover a long look, touches his sleeve. JOY, slipping
behind the hollow tree, has gone.]

You can't act in a case like this as if you 'd only a principle to consider. It 's the—
the special circumstances.

MRS. GWYN. [With a faint smile.] But you'll be glad to get the money won't
    you?

LEVER. By George! if you're going to take it like this, Molly

MRS. GWYN. Don't!

LEVER. We may not sell after all, dear, we may find it turn out trumps.

MRS. GWYN. [With a shiver.] I don't want to hear any more. I know women
    don't understand. [Impulsively.] It's only that I can't bear any
    one should think that you——

LEVER. [Distressed.] For goodness sake don't look like that, Molly! Of course,
    I'll speak to your Uncle. I'll stop him somehow, even if I have to make
    a fool of myself. I 'll do anything you want——

MRS. GWYN. I feel as if I were being smothered here.

LEVER. It 's only for one day.

MRS. GWYN. [With sudden tenderness.] It's not your fault, dear. I ought to have known how it would be. Well, let's go in!

[She sets her lips, and walks towards the house with LEVER following. But no sooner has she disappeared than JOY comes running after; she stops, as though throwing down a challenge. Her cheeks and ears are burning.]

JOY. Mother!

[After a moment MRS. GWYN reappears in the opening of the wall.]

MRS. GWYN. Oh! here you are!

JOY. [Breathlessly.] Yes.

MRS. GWYN. [Uncertainly.] Where—have you been? You look dreadfully hot; have you been running?

JOY. Yes——no.

MRS. GWYN. [Looking at her fixedly.] What's the matter—you 're trembling! [Softly.] Are n't you well, dear?

JOY. Yes—I don't know.

MRS. GWYN. What is it, darling?

JOY. [Suddenly clinging to her.] Oh! Mother!

MRS. GWYN. I don't understand.

JOY. [Breathlessly.] Oh, Mother, let me go back home with you now at once—
— MRS. GWYN. [Her face hardening.] Why? What on earth——

JOY. I can't stay here.

MRS. GWYN. But why?

JOY. I want to be with you—Oh! Mother, don't you love me?

MRS. GWYN. [With a faint smile.] Of course I love you, Joy.

JOY. Ah! but you love him more.

MRS. GWYN. Love him—whom?

JOY. Oh! Mother, I did n't—[She tries to take her Mother's hand, but fails.] Oh! don't.

MRS. GWYN. You'd better explain what you mean, I think.

JOY. I want to get you to—he—he 's—he 'snot——!

MRS. GWYN. [Frigidly.] Really, Joy!

JOY. [Passionately.] I'll fight against him, and I know there's something wrong about——

[She stops.]

MRS. GWYN. About what?

JOY. Let's tell Uncle Tom, Mother, and go away.

MRS. GWYN. Tell Uncle—Tom—what?

JOY. [Looking down and almost whispering.] About—about—the mine.

MRS. GWYN. What about the mine? What do you mean? [Fiercely.] Have you been spying on me?

JOY. [Shrinking.] No! oh, no!

MRS. GWYN. Where were you?

JOY. [Just above her breath.] I—I heard something.

MRS. GWYN. [Bitterly.] But you were not spying?

JOY. I was n't—I wasn't! I didn't want—to hear. I only heard a little. I could-
n't help listening, Mother.

MRS. GWYN. [With a little laugh.] Couldn't help listening?

JOY. [Through her teeth.] I hate him. I didn't mean to listen, but I hate him.

MRS. GWYN. I see. Why do you hate him?

[There is a silence.]

JOY. He—he——[She stops.]

MRS. GWYN. Yes?

JOY. [With a sort of despair.] I don't know. Oh! I don't know! But I feel——

MRS. GWYN. I can't reason with you. As to what you heard, it 's— ridiculous.

JOY. It 's not that. It 's—it 's you!

MRS. GWYN. [Stonily.] I don't know what you mean.

JOY. [Passionately.] I wish Dad were here!

MRS. GWYN. Do you love your Father as much as me?

JOY. Oh! Mother, no-you know I don't.

MRS. GWYN. [Resentfully.] Then why do you want him?

JOY. [Almost under her breath.] Because of that man.

MRS. GWYN. Indeed!

JOY. I will never—never make friends with him.

MRS. GWYN. [Cuttingly.] I have not asked you to.

JOY. [With a blind movement of her hand.] Oh, Mother!

[MRS. GWYN half turns away.]

Mother—won't you? Let's tell Uncle Tom and go away from him?

MRS. GWYN. If you were not, a child, Joy, you wouldn't say such things.

JOY. [Eagerly.] I'm not a child, I'm—I'm a woman. I am.

MRS. GWYN. No! You—are—not a woman, Joy.

[She sees joy throw up her arms as though warding off a blow, and turning finds that LEVER is standing in the opening of the wall.]

LEVER. [Looking from face to face.] What's the matter? [There is no answer.] What is it, Joy?

JOY. [Passionately.] I heard you, I don't care who knows. I'd listen again.

LEVER. [Impassively.] Ah! and what did I say that was so very dreadful?

JOY. You're a—a—you 're a—coward!

MRS. GWYN. [With a sort of groan.] Joy!

LEVER. [Stepping up to JOY, and standing with his hands behind him— in a low voice.] Now hit me in the face—hit me—hit me as hard as you can. Go on, Joy, it'll do you good.

[Joy raises her clenched hand, but drops it, and hides her face.]

Why don't you? I'm not pretending!

[Joy makes no sign.]

Come, joy; you'll make yourself ill, and that won't help, will it?

[But joy still makes no sign.]

[With determination.] What's the matter? now come—tell me!

JOY. [In a stifled, sullen voice.] Will you leave my mother alone?

MRS. GWYN. Oh! my dear Joy, don't be silly!

JOY. [Wincing; then with sudden passion.] I defy you—I defy you! [She rushes from their sight.]

MRS. GWYN. [With a movement of distress.] Oh!

LEVER. [Turning to MRS. GWYN with a protecting gesture.] Never mind, dear! It'll be—it'll be all right!

[But the expression of his face is not the expression of his words.]

The curtain falls.

ACT III

It is evening; a full yellow moon is shining through the branches of the hollow tree. The Chinese lanterns are alight. There is dancing in the house; the music sounds now loud, now soft. MISS BEECH is sitting on the rustic seat in a black bunchy evening dress, whose inconspicuous opening is inlaid with white. She slowly fans herself.

DICK comes from the house in evening dress. He does not see Miss BEECH.

DICK. Curse! [A short silence.] Curse!

MISS BEECH. Poor young man!

DICK. [With a start.] Well, Peachey, I can't help it [He fumbles off his gloves.]

MISS BEECH. Did you ever know any one that could?

DICK. [Earnestly.] It's such awfully hard lines on Joy. I can't get her out of my head, lying there with that beastly headache while everybody's jigging round.

MISS BEECH. Oh! you don't mind about yourself—noble young man!

DICK. I should be a brute if I did n't mind more for her.

MISS BEECH. So you think it's a headache, do you?

DICK. Did n't you hear what Mrs. Gwyn said at dinner about the sun? [With inspiration.] I say, Peachey, could n't you—could n't you just go up and give her a message from me, and find out if there 's anything she wants, and say how brutal it is that she 's seedy; it would be most awfully decent of you. And tell her the dancing's no good without her. Do, Peachey, now do! Ah! and look here!

[He dives into the hollow of the tree, and brings from out of it a pail of water in which are placed two bottles of champagne, and some yellow irises—he takes the irises.]

You might give her these. I got them specially for her, and I have n't had a chance.

MISS BEECH. [Lifting a bottle.] What 's this?

DICK. Fizz. The Colonel brought it from the George. It 's for supper; he put it in here because of—[Smiling faintly]—Mrs. Hope, I think. Peachey, do take her those irises.

MISS. BEECH. D' you think they'll do her any good?

DICK. [Crestfallen.] I thought she'd like—I don't want to worry her—you might try.

[MISS BEECH shakes her head.]

Why not?

MISS BEECH. The poor little creature won't let me in.

DICK. You've been up then!

MISS BEECH. [Sharply.] Of course I've been up. I've not got a stone for my heart, young man!

DICK. All right! I suppose I shall just have to get along somehow.

MISS BEECH. [With devilry.] That's what we've all got to do.

DICK. [Gloomily.] But this is too brutal for anything!

MISS BEECH. Worse than ever happened to any one!

DICK. I swear I'm not thinking of myself.

MISS BEECH. Did y' ever know anybody that swore they were?

DICK. Oh! shut up!

MISS BEECH. You'd better go in and get yourself a partner.

DICK. [With pale desperation.] Look here, Peachey, I simply loathe all those girls.

MISS BEECH. Ah-h! [Ironically.] Poor lot, are n't they?

DICK. All right; chaff away, it's good fun, isn't it? It makes me sick to dance when Joy's lying there. Her last night, too!

MISS BEECH. [Sidling to him.] You're a good young man, and you 've got a good heart.

[She takes his hand, and puts it to her cheek.]

DICK. Peachey—I say, Peachey d' you think there 's—I mean d' you think there'll ever be any chance for me?

MISS BEECH. I thought that was coming! I don't approve of your making love at your time of life; don't you think I 'm going to encourage you.

DICK. But I shall be of age in a year; my money's my own, it's not as if I had to ask any one's leave; and I mean, I do know my own mind.

MISS BEECH. Of course you do. Nobody else would at your age, but you do.

DICK. I would n't ask her to promise, it would n't be fair when she 's so young, but I do want her to know that I shall never change.

MISS BEECH. And suppose—only suppose—she's fond of you, and says she'll never change.

DICK. Oh! Peachey! D' you think there's a chance of that—do you?

MISS BEECH. A-h-h!

DICK. I wouldn't let her bind herself, I swear I wouldn't. [Solemnly.] I'm not such a selfish brute as you seem to think.

MISS BEECH. [Sidling close to him and in a violent whisper.] Well— have a go!

DICK. Really? You are a brick, Peachey!

[He kisses her.]

MISS BEACH. [Yielding pleasurably; then remembering her principles.] Don't you ever say I said so! You're too young, both of you.

DICK. But it is exceptional—I mean in my case, is n't it?

[The COLONEL and MRS. GWYN are coming down the lawn.]

MISS BEECH. Oh! very!

[She sits beneath the tree and fans herself.]

COLONEL. The girls are all sitting out, Dick! I've been obliged to dance myself. Phew!

[He mops his brow.]

[DICK swinging round goes rushing off towards the house.]

[Looking after him.] Hallo! What's the matter with him? Cooling your heels, Peachey? By George! it's hot. Fancy the poor devils in London on a night like this, what? [He sees the moon.] It's a full moon. You're lucky to be down here, Molly.

MRS. GWYN. [In a low voice.] Very!

MISS BEECH. Oh! so you think she's lucky, do you?

COLONEL. [Expanding his nostrils.] Delicious scent to-night! Hay and roses—delicious.

[He seats himself between them.]

A shame that poor child has knocked up like this. Don't think it was the sun myself—more likely neuralgic—she 's subject to neuralgia, Molly.

MRS. GWYN. [Motionless.] I know.

COLONEL. Got too excited about your coming. I told Nell not to keep worrying her about her frock, and this is the result. But your Aunt — you know—she can't let a thing alone!

MISS BEECH. Ah! 't isn't neuralgia.

[MRS. GWYN looks at her quickly and averts her eyes.]

COLONEL. Excitable little thing. You don't understand her, Peachey.

MISS BEECH. Don't I?

COLONEL. She's all affection. Eh, Molly? I remember what I was like at her age, a poor affectionate little rat, and now look at me!

MISS BEECH. [Fanning herself.] I see you.

COLONEL. [A little sadly.] We forget what we were like when we were young. She's been looking forward to to-night ever since you wrote; and now to have to go to bed and miss the, dancing. Too bad!

MRS. GWYN. Don't, Uncle Tom!

COLONEL. [Patting her hand.] There, there, old girl, don't think about it. She'll be all right tomorrow.

MISS BEECH. If I were her mother I'd soon have her up.

COLONEL. Have her up with that headache! What are you talking about, Peachey?

MISS BEECH. I know a remedy.

COLONEL. Well, out with it.

MISS BEECH. Oh! Molly knows it too!

MRS. GWYN. [Staring at the ground.] It's easy to advise.

COLONEL. [Fidgetting.] Well, if you're thinking of morphia for her, don't have anything to do with it. I've always set my face against morphia; the only time I took it was in Burmah. I'd raging neuralgia for two days. I went to our old doctor, and I made him give me some. "Look here, doctor," I said, "I hate the idea of morphia, I 've never taken it, and I never want to."

MISS BEECH. [Looking at MRS. GWYN.] When a tooth hurts, you should have it out. It 's only puttin' off the evil day.

COLONEL. You say that because it was n't your own.

MISS BEECH. Well, it was hollow, and you broke your principles!

COLONEL. Hollow yourself, Peachey; you're as bad as any one!

MISS BEECH [With devilry.] Well, I know that! [She turns to MRS. GWYN.] He should have had it out! Shouldn't he, Molly?

MRS. GWYN. I—don't—judge for other people.

[She gets up suddenly, as though deprived of air.]

COLONEL. [Alarmed.] Hallo, Molly! Are n't you feeling the thing, old girl?

MISS BEECH. Let her get some air, poor creature!

COLONEL. [Who follows anxiously.] Your Aunt's got some first-rate sal volatile.

MRS. GWYN. It's all right, Uncle Tom. I felt giddy, it's nothing, now.

COLONEL. That's the dancing. [He taps his forehead.] I know what it is when you're not used to it.

MRS. GWYN. [With a sudden bitter outburst.] I suppose you think I 'm a very bad mother to be amusing myself while joy's suffering.

COLONEL. My dear girl, whatever put such a thought into your head? We all know if there were anything you could do, you'd do it at once, would n't she, Peachey?

[MISS BEECH turns a slow look on MRS. GWYN.]

MRS. GWYN. Ah! you see, Peachey knows me better.

COLONEL. [Following up his thoughts.] I always think women are wonderful. There's your Aunt, she's very funny, but if there's anything the matter with me, she'll sit up all night; but when she's ill herself, and you try to do anything for her, out she raps at once.

MRS. GWYN. [In a low voice.] There's always one that a woman will do anything for.

COLONEL. Exactly what I say. With your Aunt it's me, and by George! Molly, sometimes I wish it was n't.

MISS BEECH, [With meaning.] But is it ever for another woman!

COLONEL. You old cynic! D' you mean to say Joy wouldn't do anything on earth for her Mother, or Molly for Joy? You don't know human nature. What a wonderful night! Have n't seen such a moon for years, she's like a great, great lamp!

[MRS. GWYN hiding from Miss BEECH's eyes, rises and slips her arm through his; they stand together looking at the moon.]

Don't like these Chinese lanterns, with that moon-tawdry! eh! By Jove, Molly, I sometimes think we humans are a rubbishy lot—each of us talking and thinking of nothing but our own petty little affairs; and when you see a great thing like that up there—[Sighs.] But there's your Aunt, if I were to say a thing like that to her she 'd— she'd think me a lunatic; and yet, you know, she 's a very good woman.

MRS. GWYN. [Half clinging to him.] Do you think me very selfish, Uncle Tom?

COLONEL. My dear—what a fancy! Think you selfish—of course I don't; why should I?

MRS. GWYN. [Dully.] I don't know.

COLONEL. [Changing the subject nervously.] I like your friend, Lever, Molly. He came to me before dinner quite distressed about your Aunt, beggin' me not to take those shares. She 'll be the first to worry me, but he made such a point of it, poor chap—in the end I was obliged to say I wouldn't. I thought it showed very' nice feeling. [Ruefully.] It's a pretty tight fit to make two ends meet on my income—I've missed a good thing, all owing to your Aunt. [Dropping his voice.] I don't mind telling you, Molly, I think they've got a much finer mine there than they've any idea of.

[MRS. GWYN gives way to laughter that is very near to sobs.]

[With dignity.] I can't see what there is to laugh at.

MRS. GWYN. I don't know what's the matter with me this evening.

MISS BEECH. [In a low voice.] I do.

COLONEL. There, there! Give me a kiss, old girl! [He kisses her on the brow.] Why, your forehead's as hot as fire. I know—I know-you 're fretting about Joy. Never mind—come! [He draws her hand beneath his arm.] Let's go and have a look at the moon on the river. We all get upset at times; eh! [Lifting his hand as if he had been stung.] Why, you 're not crying, Molly! I say! Don't do that, old girl, it makes me wretched. Look here, Peachey. [Holding out the hand on which the tear has dropped.] This is dreadful!

MRS. GWYN. [With a violent effort.] It's all right, Uncle Tom!

[MISS BEECH wipes her own eyes stealthily. From the house is heard the voice of MRS. HOPE, calling "Tom."]

MISS BEECH. Some one calling you.

COLONEL. There, there, my dear, you just stay here, and cool yourself—I 'll come back—shan't be a minute. [He turns to go.]

[MRS. HOPE'S voice sounds nearer.]

[Turning back.] And Molly, old girl, don't you mind anything I said. I don't remember what it was—it must have been something, I suppose.

[He hastily retreats.]

MRS. GWYN. [In a fierce low voice.] Why do you torture me?

MISS BEECH. [Sadly.] I don't want to torture you.

MRS. GWYN, But you do. D' you think I haven't seen this coming—all these weeks. I knew she must find out some time! But even a day counts——

MISS BEECH. I don't understand why you brought him down here.

MRS. GWYN. [After staring at her, bitterly.] When day after day and night after night you've thought of nothing but how to keep them both, you might a little want to prove that it was possible, mightn't you? But you don't understand—how should you? You've never been a mother! [And fiercely.] You've never had a lov—

[MISS BEECH raises her face-it is all puckered.]

[Impulsively.] Oh, I did n't mean that, Peachey!

MISS BEECH. All right, my dear.

MRS. GWYN. I'm so dragged in two! [She sinks into a chair.] I knew it must come.

MISS BEECH. Does she know everything, Molly?

MRS. GWYN. She guesses.

MISS BEECH. [Mournfully.] It's either him or her then, my dear; one or the other you 'll have to give up.

MRS. GWYN. [Motionless.] Life's very hard on women!

MISS BEECH. Life's only just beginning for that child, Molly.

MRS. GWYN. You don't care if it ends for me!

MISS BEECH. Is it as bad as that?

MRS. GWYN. Yes.

MISS BEECH. [Rocking hey body.] Poor things! Poor things!

MRS. GWYN. Are you still fond of me?

MISS BEECH. Yes, yes, my dear, of course I am.

MRS. GWYN. In spite of my-wickedness?

[She laughs.]

MISS BEECH. Who am I to tell what's wicked and what is n't? God knows you're both like daughters to me!

MRS. GWYN. [Abruptly.] I can't.

MISS BEECH. Molly.

MRS. GWYN. You don't know what you're asking.

MISS BEECH. If I could save you suffering, my dear, I would. I hate suffering, if it 's only a fly, I hate it.

MRS. GWYN. [Turning away from her.] Life is n't fair. Peachey, go in and leave me alone.

[She leans back motionless.]

[Miss BEECH gets off her seat, and stroking MRS. GWYN's arm in passing goes silently away. In the opening of the wall she meets LEVER who is looking for his partner. They make way for each other.]

LEVER. [Going up to MRS. GWYN—gravely.] The next is our dance, Molly.

MRS. GWYN. [Unmoving.] Let's sit it out here, then.

[LEVER sits down.]

LEVER. I've made it all right with your Uncle.

MRS. GWYN. [Dully.] Oh?

LEVER. I spoke to him about the shares before dinner.

MRS. GWYN. Yes, he told me, thank you.

LEVER. There 's nothing to worry over, dear.

MRS. GWYN. [Passionately.] What does it matter about the wretched shares now? I 'm stifling.

[She throws her scarf off.]

LEVER. I don't understand what you mean by "now."

MRS. GWYN. Don't you?

LEVER. We were n't—Joy can't know—why should she? I don't believe for a minute——

MRS. GWYN. Because you don't want to.

LEVER. Do you mean she does?

MRS. GWYN. Her heart knows.

[LEVER makes a movement of discomfiture; suddenly MRS. GWYN looks at him as though to read his soul.]

I seem to bring you nothing but worry, Maurice. Are you tired of me?

LEVER. [Meeting her eyes.] No, I am not.

MRS. GWYN. Ah, but would you tell me if you were?

LEVER. [Softly.] Sufficient unto the day is the evil thereof.

[MRS. GWYN struggles to look at him, then covers her face with her hands.]

MRS. GWYN. If I were to give you up, you'd forget me in a month.

LEVER. Why do you say such things?

MRS. GWYN. If only I could believe I was necessary to you!

LEVER. [Forcing the fervour of his voice.] But you are!

MRS. GWYN. Am I? [With the ghost of a smile.] Midsummer day!

[She gives a laugh that breaks into a sob.]

[The music o f a waltz sounds from the house.]

LEVER. For God's sake, don't, Molly—I don't believe in going to meet trouble.

MRS. GWYN. It's staring me in the face.

LEVER. Let the future take care of itself!

[MRS. GWYN has turned away her face, covering it with her hands.]

Don't, Molly! [Trying to pull her hands away.] Don't!

MRS. GWYN. Oh! what shall I do?

[There is a silence; the music of the waltz sounds louder from the house.]

[Starting up.] Listen! One can't sit it out and dance it too. Which is it to be, Maurice, dancing—or sitting out? It must be one or the other, must n't it?

LEVER. Molly! Molly!

MRS. GWYN. Ah, my dear! [Standing away from him as though to show her- self.] How long shall I keep you? This is all that 's left of me.

It 's time I joined the wallflowers. [Smiling faintly.] It's time I played the mother, is n't it? [In a whisper.] It'll be all sitting out then.

LEVER. Don't! Let's go and dance, it'll do you good.

[He puts his hands on her arms, and in a gust of passion kisses her lips and throat.]

MRS. GWYN. I can't give you up—I can't. Love me, oh! love me!

[For a moment they stand so; then, with sudden remembrance of where they are, they move apart.]

LEVER. Are you all right now, darling?

MRS. GWYN. [Trying to smile.] Yes, dear—quite.

LEVER. Then let 's go, and dance. [They go.]

[For a few seconds the hollow tree stands alone; then from the house ROSE comes and enters it. She takes out a bottle of champagne, wipes it, and carries it away; but seeing MRS. GWYN's scarf lying across the chair, she fingers it, and stops, listening to the waltz. Suddenly draping it round her shoulders, she seizes the bottle of champagne, and waltzes with abandon to the music, as though avenging a long starvation of her instincts. Thus dancing, she is surprised by DICK, who has come to smoke a cigarette and think, at the spot where he was told to "have a go." ROSE, startled, stops and hugs the bottle.]

DICK. It's not claret, Rose, I should n't warm it.

[ROSE, taking off the scarf, replaces it on the chair; then with the half-warmed bottle, she retreats. DICK, in the swing, sits thinking of his fate. Suddenly from behind the hollow tree he sees Joy darting forward in her day dress with her hair about her neck, and her skirt all torn. As he springs towards her, she turns at bay.]

DICK. Joy!

JOY. I want Uncle Tom.

DICK. [In consternation.] But ought you to have got up—I thought you were ill in bed; oughtn't you to be lying down?

JOY. If have n't been in bed. Where's Uncle Tom?

DICK. But where have you been?-your dress is all torn. Look! [He touches the torn skirt.]

JOY. [Tearing it away.] In the fields. Where's Uncle Tom?

DICK. Are n't you really ill then?

[Joy shakes her head.]

DICK, [showing her the irises.] Look at these. They were the best I could get.

JOY. Don't! I want Uncle Tom!

DICK. Won't you take them?

JOY. I 've got something else to do.

DICK. [With sudden resolution.] What do you want the Colonel for?

JOY. I want him.

DICK. Alone?

JOY. Yes.

DICK. Joy, what is the matter?

JOY. I 've got something to tell him.

DICK. What? [With sudden inspiration.] Is it about Lever?

JOY. [In a low voice.] The mine.

DICK. The mine?

JOY. It 's not—not a proper one.

DICK. How do you mean, Joy?

JOY. I overheard. I don't care, I listened. I would n't if it had been anybody else, but I hate him.

DICK. [Gravely.] What did you hear?

JOY. He 's keeping back something Uncle Tom ought to know.

DICK. Are you sure?

[Joy makes a rush to pass him.]

[Barring the way.] No, wait a minute—you must! Was it something that really matters?—I don't want to know what.

JOY. Yes, it was.

DICK. What a beastly thing—are you quite certain, Joy?

JOY. [Between her teeth.] Yes.

DICK. Then you must tell him, of course, even if you did overhear. You can't stand by and see the Colonel swindled. Whom was he talking to?

JOY. I won't tell you.

DICK. [Taking her wrist.] Was it was it your Mother?

[Joy bends her head.]

But if it was your Mother, why does n't she——

JOY. Let me go!

DICK. [Still holding her.] I mean I can't see what——

JOY. [Passionately.] Let me go!

DICK. [Releasing her.] I'm thinking of your Mother, Joy. She would never—

JOY. [Covering her face.] That man!

DICK. But joy, just think! There must be some mistake. It 's so queer—it 's quite impossible!

JOY. He won't let her.

DICK. Won't let her—won't let her? But [Stopping dead, and in a very different voice.] Oh!

JOY. [Passionately.] Why d' you look at me like that? Why can't you speak?

[She waits for him to speak, but he does not.]

I'm going to show what he is, so that Mother shan't speak to him again. I can—can't I—if I tell Uncle Tom?—can't I——?

DICK. But Joy—if your Mother knows a thing like—that——

JOY. She wanted to tell—she begged him—and he would n't.

DICK. But, joy, dear, it means——

JOY. I hate him, I want to make her hate him, and I will.

DICK. But, Joy, dear, don't you see—if your Mother knows a thing like that, and does n't speak of it, it means that she—it means that you can't make her hate him—it means——If it were anybody else— but, well, you can't give your own Mother away!

JOY. How dare you! How dare you! [Turning to the hollow tree.] It is n't true— Oh! it is n't true!

DICK. [In deep distress.] Joy, dear, I never meant, I didn't really!

[He tries to pull her hands down from her face.]

JOY. [Suddenly.] Oh! go away, go away!

[MRS. GWYN is seen coming back. JOY springs into the tree. DICK quickly steals away. MRS. GWYN goes up to the chair and takes the scarf that she has come for, and is going again when JOY steals out to her.]

Mother!

[MRS. GWYN stands looking at her with her teeth set on her lower lip.]

Oh! Mother, it is n't true?

MRS. GWYN. [Very still.] What is n't true?

JOY. That you and he are——

[Searching her Mother's face, which is deadly still. In a whisper.]

Then it is true. Oh!

MRS. GWYN. That's enough, Joy! What I am is my affair—not yours— do you
        understand?

JOY. [Low and fierce.] Yes, I do.

MRS. GWYN. You don't. You're only a child.

JOY. [Passionately.] I understand that you've hurt [She stops.]

MRS. GWYN. Do you mean your Father?

JOY. [Bowing her head.] Yes, and—and me. [She covers her face.] I'm—I'm
        ashamed.

MRS. GWYN. I brought you into the world, and you say that to me? Have I
        been a bad mother to you?

JOY. [In a smothered voice.] Oh! Mother!

MRS. GWYN. Ashamed? Am I to live all my life like a dead woman because
        you're ashamed? Am I to live like the dead because you 're a
        child that knows nothing of life? Listen, Joy, you 'd better
        understand this once for all. Your Father has no right over me
        and he knows it. We 've been hateful to each other for years.
        Can you understand that? Don't cover your face like a child—
        look at me.

[Joy drops her hands, and lifts her face. MRS. GWYN looks back at her, her lips are quivering; she goes on speaking with stammering rapidity.]

D' you think—because I suffered when you were born and because I 've suffered since with every ache you ever had, that that gives you the right to dictate to me now? [In a dead voice.] I've been unhappy enough and I shall be unhappy enough in the time to come. [Meeting the hard wonder in Joy's face.] Oh! you untouched things, you're as hard and cold as iron!

JOY. I would do anything for you, Mother.

MRS. GWYN. Except—let me live, Joy. That's the only thing you won't do for me, I quite understand.

JOY. Oh! Mother, you don't understand—I want you so; and I seem to be nothing to you now.

MRS. GWYN. Nothing to me? [She smiles.]

JOY. Mother, darling, if you're so unhappy let's forget it all, let's go away and I 'll be everything to you, I promise.

MRS. GWYN. [With the ghost of a laugh.] Ah, Joy!

JOY. I would try so hard.

MRS. GWYN. [With the same quivering smile.] My darling, I know you would, until you fell in love yourself.

JOY. Oh, Mother, I wouldn't, I never would, I swear it.

MRS. GWYN. There has never been a woman, joy, that did not fall in love.

JOY. [In a despairing whisper.] But it 's wrong of you it's wicked!

MRS. GWYN. If it's wicked, I shall pay for it, not you!

JOY. But I want to save you, Mother!

MRS. GWYN. Save me? [Breaking into laughter.]

JOY. I can't bear it that you—if you 'll only—I'll never leave you. You think I
    don't know what I 'm saying, but I do, because even now I—I half love
    somebody. Oh, Mother! [Pressing her breast.] I feel—I feel so awful—as
    if everybody knew.

MRS. GWYN.   You think I'm a monster to hurt you. Ah! yes! You'll under-
    stand better some day.

JOY. [In a sudden outburst of excited fear.] I won't believe it— I—I—can't—
    you're deserting me, Mother.

MRS. GWYN. Oh, you untouched things! You——

[Joy' looks up suddenly, sees her face, and sinks down on her knees.]

JOY. Mother—it 's for me!

GWYN. Ask for my life, JOY—don't be afraid.

[Joy turns her face away. MRS. GWYN bends suddenly and touches her daughter's hair; JOY shrinks from that touch.]

[Recoiling as though she had been stung.] I forgot—I 'm deserting you.

[And swiftly without looking back she goes away. Joy, left alone under the hollow
tree, crouches lower, and her shoulders shake. Here DICK finds her, when he
hears no longer any sound o f voices. He falls on his knees beside her.]

DICK. Oh! Joy; dear, don't cry. It's so dreadful to see you! I 'd do anything not
    to see you cry! Say something.

[Joy is still for a moment, then the shaking of the shoulders begins again.]

Joy, darling! It's so awful, you 'll make yourself ill, and it is n't worth it, really. I
'd do anything to save you pain—won't you stop just for a minute?

[Joy is still again.]

Nothing in the world 's worth your crying, Joy. Give me just a little look!

JOY. [Looking; in a smothered voice.] Don't!

DICK. You do look so sweet! Oh, Joy, I'll comfort you, I'll take it all on myself.
    I know all about it.

[Joy gives a sobbing laugh]

I do. I 've had trouble too, I swear I have. It gets better, it does really.

JOY. You don't know—it's—it's——

DICK. Don't think about it! No, no, no! I know exactly what it's like. [He
    strokes her arm.]

JOY. [Shrinking, in a whisper.] You mustn't.

[The music of a waltz is heard again.]

DICK. Look here, joy! It's no good, we must talk it over calmly.

JOY. You don't see! It's the—it 's the disgrace——

DICK. Oh! as to disgrace—she's your Mother, whatever she does; I'd like to see
    anybody say anything about her—[viciously]—I'd punch his head.

JOY. [Gulping her tears.] That does n't help.

DICK. But if she doesn't love your Father——

JOY. But she's married to him!

DICK. [Hastily.] Yes, of course, I know, marriage is awfully important; but a
    man understands these things.

[Joy looks at him. Seeing the impression he has made, he tries again.]

I mean, he understands better than a woman. I've often argued about moral questions with men up at Oxford.

JOY. [Catching at a straw.] But there's nothing to argue about.

DICK. [Hastily.] Of course, I believe in morals.

[They stare solemnly at each other.]

Some men don't. But I can't help seeing marriage is awfully important.

JOY. [Solemnly.] It's sacred.

DICK. Yes, I know, but there must be exceptions, Joy.

JOY. [Losing herself a little in the stress of this discussion.] How can there be exceptions if a thing 's sacred?

DICK. [Earnestly.] All rules have exceptions; that's true, you know; it's a proverb.

JOY. It can't be true about marriage—how can it when——?

DICK. [With intense earnestness.] But look here, Joy, I know a really clever man—an author. He says that if marriage is a failure people ought to be perfectly free; it isn't everybody who believes that marriage is everything. Of course, I believe it 's sacred, but if it's a failure, I do think it seems awful—don't you?

JOY. I don't know—yes—if—[Suddenly] But it's my own Mother!

DICK. [Gravely.] I know, of course. I can't expect you to see it in your own case like this. [With desperation.] But look here, Joy, this'll show you! If a person loves a person, they have to decide, have n't they? Well, then, you see, that 's what your Mother's done.

JOY. But that does n't show me anything!

DICK. But it does. The thing is to look at it as if it was n't yourself. If it had been you and me in love, Joy, and it was wrong, like them, of course [ruefully] I know you'd have decided right. [Fiercely.] But I swear I should have decided wrong. [Triumphantly.] That 's why I feel I understand your Mother.

JOY. [Brushing her sleeve across her eyes.] Oh, Dick, you are so sweet—and—and—funny!

DICK. [Sliding his arm about her.] I love you, Joy, that 's why, and I 'll love you
        till you don't feel it any more. I will. I'll love you all day and every day;
        you shan't miss anything, I swear it. It 's such a beautiful night—it 's on
        purpose. Look' [JOY looks; he looks at her.] But it 's not so beautiful as
        you.

JOY. [Bending her head.] You mustn't. I don't know—what's coming?

DICK. [Sidling closer.] Are n't your knees tired, darling? I—I can't get near you
properly.

JOY. [With a sob.] Oh! Dick, you are a funny—comfort!

DICK. We'll stick together, Joy, always; nothing'll matter then.

[They struggle to their feet-the waltz sounds louder.]

You're missing it all! I can't bear you to miss the dancing. It seems so queer!
Couldn't we? Just a little turn?

JOY. No, no?

DICK. Oh! try!

[He takes her gently by the waist, she shrinks back.]

JOY. [Brokenly.] No-no! Oh! Dick-to-morrow 'll be so awful.

DICK. To-morrow shan't hurt you, Joy; nothing shall ever hurt you again.

[She looks at him, and her face changes; suddenly she buries it against his shoulder.]

[They stand so just a moment in the moon light; then turning to the river move
slowly out of sight. Again the hollow tree is left alone. The music of the waltz has
stopped. The voices of MISS BEECH and the COLONEL are heard approaching from the house. They appear in the opening of the wall. The COLONEL
carries a pair of field glasses with which to look at the Moon.]

COLONEL. Charming to see Molly dance with Lever, their steps go so well
            together! I can always tell when a woman's enjoying herself,
            Peachey.

MISS BEECH. [Sharply.] Can you? You're very clever.

COLONEL. Wonderful, that moon! I'm going to have a look at her! Splendid glasses these, Peachy [he screws them out], not a better pair in England. I remember in Burmah with these glasses I used to be able to tell a man from a woman at two miles and a quarter. And that's no joke, I can tell you. [But on his way to the moon, he has taken a survey of the earth to the right along the river. In a low but excited voice] I say, I say—is it one of the maids—the baggage! Why! It's Dick! By George, she's got her hair down, Peachey! It's Joy!

[MISS BEECH goes to look. He makes as though to hand the glasses to her, but puts them to his own eyes instead— excitedly.]

It is! What about her headache? By George, they're kissing. I say, Peachey! I shall have to tell Nell!

MISS BEECH. Are you sure they're kissing? Well, that's some comfort.

COLONEL. They're at the stile now. Oughtn't I to stop them, eh? [He stands on tiptoe.] We must n't spy on them, dash it all. [He drops the glasses.] They're out of sight now.

MISS BEECH. [To herself.] He said he wouldn't let her.

COLONEL. What! have you been encouraging them!

MISS BEECH. Don't be in such a hurry!

[She moves towards the hollow tree.]

COLONEL. [Abstractedly.] By George, Peachey, to think that Nell and I were once—Poor Nell! I remember just such a night as this

[He stops, and stares before him, sighing.]

MISS BEECH, [Impressively.] It's a comfort she's got that good young man. She's found out that her mother and this Mr. Lever are—you know.

COLONEL. [Losing all traces of his fussiness, and drawing himself up as though he were on parade.] You tell me that my niece?

MISS BEECH. Out of her own mouth!

COLONEL. [Bowing his head.] I never would have believed she'd have forgotten herself.

MISS BEECH. [Very solemnly.] Ah, my dear! We're all the same; we're all as hollow as that tree! When it's ourselves it's always a special case!

[The COLONEL makes a movement of distress, and Miss BEECH goes to him.]

Don't you take it so to heart, my dear!

[A silence.]

COLONEL. [Shaking his head.] I couldn't have believed Molly would forget that child.

MISS BEECH. [Sadly.] They must go their own ways, poor things! She can't put herself in the child's place, and the child can't put herself in Molly's. A woman and a girl—there's the tree of life between them!

COLONEL. [Staring into the tree to see indeed if that were the tree alluded to.] It's a grief to me, Peachey, it's a grief! [He sinks into a chair, stroking his long moustaches. Then to avenge his hurt.] Shan't tell Nell—dashed if I do anything to make the trouble worse!

MISS BEECH. [Nodding.] There's suffering enough, without adding to it with our trumpery judgments! If only things would last between them!

COLONEL. [Fiercely.] Last! By George, they'd better——

[He stops, and looking up with a queer sorry look.]

I say, Peachey Life's very funny!

MISS BEECH. Men and women are! [Touching his forehead tenderly.] There, there—take care of your poor, dear head! Tsst! The blessed innocents!

[She pulls the COLONEL'S sleeve. They slip away towards the house, as JOY and DICK come back. They are still linked together, and stop by the hollow tree.]

JOY. [In a whisper.] Dick, is love always like this?

DICK. [Putting his arms around her, with conviction.] It's never been like this before. It's you and me!

[He kisses her on the lips.]

The curtain falls.

STRIFE

A DRAMA IN THREE ACTS

PERSONS OF THE PLAY

JOHN ANTHONY, Chairman of the Trenartha Tin Plate Works
EDGAR ANTHONY, his Son

FREDERIC H. WILDER,
WILLIAM SCANTLEBURY,| Directors Of the same
OLIVER WANKLIN,

HENRY TENCH, Secretary of the same
FRANCIS UNDERWOOD, C.E., Manager of the same
SIMON HARNESS, a Trades Union official

DAVID ROBERTS,
JAMES GREEN,
JOHN BULGIN, |the workmen's committee
HENRY THOMAS,
GEORGE ROUS,

HENRY ROUS,
LEWIS,
JAGO,
EVANS,   workman at the Trenartha Tin Plate Works
A BLACKSMITH,
DAVIES,
A RED-HAIRED YOUTH.
BROWN

FROST, valet to John Anthony
ENID UNDERWOOD, Wife of Francis Underwood, daughter of John
Anthony
ANNIE ROBERTS, wife of David Roberts
MADGE THOMAS, daughter of Henry Thomas

MRS. ROUS, mother of George and Henry Rous
MRS. BULGIN, wife of John Bulgin
MRS. YEO, wife of a workman
A PARLOURMAID to the Underwoods
JAN, Madge's brother, a boy of ten
A CROWD OF MEN ON STRIKE

The action takes place on February 7th between the hours of noon and six in the afternoon, close to the Trenartha Tin Plate Works, on the borders of England and Wales, where a strike has been in progress throughout the winter.

ACT I

It is noon. In the Underwoods' dining-room a bright fire is burning. On one side of the fireplace are double-doors leading to the drawing-room, on the other side a door leading to the hall. In the centre of the room a long dining-table without a cloth is set out as a Board table. At the head of it, in the Chairman's seat, sits JOHN ANTHONY, an old man, big, clean-shaven, and high-coloured, with thick white hair, and thick dark eyebrows. His movements are rather slow and feeble, but his eyes are very much alive. There is a glass of water by his side. On his right sits his son EDGAR, an earnest-looking man of thirty, reading a newspaper. Next him WANKLIN, a man with jutting eyebrows, and silver-streaked light hair, is bending over transfer papers. TENCH, the Secretary, a short and rather humble, nervous man, with side whiskers, stands helping him. On WANKLIN'S right sits UNDERWOOD, the Manager, a quiet man, with along, stiff jaw, and steady eyes. Back to the fire is SCANTLEBURY, a very large, pale, sleepy man, with grey hair, rather bald. Between him and the Chairman are two empty chairs.

WILDER. [Who is lean, cadaverous, and complaining, with drooping grey moustaches, stands before the fire.] I say, this fire's the devil! Can I have a screen, Tench?

SCANTLEBURY. A screen, ah!

TENCH. Certainly, Mr. Wilder. [He looks at UNDERWOOD.] That is— perhaps the Manager—perhaps Mr. Underwood——

SCANTLEBURY. These fireplaces of yours, Underwood——

UNDERWOOD. [Roused from studying some papers.] A screen? Rather! I'm
                        sorry. [He goes to the door with a little smile.] We're not
                        accustomed to complaints of too much fire down here just
                        now.

[He speaks as though he holds a pipe between his teeth, slowly, ironically.]

WILDER. [In an injured voice.] You mean the men. H'm!

[UNDERWOOD goes out.]

SCANTLEBURY. Poor devils!

WILDER. It's their own fault, Scantlebury.

EDGAR. [Holding out his paper.] There's great distress among them, according
                to the Trenartha News.

WILDER. Oh, that rag! Give it to Wanklin. Suit his Radical views. They call
                us monsters, I suppose. The editor of that rubbish ought to be shot.

EDGAR. [Reading.] "If the Board of worthy gentlemen who control the
                Trenartha Tin Plate Works from their arm-chairs in London would
                condescend to come and see for themselves the conditions prevailing
                amongst their work-people during this strike——"

WILDER. Well, we have come.

EDGAR. [Continuing.] "We cannot believe that even their leg-of- mutton
                hearts would remain untouched."

[WANKLIN takes the paper from him.]

WILDER. Ruffian! I remember that fellow when he had n't a penny to his name;
                little snivel of a chap that's made his way by black- guarding every-
                body who takes a different view to himself.

[ANTHONY says something that is not heard.]

WILDER. What does your father say?

EDGAR. He says "The kettle and the pot."

WILDER. H'm!

[He sits down next to SCANTLEBURY.]

SCANTLEBURY. [Blowing out his cheeks.] I shall boil if I don't get that screen.

[UNDERWOOD and ENID enter with a screen, which they place before the fire. ENID is tall; she has a small, decided face, and is twenty-eight years old.]

ENID. Put it closer, Frank. Will that do, Mr. Wilder? It's the highest we've got.

WILDER. Thanks, capitally.

SCANTLEBURY. [Turning, with a sigh of pleasure.] Ah! Merci, Madame!

ENID. Is there anything else you want, Father? [ANTHONY shakes his head.] Edgar—anything?

EDGAR. You might give me a "J" nib, old girl.

ENID. There are some down there by Mr. Scantlebury.

SCANTLEBURY. [Handing a little box of nibs.] Ah! your brother uses "J's." What does the manager use? [With expansive politeness.] What does your husband use, Mrs. Underwood?

UNDERWOOD. A quill!

SCANTLEBURY. The homely product of the goose. [He holds out quills.]

UNDERWOOD. [Drily.] Thanks, if you can spare me one. [He takes a quill.] What about lunch, Enid?

ENID. [Stopping at the double-doors and looking back.] We're going to have lunch here, in the drawing-room, so you need n't hurry with your meeting.

[WANKLIN and WILDER bow, and she goes out.]

SCANTLEBURY. [Rousing himself, suddenly.] Ah! Lunch! That hotel—
Dreadful! Did you try the whitebait last night? Fried fat!

WILDER. Past twelve! Are n't you going to read the minutes, Tench?

TENCH. [Looking for the CHAIRMAN'S assent, reads in a rapid and monot-
onous voice.] "At a Board Meeting held the 31st of January at the
Company's Offices, 512, Cannon Street, E.C. Present—Mr.
Anthony in the chair, Messrs. F. H. Wilder, William Scantlebury,
Oliver Wanklin, and Edgar Anthony. Read letters from the Manager
dated January 20th, 23d, 25th, 28th, relative to the strike at the
Company's Works. Read letters to the Manager of January 21st,
24th, 26th, 29th. Read letter from Mr. Simon Harness, of the
Central Union, asking for an interview with the Board. Read letter
from the Men's Committee, signed David Roberts, James Green, John
Bulgin, Henry Thomas, George Rous, desiring conference with the
Board; and it was resolved that a special Board Meeting be called for
February 7th at the house of the Manager, for the purpose of dis-
cussing the situation with Mr. Simon Harness and the Men's
Committee on the spot. Passed twelve transfers, signed and sealed
nine certificates and one balance certificate."

[He pushes the book over to the CHAIRMAN.]

ANTHONY. [With a heavy sigh.] If it's your pleasure, sign the same.

[He signs, moving the pen with difficulty.]

WANKLIN. What's the Union's game, Tench? They have n't made up their split
with the men. What does Harness want this interview for?

TENCH. Hoping we shall come to a compromise, I think, sir; he's having a
meeting with the men this afternoon.

WILDER. Harness! Ah! He's one of those cold-blooded, cool-headed chaps. I
distrust them. I don't know that we didn't make a mistake to come
down. What time'll the men be here?

UNDERWOOD. Any time now.

WILDER. Well, if we're not ready, they'll have to wait—won't do them any harm to cool their heels a bit.

SCANTLEBURY. [Slowly.] Poor devils! It's snowing. What weather!

UNDERWOOD. [With meaning slowness.] This house'll be the warmest place they've been in this winter.

WILDER. Well, I hope we're going to settle this business in time for me to catch the 6.30. I've got to take my wife to Spain to-morrow. [Chattily.] My old father had a strike at his works in '69 ; just such a February as this. They wanted to shoot him.

WANKLIN. What! In the close season?

WILDER. By George, there was no close season for employers then! He used to go down to his office with a pistol in his pocket.

SCANTLEBURY. [Faintly alarmed.] Not seriously?

WILDER. [With finality.] Ended in his shootin' one of 'em in the legs.

SCANTLEBURY. [Unavoidably feeling his thigh.] No? Which?

ANTHONY. [Lifting the agenda paper.] To consider the policy of the Board in relation to the strike. [There is a silence.]

WILDER. It's this infernal three-cornered duel—the Union, the men, and our-selves.

WANKLIN. We need n't consider the Union.

WILDER. It's my experience that you've always got to, consider the Union, con-found them! If the Union were going to withdraw their support from the men, as they've done, why did they ever allow them to strike at all?

EDGAR. We've had that over a dozen times.

WILDER. Well, I've never understood it! It's beyond me. They talk of the engineers' and furnace-men's demands being excessive—so they are—but
that's not enough to make the Union withdraw their support. What's
behind it?

UNDERWOOD. Fear of strikes at Harper's and Tinewell's.

WILDER. [With triumph.] Afraid of other strikes—now, that's a reason! Why
could n't we have been told that before?

UNDERWOOD. You were.

TENCH. You were absent from the Board that day, sir.

SCANTLEBURY. The men must have seen they had no chance when the Union
gave them up. It's madness.

UNDERWOOD. It's Roberts!

WILDER. Just our luck, the men finding a fanatical firebrand like Roberts for
leader. [A pause.]

WANKLIN. [Looking at ANTHONY.] Well?

WILDER. [Breaking in fussily.] It's a regular mess. I don't like the position we're
in; I don't like it; I've said so for a long time. [Looking at
WANKLIN.] When Wanklin and I came down here before
Christmas it looked as if the men must collapse. You thought so too,
Underwood.

UNDERWOOD. Yes.

WILDER. Well, they haven't! Here we are, going from bad to worse losing our
customers—shares going down!

SCANTLEBURY. [Shaking his head.] M'm! M'm!

WANKLIN. What loss have we made by this strike, Tench?

TENCH. Over fifty thousand, sir!

SCANTLEBURY, [Pained.] You don't say!

WILDER. We shall never got it back.

TENCH. No, sir.

WILDER. Who'd have supposed the men were going to stick out like this—nobody suggested that. [Looking angrily at TENCH.]

SCANTLEBURY. [Shaking his head.] I've never liked a fight—never shall.

ANTHONY. No surrender! [All look at him.]

WILDER. Who wants to surrender? [ANTHONY looks at him.] I—I want to act reasonably. When the men sent Roberts up to the Board in December—then was the time. We ought to have humoured him; instead of that the Chairman—[Dropping his eyes before ANTHONY'S]—er—we snapped his head off. We could have got them in then by a little tact.

ANTHONY. No compromise!

WILDER. There we are! This strike's been going on now since October, and as far as I can see it may last another six months. Pretty mess we shall be in by then. The only comfort is, the men'll be in a worse!

EDGAR. [To UNDERWOOD.] What sort of state are they really in, Frank?

UNDERWOOD. [Without expression.] Damnable!

WILDER. Well, who on earth would have thought they'd have held on like this without support!

UNDERWOOD. Those who know them.

WILDER. I defy any one to know them! And what about tin? Price going up daily. When we do get started we shall have to work off our contracts at the top of the market.

WANKLIN. What do you say to that, Chairman?

ANTHONY. Can't be helped!

WILDER. Shan't pay a dividend till goodness knows when!

SCANTLEBURY. [With emphasis.] We ought to think of the shareholders. [Turning heavily.] Chairman, I say we ought to think of the shareholders. [ANTHONY mutters.]

SCANTLEBURY. What's that?

TENCH. The Chairman says he is thinking of you, sir.

SCANTLEBURY. [Sinking back into torpor.] Cynic!

WILDER. It's past a joke. I don't want to go without a dividend for years if the Chairman does. We can't go on playing ducks and drakes with the Company's prosperity.

EDGAR. [Rather ashamedly.] I think we ought to consider the men.

[All but ANTHONY fidget in their seats.]

SCANTLEBURY. [With a sigh.] We must n't think of our private feelings, young man. That'll never do.

EDGAR. [Ironically.] I'm not thinking of our feelings. I'm thinking of the men's.

WILDER. As to that—we're men of business.

WANKLIN. That is the little trouble.

EDGAR. There's no necessity for pushing things so far in the face of all this suffering—it's—it's cruel.

[No one speaks, as though EDGAR had uncovered something whose existence no man prizing his self-respect could afford to recognise.]

WANKLIN. [With an ironical smile.] I'm afraid we must n't base our policy on luxuries like sentiment.

EDGAR. I detest this state of things.

ANTHONY. We did n't seek the quarrel.

EDGAR. I know that sir, but surely we've gone far enough.

ANTHONY. No. [All look at one another.]

WANKLIN. Luxuries apart, Chairman, we must look out what we're doing.

ANTHONY. Give way to the men once and there'll be no end to it.

WANKLIN. I quite agree, but——

[ANTHONY Shakes his head]

You make it a question of bedrock principle?

[ANTHONY nods.]

Luxuries again, Chairman! The shares are below par.

WILDER. Yes, and they'll drop to a half when we pass the next dividend.

SCANTLEBURY. [With alarm.] Come, come! Not so bad as that.

WILDER. [Grimly.] You'll see! [Craning forward to catch ANTHONY'S speech.] I didn't catch——

TENCH. [Hesitating.] The Chairman says, sir, "Fais que—que—devra."

EDGAR. [Sharply.] My father says: "Do what we ought—and let things rip."

WILDER. Tcha!

SCANTLEBURY. [Throwing up his hands.] The Chairman's a Stoic—I always said the Chairman was a Stoic.

WILDER. Much good that'll do us.

WANKLIN. [Suavely.] Seriously, Chairman, are you going to let the ship sink under you, for the sake of—a principle?

ANTHONY. She won't sink.

SCANTLEBURY. [With alarm.] Not while I'm on the Board I hope.

ANTHONY. [With a twinkle.] Better rat, Scantlebury.

SCANTLEBURY. What a man!

ANTHONY. I've always fought them; I've never been beaten yet.

WANKLIN. We're with you in theory, Chairman. But we're not all made of cast-iron.

ANTHONY. We've only to hold on.

WILDER. [Rising and going to the fire.] And go to the devil as fast as we can!

ANTHONY. Better go to the devil than give in!

WILDER. [Fretfully.] That may suit you, sir, but it does n't suit me, or any one else I should think.

[ANTHONY looks him in the face-a silence.]

EDGAR. I don't see how we can get over it that to go on like this means starvation to the men's wives and families.

[WILDER turns abruptly to the fire, and SCANTLEBURY puts out a hand to push the idea away.]

WANKLIN. I'm afraid again that sounds a little sentimental.

EDGAR. Men of business are excused from decency, you think?

WILDER. Nobody's more sorry for the men than I am, but if they [lashing himself] choose to be such a pig-headed lot, it's nothing to do with us; we've quite enough on our hands to think of ourselves and the shareholders.

EDGAR. [Irritably.] It won't kill the shareholders to miss a dividend or two; I don't see that that's reason enough for knuckling under.

SCANTLEBURY. [With grave discomfort.] You talk very lightly of your dividends, young man; I don't know where we are.

WILDER. There's only one sound way of looking at it. We can't go on ruining ourselves with this strike.

ANTHONY. No caving in!

SCANTLEBURY. [With a gesture of despair.] Look at him!

[ANTHONY'S leaning back in his chair. They do look at him.]

WILDER. [Returning to his seat.] Well, all I can say is, if that's the Chairman's view, I don't know what we've come down here for.

ANTHONY. To tell the men that we've got nothing for them—— [Grimly.] They won't believe it till they hear it spoken in plain English.

WILDER. H'm! Shouldn't be a bit surprised if that brute Roberts had n't got us down here with the very same idea. I hate a man with a grievance.

EDGAR. [Resentfully.] We didn't pay him enough for his discovery. I always said that at the time.

WILDER. We paid him five hundred and a bonus of two hundred three years later. If that's not enough! What does he want, for goodness' sake?

TENCH. [Complainingly.] Company made a hundred thousand out of his brains, and paid him seven hundred—that's the way he goes on, sir.

WILDER. The man's a rank agitator! Look here, I hate the Unions. But now we've got Harness here let's get him to settle the whole thing.

ANTHONY. No! [Again they look at him.]

UNDERWOOD. Roberts won't let the men assent to that.

SCANTLEBURY. Fanatic! Fanatic!

WILDER. [Looking at ANTHONY.] And not the only one! [FROST enters from the hall.]

FROST. [To ANTHONY.] Mr. Harness from the Union, waiting, sir. The men
    are here too, sir.

[ANTHONY nods. UNDERWOOD goes to the door, returning with HAR-
NESS, a pale, clean-shaven man with hollow cheeks, quick eyes, and lantern
jaw—FROST has retired.]

UNDERWOOD. [Pointing to TENCH'S chair.] Sit there next the Chairman,
Harness, won't you?

[At HARNESS'S appearance, the Board have drawn together, as it were, and
turned a little to him, like cattle at a dog.]

HARNESS. [With a sharp look round, and a bow.] Thanks! [He sits—- his
    accent is slightly nasal.] Well, gentlemen, we're going to do busi-
    ness at last, I hope.

WILDER. Depends on what you call business, Harness. Why don't you make
    the men come in?

HARNESS. [Sardonically.] The men are far more in the right than you are. The
    question with us is whether we shan't begin to support them again.

[He ignores them all, except ANTHONY, to whom he turns in speaking.]

ANTHONY. Support them if you like; we'll put in free labour and have done
    with it.

HARNESS. That won't do, Mr. Anthony. You can't get free labour, and you
    know it.

ANTHONY. We shall see that.

HARNESS. I'm quite frank with you. We were forced to withhold our support
    from your men because some of their demands are in excess of cur-
    rent rates. I expect to make them withdraw those demands to-day:
    if they do, take it straight from me, gentlemen, we shall back them
    again at once. Now, I want to see something fixed upon before I
    go back to-night. Can't we have done with this old-fashioned tug-
    of-war business? What good's it doing you? Why don't you recog-

nise once for all that these people are men like yourselves, and want what's good for them just as you want what's good for you [Bitterly.] Your motor-cars, and champagne, and eight-course dinners.

ANTHONY. If the men will come in, we'll do something for them.

HARNESS. [Ironically.] Is that your opinion too, sir—and yours— and yours? [The Directors do not answer.] Well, all I can say is: It's a kind of high and mighty aristocratic tone I thought we'd grown out of—seems I was mistaken.

ANTHONY. It's the tone the men use. Remains to be seen which can hold out longest—they without us, or we without them.

HARNESS. As business men, I wonder you're not ashamed of this waste of force, gentlemen. You know what it'll all end in.

ANTHONY. What?

HARNESS. Compromise—it always does.

SCANTLEBURY. Can't you persuade the men that their interests are the same as ours?

HARNESS. [Turning, ironically.] I could persuade them of that, sir, if they were.

WILDER. Come, Harness, you're a clever man, you don't believe all the Socialistic claptrap that's talked nowadays. There 's no real difference between their interests and ours.

HARNESS. There's just one very simple question I'd like to put to you. Will you pay your men one penny more than they force you to pay them?

[WILDER is silent.]

WANKLIN. [Chiming in.] I humbly thought that not to pay more than was necessary was the A B C of commerce.

HARNESS. [With irony.] Yes, that seems to be the A B C of commerce, sir; and the A B C of commerce is between your interests and the men's.

SCANTLEBURY. [Whispering.] We ought to arrange something.

HARNESS. [Drily.] Am I to understand then, gentlemen, that your Board is
     going to make no concessions?

[WANKLIN and WILDER bend forward as if to speak, but stop.]

ANTHONY. [Nodding.] None.

[WANKLIN and WILDER again bend forward, and SCANTLEBURY gives an
     unexpected grunt.]

HARNESS. You were about to say something, I believe?

[But SCANTLEBURY says nothing.]

EDGAR. [Looking up suddenly.] We're sorry for the state of the men.

HARNESS. [Icily.] The men have no use for your pity, sir. What they want is
     justice.

ANTHONY. Then let them be just.

HARNESS. For that word "just" read "humble," Mr. Anthony. Why should
     they be humble? Barring the accident of money, are n't they as
     good men as you?

ANTHONY. Cant!

HARNESS. Well, I've been five years in America. It colours a man's notions.

SCANTLEBURY. [Suddenly, as though avenging his uncompleted grunt.] Let's
     have the men in and hear what they've got to say!

[ANTHONY nods, and UNDERWOOD goes out by the single door.]

HARNESS. [Drily.] As I'm to have an interview with them this afternoon, gen-
     tlemen, I 'll ask you to postpone your final decision till that's over.

[Again ANTHONY nods, and taking up his glass drinks.]

[UNDERWOOD comes in again, followed by ROBERTS, GREEN, BULGIN, THOMAS, ROUS. They file in, hat in hand, and stand silent in a row. ROBERTS is lean, of middle height, with a slight stoop. He has a little rat-gnawn, brown-grey beard, moustaches, high cheek-bones, hollow cheeks, small fiery eyes. He wears an old and grease-stained blue serge suit, and carries an old bowler hat. He stands nearest the Chairman. GREEN, next to him, has a clean, worn face, with a small grey goatee beard and drooping moustaches, iron spectacles, and mild, straightforward eyes. He wears an overcoat, green with age, and a linen collar. Next to him is BULGIN, a tall, strong man, with a dark moustache, and fighting jaw, wearing a red muffler, who keeps changing his cap from one hand to the other. Next to him is THOMAS, an old man with a grey moustache, full beard, and weatherbeaten, bony face, whose overcoat discloses a lean, plucked-looking neck. On his right, ROUS, the youngest of the five, looks like a soldier; he has a glitter in his eyes.]

UNDERWOOD. [Pointing.] There are some chairs there against the wall, Roberts; won't you draw them up and sit down?

ROBERTS. Thank you, Mr. Underwood—we'll stand in the presence of the Board. [He speaks in a biting and staccato voice, rolling his r's, pronouncing his a's like an Italian a, and his consonants short and crisp.] How are you, Mr. Harness? Did n't expect t' have the pleasure of seeing you till this afternoon.

HARNESS. [Steadily.] We shall meet again then, Roberts.

ROBERTS. Glad to hear that; we shall have some news for you to take to your people.

ANTHONY. What do the men want?

ROBERTS. [Acidly.] Beg pardon, I don't quite catch the Chairman's remark.

TENCH. [From behind the Chairman's chair.] The Chairman wishes to know what the men have to say.

ROBERTS. It's what the Board has to say we've come to hear. It's for the Board to speak first.

ANTHONY. The Board has nothing to say.

ROBERTS. [Looking along the line of men.] In that case we're wasting the
    Directors' time. We'll be taking our feet off this pretty carpet.

[He turns, the men move slowly, as though hypnotically influenced.]

WANKLIN: [Suavely.] Come, Roberts, you did n't give us this long cold journey
    for the pleasure of saying that.

THOMAS. [A pure Welshman.] No, sir, an' what I say iss——

ROBERTS.[Bitingly.] Go on, Henry Thomas, go on. You 're better able to speak
    to the—Directors than me. [THOMAS is silent.]

TENCH. The Chairman means, Roberts, that it was the men who asked for the
    conference, the Board wish to hear what they have to say.

ROBERTS. Gad! If I was to begin to tell ye all they have to say, I wouldn't be
    finished to-day. And there'd be some that'd wish they'd never left
    their London palaces.

HARNESS. What's your proposition, man? Be reasonable.

ROBERTS. You want reason Mr. Harness? Take a look round this afternoon
    before the meeting. [He looks at the men; no sound escapes them.]
    You'll see some very pretty scenery.

HARNESS. All right my friend; you won't put me off.

ROBERTS. [To the men.] We shan't put Mr. Harness off. Have some cham-
    pagne with your lunch, Mr. Harness; you'll want it, sir.

HARNESS. Come, get to business, man!

THOMAS. What we're asking, look you, is just simple justice.

ROBERTS. [Venomously.] Justice from London? What are you talking about,
    Henry Thomas? Have you gone silly? [THOMAS is silent.] We
    know very well what we are—discontented dogs—never satisfied.
    What did the Chairman tell me up in London? That I did n't know
    what I was talking about. I was a foolish, uneducated man, that
    knew nothing of the wants of the men I spoke for,

EDGAR. Do please keep to the point.

ANTHONY. [Holding up his hand.] There can only be one master, Roberts.

ROBERTS. Then, be Gad, it'll be us.

[There is a silence; ANTHONY and ROBERTS stare at one another.]

UNDERWOOD. If you've nothing to say to the Directors, Roberts, perhaps you 'll let Green or Thomas speak for the men.

[GREEN and THOMAS look anxiously at ROBERTS, at each other, and the other men.]

GREEN. [An Englishman.] If I'd been listened to, gentlemen——

THOMAS. What I'fe got to say iss what we'fe all got to say——

ROBERTS. Speak for yourself, Henry Thomas.

SCANTLEBURY. [With a gesture of deep spiritual discomfort.] Let the poor men call their souls their own!

ROBERTS. Aye, they shall keep their souls, for it's not much body that you've left them, Mr. [with biting emphasis, as though the word were an offence] Scantlebury! [To the men.] Well, will you speak, or shall I speak for you?

ROUS. [Suddenly.] Speak out, Roberts, or leave it to others.

ROBERTS. [Ironically.] Thank you, George Rous. [Addressing himself to ANTHONY.] The Chairman and Board of Directors have honoured us by leaving London and coming all this way to hear what we've got to say; it would not be polite to keep them any longer waiting.

WILDER. Well, thank God for that!

ROBERTS. Ye will not dare to thank Him when I have done, Mr. Wilder, for all your piety. May be your God up in London has no time to listen to the working man. I'm told He is a wealthy God; but if he listens to what I tell Him, He will know more than ever He learned in Kensington.

HARNESS. Come, Roberts, you have your own God. Respect the God of other men.

ROBERTS. That's right, sir. We have another God down here; I doubt He is rather different to Mr. Wilder's. Ask Henry Thomas; he will tell you whether his God and Mr. Wilder's are the same.

[THOMAS lifts his hand, and cranes his head as though to prophesy.]

WANKLIN. For goodness' sake, let 's keep to the point, Roberts.

ROBERTS. I rather think it is the point, Mr. Wanklin. If you can get the God of Capital to walk through the streets of Labour, and pay attention to what he sees, you're a brighter man than I take you for, for all that you're a Radical.

ANTHONY. Attend to me, Roberts! [Roberts is silent.] You are here to speak for the men, as I am here to speak for the Board.

[He looks slowly round.]

[WILDER, WANKLIN, and SCANTLEBURY make movements of uneasiness, and EDGAR gazes at the floor. A faint smile comes on HARNESS'S face.]

Now then, what is it?

ROBERTS. Right, Sir!

[Throughout all that follows, he and ANTHONY look fixedly upon each other. Men and Directors show in their various ways suppressed uneasiness, as though listening to words that they themselves would not have spoken.]

The men can't afford to travel up to London; and they don't trust you to believe what they say in black and white. They know what the post is [he darts a look at UNDERWOOD and TENCH], and what Directors' meetings are: "Refer it to the manager—let the manager advise us on the men's condition. Can we squeeze them a little more?"

UNDERWOOD. [In a low voice.] Don't hit below the belt, Roberts!

ROBERTS. Is it below the belt, Mr. Underwood? The men know. When I came up to London, I told you the position straight. An' what came of it? I was told I did n't know what I was talkin' about. I can't afford to travel up to London to be told that again.

ANTHONY. What have you to say for the men?

ROBERTS. I have this to say—and first as to their condition. Ye shall 'ave no need to go and ask your manager. Ye can't squeeze them any more. Every man of us is well-nigh starving. [A surprised murmur rises from the men. ROBERTS looks round.] Ye wonder why I tell ye that? Every man of us is going short. We can't be no worse off than we've been these weeks past. Ye need n't think that by waiting ye'll drive us to come in. We'll die first, the whole lot of us. The men have sent for ye to know, once and for all, whether ye are going to grant them their demands. I see the sheet of paper in the Secretary's hand. [TENCH moves nervously.] That's it, I think, Mr. Tench. It's not very large.

TENCH. [Nodding.] Yes.

ROBERTS. There's not one sentence of writing on that paper that we can do without.

[A movement amongst the men. ROBERTS turns on them sharply.]

Isn't that so?

[The men assent reluctantly. ANTHONY takes from TENCH the paper and peruses it.]

Not one single sentence. All those demands are fair. We have not. asked anything that we are not entitled to ask. What I said up in London, I say again now: there is not anything on that piece of paper that a just man should not ask, and a just man give.

[A pause.]

ANTHONY. There is not one single demand on this paper that we will grant.

[In the stir that follows on these words, ROBERTS watches the Directors and ANTHONY the men. WILDER gets up abruptly and goes over to the fire.]

ROBERTS. D' ye mean that?

ANTHONY. I do.

[WILDER at the fire makes an emphatic movement of disgust.]

ROBERTS. [Noting it, with dry intensity.] Ye best know whether the condition
        of the Company is any better than the condition of the men.
        [Scanning the Directors' faces.] Ye best know whether ye can
        afford your tyranny—but this I tell ye: If ye think the men will give
        way the least part of an inch, ye're making the worst mistake ye ever
        made. [He fixes his eyes on SCANTLEBURY.] Ye think because
        the Union is not supporting us—more shame to it!—that we'll be
        coming on our knees to you one fine morning. Ye think because
        the men have got their wives an' families to think of—that it's just
        a question of a week or two——

ANTHONY. It would be better if you did not speculate so much on what we
        think.

ROBERTS. Aye! It's not much profit to us! I will say this for you, Mr.
        Anthony—ye know your own mind! [Staying at ANTHONY.] I
        can reckon on ye!

ANTHONY. [Ironically.] I am obliged to you!

ROBERTS. And I know mine. I tell ye this: The men will send their wives and
        families where the country will have to keep them; an' they will
        starve sooner than give way. I advise ye, Mr. Anthony, to prepare
        yourself for the worst that can happen to your Company. We are
        not so ignorant as you might suppose. We know the way the cat is
        jumping. Your position is not all that it might be—not exactly!

ANTHONY. Be good enough to allow us to judge of our position for ourselves.
        Go back, and reconsider your own.

ROBERTS. [Stepping forward.] Mr. Anthony, you are not a young man now;
        from the time I remember anything ye have been an enemy to

every man that has come into your works. I don't say that ye're a mean man, or a cruel man, but ye've grudged them the say of any word in their own fate. Ye've fought them down four times. I've heard ye say ye love a fight—mark my words—ye're fighting the last fight yell ever fight

[TENCH touches ROBERTS'S sleeve.]

UNDERWOOD. Roberts! Roberts!

ROBERTS. Roberts! Roberts! I must n't speak my mind to the Chairman, but the Chairman may speak his mind to me!

WILDER. What are things coming to?

ANTHONY, [With a grim smile at WILDER.] Go on, Roberts; say what you like!

ROBERTS. [After a pause.] I have no more to say.

ANTHONY. The meeting stands adjourned to five o'clock.

WANKLIN. [In a low voice to UNDERWOOD.] We shall never settle anything like this.

ROBERTS. [Bitingly.] We thank the Chairman and Board of Directors for their gracious hearing.

[He moves towards the door; the men cluster together stupefied; then ROUS, throwing up his head, passes ROBERTS and goes out. The others follow.]

ROBERTS. [With his hand on the door—maliciously.] Good day, gentlemen! [He goes out.]

HARNESS. [Ironically.] I congratulate you on the conciliatory spirit that's been displayed. With your permission, gentlemen, I'll be with you again at half-past five. Good morning!

[He bows slightly, rests his eyes on ANTHONY, who returns his stare unmoved, and, followed by UNDERWOOD, goes out. There is a moment of uneasy silence. UNDERWOOD reappears in the doorway.]

WILDER. [With emphatic disgust.] Well!

[The double-doors are opened.]

ENID. [Standing in the doorway.] Lunch is ready.

[EDGAR, getting up abruptly, walks out past his sister.]

WILDER. Coming to lunch, Scantlebury?

SCANTLEBURY. [Rising heavily.] I suppose so, I suppose so. It's the only thing
          we can do.

[They go out through the double-doors.]

WANKLIN. [In a low voice.] Do you really mean to fight to a finish, Chairman?

[ANTHONY nods.]

WANKLIN. Take care! The essence of things is to know when to stop.

[ANTHONY does not answer.]

WANKLIN. [Very gravely.] This way disaster lies. The ancient Trojans were
          fools to your father, Mrs. Underwood. [He goes out through the
          double-doors.]

ENID. I want to speak to father, Frank.

[UNDERWOOD follows WANKLIN Out. TENCH, passing round the table,
is restoring order to the scattered pens and papers.]

ENID. Are n't you coming, Dad?

[ANTHONY Shakes his head. ENID looks meaningly at TENCH.]

ENID. Won't you go and have some lunch, Mr. Tench?

TENCH. [With papers in his hand.] Thank you, ma'am, thank you! [He goes
          slowly, looking back.]

ENID. [Shutting the doors.] I do hope it's settled, Father!

ANTHONY. No!

ENID. [Very disappointed.] Oh! Have n't you done anything!

[ANTHONY shakes his head.]

ENID. Frank says they all want to come to a compromise, really, except that man Roberts.

ANTHONY. I don't.

ENID. It's such a horrid position for us. If you were the wife of the manager, and lived down here, and saw it all. You can't realise, Dad!

ANTHONY. Indeed?

ENID. We see all the distress. You remember my maid Annie, who married Roberts? [ANTHONY nods.] It's so wretched, her heart's weak; since the strike began, she has n't even been getting proper food. I know it for a fact, Father.

ANTHONY. Give her what she wants, poor woman!

ENID. Roberts won't let her take anything from us.

ANTHONY. [Staring before him.] I can't be answerable for the men's obstinacy.

ENID. They're all suffering. Father! Do stop it, for my sake!

ANTHONY. [With a keen look at her.] You don't understand, my dear.

ENID. If I were on the Board, I'd do something.

ANTHONY. What would you do?

ENID. It's because you can't bear to give way. It's so——

ANTHONY. Well?

ENID. So unnecessary.

ANTHONY. What do you know about necessity? Read your novels, play your music, talk your talk, but don't try and tell me what's at the bottom of a struggle like this.

ENID. I live down here, and see it.

ANTHONY. What d' you imagine stands between you and your class and these men that you're so sorry for?

ENID. [Coldly.] I don't know what you mean, Father.

ANTHONY. In a few years you and your children would be down in the condition they're in, but for those who have the eyes to see things as they are and the backbone to stand up for themselves.

ENID. You don't know the state the men are in.

ANTHONY. I know it well enough.

ENID. You don't, Father; if you did, you would n't

ANTHONY. It's you who don't know the simple facts of the position. What sort of mercy do you suppose you'd get if no one stood between you and the continual demands of labour? This sort of mercy— [He puts his hand up to his throat and squeezes it.] First would go your sentiments, my dear; then your culture, and your comforts would be going all the time!

ENID. I don't believe in barriers between classes.

ANTHONY. You—don't—believe—in—barriers—between the classes?

ENID. [Coldly.] And I don't know what that has to do with this question.

ANTHONY. It will take a generation or two for you to understand.

ENID. It's only you and Roberts, Father, and you know it!

[ANTHONY thrusts out his lower lip.]

It'll ruin the Company.

ANTHONY. Allow me to judge of that.

ENID. [Resentfully.] I won't stand by and let poor Annie Roberts suffer like this! And think of the children, Father! I warn you.

ANTHONY. [With a grim smile.] What do you propose to do?

ENID. That's my affair.

[ANTHONY only looks at her.]

ENID. [In a changed voice, stroking his sleeve.] Father, you know you oughtn't to have this strain on you—you know what Dr. Fisher said!

ANTHONY. No old man can afford to listen to old women.

ENID. But you have done enough, even if it really is such a matter of principle with you.

ANTHONY. You think so?

ENID. Don't Dad! [Her face works.] You—you might think of us!

ANTHONY. I am.

ENID. It'll break you down.

ANTHONY. [Slowly.] My dear, I am not going to funk; on that you may rely.

[Re-enter TENCH with papers; he glances at them, then plucking up courage.]

TENCH. Beg pardon, Madam, I think I'd rather see these papers were disposed of before I get my lunch.

[ENID, after an impatient glance at him, looks at her father, turns suddenly, and goes into the drawing-room.]

TENCH. [Holding the papers and a pen to ANTHONY, very nervously.] Would you sign these for me, please sir?

[ANTHONY takes the pen and signs.]

TENCH. [Standing with a sheet of blotting-paper behind EDGAR'S chair, begins speaking nervously.] I owe my position to you, sir.

ANTHONY. Well?

TENCH. I'm obliged to see everything that's going on, sir; I—I depend upon the Company entirely. If anything were to happen to it, it'd be disastrous for me. [ANTHONY nods.] And, of course, my wife's just had another; and so it makes me doubly anxious just now. And the rates are really terrible down our way.

ANTHONY. [With grim amusement.] Not more terrible than they are up mine.

TENCH. No, Sir? [Very nervously.] I know the Company means a great deal to you, sir.

ANTHONY. It does; I founded it.

TENCH. Yes, Sir. If the strike goes on it'll be very serious. I think the Directors are beginning to realise that, sir.

ANTHONY. [Ironically.] Indeed?

TENCH. I know you hold very strong views, sir, and it's always your habit to look things in the face; but I don't think the Directors— like it, sir, now they—they see it.

ANTHONY. [Grimly.] Nor you, it seems.

TENCH. [With the ghost of a smile.] No, sir; of course I've got my children, and my wife's delicate; in my position I have to think of these things.

[ANTHONY nods.]

It was n't that I was going to say, sir, if you'll excuse me—— [hesitates]

ANTHONY. Out with it, then!

TENCH. I know—from my own father, sir, that when you get on in life you do feel things dreadfully——

ANTHONY. [Almost paternally.] Come, out with it, Trench!

TENCH. I don't like to say it, sir.

ANTHONY. [Stonily.] You Must.

TENCH. [After a pause, desperately bolting it out.] I think the Directors are going to throw you over, sir.

ANTHONY. [Sits in silence.] Ring the bell!

[TENCH nervously rings the bell and stands by the fire.]

TENCH. Excuse me for saying such a thing. I was only thinking of you, sir.

[FROST enters from the hall, he comes to the foot of the table, and looks at ANTHONY; TENCH coveys his nervousness by arranging papers.]

ANTHONY. Bring me a whiskey and soda.

FROST. Anything to eat, sir?

[ANTHONY shakes his head. FROST goes to the sideboard, and prepares the drink.]

TENCH. [In a low voice, almost supplicating.] If you could see your way, sir, it would be a great relief to my mind, it would indeed. [He looks up at ANTHONY, who has not moved.] It does make me so very anxious. I haven't slept properly for weeks, sir, and that's a fact.

[ANTHONY looks in his face, then slowly shakes his head.]

[Disheartened.] No, Sir? [He goes on arranging papers.]

[FROST places the whiskey and salver and puts it down by ANTHONY'S right hand. He stands away, looking gravely at ANTHONY.]

FROST. Nothing I can get you, sir?

[ANTHONY shakes his head.]

You're aware, sir, of what the doctor said, sir?

ANTHONY. I am.

[A pause. FROST suddenly moves closer to him, and speaks in a low voice.]

FROST. This strike, sir; puttin' all this strain on you. Excuse me, sir, is it—is it
       worth it, sir?

[ANTHONY mutters some words that are inaudible.]

Very good, sir!

[He turns and goes out into the hall. TENCH makes two attempts to speak; but
meeting his Chairman's gaze he drops his eyes, and, turning dismally, he too goes
out. ANTHONY is left alone. He grips the glass, tilts it, and drinks deeply; then
sets it down with a deep and rumbling sigh, and leans back in his chair.]

The curtain falls.

ACT II

It is half-past three. In the kitchen of Roberts's cottage a meagre little fire is burning. The room is clean and tidy, very barely furnished, with a brick floor and
white-washed walls, much stained with smoke. There is a kettle on the fire. A
door opposite the fireplace opens inward from a snowy street. On the wooden
table are a cup and saucer, a teapot, knife, and plate of bread and cheese. Close
to the fireplace in an old arm-chair, wrapped in a rug, sits MRS. ROBERTS, a
thin and dark-haired woman about thirty-five, with patient eyes. Her hair is not
done up, but tied back with a piece of ribbon. By the fire, too, is MRS. YEO; a
red-haired, broad-faced person. Sitting near the table is MRS. ROUS, an old
lady, ashen-white, with silver hair; by the door, standing, as if about to go, is
MRS. BULGIN, a little pale, pinched-up woman. In a chair, with her elbows
resting on the table, avid her face resting in her hands, sits MADGE THOMAS,
a good-looking girl, of twenty-two, with high cheekbones, deep-set eyes, and dark
untidy hair. She is listening to the talk, but she neither speaks nor moves.

MRS. YEO. So he give me a sixpence, and that's the first bit o' money I seen this
     week. There an't much 'eat to this fire. Come and warm yerself
     Mrs. Rous, you're lookin' as white as the snow, you are.

MRS. ROUS. [Shivering—placidly.] Ah! but the winter my old man was took
     was the proper winter. Seventy-nine that was, when none of you

was hardly born—not Madge Thomas, nor Sue Bulgin. [Looking at them in turn.] Annie Roberts, 'ow old were you, dear?

MRS ROBERTS. Seven, Mrs. Rous.

MRS. ROUS. Seven—well, there! A tiny little thing!

MRS. YEO. [Aggressively.] Well, I was ten myself, I remembers it.

MRS. ROUS. [Placidly.] The Company hadn't been started three years. Father was workin' on the acid, that's 'ow he got 'is pisoned-leg. I kep' sayin' to 'im, "Father, you've got a pisoned leg." "Well," 'e said, "Mother, pison or no pison, I can't afford to go a-layin' up." An' two days after, he was on 'is back, and never got up again. It was Providence! There was n't none o' these Compensation Acts then.

MRS. YEO. Ye had n't no strike that winter! [With grim humour.] This winter's 'ard enough for me. Mrs. Roberts, you don't want no 'arder winter, do you? Wouldn't seem natural to 'ave a dinner, would it, Mrs. Bulgin?

MRS. BULGIN. We've had bread and tea last four days.

MRS. YEO. You got that Friday's laundry job?

MRS. BULGIN. [Dispiritedly.] They said they'd give it me, but when I went last Friday, they were full up. I got to go again next week.

MRS. YEO. Ah! There's too many after that. I send Yeo out on the ice to put on the gentry's skates an' pick up what 'e can. Stops 'im from broodin' about the 'ouse.

MRS. BULGIN. [In a desolate, matter-of-fact voice.] Leavin' out the men—it's bad enough with the children. I keep 'em in bed, they don't get so hungry when they're not running about; but they're that restless in bed they worry your life out.

MRS. YEO. You're lucky they're all so small. It 's the goin' to school that makes 'em 'ungry. Don't Bulgin give you anythin'?

MRS. BULGIN. [Shakes her head, then, as though by afterthought.] Would if he could, I s'pose.

MRS. YEO. [Sardonically.] What! 'Ave n't 'e got no shares in the Company?

MRS. ROUS. [Rising with tremulous cheerfulness.] Well, good-bye, Annie Roberts, I'm going along home.

MRS. ROBERTS. Stay an' have a cup of tea, Mrs. Rous?

MRS. ROUS. [With the faintest smile.] Roberts 'll want 'is tea when he comes in. I'll just go an' get to bed; it's warmer there than anywhere.

[She moves very shakily towards the door.]

MRS. YEO. [Rising and giving her an arm.] Come on, Mother, take my arm; we're all going' the same way.

MRS. ROUS. [Taking the arm.]Thank you, my dearies!

[THEY go out, followed by MRS. BULGIN.]

MADGE. [Moving for the first time.] There, Annie, you see that! I told George Rous, "Don't think to have my company till you've made an end of all this trouble. You ought to be ashamed," I said, "with your own mother looking like a ghost, and not a stick to put on the fire. So long as you're able to fill your pipes, you'll let us starve." "I 'll take my oath, Madge," he said, "I 've not had smoke nor drink these three weeks!" "Well, then, why do you go on with it?" "I can't go back on Roberts!" . . . That's it! Roberts, always Roberts! They'd all drop it but for him. When he talks it's the devil that comes into them.

[A silence. MRS. ROBERTS makes a movement of pain.]

Ah! You don't want him beaten! He's your man. With everybody like their own shadows! [She makes a gesture towards MRS. ROBERTS.] If ROUS wants me he must give up Roberts. If he gave him up—they all would. They're only waiting for a lead. Father's against him— they're all against him in their hearts.

MRS. ROBERTS. You won't beat Roberts!

[They look silently at each other.]

MADGE. Won't I? The cowards—when their own mothers and their own children don't know where to turn.

MRS. ROBERTS. Madge!

MADGE. [Looking searchingly at MRS. ROBERTS.] I wonder he can look you in the face. [She squats before the fire, with her hands out to the flame.] Harness is here again. They'll have to make up their minds to-day.

MRS. ROBERTS. [In a soft, slow voice, with a slight West-country burr.] Roberts will never give up the furnace-men and engineers. 'T wouldn't be right.

MADGE. You can't deceive me. It's just his pride.

[A tapping at the door is heard, the women turn as ENID enters. She wears a round fur cap, and a jacket of squirrel's fur. She closes the door behind her.]

ENID. Can I come in, Annie?

MRS. ROBERTS. [Flinching.] Miss Enid! Give Mrs. Underwood a chair, Madge!

[MADGE gives ENID the chair she has been sitting on.]

ENID. Thank you!

ENID. Are you any better?

MRS. ROBERTS. Yes, M'm; thank you, M'm.

ENID. [Looking at the sullen MADGE as though requesting her departure.] Why did you send back the jelly? I call that really wicked of you!

MRS. ROBERTS. Thank you, M'm, I'd no need for it.

ENID. Of course! It was Roberts's doing, wasn't it? How can he let all this suffering go on amongst you?

MADGE. [Suddenly.] What suffering?

ENID. [Surprised.] I beg your pardon!

MADGE. Who said there was suffering?

MRS. ROBERTS. Madge!

MADGE. [Throwing her shawl over her head.] Please to let us keep ourselves to ourselves. We don't want you coming here and spying on us.

ENID. [Confronting her, but without rising.] I did n't speak to you.

MADGE. [In a low, fierce voice.] Keep your kind feelings to yourself. You think you can come amongst us, but you're mistaken. Go back and tell the Manager that.

ENID. [Stonily.] This is not your house.

MADGE. [Turning to the door.] No, it is not my house; keep clear of my house, Mrs. Underwood.

[She goes out. ENID taps her fingers on the table.]

MRS. ROBERTS. Please to forgive Madge Thomas, M'm; she's a bit upset to-day.

[A pause.]

ENID. [Looking at her.] Oh, I think they're so stupid, all of them.

MRS. ROBERTS. [With a faint smile]. Yes, M'm.

ENID. Is Roberts out?

MRS. ROBERTS. Yes, M'm.

ENID. It is his doing, that they don't come to an agreement. Now is n't it, Annie?

MRS. ROBERTS. [Softly, with her eyes on ENID, and moving the fingers of one hand continually on her breast.] They do say that your father, M'm——

ENID. My father's getting an old man, and you know what old men are.

MRS. ROBERTS. I am sorry, M'm.

ENID. [More softly.] I don't expect you to feel sorry, Annie. I know it's his fault as well as Roberts's.

MRS. ROBERTS. I'm sorry for any one that gets old, M'm; it 's dreadful to get old, and Mr. Anthony was such a fine old man, I always used to think.

ENID. [Impulsively.] He always liked you, don't you remember? Look here, Annie, what can I do? I do so want to know. You don't get what you ought to have. [Going to the fire, she takes the kettle off, and looks for coals.] And you're so naughty sending back the soup and things.

MRS. ROBERTS. [With a faint smile.] Yes, M'm?

ENID. [Resentfully.] Why, you have n't even got coals?

MRS. ROBERTS. If you please, M'm, to put the kettle on again; Roberts won't have long for his tea when he comes in. He's got to meet the men at four.

ENID. [Putting the kettle on.] That means he'll lash them into a fury again. Can't you stop his going, Annie?

[MRS. ROBERTS smiles ironically.]

Have you tried?

[A silence.]

Does he know how ill you are?

MRS. ROBERTS. It's only my weak 'eard, M'm.

ENID. You used to be so well when you were with us.

MRS. ROBERTS. [Stiffening.] Roberts is always good to me.

ENID. But you ought to have everything you want, and you have nothing!

MRS. ROBERTS. [Appealingly.] They tell me I don't look like a dyin' woman?

ENID. Of course you don't; if you could only have proper—- Will you see my doctor if I send him to you? I'm sure he'd do you good.

MRS. ROBERTS. [With faint questioning.] Yes, M'm.

ENID. Madge Thomas ought n't to come here; she only excites you. As if I did n't know what suffering there is amongst the men! I do feel for them dreadfully, but you know they have gone too far.

MRS. ROBERTS. [Continually moving her fingers.] They say there's no other way to get better wages, M'm.

ENID. [Earnestly.] But, Annie, that's why the Union won't help them. My husband's very sympathetic with the men, but he says they are not underpaid.

MRS. ROBERTS. No, M'm?

ENID. They never think how the Company could go on if we paid the wages they want.

MRS. ROBERTS. [With an effort.] But the dividends having been so big, M'm.

ENID. [Takes aback.] You all seem to think the shareholders are rich men, but they're not—most of them are really no better off than working men.

[MRS. ROBERTS smiles.]

They have to keep up appearances.

MRS. ROBERTS. Yes, M'm?

ENID. You don't have to pay rates and taxes, and a hundred other things that they do. If the men did n't spend such a lot in drink and betting they'd be quite well off!

MRS. ROBERTS. They say, workin' so hard, they must have some pleasure.

ENID. But surely not low pleasure like that.

MRS. ROBERTS. [A little resentfully.] Roberts never touches a drop; and he's
        never had a bet in his life.

ENID. Oh! but he's not a com——I mean he's an engineer—— a superior man.

MRS. ROBERTS. Yes, M'm. Roberts says they've no chance of other pleasures.

ENID. [Musing.] Of course, I know it's hard.

MRS. ROBERTS. [With a spice of malice.] And they say gentlefolk's just as bad.

ENID. [With a smile.] I go as far as most people, Annie, but you know, your-
    self, that's nonsense.

MRS. ROBERTS. [With painful effort.] A lot 'o the men never go near the
        Public; but even they don't save but very little, and that goes
        if there's illness.

ENID. But they've got their clubs, have n't they?

MRS. ROBERTS. The clubs only give up to eighteen shillin's a week, M'm, and
        it's not much amongst a family. Roberts says workin' folk
        have always lived from hand to mouth. Sixpence to-day is
        worth more than a shillin' to-morrow, that's what they say.

ENID. But that's the spirit of gambling.

MRS. ROBERTS. [With a sort of excitement.] Roberts says a working man's life
        is all a gamble, from the time 'e 's born to the time 'e dies.

[ENID leans forward, interested. MRS. ROBERTS goes on with a growing
excitement that culminates in the personal feeling of the last words.]

He says, M'm, that when a working man's baby is born, it's a toss-up from breath
to breath whether it ever draws another, and so on all 'is life; an' when he comes
to be old, it's the workhouse or the grave. He says that without a man is very near,
and pinches and stints 'imself and 'is children to save, there can't be neither sur-

plus nor security. That's why he wouldn't have no children [she sinks back], not though I wanted them.

ENID. Yes, yes, I know!

MRS. ROBERTS. No you don't, M'm. You've got your children, and you'll never need to trouble for them.

ENID. [Gently.] You oughtn't to be talking so much, Annie. [Then, in spite of herself.] But Roberts was paid a lot of money, was n't he, for discovering that process?

MRS. ROBERTS. [On the defensive.] All Roberts's savin's have gone. He 's always looked forward to this strike. He says he's no right to a farthing when the others are suffering. 'T is n't so with all o' them! Some don't seem to care no more than that—so long as they get their own.

ENID. I don't see how they can be expected to when they 're suffering like this. [In a changed voice.] But Roberts ought to think of you! It's all terrible——! The kettle's boiling. Shall I make the tea? [She takes the teapot and, seeing tea there, pours water into it.] Won't you have a cup?

MRS. ROBERTS. No, thank you, M'm. [She is listening, as though for footsteps.] I'd—sooner you did n't see Roberts, M'm, he gets so wild.

ENID. Oh! but I must, Annie; I'll be quite calm, I promise.

MRS. ROBERTS. It's life an' death to him, M'm.

ENID. [Very gently.] I'll get him to talk to me outside, we won't excite you.

MRS. ROBERTS. [Faintly.] No, M'm.

[She gives a violent start. ROBERTS has come in, unseen.]

ROBERTS. [Removing his hat—with subtle mockery.] Beg pardon for coming in; you're engaged with a lady, I see.

ENID. Can I speak to you, Mr. Roberts?

ROBERTS. Whom have I the pleasure of addressing, Ma'am?

ENID. But surely you know me! I 'm Mrs. Underwood.

ROBERTS. [With a bow of malice.] The daughter of our Chairman.

ENID. [Earnestly.] I've come on purpose to speak to you; will you come outside a minute?

[She looks at MRS. ROBERTS.]

ROBERTS. [Hanging up his hat.] I have nothing to say, Ma'am.

ENID. But I must speak to you, please.

[She moves towards the door.]

ROBERTS. [With sudden venom.] I have not the time to listen!

MRS. ROBERTS. David!

ENID. Mr. Roberts, please!

ROBERTS. [Taking off his overcoat.] I am sorry to disoblige a lady- Mr. Anthony's daughter.

ENID. [Wavering, then with sudden decision.] Mr. Roberts, I know you've another meeting of the men.

[ROBERTS bows.]

I came to appeal to you. Please, please, try to come to some compromise; give way a little, if it's only for your own sakes!

ROBERTS. [Speaking to himself.] The daughter of Mr. Anthony begs me to give way a little, if it's only for our own sakes!

ENID. For everybody's sake; for your wife's sake.

ROBERTS. For my wife's sake, for everybody's sake—for the sake of Mr. Anthony.

ENID. Why are you so bitter against my father? He has never done anything to you.

ROBERTS. Has he not?

ENID. He can't help his views, any more than you can help yours.

ROBERTS. I really did n't know that I had a right to views!

ENID. He's an old man, and you——

[Seeing his eyes fixed on her, she stops.]

ROBERTS. [Without raising his voice.] If I saw Mr. Anthony going to die, and I could save him by lifting my hand, I would not lift the little finger of it.

ENID. You—you——[She stops again, biting her lips.]

ROBERTS. I would not, and that's flat!

ENID. [Coldly.] You don't mean what you say, and you know it!

ROBERTS. I mean every word of it.

ENID. But why?

ROBERTS. [With a flash.] Mr. Anthony stands for tyranny! That's why!

ENID. Nonsense!

[MRS. ROBERTS makes a movement as if to rise, but sinks back in her chair.]

ENID. [With an impetuous movement.] Annie!

ROBERTS. Please not to touch my wife!

ENID. [Recoiling with a sort of horror.] I believe—you are mad.

ROBERTS. The house of a madman then is not the fit place for a lady.

ENID. I 'm not afraid of you.

ROBERTS. [Bowing.] I would not expect the daughter of Mr. Anthony to be
        afraid. Mr. Anthony is not a coward like the rest of them.

ENID. [Suddenly.] I suppose you think it brave, then, to go on with the strug-
        gle.

ROBERTS. Does Mr. Anthony think it brave to fight against women and chil-
        dren? Mr. Anthony is a rich man, I believe; does he think it brave
        to fight against those who have n't a penny? Does he think it brave
        to set children crying with hunger, an' women shivering with cold?

ENID. [Putting up her hand, as though warding off a blow.] My father is act-
        ing on his principles, and you know it!

ROBERTS. And so am I!

ENID. You hate us; and you can't bear to be beaten!

ROBERTS. Neither can Mr. Anthony, for all that he may say.

ENID. At any rate you might have pity on your wife.

[MRS. ROBERTS who has her hand pressed to her heart, takes it away, and tries
to calm her breathing.]

ROBERTS. Madam, I have no more to say.

[He takes up the loaf. There is a knock at the door, and UNDERWOOD comes
in. He stands looking at them, ENID turns to him, then seems undecided.]

UNDERWOOD. Enid!

ROBERTS. [Ironically.] Ye were not needing to come for your wife, Mr.
        Underwood. We are not rowdies.

UNDERWOOD. I know that, Roberts. I hope Mrs. Roberts is better.

[ROBERTS turns away without answering. Come, Enid!]

ENID. I make one more appeal to you, Mr. Roberts, for the sake of your wife.

ROBERTS. [With polite malice.] If I might advise ye, Ma'am—make it for the sake of your husband and your father.

[ENID, suppressing a retort, goes out. UNDERWOOD opens the door for her and follows. ROBERTS, going to the fire, holds out his hands to the dying glow.]

ROBERTS. How goes it, my girl? Feeling better, are you?

[MRS. ROBERTS smiles faintly. He brings his overcoat and wraps it round her.]

[Looking at his watch.] Ten minutes to four! [As though inspired.] I've seen their faces, there's no fight in them, except for that one old robber.

MRS. ROBERTS. Won't you stop and eat, David? You've 'ad nothing all day!

ROBERTS. [Putting his hand to his throat.] Can't swallow till those old sharks are out o' the town: [He walks up and down.] I shall have a bother with the men—there's no heart in them, the cowards. Blind as bats, they are—can't see a day before their noses.

MRS. ROBERTS. It's the women, David.

ROBERTS. Ah! So they say! They can remember the women when their own bellies speak! The women never stop them from the drink; but from a little suffering to themselves in a sacred cause, the women stop them fast enough.

MRS. ROBERTS. But think o' the children, David.

ROBERTS. Ah! If they will go breeding themselves for slaves, without a thought o' the future o' them they breed——

MRS. ROBERTS. [Gasping.] That's enough, David; don't begin to talk of that—I won't—I can't——

ROBERTS. [Staring at her.] Now, now, my girl!

MRS. ROBERTS. [Breathlessly.] No, no, David—I won't!

ROBERTS. There, there! Come, come! That's right! [Bitterly.] Not one penny
will they put by for a day like this. Not they! Hand to mouth—
Gad!—I know them! They've broke my heart. There was no
holdin' them at the start, but now the pinch 'as come.

MRS. ROBERTS. How can you expect it, David? They're not made of iron.

ROBERTS. Expect it? Wouldn't I expect what I would do meself? Wouldn't I
starve an' rot rather than give in? What one man can do, another
can.

MRS. ROBERTS. And the women?

ROBERTS. This is not women's work.

MRS. ROBERTS. [With a flash of malice.] No, the women may die for all you
care. That's their work.

ROBERTS. [Averting his eyes.] Who talks of dying? No one will die till we
have beaten these——

[He meets her eyes again, and again turns his away. Excitedly.]

This is what I've been waiting for all these months. To get the old robbers down,
and send them home again without a farthin's worth o' change. I 've seen their
faces, I tell you, in the valley of the shadow of defeat.

[He goes to the peg and takes down his hat.]

MRS. ROBERTS. [Following with her eyes-softly.] Take your overcoat, David;
it must be bitter cold.

ROBERTS. [Coming up to her-his eyes are furtive.] No, no! There, there, stay
quiet and warm. I won't be long, my girl.

MRS. ROBERTS. [With soft bitterness.] You'd better take it.

[She lifts the coat. But ROBERTS puts it back, and wraps it round her. He tries
to meet her eyes, but cannot. MRS. ROBERTS stays huddled in the coat, her
eyes, that follow him about, are half malicious, half yearning. He looks at his

watch again, and turns to go. In the doorway he meets JAN THOMAS, a boy of ten in clothes too big for him, carrying a penny whistle.]

ROBERTS. Hallo, boy!

[He goes. JAN stops within a yard of MRS. ROBERTS, and stares at her without a word.]

MRS. ROBERTS. Well, Jan!

JAN. Father 's coming; sister Madge is coming.

[He sits at the table, and fidgets with his whistle; he blows three vague notes; then imitates a cuckoo.]

[There is a tap on the door. Old THOMAS comes in.]

THOMAS. A very coot tay to you, Ma'am. It is petter that you are.

MRS. ROBERTS. Thank you, Mr. Thomas.

THOMAS. [Nervously.] Roberts in?

MRS. ROBERTS. Just gone on to the meeting, Mr. Thomas.

THOMAS. [With relief, becoming talkative.] This is fery unfortunate, look you! I came to tell him that we must make terms with London. It is a fery great pity he is gone to the meeting. He will be kicking against the pricks, I am thinking.

MRS. ROBERTS. [Half rising.] He'll never give in, Mr. Thomas.

THOMAS. You must not be fretting, that is very pat for you. Look you, there iss hartly any mans for supporting him now, but the engineers and George Rous. [Solemnly.] This strike is no longer Going with Chapel, look you! I have listened carefully, an' I have talked with her.

[JAN blows.]

Sst! I don't care what th' others say, I say that Chapel means us to be stopping the trouple, that is what I make of her; and it is my opinion that this is the fery best thing for all of us. If it was n't my opinion, I ton't say but it is my opinion, look you.

MRS. ROBERTS. [Trying to suppress her excitement.] I don't know what'll come to Roberts, if you give in.

THOMAS. It iss no disgrace whateffer! All that a mortal man coult do he hass tone. It iss against Human Nature he hass gone; fery natural any man may do that; but Chapel has spoken and he must not go against her.

[JAN imitates the cuckoo.]

Ton't make that squeaking! [Going to the door.] Here iss my daughter come to sit with you. A fery goot day, Ma'am—no fretting —rememper!

[MADGE comes in and stands at the open door, watching the street.]

MADGE. You'll be late, Father; they're beginning. [She catches him by the sleeve.] For the love of God, stand up to him, Father—this time!

THOMAS. [Detaching his sleeve with dignity.] Leave me to do what's proper, girl!

[He goes out. MADGE, in the centre of. the open doorway, slowly moves in, as though before the approach of some one.]

ROUS. [Appearing in the doorway.] Madge!

[MADGE stands with her back to MRS. ROBERTS, staring at him with her head up and her hands behind her.]

ROUS. [Who has a fierce distracted look.] Madge! I'm going to the meeting.

[MADGE, without moving, smiles contemptuously.]

D' ye hear me?

[They speak in quick low voices.]

MADGE. I hear! Go, and kill your own mother, if you must.

[ROUS seizes her by both her arms. She stands rigid, with her head bent back. He releases her, and he too stands motionless.]

ROUS. I swore to stand by Roberts. I swore that! Ye want me to go back on what I've sworn.

MADGE. [With slow soft mockery.] You are a pretty lover!

ROUS. Madge!

MADGE. [Smiling.] I've heard that lovers do what their girls ask them—

[JAN sounds the cuckoo's notes]

—but that's not true, it seems!

ROUS. You'd make a blackleg of me!

MADGE. [With her eyes half-closed.] Do it for me!

ROUS. [Dashing his hand across his brow.] Damn! I can't!

MADGE. [Swiftly.] Do it for me!

ROUS. [Through his teeth.] Don't play the wanton with me!

MADGE. [With a movement of her hand towards JAN—quick and low.] I would be that for the children's sake!

ROUS. [In a fierce whisper.] Madge! Oh, Madge!

MADGE. [With soft mockery.] But you can't break your word for me!

ROUS. [With a choke.] Then, Begod, I can!

[He turns and rushes off.]

[MADGE Stands, with a faint smile on her face, looking after him. She turns to MRS. ROBERTS.]

MADGE. I have done for Roberts!

MRS. ROBERTS. [Scornfully.] Done for my man, with that——! [She sinks
        back.]

MADGE. [Running to her, and feeling her hands.] You're as cold as a stone! You
        want a drop of brandy. Jan, run to the "Lion"; say, I sent you for Mrs.
        Roberts.

MRS. ROBERTS. [With a feeble movement.] I'll just sit quiet, Madge. Give
        Jan—his—tea.

MADGE. [Giving JAN a slice of bread.] There, ye little rascal. Hold your pip-
        ing. [Going to the fire, she kneels.] It's going out.

MRS. ROBERTS. [With a faint smile.] 'T is all the same!

[JAN begins to blow his whistle.]

MADGE. Tsht! Tsht!—you

[JAN Stops.]

MRS. ROBERTS. [Smiling.] Let 'im play, Madge.

MADGE. [On her knees at the fire, listening.] Waiting an' waiting. I've no
        patience with it; waiting an' waiting—that's what a woman has to do!
        Can you hear them at it—I can!

[JAN begins again to play his whistle; MADGE gets up; half tenderly she ruffles
his hair; then, sitting, leans her elbows on the table, and her chin on her hands.
Behind her, on MRS. ROBERTS'S face the smile has changed to horrified surprise. She makes a sudden movement, sitting forward, pressing her hands against
her breast. Then slowly she sinks' back; slowly her face loses the look of pain, the
smile returns. She fixes her eyes again on JAN, and moves her lips and finger to
the tune.]

The curtain falls.

SCENE II

It is past four. In a grey, failing light, an open muddy space is crowded with work-men. Beyond, divided from it by a barbed- wire fence, is the raised towing-path of a canal, on which is moored a barge. In the distance are marshes and snow-covered hills. The "Works" high wall runs from the canal across the open space, and ivy the angle of this wall is a rude platform of barrels and boards. On it, HARNESS is standing. ROBERTS, a little apart from the crowd, leans his back against the wall. On the raised towing-path two bargemen lounge and smoke indifferently.

HARNESS. [Holding out his hand.] Well, I've spoken to you straight. If I speak
            till to-morrow I can't say more.

JAGO. [A dark, sallow, Spanish-looking man with a short, thin beard.] Mister,
            want to ask you! Can they get blacklegs?

BULGIN. [Menacing.] Let 'em try.

[There are savage murmurs from the crowd.]

BROWN. [A round-faced man.] Where could they get 'em then?

EVANS. [A small, restless, harassed man, with a fighting face.] There's always
            blacklegs; it's the nature of 'em. There's always men that'll save their
            own skins.

[Another savage murmur. There is a movement, and old THOMAS, joining the crowd, takes his stand in front.]

HARNESS. [Holding up his hand.] They can't get them. But that won't help
            you. Now men, be reasonable. Your demands would have brought
            on us the burden of a dozen strikes at a time when we were not
            prepared for them. The Unions live by justice, not to one, but all.
            Any fair man will tell you—you were ill-advised! I don't say you go
            too far for that which you're entitled to, but you're going too far for
            the moment; you've dug a pit for yourselves. Are you to stay there,
            or are you to climb out? Come!

LEWIS. [A clean-cut Welshman with a dark moustache.] You've hit it, Mister!
            Which is it to be?

[Another movement in the crowd, and ROUS, coming quickly, takes his stand next THOMAS.]

HARNESS. Cut your demands to the right pattern, and we 'll see you through; refuse, and don't expect me to waste my time coming down here again. I 'm not the sort that speaks at random, as you ought to know by this time. If you're the sound men I take you for—no matter who advises you against it—[he fixes his eyes on ROBERTS] you 'll make up your minds to come in, and trust to us to get your terms. Which is it to be? Hands together, and victory—or—the starvation you've got now?

[A prolonged murmur from the crowd.]

JAGO. [Sullenly.] Talk about what you know.

HARNESS. [Lifting his voice above the murmur.] Know? [With cold passion.] All that you've been through, my friend, I 've been through—I was through it when I was no bigger than [pointing to a youth] that shaver there; the Unions then were n't what they are now. What's made them strong? It's hands together that 's made them strong. I 've been through it all, I tell you, the brand's on my soul yet. I know what you 've suffered—there's nothing you can tell me that I don't know; but the whole is greater than the part, and you are only the part. Stand by us, and we will stand by you.

[Quartering them with his eyes, he waits. The murmuring swells; the men form little groups. GREEN, BULGIN, and LEWIS talk together.]

LEWIS. Speaks very sensible, the Union chap.

GREEN. [Quietly.] Ah! if I 'd a been listened to, you'd 'ave 'eard sense these two months past.

[The bargemen are seen laughing.]

LEWIS. [Pointing.] Look at those two blanks over the fence there!

BULGIN. [With gloomy violence.] They'd best stop their cackle, or I 'll break their jaws.

JAGO. [Suddenly.] You say the furnace men's paid enough?

HARNESS. I did not say they were paid enough; I said they were paid as much
        as the furnace men in similar works elsewhere.

EVANS. That's a lie! [Hubbub.] What about Harper's?

HARNESS. [With cold irony.] You may look at home for lies, my man. Harper's
        shifts are longer, the pay works out the same.

HENRY ROUS. [A dark edition of his brother George.] Will ye support us in
        double pay overtime Saturdays?

HARNESS. Yes, we will.

JAGO. What have ye done with our subscriptions?

HARNESS. [Coldly.] I have told you what we will do with them.

EVANS. Ah! will, it's always will! Ye'd have our mates desert us. [Hubbub.]

BULGIN. [Shouting.] Hold your row!

[EVANS looks round angrily.]

HARNESS. [Lifting his voice.] Those who know their right hands from their
        lefts know that the Unions are neither thieves nor traitors. I 've said
        my say. Figure it out, my lads; when you want me you know where
        I shall be.

[He jumps down, the crowd gives way, he passes through them, and goes away. A
BARGEMAN looks after him jerking his pipe with a derisive gesture. The men
close up in groups, and many looks are cast at ROBERTS, who stands alone
against the wall.]

EVANS. He wants ye to turn blacklegs, that's what he wants. He wants ye to go
        back on us. Sooner than turn blackleg—I 'd starve, I would.

BULGIN. Who's talkin' o' blacklegs—mind what you're saying, will you?

BLACKSMITH. [A youth with yellow hair and huge arms.] What about the
         women?

EVANS. They can stand what we can stand, I suppose, can't they?

BLACKSMITH. Ye've no wife?

EVANS. An' don't want one!

THOMAS. [Raising his voice.] Aye! Give us the power to come to terms with
         London, lads.

DAVIES. [A dark, slow-fly, gloomy man.] Go up the platform, if you got any-
         thing to say, go up an' say it.

[There are cries of "Thomas!" He is pushed towards the platform; he ascends it
with difficulty, and bares his head, waiting for silence. A hush.]

RED-HAIRED YOUTH. [suddenly.] Coot old Thomas!

[A hoarse laugh; the bargemen exchange remarks; a hush again, and THOMAS
begins speaking.]

THOMAS. We are all in the tepth together, and it iss Nature that has put us
         there.

HENRY ROUS. It's London put us there!

EVANS. It's the Union.

THOMAS. It iss not Lonton; nor it iss not the Union—it iss Nature. It iss no
         disgrace whateffer to a potty to give in to Nature. For this Nature
         iss a fery pig thing; it is pigger than what a man is. There iss more
         years to my hett than to the hett of any one here. It is fery pat, look
         you, this Going against Nature. It is pat to make other potties suf-
         fer, when there is nothing to pe cot py it.

[A laugh. THOMAS angrily goes on.]

What are ye laughing at? It is pat, I say! We are fighting for a principle; there is
no potty that shall say I am not a peliever in principle. Putt when Nature says
"No further," then it is no coot snapping your fingers in her face.

[A laugh from ROBERTS, and murmurs of approval.]

This Nature must pe humort. It is a man's pisiness to pe pure, honest, just, and merciful. That's what Chapel tells you. [To ROBERTS, angrily.] And, look you, David Roberts, Chapel tells you ye can do that without Going against Nature.

JAGO. What about the Union?

THOMAS. I ton't trust the Union; they haf treated us like tirt. "Do what we tell you," said they. I haf peen captain of the furnace- men twenty years, and I say to the Union—[excitedly]—"Can you tell me then, as well as I can tell you, what iss the right wages for the work that these men do?" For fife and twenty years I haf paid my moneys to the Union and—[with great excitement]—for nothings! What iss that but roguery, for all that this Mr. Harness says!

EVANS. Hear, hear.

HENRY ROUS. Get on with you! Cut on with it then!

THOMAS. Look you, if a man toes not trust me, am I going to trust him?

JAGO. That's right.

THOMAS. Let them alone for rogues, and act for ourselves.

[Murmurs.]

BLACKSMITH. That's what we been doin', haven't we?

THOMAS. [With increased excitement.] I wass brought up to do for meself. I wass brought up to go without a thing, if I hat not moneys to puy it. There iss too much, look you, of doing things with other peo- ple's moneys. We haf fought fair, and if we haf peen beaten, it iss no fault of ours. Gif us the power to make terms with London for ourself; if we ton't succeed, I say it iss petter to take our peating like men, than to tie like togs, or hang on to others' coat-tails to make them do our pisiness for us!

EVANS. [Muttering.] Who wants to?

THOMAS. [Craning.] What's that? If I stand up to a potty, and he knocks me town, I am not to go hollering to other potties to help me; I am to stand up again; and if he knocks me town properly, I am to stay there, is n't that right?

[Laughter.]

JAGO. No Union!

HENRY ROUS. Union!

[Murmurs.]

[Others take up the shout.]

EVANS. Blacklegs!

[BULGIN and the BLACKSMITH shake their fists at EVANS.]

THOMAS. [With a gesture.] I am an olt man, look you.

[A sudden silence, then murmurs again.]

LEWIS. Olt fool, with his "No Union!"

BULGIN. Them furnace chaps! For twopence I 'd smash the faces o' the lot of them.

GREEN. If I'd a been listened to at the first!

THOMAS. [Wiping his brow.] I'm comin' now to what I was going to say——

DAVIES. [Muttering.] An' time too!

THOMAS. [Solemnly.] Chapel says: Ton't carry on this strife! Put an end to it!

JAGO. That's a lie! Chapel says go on!

THOMAS. [Scornfully.] Inteet! I haf ears to my head.

RED-HAIRED YOUTH. Ah! long ones!

[A laugh.]

JAGO. Your ears have misbeled you then.

THOMAS. [Excitedly.] Ye cannot be right if I am, ye cannot haf it both ways.

RED-HAIRED YOUTH. Chapel can though!

["The Shaver" laughs; there are murmurs from the crowd.]

THOMAS. [Fixing his eyes on "The Shaver."] Ah! ye 're Going the roat to tam-
            nation. An' so I say to all of you. If ye co against Chapel I will not
            pe with you, nor will any other Got-fearing man.

[He steps down from the platform. JAGO makes his way towards it. There are
cries of "Don't let 'im go up!"]

JAGO. Don't let him go up? That's free speech, that is. [He goes up.] I ain't got
          much to say to you. Look at the matter plain; ye 've come the road this
          far, and now you want to chuck the journey. We've all been in one boat;
          and now you want to pull in two. We engineers have stood by you; ye
          're ready now, are ye, to give us the go-by? If we'd aknown that before,
          we'd not a-started out with you so early one bright morning! That's all I
          've got to say. Old man Thomas a'n't got his Bible lesson right. If you
          give up to London, or to Harness, now, it's givin' us the chuck—to save
          your skins—you won't get over that, my boys; it's a dirty thing to do.

[He gets down; during his little speech, which is ironically spoken, there is a restless discomfort in the crowd. ROUS, stepping forward, jumps on the platform.
He has an air of fierce distraction. Sullen murmurs of disapproval from the
crowd.]

ROUS. [Speaking with great excitement.] I'm no blanky orator, mates, but wot
            I say is drove from me. What I say is yuman nature. Can a man set an'
            see 'is mother starve? Can 'e now?

ROBERTS. [Starting forward.] Rous!

ROUS. [Staring at him fiercely.] Sim 'Arness said fair! I've changed my mind!

ROBERTS. Ah! Turned your coat you mean!

[The crowd manifests a great surprise.]

LEWIS. [Apostrophising Rous.] Hallo! What's turned him round?

ROUS. [Speaking with intense excitement.] 'E said fair. "Stand by us," 'e said, "and we'll stand by you." That's where we've been makin' our mistake this long time past; and who's to blame fort? [He points at ROBERTS] That man there! "No," 'e said, "fight the robbers," 'e said, "squeeze the breath out o' them!" But it's not the breath out o' them that's being squeezed; it's the breath out of us and ours, and that's the book of truth. I'm no orator, mates, it's the flesh and blood in me that's speakin', it's the heart o' me. [With a menacing, yet half-ashamed movement towards ROBERTS.] He'll speak to you again, mark my words, but don't ye listen. [The crowd groans.] It's hell fire that's on that man's tongue. [ROBERTS is seen laughing.] Sim 'Arness is right. What are we without the Union—handful o' parched leaves—a puff o' smoke. I'm no orator, but I say: Chuck it up! Chuck it up! Sooner than go on starving the women and the children.

[The murmurs of acquiescence almost drown the murmurs of dissent.]

EVANS. What's turned you to blacklegging?

ROUS. [With a furious look.] Sim 'Arness knows what he's talking about. Give us power to come to terms with London; I'm no orator, but I say—have done wi' this black misery!

[He gives his muter a twist, jerks his head back, and jumps off the platform. The crowd applauds and surges forward. Amid cries of "That's enough!" "Up Union!" "Up Harness!" ROBERTS quietly ascends the platform. There is a moment of silence.]

BLACKSMITH. We don't want to hear you. Shut it!

HENRY Rous. Get down!

[Amid such cries they surge towards the platform.]

EVANS. [Fiercely.] Let 'im speak! Roberts! Roberts!

BULGIN. [Muttering.] He'd better look out that I don't crack his skull.

[ROBERTS faces the crowd, probing them with his eyes till they gradually become silent. He begins speaking. One of the bargemen rises and stands.]

ROBERTS. You don't want to hear me, then? You'll listen to Rous and to that old man, but not to me. You'll listen to Sim Harness of the Union that's treated you so fair; maybe you'll listen to those men from London? Ah! You groan! What for? You love their feet on your necks, don't you? [Then as BULGIN elbows his way towards the platform, with calm bathos.] You'd like to break my jaw, John Bulgin. Let me speak, then do your smashing, if it gives you pleasure. [BULGIN Stands motionless and sullen.] Am I a liar, a coward, a traitor? If only I were, ye'd listen to me, I'm sure. [The murmurings cease, and there is now dead silence.] Is there a man of you here that has less to gain by striking? Is there a man of you that had more to lose? Is there a man of you that has given up eight hundred pounds since this trouble here began? Come now, is there? How much has Thomas given up—ten pounds or five, or what? You listened to him, and what had he to say? "None can pretend," he said, "that I'm not a believer in principle—[with biting irony]—but when Nature says: 'No further, 't es going agenst Nature.'" I tell you if a man cannot say to Nature: "Budge me from this if ye can!"— [with a sort of exaltation]his principles are but his belly. "Oh, but," Thomas says, "a man can be pure and honest, just and merciful, and take off his hat to Nature! "I tell you Nature's neither pure nor honest, just nor merciful. You chaps that live over the hill, an' go home dead beat in the dark on a snowy night—don't ye fight your way every inch of it? Do ye go lyin' down an' trustin' to the tender mercies of this merciful Nature? Try it and you'll soon know with what ye've got to deal. 'T es only by that—[he strikes a blow with his clenched fist]—in Nature's face that a man can be a man. "Give in," says Thomas, "go down on your knees; throw up your foolish fight, an' perhaps," he said, "perhaps your enemy will chuck you down a crust."

JAGO. Never!

EVANS. Curse them!

THOMAS. I nefer said that.

ROBERTS. [Bitingly.] If ye did not say it, man, ye meant it. An' what did ye say
          about Chapel? "Chapel's against it," ye said. "She 's against it!"
          Well, if Chapel and Nature go hand in hand, it's the first I've ever
          heard of it. That young man there— [pointing to ROUS]—said I
          'ad 'ell fire on my tongue. If I had I would use it all to scorch and
          wither this talking of surrender. Surrendering 's the work of cow-
          ards and traitors.

HENRY ROUS. [As GEORGE ROUS moves forward.] Go for him, George—
          don't stand his lip!

ROBERTS. [Flinging out his finger.] Stop there, George Rous, it's no time this
          to settle personal matters. [ROUS stops.] But there was one other
          spoke to you—Mr. Simon Harness. We have not much to thank
          Mr. Harness and the Union for. They said to us "Desert your
          mates, or we'll desert you." An' they did desert us.

EVANS. They did.

ROBERTS. Mr. Simon Harness is a clever man, but he has come too late. [With
          intense conviction.] For all that Mr. Simon Harness says, for all
          that Thomas, Rous, for all that any man present here can say—
          We've won the fight!

[The crowd sags nearer, looking eagerly up.]

[With withering scorn.] You've felt the pinch o't in your bellies. You've forgotten
what that fight 'as been; many times I have told you; I will tell you now this once
again. The fight o' the country's body and blood against a blood-sucker. The
fight of those that spend themselves with every blow they strike and every breath
they draw, against a thing that fattens on them, and grows and grows by the law
of merciful Nature. That thing is Capital! A thing that buys the sweat o' men's
brows, and the tortures o' their brains, at its own price. Don't I know that?
Wasn't the work o' my brains bought for seven hundred pounds, and has n't one
hundred thousand pounds been gained them by that seven hundred without the
stirring of a finger. It is a thing that will take as much and give you as little as it
can. That's Capital! A thing that will say—"I'm very sorry for you, poor fellows—you have a cruel time of it, I know," but will not give one sixpence of its

dividends to help you have a better time. That's Capital! Tell me, for all their talk, is there one of them that will consent to another penny on the Income Tax to help the poor? That's Capital! A white-faced, stony-hearted monster! Ye have got it on its knees; are ye to give up at the last minute to save your miserable bodies pain? When I went this morning to those old men from London, I looked into their very 'earts. One of them was sitting there—Mr. Scantlebury, a mass of flesh nourished on us: sittin' there for all the world like the shareholders in this Company, that sit not moving tongue nor finger, takin' dividends a great dumb ox that can only be roused when its food is threatened. I looked into his eyes and I saw he was afraid—afraid for himself and his dividends; afraid for his fees, afraid of the very shareholders he stands for; and all but one of them's afraid—like children that get into a wood at night, and start at every rustle of the leaves. I ask you, men—[he pauses, holding out his hand till there is utter silence]—give me a free hand to tell them: "Go you back to London. The men have nothing for you!" [A murmuring.] Give me that, an' I swear to you, within a week you shall have from London all you want.

EVANS, JAGO, and OTHERS. A free hand! Give him a free hand! Bravo-bravo!

ROBERTS. 'T is not for this little moment of time we're fighting [the murmuring dies], not for ourselves, our own little bodies, and their wants, 't is for all those that come after throughout all time. [With intense sadness.] Oh! men—for the love o' them, don't roll up another stone upon their heads, don't help to blacken the sky, an' let the bitter sea in over them. They're welcome to the worst that can happen to me, to the worst that can happen to us all, are n't they—are n't they? If we can shake [passionately] that white-faced monster with the bloody lips, that has sucked the life out of ourselves, our wives, and children, since the world began. [Dropping the note of passion but with the utmost weight and intensity.] If we have not the hearts of men to stand against it breast to breast, and eye to eye, and force it backward till it cry for mercy, it will go on sucking life; and we shall stay forever what we are [in almost a whisper], less than the very dogs.

[An utter stillness, and ROBERTS stands rocking his body slightly, with his eyes burning the faces of the crowd.]

EVANS and JAGO. [Suddenly.] Roberts! [The shout is taken up.]

[There is a slight movement in the crowd, and MADGE passing below the tow-ing-path, stops by the platform, looking up at ROBERTS. A sudden doubting silence.]

ROBERTS. "Nature," says that old man, "give in to Nature." I tell you, strike
　　　　　your blow in Nature's face—an' let it do its worst!

[He catches sight of MADGE, his brows contract, he looks away.]

MADGE. [In a low voice-close to the platform.] Your wife's dying!

[ROBERTS glares at her as if torn from some pinnacle of exaltation.]

ROBERTS. [Trying to stammer on.] I say to you—answer them—answer
　　　　　them——

[He is drowned by the murmur in the crowd.]

THOMAS. [Stepping forward.] Ton't you hear her, then?

ROBERTS. What is it? [A dead silence.]

THOMAS. Your wife, man!

[ROBERTS hesitates, then with a gesture, he leaps down, and goes away below
　　　　　the towing-path, the men making way for him. The standing barge-
　　　　　man opens and prepares to light a lantern. Daylight is fast failing.]

MADGE. He need n't have hurried! Annie Roberts is dead. [Then in the silence,
　　　　　passionately.] You pack of blinded hounds! How many more women
　　　　　are you going to let to die?

[The crowd shrinks back from her, and breaks up in groups, with a confused,
uneasy movement. MADGE goes quickly away below the towing-path. There is
a hush as they look after her.]

LEWIS. There's a spitfire, for ye!

BULGIN. [Growling.] I'll smash 'er jaw.

GREEN. If I'd a-been listened to, that poor woman——

THOMAS. It's a judgment on him for going against Chapel. I tolt him how 't would be!

EVANS. All the more reason for sticking by 'im. [A cheer.] Are you goin' to desert him now 'e 's down? Are you going to chuck him over, now 'e 's lost 'is wife?

[The crowd is murmuring and cheering all at once.]

ROUS. [Stepping in front of platform.] Lost his wife! Aye! Can't ye see? Look at home, look at your own wives! What's to save them? Ye'll have the same in all your houses before long!

LEWIS. Aye, aye!

HENRY ROUS. Right! George, right!

[There are murmurs of assent.]

ROUS. It's not us that's blind, it's Roberts. How long will ye put up with 'im!

HENRY, ROUS, BULGIN, DAVIES. Give 'im the chuck!

[The cry is taken up.]

EVANS. [Fiercely.] Kick a man that's down? Down?

HENRY ROUS. Stop his jaw there!

[EVANS throws up his arm at a threat from BULGIN. The bargeman, who has lighted the lantern, holds it high above his head.]

ROUS. [Springing on to the platform.] What brought him down then, but 'is own black obstinacy? Are ye goin' to follow a man that can't see better than that where he's goin'?

EVANS. He's lost 'is wife.

ROUS. An' who's fault's that but his own. 'Ave done with 'im, I say, before he's killed your own wives and mothers.

DAVIES. Down 'im!

HENRY ROUS. He's finished!

BROWN. We've had enough of 'im!

BLACKSMITH. Too much!

[The crowd takes up these cries, excepting only EVANS, JAGO, and GREEN, who is seen to argue mildly with the BLACKSMITH.]

ROUS. [Above the hubbub.] We'll make terms with the Union, lads.

[Cheers.]

EVANS. [Fiercely.] Ye blacklegs!

BULGIN. [Savagely-squaring up to him.] Who are ye callin' blacklegs, Rat?

[EVANS throws up his fists, parries the blow, and returns it. They fight. The bargemen are seen holding up the lantern and enjoying the sight. Old THOMAS steps forward and holds out his hands.]

THOMAS. Shame on your strife!

[The BLACKSMITH, BROWN, LEWIS, and the RED-HAIRED YOUTH pull EVANS and BULGIN apart. The stage is almost dark.]

The curtain falls.

ACT III

It is five o'clock. In the UNDERWOODS' drawing-room, which is artistically furnished, ENID is sitting on the sofa working at a baby's frock. EDGAR, by a little spindle-legged table in the centre of the room, is fingering a china-box. His eyes are fixed on the double-doors that lead into the dining-room.

EDGAR. [Putting down the china-box, and glancing at his watch.] Just on five, they're all in there waiting, except Frank. Where's he?

ENID. He's had to go down to Gasgoyne's about a contract. Will you want him?

EDGAR. He can't help us. This is a director's job. [Motioning towards a single door half hidden by a curtain.] Father in his room?

ENID. Yes.

EDGAR. I wish he'd stay there, Enid.

[ENID looks up at him. This is a beastly business, old girl?]

[He takes up the little box again and turns it over and over.]

ENID. I went to the Roberts's this afternoon, Ted.

EDGAR. That was n't very wise.

ENID. He's simply killing his wife.

EDGAR. We are you mean.

ENID. [Suddenly.] Roberts ought to give way!

EDGAR. There's a lot to be said on the men's side.

ENID. I don't feel half so sympathetic with them as I did before I went. They just set up class feeling against you. Poor Annie was looking dread fully bad—fire going out, and nothing fit for her to eat.

[EDGAR walks to and fro.]

But she would stand up for Roberts. When you see all this wretchedness going on and feel you can do nothing, you have to shut your eyes to the whole thing.

EDGAR. If you can.

ENID. When I went I was all on their side, but as soon as I got there I began to feel quite different at once. People talk about sympathy with the working classes, they don't know what it means to try and put it into practice. It seems hopeless.

EDGAR. Ah! well.

ENID. It's dreadful going on with the men in this state. I do hope the Dad will make concessions.

EDGAR. He won't. [Gloomily.] It's a sort of religion with him. Curse it! I know what's coming! He'll be voted down.

ENID. They would n't dare!

EDGAR. They will—they're in a funk.

ENID. [Indignantly.] He'd never stand it!

EDGAR. [With a shrug.] My dear girl, if you're beaten in a vote, you've got to stand it.

ENID. Oh! [She gets up in alarm.] But would he resign?

EDGAR. Of course! It goes to the roots of his beliefs.

ENID. But he's so wrapped up in this company, Ted! There'd be nothing left for him! It'd be dreadful!

[EDGAR shrugs his shoulders.]

Oh, Ted, he's so old now! You must n't let them!

EDGAR. [Hiding his feelings in an outburst.] My sympathies in this strike are all on the side of the men.

ENID. He's been Chairman for more than thirty years! He made the whole thing! And think of the bad times they've had; it's always been he who pulled them through. Oh, Ted, you must!

EDGAR. What is it you want? You said just now you hoped he'd make concessions. Now you want me to back him in not making them. This is n't a game, Enid!

ENID. [Hotly.] It is n't a game to me that the Dad's in danger of losing all he cares about in life. If he won't give way, and he's beaten, it'll simply break him down!

EDGAR. Did n't you say it was dreadful going on with the men in this state?

ENID. But can't you see, Ted, Father'll never get over it! You must stop them somehow. The others are afraid of him. If you back him up——

EDGAR. [Putting his hand to his head.] Against my convictions— against yours! The moment it begins to pinch one personally——

ENID. It is n't personal, it's the Dad!

EDGAR. Your family or yourself, and over goes the show!

ENID. [Resentfully.] If you don't take it seriously, I do.

EDGAR. I am as fond of him as you are; that's nothing to do with it.

ENID. We can't tell about the men; it's all guess-work. But we know the Dad might have a stroke any day. D' you mean to say that he isn't more to you than—

EDGAR. Of course he is.

ENID. I don't understand you then.

EDGAR. H'm!

ENID. If it were for oneself it would be different, but for our own Father! You don't seem to realise.

EDGAR. I realise perfectly.

ENID. It's your first duty to save him.

EDGAR. I wonder.

ENID. [Imploring.] Oh, Ted? It's the only interest he's got left; it'll be like a death-blow to him!

EDGAR. [Restraining his emotion.] I know.

ENID. Promise!

EDGAR. I'll do what I can.

[He turns to the double-doors.]

[The curtained door is opened, and ANTHONY appears. EDGAR opens the double-doors, and passes through.]

[SCANTLEBURY'S voice is faintly heard: "Past five; we shall never get through—have to eat another dinner at that hotel!" The doors are shut. ANTHONY walks forward.]

ANTHONY. You've been seeing Roberts, I hear.

ENID. Yes.

ANTHONY. Do you know what trying to bridge such a gulf as this is like?

[ENID puts her work on the little table, and faces him.]

Filling a sieve with sand!

ENID. Don't!

ANTHONY.   You think with your gloved hands you can cure the trouble of the century.

[He passes on.]

ENID. Father!

[ANTHONY Stops at the double doors.]

I'm only thinking of you!

ANTHONY. [More softly.] I can take care of myself, my dear.

ENID.   Have you thought what'll happen if you're beaten— [she points]—in there?

ANTHONY. I don't mean to be.

ENID. Oh! Father, don't give them a chance. You're not well; need you go to the meeting at all?

ANTHONY. [With a grim smile.] Cut and run?

ENID. But they'll out-vote you!

ANTHONY. [Putting his hand on the doors.] We shall see!

ENID. I beg you, Dad! Won't you?

[ANTHONY looks at her softly.]

[ANTHONY shakes his head. He opens the doors. A buzz of voices comes in.]

SCANTLEBURY. Can one get dinner on that 6.30 train up?

TENCH. No, Sir, I believe not, sir.

WILDER. Well, I shall speak out; I've had enough of this.

EDGAR. [Sharply.] What?

[It ceases instantly. ANTHONY passes through, closing the doors behind him. ENID springs to them with a gesture of dismay. She puts her hand on the knob, and begins turning it; then goes to the fireplace, and taps her foot on the fender. Suddenly she rings the bell. FROST comes in by the door that leads into the hall.]

FROST. Yes, M'm?

ENID. When the men come, Frost, please show them in here; the hall 's cold.

FROST. I could put them in the pantry, M'm.

ENID. No. I don't want to—to offend them; they're so touchy.

FROST. Yes, M'm. [Pause.] Excuse me, Mr. Anthony's 'ad nothing to eat all day.

ENID. I know Frost.

FROST. Nothin' but two whiskies and sodas, M'm.

ENID. Oh! you oughtn't to have let him have those.

FROST. [Gravely.] Mr. Anthony is a little difficult, M'm. It's not as if he were a younger man, an' knew what was good for 'im; he will have his own way.

ENID. I suppose we all want that.

FROST. Yes, M'm. [Quietly.] Excuse me speakin' about the strike. I'm sure if the other gentlemen were to give up to Mr. Anthony, and quietly let the men 'ave what they want, afterwards, that'd be the best way. I find that very useful with him at times, M'm.

[ENID shakes hey head.]

If he's crossed, it makes him violent. [with an air of discovery], and I've noticed in my own case, when I'm violent I'm always sorry for it afterwards.

ENID. [With a smile.] Are you ever violent, Frost?

FROST. Yes, M'm; oh! sometimes very violent.

ENID. I've never seen you.

FROST. [Impersonally.] No, M'm; that is so.

[ENID fidgets towards the back of the door.]

[With feeling.] Bein' with Mr. Anthony, as you know, M'm, ever since I was fifteen, it worries me to see him crossed like this at his age. I've taken the liberty to speak to Mr. Wanklin [dropping his voice]— seems to be the most sensible of the gentlemen—but 'e said to me: "That's all very well, Frost, but this strike's a very serious thing," 'e said. "Serious for all parties, no doubt," I said, "but yumour 'im, sir," I said, "yumour 'im. It's like this, if a man comes to a stone wall, 'e does n't drive 'is 'ead against it, 'e gets over it." "Yes," 'e said, "you'd better tell your master that." [FROST looks at his nails.] That's where it is, M'm. I said to Mr. Anthony this morning: "Is it worth it, sir?" "Damn it," he said to me, "Frost! Mind your own business, or take a month's notice!" Beg pardon, M'm, for using such a word.

ENID. [Moving to the double-doors, and listening.] Do you know that man Roberts, Frost?

FROST. Yes, M'm; that's to say, not to speak to. But to look at 'im you can tell what he's like.

ENID. [Stopping.] Yes?

FROST. He's not one of these 'ere ordinary 'armless Socialists. 'E's violent; got a fire inside 'im. What I call "personal." A man may 'ave what opinions 'e likes, so long as 'e 's not personal; when 'e 's that 'e 's not safe.

ENID. I think that's what my father feels about Roberts.

FROST. No doubt, M'm, Mr. Anthony has a feeling against him.

[ENID glances at him sharply, but finding him in perfect earnest, stands biting her lips, and looking at the double- doors.]

It 's, a regular right down struggle between the two. I've no patience with this Roberts, from what I 'ear he's just an ordinary workin' man like the rest of 'em. If he did invent a thing he's no worse off than 'undreds of others. My brother invented a new kind o' dumb-waiter—nobody gave him anything for it, an' there it is, bein' used all over the place.

[ENID moves closer to the double-doors.]

There's a kind o' man that never forgives the world, because 'e wasn't born a gentleman. What I say is—no man that's a gentleman looks down on another because 'e 'appens to be a class or two above 'im, no more than if 'e 'appens to be a class or two below.

ENID. [With slight impatience.] Yes, I know, Frost, of course. Will you please go in and ask if they'll have some tea; say I sent you.

FROST. Yes, M'm.

[He opens the doors gently and goes in. There is a momentary sound of earnest, gather angry talk.]

WILDER. I don't agree with you.

WANKLIN. We've had this over a dozen times.

EDGAR. [Impatiently.] Well, what's the proposition?

SCANTLEBURY. Yes, what does your father say? Tea? Not for me, not for me!

WANKLIN. What I understand the Chairman to say is this——

[FROST re-enters closing the door behind him.]

ENID. [Moving from the door.] Won't they have any tea, Frost?

[She goes to the little table, and remains motionless, looking at the baby's frock.]

[A parlourmaid enters from the hall.]

PARLOURMAID. A Miss Thomas, M'm

ENID. [Raising her head.] Thomas? What Miss Thomas—d' you mean a——?

PARLOURMAID. Yes, M'm.

ENID. [Blankly.] Oh! Where is she?

PARLOURMAID. In the porch.

ENID. I don't want——[She hesitates.]

FROST. Shall I dispose of her, M'm?

ENID. I 'll come out. No, show her in here, Ellen.

[The PARLOUR MAID and FROST go out. ENID pursing her lips, sits at the little table, taking up the baby's frock. The PARLOURMAID ushers in MADGE THOMAS and goes out; MADGE stands by the door.]

ENID. Come in. What is it. What have you come for, please?

MADGE. Brought a message from Mrs. Roberts.

ENID. A message? Yes.

MADGE. She asks you to look after her mother.

ENID. I don't understand.

MADGE. [Sullenly.] That's the message.

ENID. But—what—why?

MADGE. Annie Roberts is dead.

[There is a silence.]

ENID. [Horrified.] But it's only a little more than an hour since I saw her.

MADGE. Of cold and hunger.

ENID. [Rising.] Oh! that's not true! the poor thing's heart—— What makes you look at me like that? I tried to help her.

MADGE. [With suppressed savagery.] I thought you'd like to know.

ENID. [Passionately.] It's so unjust! Can't you see that I want to help you all?

MADGE. I never harmed any one that had n't harmed me first.

ENID. [Coldly.] What harm have I done you? Why do you speak to me like that?

MADGE. [With the bitterest intensity.] You come out of your comfort to spy on us! A week of hunger, that's what you want!

ENID. [Standing her ground.] Don't talk nonsense!

MADGE. I saw her die; her hands were blue with the cold.

ENID. [With a movement of grief.] Oh! why wouldn't she let me help her? It's such senseless pride!

MADGE. Pride's better than nothing to keep your body warm.

ENID. [Passionately.] I won't talk to you! How can you tell what I feel? It's not my fault that I was born better off than you.

MADGE. We don't want your money.

ENID. You don't understand, and you don't want to; please to go away!

MADGE. [Balefully.] You've killed her, for all your soft words, you and your father

ENID. [With rage and emotion.] That's wicked! My father is suffering himself through this wretched strike.

MADGE. [With sombre triumph.] Then tell him Mrs. Roberts is dead! That 'll make him better.

ENID. Go away!

MADGE. When a person hurts us we get it back on them.

[She makes a sudden and swift movement towards ENID, fixing her eyes on the child's frock lying across the little table. ENID snatches the frock up, as though it were the child itself. They stand a yard apart, crossing glances.]

MADGE. [Pointing to the frock with a little smile.] Ah! You felt that! Lucky it's her mother—not her children—you've to look after, is n't it. She won't trouble you long!

ENID. Go away!

MADGE. I've given you the message.

[She turns and goes out into the hall. ENID, motionless till she has gone, sinks down at the table, bending her head over the frock, which she is still clutching to her. The double-doors are opened, and ANTHONY comes slowly in; he passes his daughter, and lowers himself into an arm-chair. He is very flushed.]

ENID. [Hiding her emotion-anxiously.] What is it, Dad?

[ANTHONY makes a gesture, but does not speak.]

Who was it?

[ANTHONY does not answer. ENID going to the double-doors meets EDGAR Coming in. They speak together in low tones.]

What is it, Ted?

EDGAR. That fellow Wilder! Taken to personalities! He was downright insulting.

ENID. What did he say?

EDGAR. Said, Father was too old and feeble to know what he was doing! The Dad's worth six of him!

ENID. Of course he is.

[They look at ANTHONY.]

[The doors open wider, WANKLIN appears With SCANTLEBURY.]

SCANTLEBURY. [Sotto voce.] I don't like the look of this!

WANKLIN. [Going forward.] Come, Chairman! Wilder sends you his apolo-
gies. A man can't do more.

[WILDER, followed by TENCH, comes in, and goes to ANTHONY.]

WILDER. [Glumly.] I withdraw my words, sir. I'm sorry.

[ANTHONY nods to him.]

ENID. You have n't come to a decision, Mr. Wanklin?

[WANKLIN shakes his head.]

WANKLIN. We're all here, Chairman; what do you say? Shall we get on with
the business, or shall we go back to the other room?

SCANTLEBURY. Yes, yes; let's get on. We must settle something.

[He turns from a small chair, and settles himself suddenly in the largest chair with
a sigh of comfort.]

[WILDER and WANKLIN also sit; and TENCH, drawing up a straight- backed
chair close to his Chairman, sits on the edge of it with the minute-book and a sty-
lographic pen.]

ENID. [Whispering.] I want to speak to you a minute, Ted.

[They go out through the double-doors.]

WANKLIN. Really, Chairman, it's no use soothing ourselves with a sense of false
security. If this strike's not brought to an end before the General
Meeting, the shareholders will certainly haul us over the coals.

SCANTLEBURY. [Stirring.] What—what's that?

WANKLIN. I know it for a fact.

ANTHONY. Let them!

WILDER. And get turned out?

WANKLIN. [To ANTHONY.] I don't mind martyrdom for a policy in which
        I believe, but I object to being burnt for some one else's principles.

SCANTLEBURY. Very reasonable—you must see that, Chairman.

ANTHONY. We owe it to other employers to stand firm.

WANKLIN. There's a limit to that.

ANTHONY. You were all full of fight at the start.

SCANTLEBURY. [With a sort of groan.] We thought the men would give in,
        but they-have n't!

ANTHONY. They will!

WILDER. [Rising and pacing up and down.] I can't have my reputation as a man
        of business destroyed for the satisfaction of starving the men out.
        [Almost in tears.] I can't have it! How can we meet the shareholders
        with things in the state they are?

SCANTLEBURY. Hear, hear—hear, hear!

WILDER. [Lashing himself.] If any one expects me to say to them I've lost you
        fifty thousand pounds and sooner than put my pride in my pocket I'll
        lose you another. [Glancing at ANTHONY.] It's—it's unnatural! I
        don't want to go against you, sir.

WANKLIN. [Persuasively.] Come Chairman, we 're not free agents. We're part
        of a machine. Our only business is to see the Company earns as
        much profit as it safely can. If you blame me for want of princi-
        ple: I say that we're Trustees. Reason tells us we shall never get back

in the saving of wages what we shall lose if we continue this strug-gle—really, Chairman, we must bring it to an end, on the best terms we can make.

ANTHONY. No.

[There is a pause of general dismay.]

WILDER. It's a deadlock then. [Letting his hands drop with a sort of despair.] Now I shall never get off to Spain!

WANKLIN. [Retaining a trace of irony.] You hear the consequences of your victory, Chairman?

WILDER. [With a burst of feeling.] My wife's ill!

SCANTLEBURY. Dear, dear! You don't say so.

WILDER. If I don't get her out of this cold, I won't answer for the consequences.

[Through the double-doors EDGAR comes in looking very grave.]

EDGAR. [To his Father.] Have you heard this, sir? Mrs. Roberts is dead!

[Every one stages at him, as if trying to gauge the importance of this news.]

Enid saw her this afternoon, she had no coals, or food, or anything. It's enough!

[There is a silence, every one avoiding the other's eyes, except ANTHONY, who stares hard at his son.]

SCANTLEBURY. You don't suggest that we could have helped the poor thing?

WILDER. [Flustered.] The woman was in bad health. Nobody can say there's any responsibility on us. At least—not on me.

EDGAR. [Hotly.] I say that we are responsible.

ANTHONY. War is war!

EDGAR. Not on women!

WANKLIN. It not infrequently happens that women are the greatest sufferers.

EDGAR. If we knew that, all the more responsibility rests on us.

ANTHONY. This is no matter for amateurs.

EDGAR. Call me what you like, sir. It's sickened me. We had no right to carry things to such a length.

WILDER. I don't like this business a bit—that Radical rag will twist it to their own ends; see if they don't! They'll get up some cock and bull story about the poor woman's dying from starvation. I wash my hands of it.

EDGAR. You can't. None of us can.

SCANTLEBURY. [Striking his fist on the arm of his chair.] But I protest against this!

EDGAR. Protest as you like, Mr. Scantlebury, it won't alter facts.

ANTHONY. That's enough.

EDGAR. [Facing him angrily.] No, sir. I tell you exactly what I think. If we pretend the men are not suffering, it's humbug; and if they're suffering, we know enough of human nature to know the women are suffering more, and as to the children—well—it's damnable!

[SCANTLEBURY rises from his chair.]

I don't say that we meant to be cruel, I don't say anything of the sort; but I do say it's criminal to shut our eyes to the facts. We employ these men, and we can't get out of it. I don't care so much about the men, but I'd sooner resign my position on the Board than go on starving women in this way.

[All except ANTHONY are now upon their feet, ANTHONY sits grasping the arms of his chair and staring at his son.]

SCANTLEBURY. I don't—I don't like the way you're putting it, young sir.

WANKLIN. You're rather overshooting the mark.

WILDER. I should think so indeed!

EDGAR. [Losing control.] It's no use blinking things! If you want to have the death of women on your hands—I don't!

SCANTLEBURY. Now, now, young man!

WILDER. On our hands? Not on mine, I won't have it!

EDGAR. We are five members of this Board; if we were four against it, why did we let it drift till it came to this? You know perfectly well why—because we hoped we should starve the men out. Well, all we've done is to starve one woman out!

SCANTLEBURY. [Almost hysterically.] I protest, I protest! I'm a humane man—we're all humane men!

EDGAR. [Scornfully.] There's nothing wrong with our humanity. It's our imaginations, Mr. Scantlebury.

WILDER. Nonsense! My imagination's as good as yours.

EDGAR. If so, it is n't good enough.

WILDER. I foresaw this!

EDGAR. Then why didn't you put your foot down!

WILDER. Much good that would have done.

[He looks at ANTHONY.]

EDGAR. If you, and I, and each one of us here who say that our imaginations are so good—

SCANTLEBURY. [Flurried.] I never said so.

EDGAR. [Paying no attention.]—had put our feet down, the thing would have been ended long ago, and this poor woman's life wouldn't have been crushed out of her like this. For all we can tell there may be a dozen other starving women.

SCANTLEBURY. For God's sake, sir, don't use that word at a—at a Board meeting; it's—it's monstrous.

EDGAR. I will use it, Mr. Scantlebury.

SCANTLEBURY. Then I shall not listen to you. I shall not listen! It's painful to me.

[He covers his ears.]

WANKLIN. None of us are opposed to a settlement, except your Father.

EDGAR. I'm certain that if the shareholders knew——

WANKLIN. I don't think you'll find their imaginations are any better than ours. Because a woman happens to have a weak heart——

EDGAR. A struggle like this finds out the weak spots in everybody. Any child knows that. If it hadn't been for this cut-throat policy, she need n't have died like this; and there would n't be all this misery that any one who is n't a fool can see is going on.

[Throughout the foregoing ANTHONY has eyed his son; he now moves as though to rise, but stops as EDGAR speaks again.]

I don't defend the men, or myself, or anybody.

WANKLIN. You may have to! A coroner's jury of disinterested sympathisers may say some very nasty things. We mustn't lose sight of our position.

SCANTLEBURY. [Without uncovering his ears.] Coroner's jury! No, no, it's not a case for that!

EDGAR. I 've had enough of cowardice.

WANKLIN. Cowardice is an unpleasant word, Mr. Edgar Anthony. It will look very like cowardice if we suddenly concede the men's demands when a thing like this happens; we must be careful!

WILDER. Of course we must. We've no knowledge of this matter, except a rumour. The proper course is to put the whole thing into the hands of Harness to settle for us; that's natural, that's what we should have come to any way.

SCANTLEBURY. [With dignity.] Exactly! [Turning to EDGAR.] And as to you, young sir, I can't sufficiently express my—my distaste for the way you've treated the whole matter. You ought to withdraw! Talking of starvation, talking of cowardice! Considering what our views are! Except your own is—is one of goodwill—it's most irregular, it's most improper, and all I can say is it's—it's given me pain——

[He places his hand over his heart.]

EDGAR. [Stubbornly.] I withdraw nothing.

[He is about to say mote when SCANTLEBURY once more coveys up his ears. TENCH suddenly makes a demonstration with the minute- book. A sense of having been engaged in the unusual comes over all of them, and one by one they resume their seats. EDGAR alone remains on his feet.]

WILDER. [With an air of trying to wipe something out.] I pay no attention to what young Mr. Anthony has said. Coroner's jury! The idea's preposterous. I—I move this amendment to the Chairman's Motion: That the dispute be placed at once in the hands of Mr. Simon Harness for settlement, on the lines indicated by him this morning. Any one second that?

[TENCH writes in his book.]

WANKLIN. I do.

WILDER. Very well, then; I ask the Chairman to put it to the Board.

ANTHONY. [With a great sigh-slowly.] We have been made the subject of an attack. [Looking round at WILDER and SCANTLEBURY with ironical contempt.] I take it on my shoulders. I am seventy-six years old. I have been Chairman of this Company since its inception two-and- thirty years ago. I have seen it pass through good and evil report. My connection with it began in the year that this young man was born.

[EDGAR bows his head. ANTHONY, gripping his chair, goes on.]

I have had do to with "men" for fifty years; I've always stood up to them; I have never been beaten yet. I have fought the men of this Company four times, and four times I have beaten them. It has been said that I am not the man I was. [He looks at Wilder.] However that may be, I am man enough to stand to my guns.

[His voice grows stronger. The double-doors are opened. ENID slips in, followed by UNDERWOOD, who restrains her.]

The men have been treated justly, they have had fair wages, we have always been ready to listen to complaints. It has been said that times have changed; if they have, I have not changed with them. Neither will I. It has been said that masters and men are equal! Cant! There can only be one master in a house! Where two men meet the better man will rule. It has been said that Capital and Labour have the same interests. Cant! Their interests are as wide asunder as the poles. It has been said that the Board is only part of a machine. Cant! We are the machine; its brains and sinews; it is for us to lead and to determine what is to be done, and to do it without fear or favour. Fear of the men! Fear of the shareholders! Fear of our own shadows! Before I am like that, I hope to die.

[He pauses, and meeting his son's eyes, goes on.]

There is only one way of treating "men"—with the iron hand. This half and half business, the half and half manners of this generation, has brought all this upon us. Sentiment and softness, and what this young man, no doubt, would call his social policy. You can't eat cake and have it! This middle-class sentiment, or socialism, or whatever it may be, is rotten. Masters are masters, men are men! Yield one demand, and they will make it six. They are [he smiles grimly] like Oliver Twist, asking for more. If I were in their place I should be the same. But I am not in their place. Mark my words: one fine morning, when you have given way here, and given way there—you will find you have parted with the ground beneath your feet, and are deep in the bog of bankruptcy; and with you, floundering in that bog, will be the very men you have given way to. I have been accused of being a domineering tyrant, thinking only of my pride—I am thinking of the future of this country, threatened with the black waters of confusion, threatened with mob government, threatened with what I cannot see. If by any conduct of mine I help to bring this on us, I shall be ashamed to look my fellows in the face.

[ANTHONY stares before him, at what he cannot see, and there is perfect stillness. FROST comes in from the hall, and all but ANTHONY look round at him
uneasily.]

FROST. [To his master.] The men are here, sir. [ANTHONY makes a gesture
of dismissal.] Shall I bring them in, sir?

ANTHONY. Wait!

[FROST goes out, ANTHONY turns to face his son.]

I come to the attack that has been made upon me.

[EDGAR, with a gesture of deprecation, remains motionless with his head a little bowed.]

A woman has died. I am told that her blood is on my hands; I am told that on
my hands is the starvation and the suffering of other women and of children.

EDGAR. I said "on our hands," sir.

ANTHONY. It is the same. [His voice grows stronger and stronger, his feeling
is more and more made manifest.] I am not aware that if my adver-
sary suffer in a fair fight not sought by me, it is my fault. If I fall
under his feet—as fall I may—I shall not complain. That will be
my look-out—and this is—his. I cannot separate, as I would, these
men from their women and children. A fair fight is a fair fight! Let
them learn to think before they pick a quarrel!

EDGAR. [In a low voice.] But is it a fair fight, Father? Look at them, and look
at us! They've only this one weapon!

ANTHONY. [Grimly.] And you're weak-kneed enough to teach them how to
use it! It seems the fashion nowadays for men to take their enemy's
side. I have not learnt that art. Is it my fault that they quarrelled
with their Union too?

EDGAR. There is such a thing as Mercy.

ANTHONY. And justice comes before it.

EDGAR. What seems just to one man, sir, is injustice to another.

ANTHONY. [With suppressed passion.] You accuse me of injustice—of what
          amounts to inhumanity—of cruelty?

[EDGAR makes a gesture of horror—a general frightened movement.]

WANKLIN. Come, come, Chairman.

ANTHONY. [In a grim voice.] These are the words of my own son. They are
          the words of a generation that I don't understand; the words of a
          soft breed.

[A general murmur. With a violent effort ANTHONY recovers his control.]

EDGAR. [Quietly.] I said it of myself, too, Father.

[A long look is exchanged between them, and ANTHONY puts out his hand
with a gesture as if to sweep the personalities away; then places it against his brow,
swaying as though from giddiness. There is a movement towards him. He moves
them back.]

ANTHONY. Before I put this amendment to the Board, I have one more word
          to say. [He looks from face to face.] If it is carried, it means that
          we shall fail in what we set ourselves to do. It means that we shall
          fail in the duty that we owe to all Capital. It means that we shall
          fail in the duty that we owe ourselves. It means that we shall be
          open to constant attack to which we as constantly shall have to
          yield. Be under no misapprehension—run this time, and you will
          never make a stand again! You will have to fly like curs before the
          whips of your own men. If that is the lot you wish for, you will
          vote for this amendment.

[He looks again, from face to face, finally resting his gaze on EDGAR; all sit with
their eyes on the ground. ANTHONY makes a gesture, and TENCH hands him
the book. He reads.]

"Moved by Mr. Wilder, and seconded by Mr. Wanklin: 'That the men's demands
be placed at once in the hands of Mr. Simon Harness for settlement on the lines
indicated by him this morning.'" [With sudden vigour.] Those in favour: Signify
the same in the usual way!

[For a minute no one moves; then hastily, just as ANTHONY is about to speak, WILDER's hand and WANKLIN'S are held up, then SCANTLEBURY'S, and last EDGAR'S who does not lift his head.]

[ANTHONY lifts his own hand.]

[In a clear voice.] The amendment is carried. I resign my position on this Board.

[ENID gasps, and there is dead silence. ANTHONY sits motionless, his head slowly drooping; suddenly he heaves as though the whole of his life had risen up within him.]

Contrary?

Fifty years! You have disgraced me, gentlemen. Bring in the men!

[He sits motionless, staring before him. The Board draws hurriedly together, and forms a group. TENCH in a frightened manner speaks into the hall. UNDER-WOOD almost forces ENID from the room.]

WILDER. [Hurriedly.] What's to be said to them? Why isn't Harness here? Ought we to see the men before he comes? I don't——

TENCH. Will you come in, please?

[Enter THOMAS, GREEN, BULGIN, and ROUS, who file up in a row past the little table. TENCH sits down and writes. All eyes are foxed on ANTHONY, who makes no sign.]

WANKLIN. [Stepping up to the little table, with nervous cordiality.] Well, Thomas, how's it to be? What's the result of your meeting?

ROUS.   Sim Harness has our answer. He'll tell you what it is. We're waiting for him. He'll speak for us.

WANKLIN. Is that so, Thomas?

THOMAS. [Sullenly.] Yes. Roberts will not pe coming, his wife is dead.

SCANTLEBURY. Yes, yes! Poor woman! Yes! Yes!

FROST. [Entering from the hall.] Mr. Harness, Sir!

[As HARNESS enters he retires.]

[HARNESS has a piece of paper in his hand, he bows to the Directors, nods towards the men, and takes his stand behind the little table in the very centre of the room.]

HARNESS. Good evening, gentlemen.

[TENCH, with the paper he has been writing, joins him, they speak together in low tones.]

WILDER. We've been waiting for you, Harness. Hope we shall come to some—

FROST. [Entering from the hall.] Roberts!

[He goes.]

[ROBERTS comes hastily in, and stands staring at ANTHONY. His face is drawn and old.]

ROBERTS. Mr. Anthony, I am afraid I am a little late, I would have been here in time but for something that—has happened. [To the men.] Has anything been said?

THOMAS. No! But, man, what made ye come?

ROBERTS. Ye told us this morning, gentlemen, to go away and reconsider our position. We have reconsidered it; we are here to bring you the men's answer. [To ANTHONY.] Go ye back to London. We have nothing for you. By no jot or tittle do we abate our demands, nor will we until the whole of those demands are yielded.

[ANTHONY looks at him but does not speak. There is a movement amongst the men as though they were bewildered.]

HARNESS. Roberts!

ROBERTS. [Glancing fiercely at him, and back to ANTHONY.] Is that clear enough for ye? Is it short enough and to the point? Ye made a mistake to think that we would come to heel. Ye may break the body, but ye cannot break the spirit. Get back to London, the men have nothing for ye?

[Pausing uneasily he takes a step towards the unmoving ANTHONY.]

EDGAR. We're all sorry for you, Roberts, but——

ROBERTS. Keep your sorrow, young man. Let your father speak!

HARNESS. [With the sheet of paper in his hand, speaking from behind the little table.] Roberts!

ROBERT. [TO ANTHONY, with passionate intensity.] Why don't ye answer?

HARNESS. Roberts!

ROBERTS. [Turning sharply.] What is it?

HARNESS. [Gravely.] You're talking without the book; things have travelled past you.

[He makes a sign to TENCH, who beckons the Directors. They quickly sign his copy of the terms.]

Look at this, man! [Holding up his sheet of paper.] "Demands conceded, with the exception of those relating to the engineers and furnace-men. Double wages for Saturday's overtime. Night-shifts as they are." These terms have been agreed. The men go back to work again to-morrow. The strike is at an end.

ROBERTS. [Reading the paper, and turning on the men. They shrink back from him, all but ROUS, who stands his ground. With deadly stillness.] Ye have gone back on me? I stood by ye to the death; ye waited for that to throw me over!

[The men answer, all speaking together.]

ROUS. It's a lie!

THOMAS. Ye were past endurance, man.

GREEN. If ye'd listen to me!

BULGIN. (Under his breath.) Hold your jaw!

ROBERTS. Ye waited for that!

HARNESS. [Taking the Director's copy of the terms, and handing his own to TENCH.] That's enough, men. You had better go.

[The men shuffle slowly, awkwardly away.]

WILDER. [In a low, nervous voice.] There's nothing to stay for now, I suppose. [He follows to the door.] I shall have a try for that train! Coming, Scantlebury?

SCANTLEBURY. [Following with WANKLIN.] Yes, yes; wait for me. [He stops as ROBERTS speaks.]

ROBERTS. [To ANTHONY.] But ye have not signed them terms! They can't make terms without their Chairman! Ye would never sign them terms! [ANTHONY looks at him without speaking.] Don't tell me ye have! for the love o' God! [With passionate appeal.] I reckoned on ye!

HARNESS. [Holding out the Director's copy of the teems.] The Board has signed!

[ROBERTS looks dully at the signatures—dashes the paper from him, and covers up his eyes.]

SCANTLEBURY. [Behind his hand to TENCH.] Look after the Chairman! He's not well; he's not well—he had no lunch. If there's any fund started for the women and children, put me down for— for twenty pounds.

[He goes out into the hall, in cumbrous haste; and WANKLIN, who has been staring at ROBERTS and ANTHONY With twitchings of his face, follows. EDGAR remains seated on the sofa, looking at the ground; TENCH, returning to the bureau, writes in his minute— book. HARNESS stands by the little table, gravely watching ROBERTS.]

ROBERTS. Then you're no longer Chairman of this Company! [Breaking into half-mad laughter.] Ah! ha-ah, ha, ha! They've thrown ye over thrown over their Chairman: Ah-ha-ha! [With a sudden dreadful calm.] So—they've done us both down, Mr. Anthony?

[ENID, hurrying through the double-doors, comes quickly to her father.]

ANTHONY. Both broken men, my friend Roberts!

HARNESS. [Coming down and laying his hands on ROBERTS'S sleeve.] For shame, Roberts! Go home quietly, man; go home!

ROBERTS. [Tearing his arm away.] Home? [Shrinking together—in a whisper.] Home!

ENID. [Quietly to her father.] Come away, dear! Come to your room

[ANTHONY rises with an effort. He turns to ROBERTS who looks at him. They stand several seconds, gazing at each other fixedly; ANTHONY lifts his hand, as though to salute, but lets it fall. The expression of ROBERTS'S face changes from hostility to wonder. They bend their heads in token of respect. ANTHONY turns, and slowly walks towards the curtained door. Suddenly he sways as though about to fall, recovers himself, and is assisted out by EDGAR and ENID; UNDERWOOD follows, but stops at the door. ROBERTS remains motionless for several seconds, staring intently after ANTHONY, then goes out into the hall.]

TENCH. [Approaching HARNESS.] It's a great weight off my mind, Mr. Harness! But what a painful scene, sir! [He wipes his brow.]

[HARNESS, pale and resolute, regards with a grim half-smile the quavering.]

TENCH. It's all been so violent! What did he mean by: "Done us both down?" If he has lost his wife, poor fellow, he oughtn't to have spoken to the Chairman like that!

HARNESS. A woman dead; and the two best men both broken!

TENCH. [Staring at him-suddenly excited.] D'you know, sir—these terms, they're the very same we drew up together, you and I, and put to both sides before the fight began? All this—all this—and—and what for?

HARNESS. [In a slow grim voice.] That's where the fun comes in!

[UNDERWOOD without turning from the door makes a gesture of assent.]

The curtain falls.

Second Series:

The Eldest Son
The Little Dream
Justice

THE ELDEST SON

PERSONS OF THE PLAY

SIR WILLIAM CHESHIRE, a baronet
LADY CHESHIRE, his wife
BILL, their eldest son
HAROLD, their second son
RONALD KEITH(in the Lancers), their son-in-law
CHRISTINE (his wife), their eldest daughter
DOT, their second daughter
JOAN, their third daughter
MABEL LANFARNE, their guest
THE REVEREND JOHN LATTER, engaged to Joan
OLD STUDDENHAM, the head-keeper
FREDA STUDDENHAM, the lady's-maid
YOUNG DUNNING, the under-keeper
ROSE TAYLOR, a village girl
JACKSON, the butler
CHARLES, a footman

TIME: The present. The action passes on December 7 and 8 at the Cheshires' country house, in one of the shires.

ACT I
      SCENE I. The hall; before dinner.
      SCENE II. The hall; after dinner.

ACT II. Lady Cheshire's morning room; after breakfast.

ACT III. The smoking-room; tea-time.

A night elapses between Acts I. and II.

ACT I

SCENE I

The scene is a well-lighted, and large, oak-panelled hall, with an air of being lived in, and a broad, oak staircase. The dining-room, drawing-room, billiard-room, all open into it; and under the staircase a door leads to the servants' quarters. In a huge fireplace a log fire is burning. There are tiger-skins on the floor, horns on the walls; and a writing-table against the wall opposite the fireplace. FREDA STUDDENHAM, a pretty, pale girl with dark eyes, in the black dress of a lady's-maid, is standing at the foot of the staircase with a bunch of white roses in one hand, and a bunch of yellow roses in the other. A door closes above, and SIR WILLIAM CHESHIRE, in evening dress, comes downstairs. He is perhaps fifty-eight, of strong build, rather bull-necked, with grey eyes, and a well-coloured face, whose choleric autocracy is veiled by a thin urbanity. He speaks before he reaches the bottom.

SIR WILLIAM. Well, Freda! Nice roses. Who are they for?

FREDA. My lady told me to give the yellow to Mrs. Keith, Sir William, and the white to Miss Lanfarne, for their first evening.

SIR WILLIAM. Capital. [Passing on towards the drawing-room] Your father coming up to-night?

FREDA. Yes.

SIR WILLIAM. Be good enough to tell him I specially want to see him here after
            dinner, will you?

FREDA. Yes, Sir William.

SIR WILLIAM. By the way, just ask him to bring the game-book in, if he's got
            it.

He goes out into the drawing-room; and FREDA stands restlessly tapping her
foot against the bottom stair. With a flutter of skirts CHRISTINE KEITH
comes rapidly down. She is a nice-looking, fresh-coloured young woman in a
low-necked dress.

CHRISTINE. Hullo, Freda! How are YOU?

FREDA. Quite well, thank you, Miss Christine—Mrs. Keith, I mean. My lady
        told me to give you these.

CHRISTINE. [Taking the roses] Oh! Thanks! How sweet of mother!

FREDA. [In a quick, toneless voice] The others are for Miss Lanfarne. My lady
        thought white would suit her better.

CHRISTINE. They suit you in that black dress.

[FREDA lowers the roses quickly.]

What do you think of Joan's engagement?

FREDA. It's very nice for her.

CHRISTINE. I say, Freda, have they been going hard at rehearsals?

FREDA. Every day. Miss Dot gets very cross, stage-managing.

CHRISTINE. I do hate learning a part. Thanks awfully for unpacking. Any
            news?

FREDA. [In the same quick, dull voice] The under-keeper, Dunning, won't
        marry Rose Taylor, after all.

CHRISTINE. What a shame! But I say that's serious. I thought there was—she was—I mean——

FREDA. He's taken up with another girl, they say.

CHRISTINE. Too bad! [Pinning the roses] D'you know if Mr. Bill's come?

FREDA. [With a swift upward look] Yes, by the six-forty.

RONALD KEITH comes slowly down, a weathered firm-lipped man, in evening dress, with eyelids half drawn over his keen eyes, and the air of a horseman.

KEITH. Hallo! Roses in December. I say, Freda, your father missed a wigging this morning when they drew blank at Warnham's spinney. Where's that litter of little foxes?

FREDA. [Smiling faintly] I expect father knows, Captain Keith.

KEITH. You bet he does. Emigration? Or thin air? What?

CHRISTINE. Studdenham'd never shoot a fox, Ronny. He's been here since the flood.

KEITH. There's more ways of killing a cat—eh, Freda?

CHRISTINE. [Moving with her husband towards the drawing-room] Young Dunning won't marry that girl, Ronny.

KEITH. Phew! Wouldn't be in his shoes, then! Sir William'll never keep a servant who's made a scandal in the village, old girl. Bill come?

As they disappear from the hall, JOHN LATTER in a clergyman's evening dress, comes sedately downstairs, a tall, rather pale young man, with something in him, as it were, both of heaven, and a drawing-room. He passes FREDA with a formal little nod. HAROLD, a fresh-cheeked, cheery-looking youth, comes down, three steps at a time.

HAROLD. Hallo, Freda! Patience on the monument. Let's have a sniff! For Miss Lanfarne? Bill come down yet?

FREDA. No, Mr. Harold.

HAROLD crosses the hall, whistling, and follows LATTER into the drawing-room. There is the sound of a scuffle above, and a voice crying: "Shut up, Dot!" And JOAN comes down screwing her head back. She is pretty and small, with large clinging eyes.

JOAN. Am I all right behind, Freda? That beast, Dot!

FREDA. Quite, Miss Joan.

DOT's face, like a full moon, appears over the upper banisters. She too comes running down, a frank figure, with the face of a rebel.

DOT. You little being!

JOAN. [Flying towards the drawing-roam, is overtaken at the door] Oh! Dot! You're pinching!

As they disappear into the drawing-room, MABEL LANFARNE, a tall girl with a rather charming Irish face, comes slowly down. And at sight of her FREDA's whole figure becomes set and meaning- full.

FREDA. For you, Miss Lanfarne, from my lady.

MABEL. [In whose speech is a touch of wilful Irishry] How sweet! [Fastening the roses] And how are you, Freda?

FREDA. Very well, thank you.

MABEL. And your father? Hope he's going to let me come out with the guns again.

FREDA. [Stolidly] He'll be delighted, I'm sure.

MABEL. Ye-es! I haven't forgotten his face-last time.

FREDA. You stood with Mr. Bill. He's better to stand with than Mr. Harold, or Captain Keith?

MABEL. He didn't touch a feather, that day.

FREDA. People don't when they're anxious to do their best.

A gong sounds. And MABEL LANFARNE, giving FREDA a rather inquisitive stare, moves on to the drawing-room. Left alone without the roses, FREDA still lingers. At the slamming of a door above, and hasty footsteps, she shrinks back against the stairs. BILL runs down, and comes on her suddenly. He is a tall, good-looking edition of his father, with the same stubborn look of veiled choler.

BILL. Freda! [And as she shrinks still further back] what's the matter? [Then at
          some sound he looks round uneasily and draws away from her] Aren't
          you glad to see me?

FREDA. I've something to say to you, Mr. Bill. After dinner.

BILL. Mister——?

She passes him, and rushes away upstairs. And BILL, who stands frowning and looking after her, recovers himself sharply as the drawing-room door is opened, and SIR WILLIAM and MISS LANFARNE come forth, followed by KEITH, DOT, HAROLD, CHRISTINE, LATTER, and JOAN, all leaning across each other, and talking. By herself, behind them, comes LADY CHESHIRE, a refined-looking woman of fifty, with silvery dark hair, and an expression at once gentle, and ironic. They move across the hall towards the dining-room.

SIR WILLIAM. Ah! Bill.

MABEL. How do you do?

KEITH. How are you, old chap?

DOT. [gloomily] Do you know your part?

HAROLD. Hallo, old man!

CHRISTINE gives her brother a flying kiss. JOAN and LATTER pause and
          look at him shyly without speech.

BILL. [Putting his hand on JOAN's shoulder] Good luck, you two! Well moth-
          er?

LADY CHESHIRE. Well, my dear boy! Nice to see you at last. What a long
          time!

She draws his arm through hers, and they move towards the dining-room.

The curtain falls.

The curtain rises again at once.

SCENE II

CHRISTINE, LADY CHESHIRE, DOT, MABEL LANFARNE, and JOAN, are returning to the hall after dinner.

CHRISTINE. [in a low voice] Mother, is it true about young Dunning and Rose Taylor?

LADY CHESHIRE. I'm afraid so, dear.

CHRISTINE. But can't they be——

DOT. Ah! ah-h! [CHRISTINE and her mother are silent.] My child, I'm not the young person.

CHRISTINE. No, of course not—only—[nodding towards JOAN and Mable].

DOT. Look here! This is just an instance of what I hate.

LADY CHESHIRE. My dear? Another one?

DOT. Yes, mother, and don't you pretend you don't understand, because you know you do.

CHRISTINE. Instance? Of what?

JOAN and MABEL have ceased talking, and listen, still at the fire.

DOT. Humbug, of course. Why should you want them to marry, if he's tired of her?

CHRISTINE. [Ironically] Well! If your imagination doesn't carry you as far as that!

DOT. When people marry, do you believe they ought to be in love with each other?

CHRISTINE. [With a shrug] That's not the point.

DOT. Oh? Were you in love with Ronny?

CHRISTINE. Don't be idiotic!

DOT. Would you have married him if you hadn't been?

CHRISTINE. Of course not!

JOAN. Dot! You are!——

DOT. Hallo! my little snipe!

LADY CHESHIRE. Dot, dear!

DOT. Don't shut me up, mother! [To JOAN.] Are you in love with John? [JOAN turns hurriedly to the fire.] Would you be going to marry him if you were not?

CHRISTINE. You are a brute, Dot.

DOT. Is Mabel in love with—whoever she is in love with?

MABEL. And I wonder who that is.

DOT. Well, would you marry him if you weren't?

MABEL. No, I would not.

DOT. Now, mother; did you love father?

CHRISTINE. Dot, you really are awful.

DOT. [Rueful and detached] Well, it is a bit too thick, perhaps.

JOAN. Dot!

DOT. Well, mother, did you—I mean quite calmly?

LADY CHESHIRE. Yes, dear, quite calmly.

DOT. Would you have married him if you hadn't? [LADY CHESHIRE shakes her head] Then we're all agreed!

MABEL. Except yourself.

DOT. [Grimly] Even if I loved him, he might think himself lucky if I married him.

MABEL. Indeed, and I'm not so sure.

DOT. [Making a face at her] What I was going to——

LADY CHESHIRE. But don't you think, dear, you'd better not?

DOT. Well, I won't say what I was going to say, but what I do say is—Why the devil——

LADY CHESHIRE. Quite so, Dot!

DOT. [A little disconcerted.] If they're tired of each other, they ought not to marry, and if father's going to make them——

CHRISTINE. You don't understand in the least. It's for the sake of the——

DOT. Out with it, Old Sweetness! The approaching infant! God bless it!

There is a sudden silence, for KEITH and LATTER are seen coming from the dining-room.

LATTER. That must be so, Ronny.

KEITH. No, John; not a bit of it!

LATTER. You don't think!

KEITH. Good Gad, who wants to think after dinner!

DOT. Come on! Let's play pool. [She turns at the billiard-room door.] Look here! Rehearsal to-morrow is directly after breakfast; from "Eccles enters breathless" to the end.

MABEL. Whatever made you choose "Caste," DOT? You know it's awfully difficult.

DOT. Because it's the only play that's not too advanced. [The girls all go into the billiard-room.]

LADY CHESHIRE. Where's Bill, Ronny?

KEITH. [With a grimace] I rather think Sir William and he are in Committee of Supply—Mem-Sahib.

LADY CHESHIRE. Oh!

She looks uneasily at the dining-room; then follows the girls out.

LATTER. [In the tone of one resuming an argument] There can't be two opinions about it, Ronny. Young Dunning's refusal is simply indefensible.

KEITH. I don't agree a bit, John.

LATTER. Of course, if you won't listen.

KEITH. [Clipping a cigar] Draw it mild, my dear chap. We've had the whole thing over twice at least.

LATTER. My point is this——

KEITH. [Regarding LATTER quizzically with his halfclosed eyes] I know—I know—but the point is, how far your point is simply professional.

LATTER. If a man wrongs a woman, he ought to right her again. There's no answer to that.

KEITH. It all depends.

LATTER. That's rank opportunism.

KEITH. Rats! Look here—Oh! hang it, John, one can't argue this out with a parson.

LATTER. [Frigidly] Why not?

HAROLD. [Who has entered from the dining-room] Pull devil, pull baker!

KEITH. Shut up, Harold!

LATTER. "To play the game" is the religion even of the Army.

KEITH. Exactly, but what is the game?

LATTER. What else can it be in this case?

KEITH. You're too puritanical, young John. You can't help it—line of country laid down for you. All drag-huntin'! What!

LATTER. [With concentration] Look here!

HAROLD. [Imitating the action of a man pulling at a horse's head] 'Come hup, I say, you hugly beast!'

KEITH. [To LATTER] You're not going to draw me, old chap. You don't see where you'd land us all. [He smokes calmly]

LATTER. How do you imagine vice takes its rise? From precisely this sort of thing of young Dunning's.

KEITH. From human nature, I should have thought, John. I admit that I don't like a fellow's leavin' a girl in the lurch; but I don't see the use in drawin' hard and fast rules. You only have to break 'em. Sir William and you would just tie Dunning and the girl up together, willy-nilly, to save appearances, and ten to one but there'll be the deuce to pay in a year's time. You can take a horse to the water, you can't make him drink.

LATTER. I entirely and absolutely disagree with you.

HAROLD. Good old John!

LATTER. At all events we know where your principles take you.

KEITH. [Rather dangerously] Where, please? [HAROLD turns up his eyes, and points downwards] Dry up, Harold!

LATTER. Did you ever hear the story of Faust?

KEITH. Now look here, John; with all due respect to your cloth, and all the politeness in the world, you may go to-blazes.

LATTER. Well, I must say, Ronny—of all the rude boors——[He turns towards the billiard-room.]

KEITH. Sorry I smashed the glass, old chap.

LATTER passes out. There comes a mingled sound through the opened door, of female voices, laughter, and the click of billiard balls, dipped of by the sudden closing of the door.

KEITH. [Impersonally] Deuced odd, the way a parson puts one's back up! Because you know I agree with him really; young Dunning ought to play the game; and I hope Sir William'll make him.

The butler JACKSON has entered from the door under the stairs followed by the keeper STUDDENHAM, a man between fifty and sixty, in a full-skirted coat with big pockets, cord breeches, and gaiters; he has a steady self respecting weathered face, with blue eyes and a short grey beard, which has obviously once been red.

KEITH. Hullo! Studdenham!

STUDDENHAM. [Touching his forehead] Evenin', Captain Keith.

JACKSON. Sir William still in the dining-room with Mr. Bill, sir?

HAROLD. [With a grimace] He is, Jackson.

JACKSON goes out to the dining-room.

KEITH. You've shot no pheasants yet, Studdenham?

STUDDENHAM. No, Sir. Only birds. We'll be doin' the spinneys and the home covert while you're down.

KEITH. I say, talkin' of spinneys——

He breaks off sharply, and goes out with HAROLD into the billiard-room. SIR WILLIAM enters from the dining-room, applying a gold toothpick to his front teeth.

SIR WILLIAM. Ah! Studdenham. Bad business this, about young Dunning!

STUDDENHAM. Yes, Sir William.

SIR WILLIAM. He definitely refuses to marry her?

STUDDENHAM. He does that.

SIR WILLIAM. That won't do, you know. What reason does he give?

STUDDENHAM. Won't say other than that he don't want no more to do with her.

SIR WILLIAM. God bless me! That's not a reason. I can't have a keeper of mine playing fast and loose in the village like this. [Turning to LADY CHESHIRE, who has come in from the billiard-room] That affair of young Dunning's, my dear.

LADY CHESHIRE. Oh! Yes! I'm so sorry, Studdenham. The poor girl!

STUDDENHAM. [Respectfully] Fancy he's got a feeling she's not his equal, now, my lady.

LADY CHESHIRE. [To herself] Yes, I suppose he has made her his superior.

SIR WILLIAM. What? Eh! Quite! Quite! I was just telling Studdenham the fellow must set the matter straight. We can't have open scandals in the village. If he wants to keep his place he must marry her at once.

LADY CHESHIRE. [To her husband in a low voice] Is it right to force them? Do you know what the girl wishes, Studdenham?

STUDDENHAM. Shows a spirit, my lady—says she'll have him—willin' or not.

LADY CHESHIRE. A spirit? I see. If they marry like that they're sure to be miserable.

SIR WILLIAM. What! Doesn't follow at all. Besides, my dear, you ought to know by this time, there's an unwritten law in these matters. They're perfectly well aware that when there are consequences, they have to take them.

STUDDENHAM. Some o' these young people, my lady, they don't put two and two together no more than an old cock pheasant.

SIR WILLIAM. I'll give him till to-morrow. If he remains obstinate, he'll have to go; he'll get no character, Studdenham. Let him know what I've said. I like the fellow, he's a good keeper. I don't want to lose him. But this sort of thing I won't have. He must toe the mark or take himself off. Is he up here to-night?

STUDDENHAM. Hangin' partridges, Sir William. Will you have him in?

SIR WILLIAM. [Hesitating] Yes—yes. I'll see him.

STUDDENHAM. Good-night to you, my lady.

LADY CHESHIRE. Freda's not looking well, Studdenham.

STUDDENHAM. She's a bit pernickitty with her food, that's where it is.

LADY CHESHIRE. I must try and make her eat.

SIR WILLIAM. Oh! Studdenham. We'll shoot the home covert first. What did we get last year?

STUDDENHAM. [Producing the game-book; but without reference to it] Two hundred and fifty-three pheasants, eleven hares, fifty-two rabbits, three woodcock, sundry.

SIR WILLIAM. Sundry? Didn't include a fox did it? [Gravely] I was seriously upset this morning at Warnham's spinney——

SUDDENHAM. [Very gravely] You don't say, Sir William; that four-year-old he
    du look a handful!

SIR WILLIAM. [With a sharp look] You know well enough what I mean.

STUDDENHAM. [Unmoved] Shall I send young Dunning, Sir William?

SIR WILLIAM gives a short, sharp nod, and STUDDENHAM retires by the
door under the stairs.

SIR WILLIAM. Old fox!

LADY CHESHIRE. Don't be too hard on Dunning. He's very young.

SIR WILLIAM. [Patting her arm] My dear, you don't understand young fellows,
    how should you?

LADY CHESHIRE. [With her faint irony] A husband and two sons not count-
    ing. [Then as the door under the stairs is opened] Bill,
    now do——

SIR WILLIAM. I'll be gentle with him. [Sharply] Come in!

LADY CHESHIRE retires to the billiard-room. She gives a look back and a half
smile at young DUNNING, a fair young man dressed in broom cords and leg-
gings, and holding his cap in his hand; then goes out.

SIR WILLIAM. Evenin', Dunning.

DUNNING. [Twisting his cap] Evenin', Sir William.

SIR WILLIAM. Studdenham's told you what I want to see you about?

DUNNING. Yes, Sir.

SIR WILLIAM. The thing's in your hands. Take it or leave it. I don't put pres-
    sure on you. I simply won't have this sort of thing on my estate.

DUNNING. I'd like to say, Sir William, that she [He stops].

SIR WILLIAM. Yes, I daresay-Six of one and half a dozen of the other. Can't go into that.

DUNNING. No, Sir William.

SIR WILLIAM. I'm quite mild with you. This is your first place. If you leave here you'll get no character.

DUNNING. I never meant any harm, sir.

SIR WILLIAM. My good fellow, you know the custom of the country.

DUNNING. Yes, Sir William, but——

SIR WILLIAM. You should have looked before you leaped. I'm not forcing you. If you refuse you must go, that's all.

DUNNING. Yes. Sir William.

SIR WILLIAM. Well, now go along and take a day to think it over.

BILL, who has sauntered moody from the diningroom, stands by the stairs listening. Catching sight of him, DUNNING raises his hand to his forelock.

DUNNING. Very good, Sir William. [He turns, fumbles, and turns again] My old mother's dependent on me——

SIR WILLIAM. Now, Dunning, I've no more to say. [Dunning goes sadly away under the stairs.]

SIR WILLIAM. [Following] And look here! Just understand this [He too goes out....]

BILL, lighting a cigarette, has approached the writing-table. He looks very glum. The billiard-room door is flung open. MABEL LANFARNE appears, and makes him a little curtsey.

MABEL. Against my will I am bidden to bring you in to pool.

BILL. Sorry! I've got letters.

MABEL. You seem to have become very conscientious.

BILL. Oh! I don't know.

MABEL. Do you remember the last day of the covert shooting?

BITS. I do.

MABEL. [Suddenly] What a pretty girl Freda Studdenham's grown!

BILL. Has she?

MABEL. "She walks in beauty."

BILL. Really? Hadn't noticed.

MABEL. Have you been taking lessons in conversation?

BILL. Don't think so.

MABEL. Oh! [There is a silence] Mr. Cheshire!

BILL. Miss Lanfarne!

MABEL. What's the matter with you? Aren't you rather queer, considering that I don't bite, and was rather a pal!

BILL. [Stolidly] I'm sorry.

Then seeing that his mother has came in from the billiard-room, he sits down at the writing-table.

LADY CHESHIRE. Mabel, dear, do take my cue. Won't you play too, Bill, and try and stop Ronny, he's too terrible?

BILL. Thanks. I've got these letters.

MABEL taking the cue passes back into the billiard-room, whence comes out the sound of talk and laughter.

LADY CHESHIRE. [Going over and standing behind her son's chair] Anything wrong, darling?

BILL. Nothing, thanks. [Suddenly] I say, I wish you hadn't asked that girl here.

LADY CHESHIRE. Mabel! Why? She's wanted for rehearsals. I thought you got on so well with her last Christmas.

BILL. [With a sort of sullen exasperation.] A year ago.

LADY CHESHIRE. The girls like her, so does your father; personally I must say I think she's rather nice and Irish.

BILL. She's all right, I daresay.

He looks round as if to show his mother that he wishes to be left alone. But LADY CHESHIRE, having seen that he is about to look at her, is not looking at him.

LADY CHESHIRE. I'm afraid your father's been talking to you, Bill.

BILL. He has.

LADY CHESHIRE. Debts? Do try and make allowances. [With a faint smile] Of course he is a little——

BILL. He is.

LADY CHESHIRE. I wish I could——

BILL. Oh, Lord! Don't you get mixed up in it!

LADY CHESHIRE. It seems almost a pity that you told him.

BILL. He wrote and asked me point blank what I owed.

LADY CHESHIRE. Oh! [Forcing herself to speak in a casual voice] I happen to have a little money, Bill—I think it would be simpler if——

BILL. Now look here, mother, you've tried that before. I can't help spending money, I never shall be able, unless I go to the Colonies, or something of the kind.

LADY CHESHIRE. Don't talk like that, dear!

BILL. I would, for two straws!

LADY CHESHIRE. It's only because your father thinks such a lot of the place, and the name, and your career. The Cheshires are all like that. They've been here so long; they're all—root.

BILL. Deuced funny business my career will be, I expect!

LADY CHESHIRE. [Fluttering, but restraining herself lest he should see] But, Bill, why must you spend more than your allowance?

BILL. Why—anything? I didn't make myself.

LADY CHESHIRE. I'm afraid we did that. It was inconsiderate, perhaps.

BILL. Yes, you'd better have left me out.

LADY CHESHIRE. But why are you so—Only a little fuss about money!

BILL. Ye-es.

LADY CHESHIRE. You're not keeping anything from me, are you?

BILL. [Facing her] No. [He then turns very deliberately to the writing things, and takes up a pen] I must write these letters, please.

LADY CHESHIRE. Bill, if there's any real trouble, you will tell me, won't you?

BILL. There's nothing whatever.

He suddenly gets up and walks about. LADY CHESHIRE, too, moves over to the fireplace, and after an uneasy look at him, turns to the fire. Then, as if trying to switch of his mood, she changes the subject abruptly.

LADY CHESHIRE. Isn't it a pity about young Dunning? I'm so sorry for Rose Taylor.

There is a silence. Stealthily under the staircase FREDA has entered, and seeing only BILL, advances to speak to him.

BILL. [Suddenly] Oh! well,—you can't help these things in the country.

As he speaks, FREDA stops dead, perceiving that he is not alone; BILL, too, catching sight of her, starts.

LADY CHESHIRE. [Still speaking to the fire] It seems dreadful to force him. I do so believe in people doing things of their own accord. [Then seeing FREDA standing so uncertainly by the stairs] Do you want me, Freda?

FREDA. Only your cloak, my lady. Shall I—begin it?

At this moment SIR WILLIAM enters from the drawing-room.

LADY CHESHIRE. Yes, yes.

SIR WILLI AM. [to the billiard-room] We'll come directly, my dear.

FREDA, with a look at BILL, has gone back whence she came; and LADY CHESHIRE goes reluctantly away into the billiard-room.

SIR WILLIAM. I shall give young Dunning short shrift. [He moves over to the fireplace and divides hip coat-tails] Now, about you, Bill! I don't want to bully you the moment you come down, but you know, this can't go on. I've paid your debts twice. Shan't pay them this time unless I see a disposition to change your mode of life. [A pause] You get your extravagance from your mother. She's very queer—[A pause]—All the Winterleighs are like that about money....

BILL. Mother's particularly generous, if that's what you mean.

SIR WILLIAM. [Drily] We will put it that way. [A pause] At the present moment you owe, as I understand it, eleven hundred pounds.

BILL. About that.

SIR WILLIAM. Mere flea-bite. [A pause] I've a proposition to make.

BILL. Won't it do to-morrow, sir?

SIR WILLIAM. "To-morrow" appears to be your motto in life.

BILL. Thanks!

SIR WILLIAM. I'm anxious to change it to-day. [BILL looks at him in silence] It's time you took your position seriously, instead of hanging about town, racing, and playing polo, and what not.

BILL. Go ahead!

At something dangerous in his voice, SIR WILLIAM modifies his attitude.

SIR, WILLIAM. The proposition's very simple. I can't suppose anything so rational and to your advantage will appeal to you, but [drily] I mention it. Marry a nice girl, settle down, and stand for the division; you can have the Dower House and fifteen hundred a year, and I'll pay your debts into the bargain. If you're elected I'll make it two thousand. Plenty of time to work up the constituency before we kick out these infernal Rads. Carpetbagger against you; if you go hard at it in the summer, it'll be odd if you don't manage to get in your three days a week, next season. You can take Rocketer and that four-year-old—he's well up to your weight, fully eight and a half inches of bone. You'll only want one other. And if Miss—if your wife means to hunt——

BILL. You've chosen my wife, then?

SIR WILLIAM. [With a quick look] I imagine, you've some girl in your mind.

BILL. Ah!

SIR WILLIAM: Used not to be unnatural at your age. I married your mother at twenty-eight. Here you are, eldest son of a family that stands for something. The more I see of the times the more I'm convinced that everybody who is anybody has got to buckle to, and save the landmarks left. Unless we're true to our caste, and prepared to work for it, the landed classes are going to go under to this infernal democratic spirit in the air. The outlook's very serious. We're threatened in a hundred ways. If you mean business, you'll want a wife. When I came into the property I should have been lost without your mother.

BILL. I thought this was coming.

SIR WILLIAM. [With a certain geniality] My dear fellow, I don't want to put a pistol to your head. You've had a slack rein so far. I've never objected to your sowing a few wild oats-so long as you- -er— [Unseen by SIR WILLIAM, BILL makes a sudden movement] Short of that—at all events, I've not inquired into your affairs. I can only judge by the—er—pecuniary evidence you've been good enough to afford me from time to time. I imagine you've lived like a good many young men in your position—I'm not blaming you, but there's a time for all things.

BILL. Why don't you say outright that you want me to marry Mabel Lanfarne?

SITS WILLIAM. Well, I do. Girl's a nice one. Good family—got a little money—rides well. Isn't she good-looking enough for you, or what?

BILL. Quite, thanks.

SIR WILLIAM. I understood from your mother that you and she were on good terms.

BILL. Please don't drag mother into it.

SIR WILLIAM. [With dangerous politeness] Perhaps you'll be good enough to state your objections.

BILL. Must we go on with this?

SIR WILLIAM. I've never asked you to do anything for me before; I expect you to pay attention now. I've no wish to dragoon you into this particular marriage. If you don't care for Miss Lanfarne, marry a girl you're fond of.

BILL. I refuse.

SIR WILLIAM. In that case you know what to look out for. [With a sudden rush of choler] You young.... [He checks himself and stands glaring at BILL, who glares back at him] This means, I suppose, that you've got some entanglement or other.

BILL. Suppose what you like, sir.

SITS WILLIAM. I warn you, if you play the blackguard——

BILL. You can't force me like young Dunning.

Hearing the raised voices LADY CHESHIRE has come back from the billiard-room.

LADY CHESHIRE. [Closing the door] What is it?

SIR WILLIAM. You deliberately refuse! Go away, Dorothy.

LADY CHESHIRE. [Resolutely] I haven't seen Bill for two months.

SIR WILLIAM. What! [Hesitating] Well—we must talk it over again.

LADY CHESHIRE. Come to the billiard-room, both of you! Bill, do finish
                     those letters!

With a deft movement she draws SIR WILLIAM toward the billiard-room, and
glances back at BILL before going out, but he has turned to the writing-table.
When the door is closed, BILL looks into the drawing-room, them opens the
door under the stairs; and backing away towards the writing-table, sits down
there, and takes up a pen. FREDA who has evidently been waiting, comes in and
stands by the table.

BILL. I say, this is dangerous, you know.

FREDA. Yes—but I must.

BILL. Well, then—[With natural recklessness] Aren't you going to kiss me?

Without moving she looks at him with a sort of miserable inquiry.

BILL. Do you know you haven't seen me for eight weeks?

FREDA. Quite—long enough—for you to have forgotten.

BILL. Forgotten! I don't forget people so soon.

FREDA. No?

BILL. What's the matter with you, Freda?

FREDA. [After a long look] It'll never be as it was.

BILL. [Jumping up] How d'you mean?

FREDA. I've got something for you. [She takes a diamond ring out of her dress and holds it out to him] I've not worn it since Cromer.

BILL. Now, look here

FREDA. I've had my holiday; I shan't get another in a hurry.

BILL. Freda!

FREDA. You'll be glad to be free. That fortnight's all you really loved me in.

BILL. [Putting his hands on her arms] I swear——

FREDA. [Between her teeth] Miss Lanfarne need never know about me.

BILL. So that's it! I've told you a dozen times—nothing's changed. [FREDA looks at him and smiles.]

BILL. Oh! very well! If you will make yourself miserable.

FREDA. Everybody will be pleased.

BILL. At what?

FREDA. When you marry her.

BILL. This is too bad.

FREDA. It's what always happens—even when it's not a—gentleman.

BILL. That's enough.

FREDA. But I'm not like that girl down in the village. You needn't be afraid I'll
say anything when—it comes. That's what I had to tell you.

BILL. What!

FREDA. I can keep a secret.

BILL. Do you mean this? [She bows her head.]

BILL. Good God!

FREDA. Father brought me up not to whine. Like the puppies when they hold
them up by their tails. [With a sudden break in her voice] Oh! Bill!

BILL. [With his head down, seizing her hands] Freda! [He breaks away from
her towards the fire] Good God!

She stands looking at him, then quietly slips away by the door under the staircase.
BILL turns to speak to her, and sees that she has gone. He walks up to the fireplace, and grips the mantelpiece.

BILL. By Jove! This is——!

The curtain falls.

ACT II

The scene is LADY CHESHIRE's morning room, at ten o'clock on the following day. It is a pretty room, with white panelled walls; and chrysanthemums and carmine lilies in bowls. A large bow window overlooks the park under a sou'-westerly sky. A piano stands open; a fire is burning; and the morning's correspondence is scattered on a writing-table. Doors opposite each other lead to the maid's workroom, and to a corridor. LADY CHESHIRE is standing in the middle of the room, looking at an opera cloak, which FREDA is holding out.

LADY CHESHIRE. Well, Freda, suppose you just give it up!

FREDA. I don't like to be beaten.

LADY CHESHIRE. You're not to worry over your work. And by the way, I promised your father to make you eat more. [FREDA smiles.]

LADY CHESHIRE. It's all very well to smile. You want bracing up. Now don't be naughty. I shall give you a tonic. And I think you had better put that cloak away.

FREDA. I'd rather have one more try, my lady.

LADY CHESHIRE. [Sitting doom at her writing-table] Very well.

FREDA goes out into her workroom, as JACKSON comes in from the corridor.

JACKSON. Excuse me, my lady. There's a young woman from the village, says
        you wanted to see her.

LADY CHESHIRE. Rose Taylor? Ask her to come in. Oh! and Jackson the car
        for the meet please at half-past ten.

JACKSON having bowed and withdrawn, LADY CHESHIRE rises with worked
signs of nervousness, which she has only just suppressed, when ROSE TAYLOR,
a stolid country girl, comes in and stands waiting by the door.

LADY CHESHIRE. Well, Rose. Do come in! [ROSE advances perhaps a cou-
        ple of steps.]

LADY CHESHIRE. I just wondered whether you'd like to ask my advice. Your
        engagement with Dunning's broken off, isn't it?

ROSE. Yes—but I've told him he's got to marry me.

LADY CHESHIRE. I see! And you think that'll be the wisest thing?

ROSE. [Stolidly] I don't know, my lady. He's got to.

LADY CHESHIRE. I do hope you're a little fond of him still.

ROSE. I'm not. He don't deserve it.

LADY CHESHIRE: And—do you think he's quite lost his affection for you?

ROSE. I suppose so, else he wouldn't treat me as he's done. He's after that—
        that—He didn't ought to treat me as if I was dead.

LADY CHESHIRE. No, no—of course. But you will think it all well over, won't
        you?

ROSE. I've a—got nothing to think over, except what I know of.

LADY CHESHIRE. But for you both t0 marry in that spirit! You know it's for
        life, Rose. [Looking into her face] I'm always ready to
        help you.

ROSE. [Dropping a very slight curtsey] Thank you, my lady, but I think he ought to marry me. I've told him he ought.

LADY CHESHIRE. [Sighing] Well, that's all I wanted to say. It's a question of your self-respect; I can't give you any real advice. But just remember that if you want a friend——

ROSE. [With a gulp] I'm not so 'ard, really. I only want him to do what's right by me.

LADY CHESHIRE. [With a little lift of her eyebrow—gently] Yes, yes—I see.

ROSE. [Glancing back at the door] I don't like meeting the servants.

LADY CHESHIRE. Come along, I'll take you out another way. [As they reach the door, DOT comes in.]

DOT. [With a glance at ROSE] Can we have this room for the mouldy rehearsal, Mother?

LADY CHESHIRE. Yes, dear, you can air it here.

Holding the door open for ROSE she follows her out. And DOT, with a book of "Caste" in her hand, arranges the room according to a diagram.

DOT. Chair—chair—table—chair—Dash! Table—piano—fire—window! [Producing a pocket comb] Comb for Eccles. Cradle?—Cradle—[She viciously dumps a waste-paper basket down, and drops a footstool into it] Brat! [Then reading from the book gloomily] "Enter Eccles breathless. Esther and Polly rise-Esther puts on lid of bandbox." Bandbox!

Searching for something to represent a bandbox, she opens the workroom door.

DOT. Freda?

FREDA comes in.

DOT. I say, Freda. Anything the matter? You seem awfully down. [FREDA does not answer.]

DOT. You haven't looked anything of a lollipop lately.

FREDA. I'm quite all right, thank you, Miss Dot.

DOT. Has Mother been givin' you a tonic?

FREDA. [Smiling a little] Not yet.

DOT. That doesn't account for it then. [With a sudden warm impulse] What is it, Freda?

FREDA. Nothing.

DOT. [Switching of on a different line of thought] Are you very busy this morning?

FREDA. Only this cloak for my lady.

DOT. Oh! that can wait. I may have to get you in to prompt, if I can't keep 'em straight. [Gloomily] They stray so. Would you mind?

FREDA. [Stolidly] I shall be very glad, Miss Dot.

DOT. [Eyeing her dubiously] All right. Let's see—what did I want?

JOAN has come in.

JOAN. Look here, Dot; about the baby in this scene. I'm sure I ought to make more of it.

DOT. Romantic little beast! [She plucks the footstool out by one ear, and holds it forth] Let's see you try!

JOAN. [Recoiling] But, Dot, what are we really going to have for the baby? I can't rehearse with that thing. Can't you suggest something, Freda?

FREDA. Borrow a real one, Miss Joan. There are some that don't count much.

JOAN. Freda, how horrible!

DOT. [Dropping the footstool back into the basket] You'll just put up with what you're given.

Then as CHRISTINE and MABEL LANFARNE Come in, FREDA turns abruptly and goes out.

DOT. Buck up! Where are Bill and Harold? [To JOAN] Go and find them, mouse-cat.

But BILL and HAROLD, followed by LATTER, are already in the doorway. They come in, and LATTER, stumbling over the waste-paper basket, takes it up to improve its position.

DOT. Drop that cradle, John! [As he picks the footstool out of it] Leave the baby in! Now then! Bill, you enter there! [She points to the workroom door where BILL and MABEL range themselves close to the piano; while HAROLD goes to the window] John! get off the stage! Now then, "Eccles enters breathless, Esther and Polly rise." Wait a minute. I know now. [She opens the workroom door] Freda, I wanted a bandbox.

HAROLD. [Cheerfully] I hate beginning to rehearse, you know, you feel such a fool.

DOT. [With her bandbox-gloomily] You'll feel more of a fool when you have begun. [To BILL, who is staring into the workroom] Shut the door. Now. [BILL shuts the door.]

LATTER. [Advancing] Look here! I want to clear up a point of psychology before we start.

DOT. Good Lord!

LATTER. When I bring in the milk—ought I to bring it in seriously— as if I were accustomed—I mean, I maintain that if I'm——

JOAN. Oh! John, but I don't think it's meant that you should——

DOT. Shut up! Go back, John! Blow the milk! Begin, begin, begin! Bill!

LATTER. [Turning round and again advancing] But I think you underrate the importance of my entrance altogether.

MABEL. Oh! no, Mr. Latter!

LATTER. I don't in the least want to destroy the balance of the scene, but I do want to be clear about the spirit. What is the spirit?

DOT. [With gloom] Rollicking!

LATTER. Well, I don't think so. We shall run a great risk, with this play, if we rollick.

DOT. Shall we? Now look here——!

MABEL. [Softly to BILL] Mr. Cheshire!

BILL. [Desperately] Let's get on!

DOT. [Waving LATTER back] Begin, begin! At last! [But JACKSON has came in.]

JACKSON. [To CHRISTINE] Studdenham says, Mm, if the young ladies want to see the spaniel pups, he's brought 'em round.

JOAN. [Starting up] Oh! come 'on, John! [She flies towards the door, followed by LATTER.]

DOT. [Gesticulating with her book] Stop! You—— [CHRISTINE and HAROLD also rush past.]

DOT. [Despairingly] First pick! [Tearing her hair] Pigs! Devils! [She rushes after them. BILL and MABEL are left alone.]

MABEL. [Mockingly] And don't you want one of the spaniel pups?

BILL. [Painfully reserved and sullen, and conscious of the workroom door] Can't keep a dog in town. You can have one, if you like. The breeding's all right.

MABEL. Sixth Pick?

BILL. The girls'll give you one of theirs. They only fancy they want 'em.

Mann. [Moving nearer to him, with her hands clasped behind her] You know, you remind me awfully of your father. Except that you're not nearly so polite. I don't understand you English-lords of the soil. The way you have of disposing of your females. [With a sudden change of voice] What was the matter with you last night? [Softly] Won't you tell me?

BILL. Nothing to tell.

MABEL. Ah! no, Mr. Bill.

BILL. [Almost succumbing to her voice—then sullenly] Worried, I suppose.

MABEL. [Returning to her mocking] Quite got over it?

BILL. Don't chaff me, please.

MABEL. You really are rather formidable.

BILL. Thanks.

MABEL, But, you know, I love to cross a field where there's a bull.

BILL. Really! Very interesting.

MABEL. The way of their only seeing one thing at a time. [She moves back as he advances] And overturning people on the journey.

BILL. Hadn't you better be a little careful?

MABEL. And never to see the hedge until they're stuck in it. And then straight from that hedge into the opposite one.

BILL. [Savagely] What makes you bait me this morning of all mornings?

MABEL. The beautiful morning! [Suddenly] It must be dull for poor Freda working in there with all this fun going on?

BILL. [Glancing at the door] Fun you call it?

MABEL, To go back to you,—now—Mr. Cheshire.

BILL. No.

MABEL,   You always make me feel so Irish. Is it because you're so English, d'you
            think? Ah! I can see him moving his ears. Now he's pawing the
            ground—He's started!

BILL. Miss Lanfarne!

MABEL.   [Still backing away from him, and drawing him on with her eyes and
            smile] You can't help coming after me! [Then with a sudden change
            to a sort of sierra gravity] Can you? You'll feel that when I've gone.

They stand quite still, looking into each other's eyes and FREDA, who has
opened the door of the workroom stares at them.

MABEL. [Seeing her] Here's the stile. Adieu, Monsieur le taureau!

She puts her hand behind her, opens the door, and slips through, leaving BILL to
turn, following the direction of her eyes, and see FREDA with the cloak still in
her hand.

BILL. [Slowly walking towards her] I haven't slept all night.

FREDA. No?

BILL. Have you been thinking it over? [FREDA gives a bitter little laugh.]

BILL. Don't! We must make a plan. I'll get you away. I won't let you suffer. I
          swear I won't.

FREDA. That will be clever.

BILL. I wish to Heaven my affairs weren't in such a mess.

FREDA. I shall be—all—right, thank you.

BILL. You must think me a blackguard. [She shakes her head] Abuse me—say
          something! Don't look like that!

FREDA. Were you ever really fond of me?

BILL. Of course I was, I am now. Give me your hands.

She looks at him, then drags her hands from his, and covers her face.

BILL. [Clenching his fists] Look here! I'll prove it. [Then as she suddenly flings her arms round his neck and clings to him] There, there!

There is a click of a door handle. They start away from each other, and see LADY CHESHIRE regarding them.

LADY CHESHIRE. [Without irony] I beg your pardon.

She makes as if to withdraw from an unwarranted intrusion, but suddenly turning, stands, with lips pressed together, waiting.

LADY CHESHIRE. Yes?

FREDA has muffled her face. But BILL turns and confronts his mother.

BILL. Don't say anything against her!

LADY CHESHIRE. [Tries to speak to him and fails—then to FREDA] Please—go!

BILL. [Taking FREDA's arm] No.

LADY CHESHIRE, after a moment's hesitation, herself moves towards the door.

BILL. Stop, mother!

LADY CHESHIRE. I think perhaps not.

BILL. [Looking at FREDA, who is cowering as though from a blow] It's a d—— d shame!

LADY CHESHIRE. It is.

BILL. [With sudden resolution] It's not as you think. I'm engaged to be married to her.

[FREDA gives him a wild stare, and turns away.]

LADY CHESHIRE. [Looking from one to the other] I don't think I—quite—understand.

BILL. [With the brutality of his mortification] What I said was plain enough.

LADY CHESHIRE. Bill!

BILL. I tell you I am going to marry her.

LADY CHESHIRE. [To FREDA] Is that true?

[FREDA gulps and remains silent.]

BILL. If you want to say anything, say it to me, mother.

LADY CHESHIRE. [Gripping the edge of a little table] Give me a chair, please. [BILL gives her a chair.]

LADY CHESHIRE. [To FREDA] Please sit down too.

FREDA sits on the piano stool, still turning her face away.

LADY CHESHIRE. [Fixing her eyes on FREDA] Now!

BILL. I fell in love with her. And she with me.

LADY CHESHIRE. When?

BILL. In the summer.

LADY CHESHIRE. Ah!

BILL. It wasn't her fault.

LADY CHESHIRE. No?

BILL. [With a sort of menace] Mother!

LADY CHESHIRE. Forgive me, I am not quite used to the idea. You say that you—are engaged?

BILL. Yes.

LADY CHESHIRE. The reasons against such an engagement have occurred to you, I suppose? [With a sudden change of tone] Bill! what does it mean?

BILL. If you think she's trapped me into this——

LADY CHESHIRE. I do not. Neither do I think she has been trapped. I think nothing. I understand nothing.

BILL. [Grimly] Good!

LADY CHESHIRE. How long has this-engagement lasted?

BILL. [After a silence] Two months.

LADY CHESHIRE. [Suddenly] This is-this is quite impossible.

BILL. You'll find it isn't.

LADY CHESHIRE. It's simple misery.

BILL. [Pointing to the workroom] Go and wait in there, Freda.

LADY CHESHIRE. [Quickly] And are you still in love with her?

FREDA, moving towards the workroom, smothers a sob.

BILL. Of course I am.

FREDA has gone, and as she goes, LADY CHESHIRE rises suddenly, forced by the intense feeling she has been keeping in hand.

LADY CHESHIRE. Bill! Oh, Bill! What does it all mean? [BILL, looking from side to aide, only shrugs his shoulders] You are not in love with her now. It's no good telling me you are.

BILL. I am.

LADY CHESHIRE. That's not exactly how you would speak if you were.

BILL. She's in love with me.

LADY CHESHIRE. [Bitterly] I suppose so.

BILL. I mean to see that nobody runs her down.

LADY CHESHIRE. [With difficulty] Bill! Am I a hard, or mean woman?

BILL. Mother!

LADY CHESHIRE. It's all your life—and—your father's—and—all of us. I want to understand—I must understand. Have you realised what an awful thins this would be for us all? It's quite impossible that it should go on.

BILL. I'm always in hot water with the Governor, as it is. She and I'll take good care not to be in the way.

LADY CHESHIRE. Tell me everything!

BILL. I have.

LADY CHESHIRE. I'm your mother, Bill.

BILL. What's the good of these questions?

LADY CHESHIRE. You won't give her away—I see!

BILL. I've told you all there is to tell. We're engaged, we shall be married quietly, and—and—go to Canada.

LADY CHESHIRE. If there weren't more than that to tell you'd be in love with her now.

BILL. I've told you that I am.

LADY CHESHIRE. You are not. [Almost fiercely] I know—I know there's more behind.

BILL. There—is—nothing.

LADY CHESHIRE. [Baffled, but unconvinced] Do you mean that your love for her has been just what it might have been for a lady?

BILL. [Bitterly] Why not?

LADY CHESHIRE. [With painful irony] It is not so as a rule.

BILL. Up to now I've never heard you or the girls say a word against Freda. This isn't the moment to begin, please.

LADY CHESHIRE. [Solemnly] All such marriages end in wretchedness. You haven't a taste or tradition in common. You don't know what marriage is. Day after day, year after year. It's no use being sentimental—for people brought up as we are to have different manners is worse than to have different souls. Besides, it's poverty. Your father will never forgive you, and I've practically nothing. What can you do? You have no profession. How are you going to stand it; with a woman who—? It's the little things.

BILL. I know all that, thanks.

LADY CHESHIRE. Nobody does till they've been through it. Marriage is hard enough when people are of the same class. [With a sudden movement towards him] Oh! my dear-before it's too late!

BILL. [After a struggle] It's no good.

LADY CHESHIRE. It's not fair to her. It can only end in her misery.

BILL. Leave that to me, please.

LADY CHESHIRE. [With an almost angry vehemence] Only the very finest can do such things. And you don't even know what trouble's like.

BILL. Drop it, please, mother.

LADY CHESHIRE. Bill, on your word of honour, are you acting of your own free will?

BILL. [Breaking away from her] I can't stand any more. [He goes out into the workroom.]

LADY CHESHIRE. What in God's name shall I do?

In her distress she walks up and doom the room, then goes to the workroom door, and opens it.

LADY CHESHIRE. Come in here, please, Freda.

After a seconds pause, FREDA, white and trembling, appears in the doorway, followed by BILL.

LADY CHESHIRE. No, Bill. I want to speak to her alone.

BILL, does not move.

LADY CHESHIRE. [Icily] I must ask you to leave us.

BILL hesitates; then shrugging his shoulders, he touches FREDA's arms, and goes back into the workroom, closing the door. There is silence.

LADY CHESHIRE. How did it come about?

FREDA. I don't know, my lady.

LADY CHESHIRE. For heaven's sake, child, don't call me that again, whatever happens. [She walks to the window, and speaks from there] I know well enough how love comes. I don't blame you. Don't cry. But, you see, it's my eldest son. [FREDA puts her hand to her breast] Yes, I know. Women always get the worst of these things. That's natural. But it's not only you is it? Does any one guess?

FREDA. No.

LADY CHESHIRE. Not even your father? [FREDA shakes her head] There's nothing more dreadful than for a woman to hang like a stone round a man's neck. How far has it gone? Tell me!

FREDA. I can't.

LADY CHESHIRE. Come!

FREDA. I—won't.

LADY CHESHIRE. [Smiling painfully]. Won't give him away? Both of you the
                         same. What's the use of that with me? Look at me! Wasn't
                         he with you when you went for your holiday this summer?

FREDA. He's—always—behaved—like—a—gentleman.

LADY CHESHIRE. Like a man you mean!

FREDA. It hasn't been his fault! I love him so.

LADY CHESHIRE turns abruptly, and begins to walk up and down the room.
                         Then stopping, she looks intently at FREDA.

LADY CHESHIRE. I don't know what to say to you. It's simple madness! It
                         can't, and shan't go on.

FREDA. [Sullenly] I know I'm not his equal, but I am—somebody.

LADY CHESHIRE. [Answering this first assertion of rights with a sudden stee-
                         liness] Does he love you now?

FREDA. That's not fair—it's not fair.

LADY CHESHIRE. If men are like gunpowder, Freda, women are not. If you've
                         lost him it's been your own fault.

FREDA. But he does love me, he must. It's only four months.

LADY CHESHIRE. [Looking down, and speaking rapidly] Listen to me. I love
                         my son, but I know him—I know all his kind of man. I've
                         lived with one for thirty years. I know the way their sens-
                         es work. When they want a thing they must have it, and
                         then—they're sorry.

FREDA. [Sullenly] He's not sorry.

LADY CHESHIRE. Is his love big enough to carry you both over everything?....
                         You know it isn't.

FREDA. If I were a lady, you wouldn't talk like that.

LADY CHESHIRE. If you were a lady there'd be no trouble before either of you. You'll make him hate you.

FREDA. I won't believe it. I could make him happy—out there.

LADY CHESHIRE. I don't want to be so odious as to say all the things you must know. I only ask you to try and put yourself in our position.

FREDA. Ah, yes!

LADY CHESHIRE. You ought to know me better than to think I'm purely selfish.

FREDA. Would you like to put yourself in my position?

LADY CHESHIRE. What!

FREDA. Yes. Just like Rose.

LADY CHESHIRE. [In a low, horror-stricken voice] Oh!

There is a dead silence, then going swiftly up to her, she looks straight into FREDA's eyes.

FREDA. [Meeting her gaze] Oh! Yes—it's the truth. [Then to Bill who has come in from the workroom, she gasps out] I never meant to tell.

BILL. Well, are you satisfied?

LADY CHESHIRE. [Below her breath] This is terrible!

BILL. The Governor had better know.

LADY CHESHIRE. Oh! no; not yet!

BILL. Waiting won't cure it!

The door from the corridor is thrown open; CHRISTINE and DOT run in with their copies of the play in their hands; seeing that something is wrong, they stand still. After a look at his mother, BILL turns abruptly, and goes back into the workroom. LADY CHESHIRE moves towards the window.

JOAN. [Following her sisters] The car's round. What's the matter?

DOT. Shut up!

SIR WILLIAM'S voice is heard from the corridor calling "Dorothy!" As LADY CHESHIRE, passing her handkerchief over her face, turns round, he enters. He is in full hunting dress: well-weathered pink, buckskins, and mahogany tops.

SIR WILLIAM. Just off, my dear. [To his daughters, genially] Rehearsin'? What! [He goes up to FREDA holding out his gloved right hand] Button that for me, Freda, would you? It's a bit stiff!

FREDA buttons the glove: LADY CHESHIRE arid the girls watching in hyp-
         notic silence.

SIR WILLIAM. Thank you! "Balmy as May"; scent ought to be first-rate. [To LADY CHESHIRE] Good-bye, my dear! Sampson's Gorse — best day of the whole year. [He pats JOAN on the shoulder] Wish you were cumin' out, Joan.

He goes out, leaving the door open, and as his footsteps and the chink of his spurs die away, FREDA turns and rushes into the workroom.

CHRISTINE. Mother! What——?

But LADY CHESHIRE waves the question aside, passes her daughter, and goes out into the corridor. The sound of a motor car is heard.

JOAN. [Running to the window] They've started—! Chris! What is it? Dot?

DOT. Bill, and her!

JOAN. But what?

DOT. [Gloomily] Heaven knows! Go away, you're not fit for this.

JOAN. [Aghast] I am fit.

DOT. I think not.

JOAN. Chris?

CHRISTINE. [In a hard voice] Mother ought to have told us.

JOAN. It can't be very awful. Freda's so good.

DOT. Call yourself in love, you milk-and-water-kitten!

CHRISTINE. It's horrible, not knowing anything! I wish Runny hadn't gone.

JOAN. Shall I fetch John?

DOT. John!

CHRISTINE. Perhaps Harold knows.

JOAN. He went out with Studdenham.

DOT. It's always like this, women kept in blinkers. Rose-leaves and humbug! That awful old man!

JOAN. Dot!

CHRISTINE. Don't talk of father like that!

DOT. Well, he is! And Bill will be just like him at fifty! Heaven help Freda, whatever she's done! I'd sooner be a private in a German regiment than a woman.

JOAN. Dot, you're awful.

DOT. You-mouse-hearted-linnet!

CHRISTINE. Don't talk that nonsense about women!

DOT. You're married and out of it; and Ronny's not one of these terrific John Bulls. [To JOAN who has opened the door] Looking for John? No good, my dear; lath and plaster.

JOAN. [From the door, in a frightened whisper] Here's Mabel!

DOT. Heavens, and the waters under the earth!

CHRISTINE. If we only knew!

MABEL comes in, the three girls are silent, with their eyes fixed on their books.

MABEL. The silent company.

DOT. [Looking straight at her] We're chucking it for to-day.

MABEL. What's the matter?

CHRISTINE. Oh! nothing.

DOT. Something's happened.

MABEL. Really! I am sorry. [Hesitating] Is it bad enough for me to go?

CHRISTINE. Oh! no, Mabel!

DOT. [Sardonically] I should think very likely.

While she is looking from face to face, BILL comes in from the workroom. He starts to walk across the room, but stops, and looks stolidly at the four girls.

BILL. Exactly! Fact of the matter is, Miss Lanfarne, I'm engaged to my mother's maid.

No one moves or speaks. Suddenly MABEL LANFARNE goes towards him, holding out her hand. BILL does not take her hand, but bows. Then after a swift glance at the girls' faces MABEL goes out into the corridor, and the three girls are left staring at their brother.

BILL. [Coolly] Thought you might like to know. [He, too, goes out into the corridor.]

CHRISTINE. Great heavens!

JOAN. How awful!

CHRISTINE. I never thought of anything as bad as that.

JOAN. Oh! Chris! Something must be done!

DOT. [Suddenly to herself] Ha! When Father went up to have his glove buttoned!

There is a sound, JACKSON has came in from the corridor.

JACKSON. [To Dot] If you please, Miss, Studdenham's brought up the other two pups. He's just outside. Will you kindly take a look at them, he says?

There is silence.

DOT. [Suddenly] We can't.

CHRISTINE. Not just now, Jackson.

JACKSON. Is Studdenham and the pups to wait, Mm?

DOT shakes her head violently. But STUDDENHAM is seen already standing in the doorway, with a spaniel puppy in either side-pocket. He comes in, and JACKSON stands waiting behind him.

STUDDENHAM. This fellow's the best, Miss DOT. [He protrudes the right-hand pocket] I was keeping him for my girl—a, proper greedy one—takes after his father.

The girls stare at him in silence.

DOT. [Hastily] Thanks, Studdenham, I see.

STUDDENHAM. I won't take 'em out in here. They're rather bold yet.

CHRISTINE. [Desperately] No, no, of course.

STUDDENHAM. Then you think you'd like him, Miss DOT? The other's got a white chest; she's a lady.

[He protrudes the left-hand pocket.]

DOT. Oh, yes! Studdenham; thanks, thanks awfully.

STUDDENHAM. Wonderful faithful creatures; follow you like a woman. You can't shake 'em off anyhow. [He protrudes the right-hand pocket] My girl, she'd set her heart on him, but she'll just have to do without.

DOT. [As though galvanised] Oh! no, I can't take it away from her.

STUDDENHAM. Bless you, she won't mind! That's settled, then. [He turns to the door. To the PUPPY] Ah! would you! Tryin' to wriggle out of it! Regular young limb! [He goes out, followed by JACKSON.]

CHRISTINE. How ghastly!

DOT. [Suddenly catching sight of the book in her hand] "Caste!" [She gives vent to a short sharp laugh.]

The curtain falls.

ACT III

It is five o'clock of the same day. The scene is the smoking-room, with walls of Leander red, covered by old steeplechase and hunting prints. Armchairs encircle a high ferulered hearth, in which a fire is burning. The curtains are not yet drawn across mullioned windows, but electric light is burning. There are two doors, leading, the one to the billiard- room, the other to a corridor. BILL is pacing up and doom; HAROLD, at the fireplace, stands looking at him with commiseration.

BILL. What's the time?

HAROLD. Nearly five. They won't be in yet, if that's any consolation. Always a
        tough meet—[softly] as the tiger said when he ate the man.

BILL. By Jove! You're the only person I can stand within a mile of me, Harold.

HAROLD. Old boy! Do you seriously think you're going to make it any better
        by marrying her?

[Bill shrugs his shoulders, still pacing the room.]

BILL. Look here! I'm not the sort that finds it easy to say things.

HAROLD. No, old man.

BILL. But I've got a kind of self-respect though you wouldn't think it!

HAROLD. My dear old chap!

BILL. This is about as low-down a thing as one could have done, I suppose—
one's own mother's maid; we've known her since she was so high. I see it
now that—I've got over the attack.

HAROLD. But, heavens! if you're no longer keen on her, Bill! Do apply your
reason, old boy.

There is silence; while BILL again paces up and dozen.

BILL. If you think I care two straws about the morality of the thing.

HAROLD. Oh! my dear old man! Of course not!

BILL. It's simply that I shall feel such a d——-d skunk, if I leave her in the lurch,
with everybody knowing. Try it yourself; you'd soon see!

HAROLD. Poor old chap!

BILL. It's not as if she'd tried to force me into it. And she's a soft little thing.
Why I ever made such a sickening ass of myself, I can't think. I never
meant—

HAROLD. No, I know! But, don't do anything rash, Bill; keep your head, old
man!

BILL. I don't see what loss I should be, if I did clear out of the country. [The
sound of cannoning billiard balls is heard] Who's that knocking the balls
about?

HAROLD. John, I expect. [The sound ceases.]

BILL. He's coming in here. Can't stand that!

As LATTER appears from the billiard-room, he goes hurriedly out.

LATTER. Was that Bill?

HAROLD. Yes.

LATTER. Well?

HAROLD. [Pacing up and down in his turn] Rat in a cage is a fool to him. This
          is the sort of thing you read of in books, John! What price your
          argument with Runny now? Well, it's not too late for you luckily.

LATTER. What do you mean?

HAROLD. You needn't connect yourself with this eccentric family!

LATTER. I'm not a bounder, Harold.

HAROLD. Good!

LATTER. It's terrible for your sisters.

HAROLD. Deuced lucky we haven't a lot of people staying here! Poor mother!
          John, I feel awfully bad about this. If something isn't done, pretty
          mess I shall be in.

LATTER. How?

HAROLD. There's no entail. If the Governor cuts Bill off, it'll all come to me.

LATTER. Oh!

HAROLD. Poor old Bill! I say, the play! Nemesis! What? Moral! Caste don't
          matter. Got us fairly on the hop.

LATTER. It's too bad of Bill. It really is. He's behaved disgracefully.

HAROLD. [Warningly] Well! There are thousands of fellows who'd never
          dream of sticking to the girl, considering what it means.

LATTER. Perfectly disgusting!

HAROLD. Hang you, John! Haven't you any human sympathy? Don't you
          know how these things come about? It's like a spark in a straw-yard.

LATTER.   One doesn't take lighted pipes into strawyards unless one's an idiot, or worse.

HAROLD.   H'm! [With a grin] You're not allowed tobacco.   In the good old days no one would h've thought anything of this.   My great-grand-father——

LATTER.   Spare me your great-grandfather.

HAROLD.   I could tell you of at least a dozen men I know who've been through this same business, and got off scot-free; and now because Bill's going to play the game, it'll smash him up.

LATTER.   Why didn't he play the game at the beginning?

HAROLD.   I can't stand your sort, John.   When a thing like this happens, all you can do is to cry out: Why didn't he—?   Why didn't she—?   What's to be done—that's the point!

LATTER.   Of course he'll have to——.

HAROLD.   Ha!

LATTER.   What do you mean by—that?

HAROLD.   Look here, John!   You feel in your bones that a marriage'll be hope-less, just as I do, knowing Bill and the girl and everything!   Now don't you?

LATTER.   The whole thing is—is most unfortunate.

HAROLD.   By Jove!   I should think it was!

As he speaks CHRISTINE and KEITH Come in from the billiard-room. He is still in splashed hunting clothes, and looks exceptionally weathered, thin-lipped, reticent.   He lights a cigarette and sinks into an armchair.   Behind them DOT and JOAN have come stealing in.

CHRISTINE.   I've told Ronny.

JOAN. This waiting for father to be told is awful.

HAROLD. [To KEITH] Where did you leave the old man?

KEITH. Clackenham. He'll be home in ten minutes.

DOT. Mabel's going. [They all stir, as if at fresh consciousness of discomfiture]. She walked into Gracely and sent herself a telegram.

HAROLD. Phew!

DOT. And we shall say good-bye, as if nothing had happened.

HAROLD. It's up to you, Ronny.

KEITH, looking at JOAN, slowly emits smoke; and LATTER passing his arm through JOAN'S, draws her away with him into the billiard-room.

KEITH. Dot?

DOT. I'm not a squeamy squirrel.

KEITH. Anybody seen the girl since?

DOT. Yes.

HAROLD. Well?

DOT. She's just sitting there.

CHRISTINE. [In a hard voice] As we're all doing.

DOT. She's so soft, that's what's so horrible. If one could only feel——!

KEITH. She's got to face the music like the rest of us.

DOT. Music! Squeaks! Ugh! The whole thing's like a concertina, and some one jigging it!

They all turn as the door opens, and a FOOTMAN enters with a tray of whiskey, gin, lemons, and soda water. In dead silence the FOOTMAN puts the tray down.

HAROLD. [Forcing his voice] Did you get a run, Ronny? [As KEITH nods]
    What point?

KEITH. Eight mile.

FOOTMAN. Will you take tea, sir?

KEITH. No, thanks, Charles!

In dead silence again the FOOTMAN goes out, and they all look after him.

HAROLD. [Below his breath] Good Gad! That's a squeeze of it!

KEITH. What's our line of country to be?

CHRISTINE. All depends on father.

KEITH. Sir William's between the devil and the deep sea, as it strikes me.

CHRISTINE. He'll simply forbid it utterly, of course.

KEITH. H'm! Hard case! Man who reads family prayers, and lessons on Sunday
    forbids son to——

CHRISTINE, Ronny!

KEITH. Great Scott! I'm not saying Bill ought to marry her. She's got to stand
    the racket. But your Dad will have a tough job to take up that posi-
    tion.

DOT. Awfully funny!

CHRISTINE. What on earth d'you mean, Dot?

DOT. Morality in one eye, and your title in the other!

CHRISTINE. Rubbish!

HAROLD. You're all reckoning without your Bill.

KEITH. Ye-es. Sir William can cut him off; no mortal power can help the title going down, if Bill chooses to be such a—— [He draws in his breath with a sharp hiss.]

HAROLD. I won't take what Bill ought to have; nor would any of you girls, I should think.

CHRISTINE and DOT. Of course not!

KEITH. [Patting his wife's arm] Hardly the point, is it?

DOT. If it wasn't for mother! Freda's just as much of a lady as most girls. Why shouldn't he marry her, and go to Canada? It's what he's really fit for.

HAROLD. Steady on, Dot!

DOT. Well, imagine him in Parliament! That's what he'll come to, if he stays here—jolly for the country!

CHRISTINE. Don't be cynical! We must find a way of stopping Bill.

DOT. Me cynical!

CHRISTINE. Let's go and beg him, Ronny!

KEITH. No earthly! The only hope is in the girl.

DOT. She hasn't the stuff in her!

HAROLD. I say! What price young Dunning! Right about face! Poor old Dad!

CHRISTINE. It's past joking, Harold!

DOT. [Gloomily] Old Studdenham's better than most relations by marriage!

KEITH. Thanks!

CHRISTINE. It's ridiculous—monstrous! It's fantastic!

HAROLD. [Holding up his hand] There's his horse going round. He's in!

They turn from listening to the sound, to see LADY CHESHIRE coming from the billiard-room. She is very pale. They all rise and DOT puts an arm round her; while KEITH pushes forward his chair. JOAN and LATTER too have come stealing back.

LADY CHESHIRE. Thank you, Ronny! [She sits down.]

DOT. Mother, you're shivering! Shall I get you a fur?

LADY CHESHIRE. No, thanks, dear!

DOT. [In a low voice] Play up, mother darling!

LADY CHESHIRE. [Straightening herself] What sort of a run, Ronny?

KEITH. Quite fair, M'm. Brazier's to Caffyn's Dyke, good straight line.

LADY CHESHIRE. And the young horse?

KEITH. Carries his ears in your mouth a bit, that's all. [Putting his hand on her shoulder] Cheer up, Mem-Sahib!

CHRISTINE. Mother, must anything be said to father? Ronny thinks it all depends on her. Can't you use your influence? [LADY CHESHIRE shakes her head.]

CHRISTINE. But, mother, it's desperate.

DOT. Shut up, Chris! Of course mother can't. We simply couldn't beg her to let us off!

CHRISTINE. There must be some way. What do you think in your heart, mother?

DOT. Leave mother alone!

CHRISTINE. It must be faced, now or never.

DOT. [In a low voice] Haven't you any self-respect?

CHRISTINE. We shall be the laughing-stock of the whole county. Oh! mother do speak to her! You know it'll be misery for both of them.

[LADY CHESHIRE bows her head] Well, then? [LADY
CHESHIRE shakes her head.]

CHRISTINE. Not even for Bill's sake?

DOT. Chris!

CHRISTINE. Well, for heaven's sake, speak to Bill again, mother! We ought all
to go on our knees to him.

LADY CHESHIRE. He's with your father now.

HAROLD. Poor old Bill!

CHRISTINE. [Passionately] He didn't think of us! That wretched girl!

LADY CHESHIRE. Chris!

CHRISTINE. There are limits!

LADY CHESHIRE. Not to self-control.

CHRISTINE. No, mother! I can't I never shall—Something must be done! You
know what Bill is. He rushes at things so, when he gets his head
down. Oh! do try! It's only fair to her, and all of us!

LADY CHESHIRE. [Painfully] There are things one can't do.

CHRISTINE. But it's Bill! I know you can make her give him up, if you'll only
say all you can. And, after all, what's coming won't affect her as
if she'd been a lady. Only you can do it, mother: Do back me up,
all of you! It's the only way!

Hypnotised by their private longing for what CHRISTINE has been urging they
have all fixed their eyes on LADY CHESHIRE, who looks from, face to face, and
moves her hands as if in physical pain.

CHRISTINE. [Softly] Mother!

LADY CHESHIRE   suddenly rises, looking towards the billiard-room door, listening. They all follow her eyes. She sits down again,

passing her hand over her lips, as SIR WILLIAM enters. His hunting clothes are splashed; his face very grim and set. He walks to the fore without a glance at any one, and stands looking down into it. Very quietly, every one but LADY CHESHIRE steals away.

LADY CHESHIRE. What have you done?

SIR WILLIAM. You there!

LADY CHESHIRE. Don't keep me in suspense!

SIR WILLIAM. The fool! My God! Dorothy! I didn't think I had a blackguard for a son, who was a fool into the bargain.

LADY CHESHIRE. [Rising] If he were a blackguard he would not be what you call a fool.

SIR WILLIAM. [After staring angrily, makes her a slight bow] Very well!

LADY CHESHIRE. [In a low voice] Bill, don't be harsh. It's all too terrible.

SIR WILLIAM. Sit down, my dear. [She resumes her seat, and he turns back to the fire.]

SIR WILLIAM. In all my life I've never been face to face with a thing like this. [Gripping the mantelpiece so hard that his hands and arms are seen shaking] You ask me to be calm. I am trying to be. Be good enough in turn not to take his part against me.

LADY CHESHIRE. Bill!

SIR WILLIAM. I am trying to think. I understand that you've known this—piece of news since this morning. I've known it ten minutes. Give me a little time, please. [Then, after a silence] Where's the girl?

LADY CHESHIRE. In the workroom.

SIR WILLIAM. [Raising his clenched fist] What in God's name is he about?

LADY CHESHIRE. What have you said to him?

SIR WILLIAM. Nothing-by a miracle. [He breaks away from the fire and walks up and down] My family goes back to the thirteenth century. Nowadays they laugh at that! I don't! Nowadays they laugh at everything—they even laugh at the word lady. I married you, and I don't .... Married his mother's maid! By George! Dorothy! I don't know what we've done to deserve this; it's a death blow! I'm not prepared to sit down and wait for it. By Gad! I am not. [With sudden fierceness] There are plenty in these days who'll be glad enough for this to happen; plenty of these d——d Socialists and Radicals, who'll laugh their souls out over what they haven't the bowels to sees a—tragedy. I say it would be a tragedy; for you, and me, and all of us. You and I were brought up, and we've brought the children up, with certain beliefs, and wants, and habits. A man's past—his traditions—he can't get rid of them. They're—they're himself! [Suddenly] It shan't go on.

LADY CHESHIRE. What's to prevent it?

SIR WILLIAM. I utterly forbid this piece of madness. I'll stop it.

LADY CHESHIRE. But the thing we can't stop.

SIR WILLIAM. Provision must be made.

LADY CHESHIRE. The unwritten law!

SIR WILLIAM. What! [Suddenly perceiving what she is alluding to] You're thinking of young—young——[Shortly] I don't see the connection.

LADY CHESHIRE. What's so awful, is that the boy's trying to do what's loyal—and we—his father and mother——!

SIR WILLIAM. I'm not going to see my eldest son ruin his life. I must think this out.

LADY CHESHIRE. [Beneath her breath] I've tried that—it doesn't help.

SIR WILLIAM.   This girl, who was born on the estate, had the run of the house—brought up with money earned from me—nothing but kindness from all of us; she's broken the common rules of gratitude and decency—she lured him on, I haven't a doubt!

LADY CHESHIRE.   [To herself] In a way, I suppose.

SIR WILLIAM.   What! It's ruin. We've always been here. Who the deuce are we if we leave this place? D'you think we could stay? Go out and meet everybody just as if nothing had happened? Good-bye to any prestige, political, social, or anything! This is the sort of business nothing can get over. I've seen it before. As to that other matter—it's soon forgotten—constantly happening—Why, my own grandfather——!

LADY CHESHIRE.   Does he help?

SIR WILLIAM.   [Stares before him in silence-suddenly] You must go to the girl. She's soft. She'll never hold out against you.

LADY CHESHIRE.   I did before I knew what was in front of her—I said all I could. I can't go again now. I can't do it, Bill.

SIR WILLIAM.   What are you going to do, then—fold your hands? [Then as LADY CHESHIRE makes a move of distress.] If he marries her, I've done with him. As far as I'm concerned he'll cease to exist. The title—I can't help. My God! Does that meet your wishes?

LADY CHESHIRE.   [With sudden fire] You've no right to put such an alternative to me. I'd give ten years of my life to prevent this marriage. I'll go to Bill. I'll beg him on my knees.

SIR WILLIAM.   Then why can't you go to the girl? She deserves no consideration. It's not a question of morality: Morality be d——d!

LADY CHESHIRE.   But not self-respect....

SIR WILLIAM.   What! You're his mother!

LADY CHESHIRE.   I've tried; I [putting her hand to her throat] can't get it out.

SIR WILLIAM. [Staring at her] You won't go to her? It's the only chance. [LADY CHESHIRE turns away.]

SIR WILLIAM. In the whole course of our married life, Dorothy, I've never known you set yourself up against me. I resent this, I warn you—I resent it. Send the girl to me. I'll do it myself.

With a look back at him LADY CHESHIRE goes out into the corridor.

SIR WILLIAM. This is a nice end to my day!

He takes a small china cup from of the mantel-piece; it breaks with the pressure of his hand, and falls into the fireplace. While he stands looking at it blankly, there is a knock.

SIR WILLIAM. Come in!

FREDA enters from the corridor.

SIR WILLIAM. I've asked you to be good enough to come, in order that— [pointing to chair]—You may sit down.

But though she advances two or three steps, she does not sit down.

SIR WILLIAM. This is a sad business.

FREDA. [Below her breath] Yes, Sir William.

SIR WILLIAM. [Becoming conscious of the depths of feeling before him] I— er—are you attached to my son?

FREDA. [In a whisper] Yes.

SIR WILLIAM. It's very painful to me to have to do this. [He turns away from her and speaks to the fire.] I sent for you—to—ask— [quickly] How old are you?

FREDA. Twenty-two.

SIR WILLIAM. [More resolutely] Do you expect me to sanction such a mad idea as a marriage?

FREDA. I don't expect anything.

SIR WILLIAM. You know—you haven't earned the right to be considered.

FREDA. Not yet!

SIR WILLIAM. What! That oughtn't to help you! On the contrary. Now brace yourself up, and listen to me!

She stands waiting to hear her sentence. SIR WILLIAM looks at her; and his glance gradually wavers.

SIR WILLIAM. I've not a word to say for my son. He's behaved like a scamp.

FREDA. Oh! no!

SIR WILLIAM. [With a silencing gesture] At the same, time—What made you forget yourself? You've no excuse, you know.

FREDA. No.

SIR WILLIAM. You'll deserve all you'll get. Confound it! To expect me to—It's intolerable! Do you know where my son is?

FREDA. [Faintly] I think he's in the billiard-room with my lady.

SIR WILLIAM. [With renewed resolution] I wanted to—to put it to you—as a—as a—what! [Seeing her stand so absolutely motionless, looking at him, he turns abruptly, and opens the billiard-room door] I'll speak to him first. Come in here, please! [To FREDA] Go in, and wait!

LADY CHESHIRE and BILL Come in, and FREDA passing them, goes into the billiard-room to wait.

SIR WILLIAM. [Speaking with a pause between each sentence] Your mother and I have spoken of this—calamity. I imagine that even you have some dim perception of the monstrous nature of it. I must tell you this: If you do this mad thing, you fend for yourself. You'll receive nothing from me now or hereafter. I consider that only due to the position our family has always held here. Your

brother will take your place. We shall—get on as best we can
without you. [There is a dead silence till he adds sharply] Well!

BILL. I shall marry her.

LADY CHESHIRE. Oh! Bill! Without love-without anything!

BILL. All right, mother! [To SIR WILLIAM] you've mistaken your man, sir.
Because I'm a rotter in one way, I'm not necessarily a rotter in all. You
put the butt end of the pistol to Dunning's head yesterday, you put the
other end to mine to-day. Well! [He turns round to go out] Let the d—
-d thing off!

LADY CHESHIRE. Bill!

BILL. [Turning to her] I'm not going to leave her in the lurch.

SIR WILLIAM. Do me the justice to admit that I have not attempted to persuade you to.

BILL. No! you've chucked me out. I don't see what else you could have done
under the circumstances. It's quite all right. But if you wanted me to
throw her over, father, you went the wrong way to work, that's all; neither you nor I are very good at seeing consequences.

SIR WILLIAM. Do you realise your position?

BILK. [Grimly] I've a fair notion of it.

SIR WILLIAM. [With a sudden outburst] You have none—not the faintest,
brought up as you've been.

BILL. I didn't bring myself up.

SIR WILLIAM. [With a movement of uncontrolled anger, to which his son
responds] You—ungrateful young dog!

LADY CHESHIRE. How can you—both? [They drop their eyes, and stand
silent.]

SIR WILLIAM. [With grimly suppressed emotion] I am speaking under the stress
of very great pain—some consideration is due to me. This is a

disaster which I never expected to have to face. It is a matter which I naturally can never hope to forget. I shall carry this down to my death. We shall all of us do that. I have had the misfortune all my life to believe in our position here—to believe that we counted for something—that the country wanted us. I have tried to do my duty by that position. I find in one moment that it is gone— smoke—gone. My philosophy is not equal to that. To countenance this marriage would be unnatural.

BILL. I know. I'm sorry. I've got her into this—I don't see any other way out. It's a bad business for me, father, as well as for you——

He stops, seeing that JACKSON has route in, and is standing there waiting.

JACKSON. Will you speak to Studdenham, Sir William? It's about young Dunning.

After a moment of dead silence, SIR WILLIAM nods, and the butler withdraws.

BILL. [Stolidly] He'd better be told.

SIR WILLIAM. He shall be.

STUDDENHAM enters, and touches his forehead to them all with a comprehensive gesture.

STUDDENHAM. Good evenin', my lady! Evenin', Sir William!

STUDDENHAM. Glad to be able to tell you, the young man's to do the proper thing. Asked me to let you know, Sir William. Banns'll be up next Sunday. [Struck by the silence, he looks round at all three in turn, and suddenly seeing that LADY CHESHIRE is shivering] Beg pardon, my lady, you're shakin' like a leaf!

BILL. [Blurting it out] I've a painful piece of news for you, Studdenham; I'm engaged to your daughter. We're to be married at once.

STUDDENHAM. I—don't—understand you—sir.

BILL. The fact is, I've behaved badly; but I mean to put it straight.

STUDDENHAM. I'm a little deaf. Did you say—my daughter?

SIR WILLIAM. There's no use mincing matters, Studdenham. It's a thunder-
bolt—young Dunning's case over again.

STUDDENHAM. I don't rightly follow. She's—You've—! I must see my
daughter. Have the goodness to send for her, m'lady.

LADY CHESHIRE goes to the billiard-room, and calls: "FREDA, come here,
please."

STUDDENHAM. [TO SIR WILLIAM] YOU tell me that my daughter's in
the position of that girl owing to your son? Men ha' been
shot for less.

BILL. If you like to have a pot at me, Studdenham you're welcome.

STUDDENHAM. [Averting his eyes from BILL at the sheer idiocy of this sequel
to his words] I've been in your service five and twenty years,
Sir William; but this is man to man—this is!

SIR WILLIAM. I don't deny that, Studdenham.

STUDDENHAM. [With eyes shifting in sheer anger] No—'twouldn't be very
easy. Did I understand him to say that he offers her marriage?

SIR WILLIAM. You did.

STUDDENHAM. [Into his beard] Well—that's something! [Moving his hands
as if wringing the neck of a bird] I'm tryin' to see the rights
o' this.

SIR WILLIAM. [Bitterly] You've all your work cut out for you, Studdenham.

Again STUDDENHAM makes the unconscious wringing movement with his
hands.

LADY CHESHIRE. [Turning from it with a sort of horror] Don't, Studdenham!
Please!

STUDDENHAM. What's that, m'lady?

LADY CHESHIRE. [Under her breath] Your—your—hands.

While STUDDENHAM is still staring at her, FREDA is seen standing in the doorway, like a black ghost.

STUDDENHAM. Come here! You! [FREDA moves a few steps towards her father] When did you start this?

FREDA. [Almost inaudibly] In the summer, father.

LADY CHESHIRE. Don't be harsh to her!

STUDDENHAM. Harsh! [His eyes again move from side to side as if pain and anger had bewildered them. Then looking sideways at FREDA, but in a gentler voice] And when did you tell him about—what's come to you?

FREDA. Last night.

STUDDENHAM. Oh! [With sudden menace] You young—! [He makes a convulsive movement of one hand; then, in the silence, seems to lose grip of his thoughts, and pits his hand up to his head] I want to clear me mind a bit—I don't see it plain at all. [Without looking at BILL] 'Tis said there's been an offer of marriage?

BILL. I've made it, I stick to it.

STUDDENHAM. Oh! [With slow, puzzled anger] I want time to get the pith o' this. You don't say anything, Sir William?

SIR WILLIAM. The facts are all before you.

STUDDENHAM. [Scarcely moving his lips] M'lady?

LADY CHESHIRE is silent.

STUDDENHAM. [Stammering] My girl was—was good enough for any man. It's not for him that's—that's to look down on her. [To

FREDA] You hear the handsome offer that's been made you? Well? [FREDA moistens her lips and tries to speak, but cannot] If nobody's to speak a word, we won't get much forrarder. I'd like for you to say what's in your mind, Sir William.

SIR WILLIAM. I—If my son marries her he'll have to make his own way.

STUDDENHAM. [Savagely] I'm not puttin' thought to that.

SIR WILLIAM. I didn't suppose you were, Studdenham. It appears to rest with your daughter. [He suddenly takes out his handkerchief, and puts it to his forehead] Infernal fires they make up here!

LADY CHESHIRE, who is again shivering desperately, as if with intense cold, makes a violent attempt to control her shuddering.

STUDDENHAM. [Suddenly] There's luxuries that's got to be paid for. [To FREDA] Speak up, now.

FREDA turns slowly and looks up at SIR WILLIAM; he involuntarily raises his hand to his mouth. Her eyes travel on to LADY CHESHIRE, who faces her, but so deadly pale that she looks as if she were going to faint. The girl's gaze passes on to BILL, standing rigid, with his jaw set.

FREDA. I want—[Then flinging her arm up over her eyes, she turns from him] No!

SIR WILLIAM. Ah!

At that sound of profound relief, STUDDENHAM, whose eyes have been following his daughter's, moves towards SIR WILLIAM, all his emotion turned into sheer angry pride.

STUDDENHAM. Don't be afraid, Sir William! We want none of you! She'll not force herself where she's not welcome. She may ha' slipped her good name, but she'll keep her proper pride. I'll have no charity marriage in my family.

SIR WILLIAM. Steady, Studdenham!

STUDDENHAM. If the young gentleman has tired of her in three months, as
            a blind man can see by the looks of him—she's not for him!

BILL. [Stepping forward] I'm ready to make it up to her.

STUDDENHAM. Keep back, there? [He takes hold of FREDA, and looks
            around him] Well! She's not the first this has happened to
            since the world began, an' she won't be the last. Come away,
            now, come away!

Taking FREDA by the shoulders, he guides her towards the door.

SIR WILLIAM. D—-n 'it, Studdenham! Give us credit for something!

STUDDENHAM. [Turning his face and eyes lighted up by a sort of smiling
            snarl] Ah! I do that, Sir William. But there's things that
            can't be undone!

He follows FREDA Out. As the door closes, SIR WILLIAM'S Calm gives way.
He staggers past his wife, and sinks heavily, as though exhausted, into a chair by
the fire. BILL, following FREDA and STUDDENHAM, has stopped at the shut
door. LADY CHESHIRE moves swiftly close to him. The door of the billiard-
room is opened, and DOT appears. With a glance round, she crosses quickly to
her mother.

DOT. [In a low voice] Mabel's just going, mother! [Almost whispering] Where's
Freda? Is it—Has she really had the pluck?

LADY CHESHIRE bending her head for "Yes," goes out into the billiard-room.
DOT clasps her hands together, and standing there in the middle of the room,
looks from her brother to her father, from her father to her brother. A quaint little pitying smile comes on her lips. She gives a faint shrug of her shoulders.

The curtain falls.

THE LITTLE DREAM

AN ALLEGORY IN SIX SCENES

CHARACTERS

SEELCHEN, a mountain girl
LAMOND, a climber
FELSMAN, a glide

CHARACTERS IN THE DREAM

THE GREAT HORN
THE COW HORN   mountains
THE WINE HORN

THE EDELWEISS
THE ALPENROSE   flowers
THE GENTIAN
THE MOUNTAIN DANDELION

VOICES AND FIGURES IN THE DREAM

COWBELLS
MOUNTAIN AIR
FAR VIEW OF ITALY
DISTANT FLUME OF STEAM
THINGS IN BOOKS
MOTH CHILDREN
THREE DANCING YOUTHS
THREE DANCING GIRLS
THE FORMS OF WORKERS
THE FORMS OF WHAT IS MADE BY WORK

SCENE I

It is just after sunset of an August evening. The scene is a room in a mountain hut, furnished only with a table, benches. and a low broad window seat. Through this window three rocky peaks are seen by the light of a moon which is slowly whitening the last hues of sunset. An oil lamp is burning. SEELCHEN, a mountain girl, eighteen years old, is humming a folk-song, and putting away in a cupboard freshly washed soup-bowls and glasses. She is dressed in a tight-fitting black velvet bodice. square-cut at the neck and partly filled in with a gay handkerchief, coloured rose-pink, blue, and golden, like the alpen-rose, the gentian, and the mountain dandelion; alabaster beads, pale as edelweiss, are round her throat; her stiffened. white linen sleeves finish at the elbow; and her full well-worn skirt is of gentian blue. The two thick plaits of her hair are crossed, and turned round her head. As she puts away the last bowl, there is a knock; and LAMOND opens the outer door. He is young, tanned, and good-looking, dressed like a climber, and carries a plaid, a ruck-sack, and an ice-axe.

LAMOND. Good evening!

SEELCHEN. Good evening, gentle Sir!

LAMOND. My name is Lamond. I'm very late I fear.

SEELCHEN. Do you wish to sleep here?

LAMOND. Please.

SEELCHEN. All the beds are full—it is a pity. I will call Mother.

LAMOND. I've come to go up the Great Horn at sunrise.

SEELCHEN. [Awed] The Great Horn! But he is impossible.

LAMOND. I am going to try that.

SEELCHEN. There is the Wine Horn, and the Cow Horn.

LAMOND. I have climbed them.

SEELCHEN. But he is so dangerous—it is perhaps—death.

LAMOND. Oh! that's all right! One must take one's chance.

SEELCHEN. And father has hurt his foot. For guide, there is only Mans
          Felsman.

LAMOND. The celebrated Felsman?

SEELCHEN. [Nodding; then looking at him with admiration] Are you that
          Herr Lamond who has climbed all our little mountains this year?

LAMOND. All but that big fellow.

SEELCHEN. We have heard of you. Will you not wait a day for father's foot?

LAMOND. Ah! no. I must go back home to-morrow.

SEELCHEN. The gracious Sir is in a hurry.

LAMOND. [Looking at her intently] Alas!

SEELCHEN. Are you from London?   Is it very big?

LAMOND. Six million souls.

SEELCHEN. Oh! [After a little pause] I have seen Cortina twice.

LAMOND. Do you live here all the year?

SEELCHEN. In winter in the valley.

LAMOND. And don't you want to see the world?

SEELCHEN. Sometimes. [Going to a door, she calls softly] Hans! [Then pointing to another door] There are seven German gentlemen asleep in there!

LAMOND. Oh God!

SEELCHEN. Please? They are here to see the sunrise. [She picks up a little book that has dropped from LAMOND'S pocket] I have read several books.

LAMOND. This is by the great English poet. Do you never make poetry here, and dream dreams, among your mountains?

SEELCHEN. [Slowly shaking her head] See! It is the full moon.

While they stand at the window looking at the moon, there enters a lean, well-built, taciturn young man dressed in Loden.

SEELCHEN. Hans!

FELSMAN. [In a deep voice] The gentleman wishes me?

SEELCHEN. [Awed] The Great Horn for to-morrow! [Whispering to him] It is the celebrated London one.

FELSMAN. The Great Horn is not possible.

LAMOND. You say that? And you're the famous Felsman?

FELSMAN. [Grimly] We start at dawn.

SEELCHEN. It is the first time for years!

LAMOND. [Placing his plaid and rucksack on the window bench] Can I sleep here?

SEELCHEN. I will see; perhaps—

[She runs out up some stairs]

FELSMAN. [Taking blankets from the cupboard and spreading them on the window seat] So!

As he goes out into the air. SEELCHEN comes slipping in again with a lighted candle.

SEELCHEN. There is still one bed. This is too hard for you.

LAMOND. Oh! thanks; but that's all right.

SEELCHEN. To please me!

LAMOND. May I ask your name?

SEELCHEN. Seelchen.

LAMOND. Little soul, that means—doesn't it?   To please you I would sleep with seven German gentlemen.

SEELCHEN. Oh! no; it is not necessary.

LAMOND. [With. a grave bow] At your service, then. [He prepares to go]

SEELCHEN. Is it very nice in towns, in the World, where you come from?

LAMOND. When I'm there I would be here; but when I'm here I would be there.

SEELCHEN. [Clasping her hands] That is like me but I am always here.

LAMOND. Ah! yes; there is no one like you in towns.

SEELCHEN. In two places one cannot be. [Suddenly] In the towns there are theatres, and there is beautiful fine work, and—dancing, and—churches—and trains—and all the things in books—and—

LAMOND. Misery.

SEELCHEN. But there is life.

LAMOND. And there is death.

SEELCHEN. To-morrow, when you have climbed—will you not come back?

LAMOND. No.

SEELCHEN. You have all the world; and I have nothing.

LAMOND. Except Felsman, and the mountains.

SEELCHEN. It is not good to eat only bread.

LAMOND. [Looking at her hard] I would like to eat you!

SEELCHEN. But I am not nice; I am full of big wants—like the cheese with holes.

LAMOND. I shall come again.

SEELCHEN. There will be no more hard mountains left to climb. And if it is not exciting, you do not care.

LAMOND. O wise little soul!

SEELCHEN. No. I am not wise. In here it is always aching.

LAMOND. For the moon?

SEELCHEN. Yes. [Then suddenly] From the big world you will remember?

LAMOND. [Taking her hand] There is nothing in the big world so sweet as this.

SEELCHEN. [Wisely] But there is the big world itself.

LAMOND. May I kiss you, for good-night?

She puts her face forward; and he kisses her cheek, and, suddenly, her lips. Then as she draws away.

LAMOND. I am sorry, little soul.

SEELCHEN. That's all right!

LAMOND. [Taking the candle] Dream well! Goodnight!

SEELCHEN. [Softly] Good-night!

FELSMAN. [Coming in from the air, and eyeing them] It is cold—it will be
          fine.

LAMOND still looking back goes up the stairs; and FELSMAN waits for him to
          pass.

SEELCHEN. [From the window seat] It was hard for him here. I thought.

He goes up to her, stays a moment looking down then bends and kisses her hun-
grily.

SEELCHEN. Art thou angry?

He does not answer, but turning out the lamp, goes into an inner room.

SEELCHEN sits gazing through the window at the peaks bathed in full moon-
          light. Then, drawing the blankets about her, she snuggles doom on
          the window seat.

SEELCHEN. [In a sleepy voice] They kissed me—both. [She sleeps]

The scene falls quite dark

SCENE II

The scene is slowly illumined as by dawn. SEELCHEN is still lying on the window seat. She sits up, freeing her face and hands from the blankets, changing the swathings of deep sleep for the filmy coverings of a dream. The wall of the hut has vanished; there is nothing between her and the three mountains veiled in mist, save a through of darkness. There, as the peaks of the mountains brighten, they are seen to have great faces.

SEELCHEN. Oh! They have faces!

The face of THE WINE HORN is the profile of a beardless youth. The face of THE COW HORN is that of a mountain shepherd. solemn, and broom, with fierce black eyes, and a black beard. Between them THE GREAT HORN, whose hair is of snow, has a high. beardless visage, as of carved bronze, like a male sphinx, serene, without cruelty. Far down below the faces of the peaks. above the trough of darkness, are peeping out the four little heads of the flowers of EDELWEISS, and GENTIAN, MOUNTAIN DANDELION, and ALPENROSE; on their heads are crowns made of their several flowers, all powdered with dewdrops; and when THE FLOWERS lift their child-faces little tinkling bells ring.

All around the peaks there is nothing but blue sky.

EDELWEISS. [In a tiny voice] Would you? Would you? Would you? Ah! ha!

GENTIAN, M. DANDELION, ALPENROSE [With their bells ranging enviously] Oo-oo-oo!

From behind the Cow HORN are heard the voices of COWBELLS and MOUNTAIN AIR:

"Clinkel-clink! Clinkel-clink!"
"Mountain air! Mountain air!"

From behind THE WINE HORN rise the rival voices Of VIEW OF ITALY, FLUME OF STEAM, and THINGS IN BOOKS:

"I am Italy! Italy!"

"See me—steam in the distance!"

"O remember the things in books!"

And all call out together, very softly, with THE FLOWERS ringing their bells. Then far away like an echo comes a sighing:

"Mountain air! Mountain air!"

And suddenly the Peak of THE COW HORN speaks in a voice as of one unaccustomed.

THE COW HORN.   Amongst kine and my black-brown sheep I Live; I am silence, and monotony; I am the solemn hills. I am fierceness, and the mountain wind; clean pasture, and wild rest. Look in my eyes. love me alone!

SEELCHEN. [Breathless] The Cow Horn! He is speaking for Felsman and the mountains. It is the half of my heart!

THE FLOWERS laugh happily.

THE COW HORN.   I stalk the eternal hills—I drink the mountain snows. My eyes are the colour of burned wine; in them lives melancholy. The lowing of the kine, the wind, the sound of falling rocks, the running of the torrents; no other talk know I. Thoughts simple, and blood hot, strength huge—the cloak of gravity.

SEELCHEN. Yes. yes! I want him. He is strong!

The voices of COWBELLS and MOUNTAIN AIR cry out together:

"Clinkel-clink! Clinkel-clink!"

"Mountain air! Mountain air!"

THE COW HORN. Little soul! Hold to me! Love me! Live with me under the stars!

SEELCHEN. [Below her breath] I am afraid.

And suddenly the Peak of THE WINE HORN speaks in a youth's voice.

THE WINE HORN. I am the will o' the wisp that dances thro' the streets; I am the cooing dove of Towns, from the plane trees and the chestnuts' shade. From day to day all changes, where I burn my incense to my thousand little gods. In white palaces I dwell, and passionate dark alleys. The life of men in crowds is mine—of lamplight in the streets at dawn. [Softly] I have a thousand loves. and never one too long; for I am nimbler than your heifers playing in the sunshine.

THE FLOWERS, ringing in alarm, cry:

"We know them!"

THE WINE HORN. I hear the rustlings of the birth and death of pleasure; and the rattling of swift wheels. I hear the hungry oaths of men; and love kisses in the airless night. Without me, little soul, you starve and die,

SEELCHEN. He is speaking for the gentle Sir, and the big world of the Town. It pulls my heart.

THE WINE HORN. My thoughts surpass in number the flowers in your meadows; they fly more swiftly than your eagles on the wind. I drink the wine of aspiration, and the drug of disillusion. Thus am I never dull!

The voices of VIEW OF ITALY, FLUME OF STEAM, and THINGS IN BOOKS are heard calling out together:

"I am Italy, Italy!"

"See me—steam in the distance!"

"O remember, remember!"

THE WINE HORN. Love me, little soul! I paint life fifty colours. I make a thousand pretty things! I twine about your heart!

SEELCHEN. He is honey!

THE FLOWERS ring their bells jealously and cry:

"Bitter! Bitter!"

THE COW HORN. Stay with me, Seelchen! I wake thee with the crystal air.

The voices of COWBELLS and MOUNTAIN AIR tiny out far away:

"Clinkel-clink! Clinkel-clink!"

"Mountain air! Mountain air!"

And THE FLOWERS laugh happily.

THE WINE HORN. Come with me, Seelchen! My fan, Variety, shall wake you!

The voices of VIEW OF ITALY, FLUME OF STEAM and THINGS IN BOOKS chant softly:

"I am Italy! Italy!"

"See me—steam in the distance!"

"O remember, remember!"

And THE FLOWERS moan.

SEELCHEN. [In grief] My heart! It is torn!

THE WINE HORN. With me, little soul, you shall race in the streets. and peep at all secrets. We will hold hands, and fly like the thistle-down.

M. DANDELION. My puff-balls fly faster!

THE WINE HORN. I will show you the sea.

GENTIAN. My blue is deeper!

THE WINE HORN. I will shower on you blushes.

ALPENROSE. I can blush redder!

THE WINE HORN. Little soul, listen! My Jewels! Silk! Velvet!

EDELWEISS. I am softer than velvet!

THE WINE HORN. [Proudly] My wonderful rags!

THE FLOWERS. [Moaning] Of those we have none.

SEELCHEN. He has all things.

THE COW HORN.   Mine are the clouds with the dark silvered wings; mine are the rocks on fire with the sun; and the dewdrops cooler than pearls. Away from my breath of snow and sweet grass, thou wilt droop, little soul.

THE WINE HORN. The dark Clove is my fragrance!

THE FLOWERS ring eagerly, and turning up their faces, cry:

"We too, smell sweet."

But the voices of VIEW OF ITALY, FLUME OF STEAM, and THINGS IN BOOKS cry out:

"I am Italy! Italy!"

"See me—steam in the distance!"

"O remember! remember!"

SEELCHEN. [Distracted] Oh! it is hard!

THE COW HORN. I will never desert thee.

THE WINE HORN.   A hundred times I will desert you, a hundred times come
                 back, and kiss you.

SEELCHEN. [Whispering] Peace for my heart!

THE COW HORN. With me thou shalt lie on the warm wild thyme.

THE FLOWERS laugh happily.

THE WINE HORN. With me you shall lie on a bed of dove's feathers.

THE FLOWERS moan.

THE WINE HORN. I will give you old wine.

THE COW HORN. I will give thee new milk.

THE WINE HORN. Hear my song!

From far away comes the sound as of mandolins.

SEELCHEN. [Clasping her breast] My heart—it is leaving me!

THE COW HORN. Hear my song!

From the distance floats the piping of a Shepherd's reed.

SEELCHEN. [Curving her hand at her ears] The piping! Ah!

THE COW HORN. Stay with me, Seelchen!

THE WINE HORN. Come with me, Seelchen!

THE COW HORN. I give thee certainty!

THE WINE HORN. I give you chance!

THE COW HORN. I give thee peace.

THE WINE HORN. I give you change.

THE COW HORN. I give thee stillness.

THE WINE HORN. I give you voice.

THE COW HORN. I give thee one love.

THE WINE HORN. I give you many.

SEELCHEN. [As if the words were torn from her heart] Both, both—I will love!

And suddenly the Peak of THE GREAT HORN speaks.

THE GREAT HORN. And both thou shalt love, little soul! Thou shalt lie on the hills with Silence; and dance in the cities with Knowledge. Both shall possess thee! The sun and the moon on the mountains shall burn thee; the lamps of the town singe thy wings. small Moth! Each shall seem all the world to thee, each shall seem as thy grave! Thy heart is a feather blown from one mouth to the other. But be not afraid! For the life of a man is for all loves in turn. 'Tis a little raft moored, then sailing out into the blue; a tune caught in a hush, then whispering on; a new-born babe, half courage and half sleep. There is a hidden rhythm. Change. Quietude. Chance. Certainty. The One. The Many. Burn on—thou pretty flame, trying to eat the world! Thou shaft come to me at last, my little soul!

THE VOICES and THE FLOWER-BELLS peal out.

SEELCHEN, enraptured, stretches her arms to embrace the sight and sound, but all fades slowly into dark sleep.

SCENE III

The dark scene again becomes glamorous. SEELCHEN is seen with her hand stretched out towards the Piazza of a little town, with a plane tree on one side, a wall on the other, and from the open doorway of an Inn a pale path of light. Over the Inn hangs a full golden moon. Against the wall, under the glimmer of a lamp, leans a youth with the face of THE WINE HORN, in a crimson dock, thrumming a mandolin, and singing:

> "Little star soul
> Through the frost fields of night
> Roaming alone, disconsolate—
> From out the cold
> I call thee in
> Striking my dark mandolin
> Beneath this moon of gold."

From the Inn comes a burst of laughter, and the sound of dancing.

SEELCHEN: [Whispering] It is the big world!

The Youth of THE WINE HORN sings On:

> "Pretty grey moth,
> Where the strange candles shine,

> Seeking for warmth, so desperate—
> Ah! fluttering dove
> I bid thee win
> Striking my dark mandolin
> The crimson flame of love."

SEELCHEN. [Gazing enraptured at the Inn] They are dancing!

As SHE speaks, from either side come moth-children, meeting and fluttering up the path of light to the Inn doorway; then wheeling aside, they form again, and again flutter forward.

SEELCHEN. [Holding out her hands] They are real! Their wings are windy.

The Youth of THE WINE HORN sings on;

> "Lips of my song,
> To the white maiden's heart
> Go ye, and whisper, passionate.
> These words that burn
> 'O listening one!
> Love that flieth past is gone
> Nor ever may return!'"

SEELCHEN runs towards him—but the light above him fades; he has become shadow. She turns bewildered to the dancing moth- children—but they vanish before her. At the door of the Inn stands LAMOND in a dark cloak.

SEELCHEN. It is you!

LAMOND. Without my little soul I am cold. Come! [He holds out his arms to her]

SEELCHEN. Shall I be safe?

LAMOND. What is safety? Are you safe in your mountains?

SEELCHEN. Where am I, here?

LAMOND. The Town.

Smiling, he points to the doorway. And silent as shadows there come dancing out, two by two, two girls and two youths. The first girl is dressed in white satin and jewels; and the first youth in black velvet. The second girl is in rags, and a shawl; and the second youth in shirt and corduroys. They dance gravely, each couple as if in a world apart.

SEELCHEN. [Whispering] In the mountains all dance together. Do they never
        change partners?

LAMOND. How could they, little one? Those are rich, these poor. But see!

A CORYBANTIC COUPLE come dancing forth. The girl has bare limbs. a flame-coloured shift, and hair bound with red flowers; the youth wears a panther-skin. They pursue not only each other. but the other girls and youths. For a moment all is a furious medley. Then the Corybantic Couple vanish into the Inn, and the first two couples are left, slowly, solemnly dancing, apart from each other as before.

SEELCHEN. [Shuddering] Shall I one day dance like that?

The Youth of THE WINE HORN appears again beneath the lamp. He strikes a loud chord; then as SEELCHEN moves towards that sound the lamp goes out; there is again only blue shadow; but the couples have disappeared into the Inn, and the doorway has grown dark.

SEELCHEN. Ah! What I do not like, he will not let me see.

LAMOND. Will you not come, then, little soul?

SEELCHEN. Always to dance?

LAMOND: Not so!

THE SHUTTERS of the houses are suddenly thrown wide. In a lighted room on
        one aide of the Inn are seen two pale men and a woman,
        amongst many clicking machines. On the other side of the
        Inn, in a forge, are visible two women and a man, but half
        clothed, making chains.

SEELCHEN. [Recoiling from both sights, in turn] How sad they look —all!
        What are they making?

In the dark doorway of the Inn a light shines out, and in it is seen a figure, visible only from the waist up, clad in gold-cloth studded with jewels, with a flushed complacent face, holding in one hand a glass of golden wine.

SEELCHEN. It is beautiful. What is it?

LAMOND. Luxury.

SEELCHEN. What is it standing on? I cannot see.

Unseen, THE WINE HORN'S mandolin twangs out.

LAMOND. For that do not look, little soul.

SEELCHEN. Can it not walk? [He shakes his head] Is that all they make here
                with their sadness?

But again the mandolin twangs out; the shutters fall over the houses; the door of the Inn grows dark.

LAMOND. What is it, then, you would have? Is it learning? There are books
                here, that, piled on each other, would reach to the stars! [But
                SEELCHEN shakes her head] There is religion so deep that no
                man knows what it means. [But SEELCHEN shakes her head]
                There is religion so shallow, you may have it by turning a handle.
                We have everything.

SEELCHEN. Is God here?

LAMOND. Who knows? Is God with your goats? [But SEELCHEN shakes her
                head] What then do you want?

SEELCHEN. Life.

The mandolin twangs out.

LAMOND. [Pointing to his breast] There is but one road to life.

SEELCHEN. Ah! but I do not love.

LAMOND.   When a feather dies, is it not loving the wind—the unknown?
When the day brings not new things, we are children of sorrow. If
darkness and light did not change, could we breathe? Child! To live
is to love, to love is to live-seeking for wonder. [And as she draws
nearer] See! To love is to peer over the edge, and, spying the little
grey flower, to climb down! It has wings; it has flown—again you
must climb; it shivers, 'tis but air in your hand—you must crawl,
you must cling, you must leap, and still it is there and not there—
for the grey flower flits like a moth, and the wind of its wings is all
you shall catch. But your eyes shall be shining, your cheeks shall be
burning, your breast shall be panting—Ah! little heart! [The scene
falls darker] And when the night comes—there it is still, thistle-
down blown on the dark, and your white hands will reach for it, and
your honey breath waft it, and never, never, shall you grasp that
wanton thing—but life shall be lovely. [His voice dies to a whisper.
He stretches out his arms]

SEELCHEN.   [Touching his breast]   I will come.

LAMOND.   [Drawing her to the dark doorway]   Love me!

SEELCHEN.   I love!

The mandolin twangs out, the doorway for a moment is all glamorous; and they
pass through. Illumined by the glimmer of the lamp the Youth of THE WINE
Hour is seen again. And slowly to the chords of his mandolin he begins to sing:

> "The windy hours through darkness fly
> Canst hear them little heart?
> New loves are born, and old loves die,
> And kissing lips must part.

"The dusky bees of passing years Canst see them, soul of mine— From flower and
flower supping tears, And pale sweet honey wine?

[His voice grown strange and passionate]

> "O flame that treads the marsh of time.
> Flitting for ever low.
> Where, through the black enchanted slime.
> We, desperate, following go

Untimely fire, we bid thee stay!
Into dark air above.
The golden gipsy thins away—
So has it been with love!"

While he is singing, the moon grows pale, and dies. It falls dark, save for the glimmer of the lamp beneath which he stands. But as his song ends, the dawn breaks over the houses, the lamp goes out—THE WINE HORN becomes shadow. Then from the doorway of the Inn, in the shrill grey light SEELCHEN comes forth. She is pale, as if wan with living; her eyes like pitch against the powdery whiteness of her face.

SEELCHEN. My heart is old.

But as she speaks, from far away is heard a faint chiming of COWBELLS; and while she stands listening, LAMOND appears in the doorway of the Inn.

LAMOND. Little soul!

SEELCHEN. You! Always you!

LAMOND. I have new wonders.

SEELCHEN. [Mournfully] No.

LAMOND. I swear it! You have not tired of me, that am never the same? It cannot be.

SEELCHEN. Listen!

The chime of THE COWBELLS is heard again.

LAMOND. [Jealously] The music' of dull sleep! Has life, then, with me been sorrow?

SEELCHEN. I do not regret.

LAMOND. Come!

SEELCHEN. [Pointing-to her breast] The bird is tired with flying. [Touching her lips] The flowers have no dew.

LAMOND. Would you leave me?

SEELCHEN. See!

There, in a streak of the dawn, against the plane tree is seen the Shepherd of THE
COW HORN, standing wrapped in his mountain cloak.

LAMOND. What is it?

SEELCHEN. He!

LAMOND. There is nothing. [He holds her fast] I have shown you the mar-
　　　　vels of my town—the gay, the bitter wonders. We have known life.
　　　　If with you I may no longer live, then let us die! See! Here are
　　　　sweet Deaths by Slumber and by Drowning!

The mandolin twangs out, and from the dim doorway of the Inn come forth the
shadowy forms. DEATH BY SLUMBER, and DEATH BY DROWNING. who
to a ghostly twanging of mandolins dance slowly towards SEELCHEN. stand
smiling at her, and as slowly dance away.

SEELCHEN. [Following] Yes. They are good and sweet.

While she moves towards the Inn. LAMOND'S face becomes transfigured with
joy. But just as she reaches the doorway. there is a distant chiming of bells and
blowing of pipes, and the Shepherd of THE COW HORN sings:

> "To the wild grass come, and the dull far roar
> Of the falling rock; to the flowery meads
> Of thy mountain home, where the eagles soar,
> And the grizzled flock in the sunshine feeds.
> To the Alp, where I, in the pale light crowned
> With the moon's thin horns, to my pasture roam;
> To the silent sky, and the wistful sound
> Of the rosy dawns——my daughter, come!"

While HE sings, the sun has risen; and SEELCHEN has turned. with parted lips,
and hands stretched out; and the forms of death have vanished.

SEELCHEN. I come.

LAMOND. [Clasping her knees] Little soul! Must I then die, like a gnat when the sun goes down? Without you I am nothing.

SEELCHEN. [Releasing herself] Poor heart—I am gone!

LAMOND. It is dark. [He covers his face with his cloak].

Then as SEELCHEN reaches the Shepherd of THE COW HORN, there is blown a long note of a pipe; the scene falls back; and there rises a far, continual, mingled sound of Cowbells, and Flower Bells, and Pipes.

SCENE IV

The scene slowly brightens with the misty flush of dawn. SEELCHEN stands on a green alp, with all around, nothing but blue sky. A slip of a crescent moon is lying on her back. On a low rock sits a brown faced GOATHERD blowing on a pipe, and the four Flower-children are dancing in their shifts of grey white. and blue, rose-pink, and burnt-gold. Their bells are ringing. as they pelt each other with flowers of their own colours; and each in turn, wheeling, flings one flower at SEELCHEN, who puts them to her lips and eyes.

SEELCHEN. The dew! [She moves towards the rock] Goatherd!

But THE FLOWERS encircle him; and when they wheel away he has vanished. She turns to THE FLOWERS, but they too vanish. The veils of mist are rising.

SEELCHEN. Gone! [She rubs her eyes; then turning once more to the rock, sees
        FELSMAN standing there, with his arms folded] Thou!

FELSMAN. So thou hast come—like a sick heifer to be healed. Was it good in
        the Town—that kept thee so long?

SEELCHEN. I do not regret.

FELSMAN. Why then return?

SEELCHEN. I was tired.

FELSMAN. Never again shalt thou go from me!

SEELCHEN. [Mocking] With what wilt thou keep me?

FELSMAN. [Grasping her] Thus.

SEELCHEN. I have known Change—I am no timid maid.

FELSMAN. [Moodily] Aye, thou art different. Thine eyes are hollow —thou art white-faced.

SEELCHEN. [Still mocking] Then what hast thou here that shall keep me?

FELSMAN. The sun.

SEELCHEN. To burn me.

FELSMAN. The air.

There is a faint wailing of wind.

SEELCHEN. To freeze me.

FELSMAN. The silence.

The noise of the wind dies away.

SEELCHEN. Yes, it is lonely.

FELSMAN. Wait! And the flowers shall dance to thee.

And to a ringing of their bells. THE FLOWERS come dancing; till, one by one, they cease, and sink down, nodding, falling asleep.

SEELCHEN. See! Even they grow sleepy here!

FELSMAN. I will call the goats to wake them.

THE GOATHERD is seen again sitting upright on his rock and piping. And there come four little brown, wild-eyed, naked Boys, with Goat's legs and feet, who dance gravely in and out of The Sleeping Flowers; and THE FLOWERS wake, spring up, and fly. Till each Goat, catching his flower has vanished, and THE GOATHERD has ceased to pipe, and lies motionless again on his rock.

FELSMAN. Love me!

SEELCHEN. Thou art rude!

FELSMAN. Love me!

SEELCHEN. Thou art grim!

FELSMAN. Aye. I have no silver tongue. Listen! This is my voice. [Sweeping his arm round all the still alp] It is quiet. From dawn to the first star all is fast. [Laying his hand on her heart] And the wings of the birds shall be still.

SEELCHEN. [Touching his eyes] Thine eyes are fierce. In them I see the wild beasts crouching. In them I see the distance. Are they always fierce?

FELSMAN. Never—to look on thee, my flower.

SEELCHEN. [Touching his hands] Thy hands are rough to pluck flowers. [She breaks away from him to the rock where THE GOATHERD is lying] See! Nothing moves! The very day stands still. Boy! [But THE GOATHERD neither stirs nor answers] He is lost in the blue. [Passionately] Boy! He will not answer me. No one will answer me here.

FELSMAN. [With fierce longing] Am I then no one?

SEELCHEN. Thou?

[The scene darkens with evening]

See! Sleep has stolen the day! It is night already.

There come the female shadow forms of SLEEP, in grey cobweb garments, waving their arms drowsily, wheeling round her.

SEELCHEN. Are you Sleep?   Dear Sleep!

Smiling, she holds out her arms to FELSMAN. He takes her swaying form. They vanish, encircled by the forms of SLEEP. It is dark, save for the light of the thin horned moon suddenly grown bright. Then on his rock, to a faint gaping THE GOATHERD sings:

> "My goat, my little speckled one.
> My yellow-eyed, sweet-smelling.
> Let moon and wind and golden sun
> And stars beyond all telling
> Make, every day, a sweeter grass.
> And multiply thy leaping!
> And may the mountain foxes pass
> And never scent thee sleeping!
> Oh! Let my pipe be clear and far.
> And let me find sweet water!
> No hawk nor udder-seeking jar
> Come near thee, little daughter!
> May fiery rocks defend, at noon,
> Thy tender feet from slipping!
> Oh! hear my prayer beneath the moon—
> Great Master, Goat-God—skipping!"

There passes in the thin moonlight the Goat-Good Pan; and with a long wail of the pipe THE GOATHERD BOY is silent. Then the moon fades, and all is black; till, in the faint grisly light of the false dawn creeping up, SEELCHEN is seen rising from the side of the sleeping FELSMAN. THE GOATHERD BOY has gone; but by the rock stands the Shepherd of THE COW HORN in his dock.

SEELCHEN.   Years, years I have slept. My spirit is hungry. [Then as she sees the Shepherd of THE COW HORN standing there] I know thee now—Life of the earth—the smell of thee, the sight of thee, the taste of thee, and all thy music. I have passed thee and gone by. [She moves away]

FELSMAN. [Waking] Where wouldst thou go?

SEELCHEN. To the edge of the world.

FELSMAN. [Rising and trying to stay her] Thou shalt not leave me!

[But against her smiling gesture he struggles as though against solidity]

SEELCHEN. Friend! The time is on me.

FELSMAN. Were my kisses, then, too rude? Was I too dull?

SEELCHEN. I do not regret.

The Youth of THE WINE HORN is seen suddenly standing opposite the motionless Shepherd of THE COW HORN; and his mandolin twangs out.

FELSMAN. The cursed music of the Town! Is it back to him thou wilt go?
            [Groping for sight of the hated figure] I cannot see.

SEELCHEN. Fear not! I go ever onward.

FELSMAN. Do not leave me to the wind in the rocks! Without thee love is
            dead, and I must die.

SEELCHEN. Poor heart! I am gone.

FELSMAN. [Crouching against the rock] It is cold.

At the blowing of the Shepherd's pipe, THE COW HORN stretches forth his hand to her. The mandolin twangs out, and THE WINE HORN holds out his hand. She stands unmoving.

SEELCHEN. Companions. I must go. In a moment it will be dawn.

In Silence THE COW HORN and THE WINE HORN, cover their faces. The false dawn dies. It falls quite dark.

SCENE V

Then a faint glow stealing up, lights the snowy head of THE GREAT HORN, and streams forth on SEELCHEN. To either aide of that path of light, like shadows. THE COW HORN and THE WINE HORN stand with cloaked heads.

SEELCHEN. Great One! I come!

The Peak of THE GREAT HORN speaks in a far-away voice, growing, with the light, clearer and stronger.

> Wandering flame, thou restless fever
> Burning all things, regretting none;
> The winds of fate are stilled for ever—
> Thy little generous life is done.
> And all its wistful wonderings cease!
> Thou traveller to the tideless sea,
> Where light and dark, and change and peace,
> Are One—Come, little soul, to MYSTERY!

SEELCHEN falling on her knees, bows her head to the ground. The glow slowly fades till the scene is black.

SCENE VI

Then as the blackness lifts, in the dim light of the false dawn filtering through the window of the mountain hut. LAMOND and FELSMAN are seen standing beside SEELCHEN looking down at her asleep on the window seat.

FELSMAN. [Putting out his hand to wake her] In a moment it will be dawn.

She stirs, and her lips move, murmuring.

LAMOND. Let her sleep. She's dreaming.

FELSMAN raises a lantern, till its light falls on her face. Then the two men move stealthily towards the door, and, as she speaks, pass out.

SEELCHEN. [Rising to her knees, and stretching out her hands with ecstasy] Great One. I come! [Waking, she looks around, and struggles to her feet] My little dream!

Through the open door, the first flush of dawn shows in the sky. There is a sound of goat-bells passing.

The curtain falls.

JUSTICE

PERSONS OF THE PLAY

JAMES HOW, solicitor
WALTER HOW, solicitor
ROBERT COKESON, their managing clerk
WILLIAM FALDER, their junior clerk
SWEEDLE, their office-boy
WISTER, a detective
COWLEY, a cashier
MR. JUSTICE FLOYD, a judge
HAROLD CLEAVER, an old advocate
HECTOR FROME, a young advocate
CAPTAIN DANSON, V.C., a prison governor
THE REV. HUGH MILLER, a prison chaplain
EDWARD CLEMENT, a prison doctor
WOODER, a chief warder
MOANEY, convict
CLIFTON, convict
O'CLEARY, convict
RUTH HONEYWILL, a woman
A NUMBER OF BARRISTERS, SOLICITERS, SPECTATORS, USHERS,
REPORTERS, JURYMEN, WARDERS, AND PRISONERS

TIME: The Present.

ACT I. The office of James and Walter How. Morning. July.

ACT II. Assizes. Afternoon. October.

ACT III. A prison. December.
SCENE I. The Governor's office.

SCENE II. A corridor.
SCENE III. A cell.

ACT IV. The office of James and Walter How. Morning. March, two years later.

CAST OF THE FIRST PRODUCTION

AT THE DUKE OF YORK'S THEATRE, FEBRUARY 21, 1910

James How	MR. SYDNEY VALENTINE
Walter How	MR. CHARLES MAUDE
Cokeson	MR. EDMUND GWENN
Falder	MR. DENNIS EADIE
The Office-boy	MR. GEORGE HERSEE
The Detective	MR. LESLIE CARTER
The Cashier	MR. C. E. VERNON
The Judge	MR. DION BOUCICAULT
The Old Advocate	MR. OSCAR ADYE
The Young Advocate	MR. CHARLES BRYANT
The Prison Governor	MR. GRENDON BENTLEY
The Prison Chaplain	MR. HUBERT HARBEN
The Prison Doctor	MR. LEWIS CASSON
Wooder	MR. FREDERICK LLOYD
Moaney	MR. ROBERT PATEMAN
Clipton	MR. O. P. HEGGIE
O'Cleary	MR. WHITFORD KANE
Ruth Honeywill	Miss EDYTH OLIVE

ACT I

The scene is the managing clerk's room, at the offices of James and Walter How, on a July morning. The room is old fashioned, furnished with well-worn mahogany and leather, and lined with tin boxes and estate plans. It has three doors. Two of them are close together in the centre of a wall. One of these two doors leads to the outer office, which is only divided from the managing clerk's room by a partition of wood and clear glass; and when the door into this outer office is opened there can be seen the wide outer door leading out on to the stone stairway of the building. The other of these two centre doors leads to the junior clerk's room. The third door is that leading to the partners' room.

The managing clerk, COKESON, is sitting at his table adding up figures in a pass-book, and murmuring their numbers to himself. He is a man of sixty, wearing spectacles; rather short, with a bald head, and an honest, pugdog face. He is dressed in a well-worn black frock-coat and pepper-and-salt trousers.

COKESON. And five's twelve, and three—fifteen, nineteen, twenty-three, thirty-two, forty-one-and carry four. [He ticks the page, and goes on murmuring] Five, seven, twelve, seventeen, twenty-four and nine, thirty-three, thirteen and carry one.

He again makes a tick. The outer office door is opened, and SWEEDLE, the office-boy, appears, closing the door behind him. He is a pale youth of sixteen, with spiky hair.

COKESON. [With grumpy expectation] And carry one.

SWEEDLE. There's a party wants to see Falder, Mr. Cokeson.

COKESON. Five, nine, sixteen, twenty-one, twenty-nine—and carry two. Send him to Morris's. What name?

SWEEDLE. Honeywill.

COKESON. What's his business?

SWEEDLE. It's a woman.

COKESON. A lady?

SWEEDLE. No, a person.

COKESON. Ask her in. Take this pass-book to Mr. James. [He closes the pass-book.]

SWEEDLE. [Reopening the door] Will you come in, please?

RUTH HONEYWILL comes in. She is a tall woman, twenty-six years old, unpretentiously dressed, with black hair and eyes, and an ivory-white, clear-cut face. She stands very still, having a natural dignity of pose and gesture.

SWEEDLE goes out into the partners' room with the pass-book.

COKESON. [Looking round at RUTH] The young man's out. [Suspiciously] State your business, please.

RUTH. [Who speaks in a matter-of-fact voice, and with a slight West-Country accent] It's a personal matter, sir.

COKESON. We don't allow private callers here. Will you leave a message?

RUTH. I'd rather see him, please.

She narrows her dark eyes and gives him a honeyed look.

COKESON. [Expanding] It's all against the rules. Suppose I had my friends here to see me! It'd never do!

RUTH. No, sir.

COKESON. [A little taken aback] Exactly! And here you are wanting to see a junior clerk!

RUTH. Yes, sir; I must see him.

COKESON. [Turning full round to her with a sort of outraged interest] But this is a lawyer's office. Go to his private address.

RUTH. He's not there.

COKESON. [Uneasy] Are you related to the party?

RUTH. No, sir.

COKESON. [In real embarrassment] I don't know what to say. It's no affair of the office.

RUTH. But what am I to do?

COKESON. Dear me! I can't tell you that.

SWEEDLE comes back. He crosses to the outer office and passes through into it, with a quizzical look at Cokeson, carefully leaving the door an inch or two open.

COKESON. [Fortified by this look] This won't do, you know, this won't do at all. Suppose one of the partners came in!

An incoherent knocking and chuckling is heard from the outer door of the outer office.

SWEEDLE. [Putting his head in] There's some children outside here.

RUTH. They're mine, please.

SWEEDLE. Shall I hold them in check?

RUTH. They're quite small, sir. [She takes a step towards COKESON]

COKESON. You mustn't take up his time in office hours; we're a clerk short as
it is.

RUTH. It's a matter of life and death.

COKESON. [Again outraged] Life and death!

SWEEDLE. Here is Falder.

FALDER has entered through the outer office. He is a pale, good-looking young
man, with quick, rather scared eyes. He moves towards the door of the clerks'
office, and stands there irresolute.

COKESON. Well, I'll give you a minute. It's not regular.

Taking up a bundle of papers, he goes out into the partners' room.

RUTH. [In a low, hurried voice] He's on the drink again, Will. He tried to cut
my throat last night. I came out with the children before he was awake.
I went round to you.

FALDER. I've changed my digs.

RUTH. Is it all ready for to-night?

FALDER. I've got the tickets. Meet me 11.45 at the booking office. For God's
sake don't forget we're man and wife! [Looking at her with tragic
intensity] Ruth!

RUTH. You're not afraid of going, are you?

FALDER. Have you got your things, and the children's?

RUTH. Had to leave them, for fear of waking Honeywill, all but one bag. I can't
go near home again.

FALDER. [Wincing] All that money gone for nothing. How much must you
have?

RUTH. Six pounds—I could do with that, I think.

FALDER. Don't give away where we're going. [As if to himself] When I get out there I mean to forget it all.

RUTH. If you're sorry, say so. I'd sooner he killed me than take you against your will.

FALDER. [With a queer smile] We've got to go. I don't care; I'll have you.

RUTH. You've just to say; it's not too late.

FALDER. It is too late. Here's seven pounds. Booking office 11.45 to-night. If you weren't what you are to me, Ruth——!

RUTH. Kiss me!

They cling together passionately, there fly apart just as COKESON re-enters the room. RUTH turns and goes out through the outer office. COKESON advances deliberately to his chair and seats himself.

COKESON. This isn't right, Falder.

FALDER. It shan't occur again, sir.

COKESON. It's an improper use of these premises.

FALDER. Yes, sir.

COKESON. You quite understand-the party was in some distress; and, having children with her, I allowed my feelings——[He opens a drawer and produces from it a tract] Just take this! "Purity in the Home." It's a well-written thing.

FALDER. [Taking it, with a peculiar expression] Thank you, sir.

COKESON. And look here, Falder, before Mr. Walter comes, have you finished up that cataloguing Davis had in hand before he left?

FALDER. I shall have done with it to-morrow, sir—for good.

COKESON. It's over a week since Davis went. Now it won't do, Falder. You're neglecting your work for private life. I shan't mention about the party having called, but——

FALDER. [Passing into his room] Thank you, sir.

COKESON stares at the door through which FALDER has gone out; then shakes his head, and is just settling down to write, when WALTER How comes in through the outer Office. He is a rather refined-looking man of thirty-five, with a pleasant, almost apologetic voice.

WALTER. Good-morning, Cokeson.

COKESON. Morning, Mr. Walter.

WALTER. My father here?

COKESON. [Always with a certain patronage as to a young man who might be doing better] Mr. James has been here since eleven o'clock.

WALTER. I've been in to see the pictures, at the Guildhall.

COKESON. [Looking at him as though this were exactly what was to be expected] Have you now—ye—es. This lease of Boulter's—am I to send it to counsel?

WALTER. What does my father say?

COKESON. 'Aven't bothered him.

WALTER. Well, we can't be too careful.

COKESON. It's such a little thing—hardly worth the fees. I thought you'd do it yourself.

WALTER. Send it, please. I don't want the responsibility.

COKESON. [With an indescribable air of compassion] Just as you like. This "right-of-way" case—we've got 'em on the deeds.

WALTER. I know; but the intention was obviously to exclude that bit of common ground.

COKESON. We needn't worry about that. We're the right side of the law.

WALTER. I don't like it,

COKESON. [With an indulgent smile] We shan't want to set ourselves up against the law. Your father wouldn't waste his time doing that.

As he speaks JAMES How comes in from the partners' room. He is a shortish man, with white side-whiskers, plentiful grey hair, shrewd eyes, and gold pince-nez.

JAMES. Morning, Walter.

WALTER. How are you, father?

COKESON. [Looking down his nose at the papers in his hand as though deprecating their size] I'll just take Boulter's lease in to young Falder to draft the instructions. [He goes out into FALDER'S room.]

WALTER. About that right-of-way case?

JAMES. Oh, well, we must go forward there. I thought you told me yesterday the firm's balance was over four hundred.

WALTER. So it is.

JAMES. [Holding out the pass-book to his son] Three—five—one, no recent cheques. Just get me out the cheque-book.

WALTER goes to a cupboard, unlocks a drawer and produces a cheque-book.

JAMES. Tick the pounds in the counterfoils. Five, fifty-four, seven, five, twenty-eight, twenty, ninety, eleven, fifty-two, seventy-one. Tally?

WALTER. [Nodding] Can't understand. Made sure it was over four hundred.

JAMES. Give me the cheque-book. [He takes the check-book and cons the counterfoils] What's this ninety?

WALTER. Who drew it?

JAMES. You.

WALTER. [Taking the cheque-book] July 7th? That's the day I went down to look over the Trenton Estate—last Friday week; I came back on the Tuesday, you remember. But look here, father, it was nine I drew a cheque for. Five guineas to Smithers and my expenses. It just covered all but half a crown.

JAMES. [Gravely] Let's look at that ninety cheque. [He sorts the cheque out from the bundle in the pocket of the pass-book] Seems all right. There's no nine here. This is bad. Who cashed that nine-pound cheque?

WALTER. [Puzzled and pained] Let's see! I was finishing Mrs. Reddy's will—only just had time; yes—I gave it to Cokeson.

JAMES. Look at that 't' 'y': that yours?

WALTER. [After consideration] My y's curl back a little; this doesn't.

JAMES. [As COKESON re-enters from FALDER'S room] We must ask him. Just come here and carry your mind back a bit, Cokeson. D'you remember cashing a cheque for Mr. Walter last Friday week—the day he went to Trenton?

COKESON. Ye-es. Nine pounds.

JAMES. Look at this. [Handing him the cheque.]

COKESON. No! Nine pounds. My lunch was just coming in; and of course I like it hot; I gave the cheque to Davis to run round to the bank. He brought it back, all gold—you remember, Mr. Walter, you wanted some silver to pay your cab. [With a certain contemptuous compassion] Here, let me see. You've got the wrong cheque.

He takes cheque-book and pass-book from WALTER.

WALTER. Afraid not.

COKESON. [Having seen for himself] It's funny.

JAMES. You gave it to Davis, and Davis sailed for Australia on Monday. Looks black, Cokeson.

COKESON. [Puzzled and upset] why this'd be a felony! No, no! there's some mistake.

JAMES. I hope so.

COKESON. There's never been anything of that sort in the office the twenty-nine years I've been here.

JAMES. [Looking at cheque and counterfoil] This is a very clever bit of work; a warning to you not to leave space after your figures, Walter.

WALTER. [Vexed] Yes, I know—I was in such a tearing hurry that afternoon.

COKESON. [Suddenly] This has upset me.

JAMES. The counterfoil altered too—very deliberate piece of swindling. What was Davis's ship?

WALTER. 'City of Rangoon'.

JAMES. We ought to wire and have him arrested at Naples; he can't be there yet.

COKESON. His poor young wife. I liked the young man. Dear, oh dear! In this office!

WALTER. Shall I go to the bank and ask the cashier?

JAMES. [Grimly] Bring him round here. And ring up Scotland Yard.

WALTER. Really?

He goes out through the outer office. JAMES paces the room. He stops and looks at COKESON, who is disconsolately rubbing the knees of his trousers.

JAMES. Well, Cokeson! There's something in character, isn't there?

COKESON. [Looking at him over his spectacles] I don't quite take you, sir.

JAMES. Your story, would sound d——d thin to any one who didn't know you.

COKESON. Ye-es! [He laughs. Then with a sudden gravity] I'm sorry for that young man. I feel it as if it was my own son, Mr. James.

JAMES. A nasty business!

COKESON. It unsettles you. All goes on regular, and then a thing like this happens. Shan't relish my lunch to-day.

JAMES. As bad as that, Cokeson?

COKESON. It makes you think. [Confidentially] He must have had temptation.

JAMES. Not so fast. We haven't convicted him yet.

COKESON. I'd sooner have lost a month's salary than had this happen. [He broods.]

JAMES. I hope that fellow will hurry up.

COKESON. [Keeping things pleasant for the cashier] It isn't fifty yards, Mr. James. He won't be a minute.

JAMES. The idea of dishonesty about this office it hits me hard, Cokeson.

He goes towards the door of the partners' room.

SWEEDLE. [Entering quietly, to COKESON in a low voice] She's popped up again, sir-something she forgot to say to Falder.

COKESON. [Roused from his abstraction] Eh? Impossible. Send her away!

JAMES. What's that?

COKESON. Nothing, Mr. James. A private matter. Here, I'll come myself. [He goes into the outer office as JAMES passes into the partners' room] Now, you really mustn't—we can't have anybody just now.

RUTH. Not for a minute, sir?

COKESON. Reely! Reely! I can't have it. If you want him, wait about; he'll be going out for his lunch directly.

RUTH. Yes, sir.

WALTER, entering with the cashier, passes RUTH as she leaves the outer office.

COKESON. [To the cashier, who resembles a sedentary dragoon] Good-morning. [To WALTER] Your father's in there.

WALTER crosses and goes into the partners' room.

COKESON. It's a nahsty, unpleasant little matter, Mr. Cowley. I'm quite ashamed to have to trouble you.

COWLEY. I remember the cheque quite well. [As if it were a liver] Seemed in perfect order.

COKESON. Sit down, won't you? I'm not a sensitive man, but a thing like this about the place—it's not nice. I like people to be open and jolly together.

COWLEY. Quite so.

COKESON. [Buttonholing him, and glancing toward the partners' room] Of course he's a young man. I've told him about it before now— leaving space after his figures, but he will do it.

COWLEY. I should remember the person's face—quite a youth.

COKESON. I don't think we shall be able to show him to you, as a matter of fact.

JAMES and WALTER have come back from the partners' room.

JAMES. Good-morning, Mr. Cowley. You've seen my son and myself, you've seen Mr. Cokeson, and you've seen Sweedle, my office-boy. It was none of us, I take it.

The cashier shakes his head with a smile.

JAMES. Be so good as to sit there. Cokeson, engage Mr. Cowley in conversation, will you?

He goes toward FALDER'S room.

COKESON. Just a word, Mr. James.

JAMES. Well?

COKESON. You don't want to upset the young man in there, do you? He's a nervous young feller.

JAMES. This must be thoroughly cleared up, Cokeson, for the sake of Falder's name, to say nothing of yours.

COKESON. [With Some dignity] That'll look after itself, sir. He's been upset once this morning; I don't want him startled again.

JAMES. It's a matter of form; but I can't stand upon niceness over a thing like this—too serious. Just talk to Mr. Cowley.

He opens the door of FALDER'S room.

JAMES. Bring in the papers in Boulter's lease, will you, Falder?

COKESON. [Bursting into voice] Do you keep dogs?

The cashier, with his eyes fixed on the door, does not answer.

COKESON. You haven't such a thing as a bulldog pup you could spare me, I suppose?

At the look on the cashier's face his jaw drops, and he turns to see FALDER standing in the doorway, with his eyes fixed on COWLEY, like the eyes of a rabbit fastened on a snake.

FALDER. [Advancing with the papers] Here they are, sir!

JAMES. [Taking them] Thank you.

FALDER. Do you want me, sir?

JAMES. No, thanks!

FALDER turns and goes back into his own room. As he shuts the door JAMES gives the cashier an interrogative look, and the cashier nods.

JAMES. Sure? This isn't as we suspected.

COWLEY. Quite. He knew me. I suppose he can't slip out of that room?

COKESON. [Gloomily] There's only the window—a whole floor and a base-ment.

The door of FALDER'S room is quietly opened, and FALDER, with his hat in his hand, moves towards the door of the outer office.

JAMES. [Quietly] Where are you going, Falder?

FALDER. To have my lunch, sir.

JAMES. Wait a few minutes, would you? I want to speak to you about this lease.

FALDER. Yes, sir. [He goes back into his room.]

COWLEY. If I'm wanted, I can swear that's the young man who cashed the cheque. It was the last cheque I handled that morning before my lunch. These are the numbers of the notes he had. [He puts a slip of paper on the table; then, brushing his hat round] Good-morn-ing!

JAMES. Good-morning, Mr. Cowley!

COWLEY. [To COKESON] Good-morning.

COKESON. [With Stupefaction] Good-morning.

The cashier goes out through the outer office. COKESON sits down in his chair, as though it were the only place left in the morass of his feelings.

WALTER. What are you going to do?

JAMES. Have him in. Give me the cheque and the counterfoil.

COKESON. I don't understand. I thought young Davis——

JAMES. We shall see.

WALTER. One moment, father: have you thought it out?

JAMES. Call him in!

COKESON. [Rising with difficulty and opening FALDER'S door; hoarsely] Step in here a minute.

FALDER. [Impassively] Yes, sir?

JAMES. [Turning to him suddenly with the cheque held out] You know this cheque, Falder?

FALDER. No, sir.

JADES. Look at it. You cashed it last Friday week.

FALDER. Oh! yes, sir; that one—Davis gave it me.

JAMES. I know. And you gave Davis the cash?

FALDER. Yes, sir.

JAMES. When Davis gave you the cheque was it exactly like this?

FALDER. Yes, I think so, sir.

JAMES. You know that Mr. Walter drew that cheque for nine pounds?

FALDER. No, sir—ninety.

JAMES. Nine, Falder.

FALDER. [Faintly] I don't understand, sir.

JAMES. The suggestion, of course, is that the cheque was altered; whether by you or Davis is the question.

FALDER. I—I

COKESON. Take your time, take your time.

FALDER. [Regaining his impassivity] Not by me, sir.

JAMES. The cheque was handed to—Cokeson by Mr. Walter at one o'clock; we know that because Mr. Cokeson's lunch had just arrived.

COKESON. I couldn't leave it.

JAMES. Exactly; he therefore gave the cheque to Davis. It was cashed by you at 1.15. We know that because the cashier recollects it for the last cheque he handled before his lunch.

FALDER. Yes, sir, Davis gave it to me because some friends were giving him a farewell luncheon.

JAMES. [Puzzled] You accuse Davis, then?

FALDER. I don't know, sir—it's very funny.

WALTER, who has come close to his father, says something to him in a low voice.

JAMES. Davis was not here again after that Saturday, was he?

COKESON. [Anxious to be of assistance to the young man, and seeing faint signs of their all being jolly once more] No, he sailed on the Monday.

JAMES. Was he, Falder?

FALDER. [Very faintly] No, sir.

JAMES. Very well, then, how do you account for the fact that this nought was added to the nine in the counterfoil on or after Tuesday?

COKESON. [Surprised] How's that?

FALDER gives a sort of lurch; he tries to pull himself together, but he has gone all to pieces.

JAMES. [Very grimly] Out, I'm afraid, Cokeson. The cheque-book remained in Mr. Walter's pocket till he came back from Trenton on Tuesday morning. In the face of this, Falder, do you still deny that you altered both cheque and counterfoil?

FALDER. No, sir—no, Mr. How. I did it, sir; I did it.

COKESON. [Succumbing to his feelings] Dear, dear! what a thing to do!

FALDER. I wanted the money so badly, sir. I didn't know what I was doing.

COKESON. However such a thing could have come into your head!

FALDER. [Grasping at the words] I can't think, sir, really! It was just a minute of madness.

JAMES. A long minute, Falder. [Tapping the counterfoil] Four days at least.

FALDER. Sir, I swear I didn't know what I'd done till afterwards, and then I hadn't the pluck. Oh! Sir, look over it! I'll pay the money back—I will, I promise.

JAMES. Go into your room.

FALDER, with a swift imploring look, goes back into his room. There is silence.

JAMES. About as bad a case as there could be.

COKESON. To break the law like that-in here!

WALTER. What's to be done?

JAMES. Nothing for it. Prosecute.

WALTER. It's his first offence.

JAMES. [Shaking his head] I've grave doubts of that. Too neat a piece of swindling altogether.

COKESON. I shouldn't be surprised if he was tempted.

JAMES. Life's one long temptation, Cokeson.

COKESON. Ye-es, but I'm speaking of the flesh and the devil, Mr. James. There was a woman come to see him this morning.

WALTER. The woman we passed as we came in just now. Is it his wife?

COKESON. No, no relation. [Restraining what in jollier circumstances would have been a wink] A married person, though.

WALTER. How do you know?

COKESON. Brought her children. [Scandalised] There they were outside the office.

JAMES. A real bad egg.

WALTER. I should like to give him a chance.

JAMES. I can't forgive him for the sneaky way be went to work— counting on our suspecting young Davis if the matter came to light. It was the merest accident the cheque-book stayed in your pocket.

WALTER. It must have been the temptation of a moment. He hadn't time.

JAMES. A man doesn't succumb like that in a moment, if he's a clean mind and habits. He's rotten; got the eyes of a man who can't keep his hands off when there's money about.

WALTER. [Dryly] We hadn't noticed that before.

JAMES. [Brushing the remark aside] I've seen lots of those fellows in my time. No doing anything with them except to keep 'em out of harm's way. They've got a blind spat.

WALTER. It's penal servitude.

COKESON. They're nahsty places-prisons.

JAMES. [Hesitating] I don't see how it's possible to spare him. Out of the question to keep him in this office—honesty's the 'sine qua non'.

COKESON. [Hypnotised] Of course it is.

JAMES. Equally out of the question to send him out amongst people who've no knowledge of his character. One must think of society.

WALTER. But to brand him like this?

JAMES. If it had been a straightforward case I'd give him another chance. It's far from that. He has dissolute habits.

COKESON. I didn't say that—extenuating circumstances.

JAMES. Same thing. He's gone to work in the most cold-blooded way to defraud his employers, and cast the blame on an innocent man. If that's not a case for the law to take its course, I don't know what is.

WALTER. For the sake of his future, though.

JAMES. [Sarcastically] According to you, no one would ever prosecute.

WALTER. [Nettled] I hate the idea of it.

COKESON. That's rather 'ex parte', Mr. Walter! We must have protection.

JAMES. This is degenerating into talk.

He moves towards the partners' room.

WALTER. Put yourself in his place, father.

JAMES. You ask too much of me.

WALTER. We can't possibly tell the pressure there was on him.

JAMES. You may depend on it, my boy, if a man is going to do this sort of thing he'll do it, pressure or no pressure; if he isn't nothing'll make him.

WALTER. He'll never do it again.

COKESON. [Fatuously] S'pose I were to have a talk with him. We don't want to be hard on the young man.

JAMES. That'll do, Cokeson. I've made up my mind. [He passes into the partners' room.]

COKESON. [After a doubtful moment] We must excuse your father. I don't want to go against your father; if he thinks it right.

WALTER. Confound it, Cokeson! why don't you back me up? You know you feel——

COKESON. [On his dignity] I really can't say what I feel.

WALTER. We shall regret it.

COKESON. He must have known what he was doing.

WALTER. [Bitterly] "The quality of mercy is not strained."

COKESON. [Looking at him askance] Come, come, Mr. Walter. We must try and see it sensible.

SWEEDLE. [Entering with a tray] Your lunch, sir.

COKESON. Put it down!

While SWEEDLE is putting it down on COKESON's table, the detective, WISTER, enters the outer office, and, finding no one there, comes to the inner doorway. He is a square, medium-sized man, clean-shaved, in a serviceable blue serge suit and strong boots.

COKESON. [Hoarsely] Here! Here! What are we doing?

WISTER. [To WALTER] From Scotland Yard, sir. Detective-Sergeant Blister.

WALTER. [Askance] Very well! I'll speak to my father.

He goes into the partners' room. JAMES enters.

JAMES. Morning! [In answer to an appealing gesture from COKESON] I'm
    sorry; I'd stop short of this if I felt I could. Open that door. [SWEE-
    DLE, wondering and scared, opens it] Come here, Mr. Falder.

As FALDER comes shrinkingly out, the detective in obedience to a sign from
JAMES, slips his hand out and grasps his arm.

FALDER. [Recoiling] Oh! no,—oh! no!

WALTER. Come, come, there's a good lad.

JAMES. I charge him with felony.

FALTER. Oh, sir! There's some one—I did it for her. Let me be till to-morrow.

JAMES motions with his hand. At that sign of hardness, FALDER becomes
rigid. Then, turning, he goes out quietly in the detective's grip. JAMES follows,
stiff and erect. SWEEDLE, rushing to the door with open mouth, pursues them
through the outer office into the corridor. When they have all disappeared
COKESON spins completely round and makes a rush for the outer office.

COKESON: [Hoarsely] Here! What are we doing?

There is silence. He takes out his handkerchief and mops the sweat from his face.
Going back blindly to his table, sits down, and stares blankly at his lunch.

The curtain falls.

ACT II

A Court of Justice, on a foggy October afternoon crowded with barristers, solicitors, reporters, ushers, and jurymen. Sitting in the large, solid dock is FALDER, with a warder on either side of him, placed there for his safe custody, but seemingly indifferent to and unconscious of his presence. FALDER is sitting exactly opposite to the JUDGE, who, raised above the clamour of the court, also seems unconscious of and indifferent to everything. HAROLD CLEAVER, the counsel for the Crown, is a dried, yellowish man, of more than middle age, in a wig worn almost to the colour of his face. HECTOR FROME, the counsel for the defence, is a young, tall man, clean shaved, in a very white wig. Among the spectators, having already given their evidence, are JAMES and WALTER HOW, and COWLEY, the cashier. WISTER, the detective, is just leaving the witness-box.

CLEAVER. That is the case for the Crown, me lud!

Gathering his robes together, he sits down.

FROME. [Rising and bowing to the JUDGE] If it please your lordship and gentlemen of the jury. I am not going to dispute the fact that the prisoner altered this cheque, but I am going to put before you evidence as to the condition of his mind, and to submit that you would not be justified in finding that he was responsible for his actions at the time. I am going to show you, in fact, that he did this in a moment of aberration, amounting to temporary insanity, caused by the violent distress under which he was labouring. Gentlemen, the prisoner is only twenty-three years old. I shall call before you a woman from whom you will learn the events that led up to this act. You will hear from her own lips the tragic circumstances of her life, the still more tragic infatuation with which she has inspired the prisoner. This woman, gentlemen, has been leading a miserable existence with a husband who habitually ill-uses her, from whom she actually goes in terror of her life. I am not, of course, saying that it's either right or desirable for a young man to fall in love with a married woman, or that it's his business to rescue her from an ogre-like husband. I'm not saying anything of the sort. But we all know the power of the passion of love; and I would ask you to remember, gentlemen, in listening to her evidence, that, married to a drunken and violent husband, she has no power to get rid of him; for, as you know, another offence besides violence is necessary to enable a woman to obtain a divorce; and of this offence it does not appear that her husband is guilty.

JUDGE. Is this relevant, Mr. Frome?

FROME. My lord, I submit, extremely—I shall be able to show your lordship that directly.

JUDGE. Very well.

FROME. In these circumstances, what alternatives were left to her? She could either go on living with this drunkard, in terror of her life; or she could apply to the Court for a separation order. Well, gentlemen, my experience of such cases assures me that this would have given her very insufficient protection from the violence of such a man; and even if effectual would very likely have reduced her either to the workhouse or the streets—for it's not easy, as she is now finding, for an unskilled woman without means of livelihood to support herself and her children without resorting either to the Poor Law or—to speak quite plainly—to the sale of her body.

JUDGE. You are ranging rather far, Mr. Frome.

FROME. I shall fire point-blank in a minute, my lord.

JUDGE. Let us hope so.

FROME. Now, gentlemen, mark—and this is what I have been leading up to—this woman will tell you, and the prisoner will confirm her, that, confronted with such alternatives, she set her whole hopes on himself, knowing the feeling with which she had inspired him. She saw a way out of her misery by going with him to a new country, where they would both be unknown, and might pass as husband and wife. This was a desperate and, as my friend Mr. Cleaver will no doubt call it, an immoral resolution; but, as a fact, the minds of both of them were constantly turned towards it. One wrong is no excuse for another, and those who are never likely to be faced by such a situation possibly have the right to hold up their hands—as to that I prefer to say nothing. But whatever view you take, gentlemen, of this part of the prisoner's story—whatever opinion you form of the right of these two young people under such circumstances to take the law into their own hands—the fact remains that this young woman in her distress, and this young man, little more than a boy, who was so devotedly attached to her, did conceive this—if you like— reprehensible design of going away together. Now, for that, of course, they required money, and—they had none. As to the actual events of the morning of July 7th, on which this cheque was altered, the events on which I rely to prove the defendant's irresponsibility —I shall allow those events to speak for themselves, through the lips of my witness. Robert Cokeson. [He turns, looks round, takes up a sheet of paper, and waits.]

COKESON is summoned into court, and goes into the witness-box, holding his hat before him. The oath is administered to him.

FROME. What is your name?

COKESON. Robert Cokeson.

FROME. Are you managing clerk to the firm of solicitors who employ the prisoner?

COKESON. Ye-es.

FROME. How long had the prisoner been in their employ?

COKESON. Two years. No, I'm wrong there—all but seventeen days.

FROME. Had you him under your eye all that time?

COKESON. Except Sundays and holidays.

FROME. Quite so. Let us hear, please, what you have to say about his general character during those two years.

COKESON. [Confidentially to the jury, and as if a little surprised at being asked] He was a nice, pleasant-spoken young man. I'd no fault to find with him—quite the contrary. It was a great surprise to me when he did a thing like that.

FROME. Did he ever give you reason to suspect his honesty?

COKESON. No! To have dishonesty in our office, that'd never do.

FROME. I'm sure the jury fully appreciate that, Mr. Cokeson.

COKESON. Every man of business knows that honesty's 'the sign qua non'.

FROME. Do you give him a good character all round, or do you not?

COKESON. [Turning to the JUDGE] Certainly. We were all very jolly and pleasant together, until this happened. Quite upset me.

FROME. Now, coming to the morning of the 7th of July, the morning on which the cheque was altered. What have you to say about his demeanour that morning?

COKESON. [To the jury] If you ask me, I don't think he was quite compos when he did it.

THE JUDGE. [Sharply] Are you suggesting that he was insane?

COKESON. Not compos.

THE JUDGE. A little more precision, please.

FROME. [Smoothly] Just tell us, Mr. Cokeson.

COKESON. [Somewhat outraged] Well, in my opinion—[looking at the JUDGE]—such as it is—he was jumpy at the time. The jury will understand my meaning.

FROME. Will you tell us how you came to that conclusion?

COKESON. Ye-es, I will. I have my lunch in from the restaurant, a chop and a potato—saves time. That day it happened to come just as Mr. Walter How handed me the cheque. Well, I like it hot; so I went into the clerks' office and I handed the cheque to Davis, the other clerk, and told him to get change. I noticed young Falder walking up and down. I said to him: "This is not the Zoological Gardens, Falder."

FROME. Do you remember what he answered?

COKESON. Ye-es: "I wish to God it were!" Struck me as funny.

FROME. Did you notice anything else peculiar?

COKESON. I did.

FROME. What was that?

COKESON. His collar was unbuttoned. Now, I like a young man to be neat. I said to him: "Your collar's unbuttoned."

FROME. And what did he answer?

COKESON. Stared at me. It wasn't nice.

THE JUDGE. Stared at you? Isn't that a very common practice?

COKESON. Ye-es, but it was the look in his eyes. I can't explain my meaning— it was funny.

FROME. Had you ever seen such a look in his eyes before?

COKESON. No. If I had I should have spoken to the partners. We can't have anything eccentric in our profession.

THE JUDGE. Did you speak to them on that occasion?

COKESON. [Confidentially] Well, I didn't like to trouble them about prime facey evidence.

FROME. But it made a very distinct impression on your mind?

COKESON. Ye-es. The clerk Davis could have told you the same.

FROME. Quite so. It's very unfortunate that we've not got him here. Now can you tell me of the morning on which the discovery of the forgery was made? That would be the 18th. Did anything happen that morning?

COKESON. [With his hand to his ear] I'm a little deaf.

FROME. Was there anything in the course of that morning—I mean before the discovery—that caught your attention?

COKESON. Ye-es—a woman.

THE JUDGE. How is this relevant, Mr. Frome?

FROME. I am trying to establish the state of mind in which the prisoner committed this act, my lord.

THE JUDGE. I quite appreciate that. But this was long after the act.

FROME. Yes, my lord, but it contributes to my contention.

THE JUDGE. Well!

FROME. You say a woman. Do you mean that she came to the office?

COKESON. Ye-es.

FROME. What for?

COKESON. Asked to see young Falder; he was out at the moment.

FROME. Did you see her?

COKESON. I did.

FROME. Did she come alone?

COKESON. [Confidentially] Well, there you put me in a difficulty. I mustn't tell you what the office-boy told me.

FROME. Quite so, Mr. Cokeson, quite so——

COKESON. [Breaking in with an air of "You are young—leave it to me"] But I think we can get round it. In answer to a question put to her by a third party the woman said to me: "They're mine, sir."

THE JUDGE. What are? What were?

COKESON. Her children. They were outside.

THE JUDGE. HOW do you know?

COKESON. Your lordship mustn't ask me that, or I shall have to tell you what I was told—and that'd never do.

THE JUDGE. [Smiling] The office-boy made a statement.

COKESON. Egg-zactly.

FROME. What I want to ask you, Mr. Cokeson, is this. In the course of her appeal to see Falder, did the woman say anything that you specially remember?

COKESON. [Looking at him as if to encourage him to complete the sentence] A leetle more, sir.

FROME. Or did she not?

COKESON. She did. I shouldn't like you to have led me to the answer.

FROME. [With an irritated smile] Will you tell the jury what it was?

COKESON. "It's a matter of life and death."

FOREMAN OF THE JURY. Do you mean the woman said that?

COKESON. [Nodding] It's not the sort of thing you like to have said to you.

FROME. [A little impatiently] Did Falder come in while she was there? [COKESON nods] And she saw him, and went away?

COKESON. Ah! there I can't follow you. I didn't see her go.

FROME. Well, is she there now?

COKESON. [With an indulgent smile] No!

FROME. Thank you, Mr. Cokeson. [He sits down.]

CLEAVER. [Rising] You say that on the morning of the forgery the prisoner was jumpy. Well, now, sir, what precisely do you mean by that word?

COKESON. [Indulgently] I want you to understand. Have you ever seen a dog that's lost its master? He was kind of everywhere at once with his eyes.

CLEAVER. Thank you; I was coming to his eyes. You called them "funny." What are we to understand by that? Strange, or what?

COKESON. Ye-es, funny.

COKESON. [Sharply] Yes, sir, but what may be funny to you may not be funny to me, or to the jury. Did they look frightened, or shy, or fierce, or what?

COKESON. You make it very hard for me. I give you the word, and you want me to give you another.

CLEAVER. [Rapping his desk] Does "funny" mean mad?

CLEAVER. Not mad, fun——

CLEAVER. Very well! Now you say he had his collar unbuttoned? Was it a hot day?

COKESON. Ye-es; I think it was.

CLEAVER. And did he button it when you called his attention to it?

COKESON. Ye-es, I think he did.

CLEAVER. Would you say that that denoted insanity?

He sits downs. COKESON, who has opened his mouth to reply, is left gaping.

FROME. [Rising hastily] Have you ever caught him in that dishevelled state before?

COKESON. No! He was always clean and quiet.

FROME. That will do, thank you.

COKESON turns blandly to the JUDGE, as though to rebuke counsel for not remembering that the JUDGE might wish to have a chance; arriving at the conclusion that he is to be asked nothing further, he turns and descends from the box, and sits down next to JAMES and WALTER.

FROME. Ruth Honeywill.

RUTH comes into court, and takes her stand stoically in the witness-box. She is sworn.

FROME. What is your name, please?

RUTH. Ruth Honeywill.

FROME. How old are you?

RUTH. Twenty-six.

FROME. You are a married woman, living with your husband? A little louder.

RUTH. No, sir; not since July.

FROME. Have you any children?

RUTH. Yes, sir, two.

FROME. Are they living with you?

RUTH. Yes, sir.

FROME. You know the prisoner?

RUTH. [Looking at him] Yes.

FROME. What was the nature of your relations with him?

RUTH. We were friends.

THE JUDGE. Friends?

RUTH. [Simply] Lovers, sir.

THE JUDGE. [Sharply] In what sense do you use that word?

RUTH. We love each other.

THE JUDGE. Yes, but——

RUTH. [Shaking her head] No, your lordship—not yet.

THE JUDGE. 'Not yet! H'm! [He looks from RUTH to FALDER] Well!

FROME. What is your husband?

RUTH. Traveller.

FROME. And what was the nature of your married life?

RUTH. [Shaking her head] It don't bear talking about.

FROME. Did he ill-treat you, or what?

RUTH. Ever since my first was born.

FROME. In what way?

RUTH. I'd rather not say. All sorts of ways.

THE JUDGE. I am afraid I must stop this, you know.

RUTH. [Pointing to FALDER] He offered to take me out of it, sir. We were going to South America.

FROME. [Hastily] Yes, quite—and what prevented you?

RUTH. I was outside his office when he was taken away. It nearly broke my heart.

FROME. You knew, then, that he had been arrested?

RUTH. Yes, sir. I called at his office afterwards, and [pointing to COKESON] that gentleman told me all about it.

FROME. Now, do you remember the morning of Friday, July 7th?

RUTH. Yes.

FROME. Why?

RUTH. My husband nearly strangled me that morning.

THE JUDGE. Nearly strangled you!

RUTH. [Bowing her head] Yes, my lord.

FROME. With his hands, or——?

RUTH. Yes, I just managed to get away from him. I went straight to my friend. It was eight o'clock.

THE JUDGE. In the morning? Your husband was not under the influence of liquor then?

RUTH. It wasn't always that.

FROME. In what condition were you?

RUTH. In very bad condition, sir. My dress was torn, and I was half choking.

FROME. Did you tell your friend what had happened?

RUTH. Yes. I wish I never had.

FROME. It upset him?

RUTH. Dreadfully.

FROME. Did he ever speak to you about a cheque?

RUTH. Never.

FROZE. Did he ever give you any money?

RUTH. Yes.

FROME. When was that?

RUTH. On Saturday.

FROME. The 8th?

RUTH. To buy an outfit for me and the children, and get all ready to start.

FROME. Did that surprise you, or not?

RUTH. What, sir?

FROME. That he had money to give you.

Ring. Yes, because on the morning when my husband nearly killed me my friend cried because he hadn't the money to get me away. He told me afterwards he'd come into a windfall.

FROME. And when did you last see him?

RUTH. The day he was taken away, sir. It was the day we were to have started.

FROME. Oh, yes, the morning of the arrest. Well, did you see him at all between the Friday and that morning? [RUTH nods] What was his manner then?

RUTH. Dumb—like—sometimes he didn't seem able to say a word.

FROME. As if something unusual had happened to him?

RUTH. Yes.

FROME. Painful, or pleasant, or what?

RUTH. Like a fate hanging over him.

FROME. [Hesitating] Tell me, did you love the prisoner very much?

RUTH. [Bowing her head] Yes.

FROME. And had he a very great affection for you?

RUTH. [Looking at FALDER] Yes, sir.

FROME. Now, ma'am, do you or do you not think that your danger and unhappiness would seriously affect his balance, his control over his actions?

RUTH. Yes.

FROME. His reason, even?

RUTH. For a moment like, I think it would.

FROME. Was he very much upset that Friday morning, or was he fairly calm?

RUTH. Dreadfully upset. I could hardly bear to let him go from me.

FROME. Do you still love him?

RUTH. [With her eyes on FALDER] He's ruined himself for me.

FROME. Thank you.

He sits down. RUTH remains stoically upright in the witness-box.

CLEAVER. [In a considerate voice] When you left him on the morning of Friday the 7th you would not say that he was out of his mind, I suppose?

RUTH. No, sir.

CLEAVER. Thank you; I've no further questions to ask you.

RUTH. [Bending a little forward to the jury] I would have done the same for
     him; I would indeed.

THE JUDGE. Please, please! You say your married life is an unhappy one?
     Faults on both sides?

RUTH. Only that I never bowed down to him. I don't see why I should, sir,
     not to a man like that.

THE JUDGE. You refused to obey him?

RUTH. [Avoiding the question] I've always studied him to keep things nice.

THE JUDGE. Until you met the prisoner—was that it?

RUTH. No; even after that.

THE JUDGE. I ask, you know, because you seem to me to glory in this affec-
     tion of yours for the prisoner.

RUTH. [Hesitating] I—I do. It's the only thing in my life now.

THE JUDGE. [Staring at her hard] Well, step down, please.

RUTH looks at FALDER, then passes quietly down and takes her seat among the
witnesses.

FROME. I call the prisoner, my lord.

FALDER leaves the dock; goes into the witness-box, and is duly sworn.

FROME. What is your name?

FALDER. William Falder.

FROME. And age?

FALDER. Twenty-three.

FROME. You are not married?

FALDER shakes his head

FROME. How long have you known the last witness?

FALDER. Six months.

FROME. Is her account of the relationship between you a correct one?

FALDER. Yes.

FROME. You became devotedly attached to her, however?

FALDER. Yes.

THE JUDGE. Though you knew she was a married woman?

FALDER. I couldn't help it, your lordship.

THE JUDGE. Couldn't help it?

FALDER. I didn't seem able to.

The JUDGE slightly shrugs his shoulders.

FROME. How did you come to know her?

FALDER. Through my married sister.

FROME. Did you know whether she was happy with her husband?

FALDER. It was trouble all the time.

FROME. You knew her husband?

FALDER. Only through her—he's a brute.

THE JUDGE. I can't allow indiscriminate abuse of a person not present.

FROME. [Bowing] If your lordship pleases. [To FALDER] You admit altering this cheque?

FALDER bows his head.

FROME. Carry your mind, please, to the morning of Friday, July the 7th, and tell the jury what happened.

FALDER. [Turning to the jury] I was having my breakfast when she came. Her dress was all torn, and she was gasping and couldn't seem to get her breath at all; there were the marks of his fingers round her throat; her arm was bruised, and the blood had got into her eyes dreadfully. It frightened me, and then when she told me, I felt—I felt—well—it was too much for me! [Hardening suddenly] If you'd seen it, having the feelings for her that I had, you'd have felt the same, I know.

FROME. Yes?

FALDER. When she left me—because I had to go to the office—I was out of my senses for fear that he'd do it again, and thinking what I could do. I couldn't work—all the morning I was like that—simply couldn't fix my mind on anything. I couldn't think at all. I seemed to have to keep moving. When Davis—the other clerk—gave me the cheque—he said: "It'll do you good, Will, to have a run with this. You seem half off your chump this morning." Then when I had it in my hand—I don't know how it came, but it just flashed across me that if I put the 'ty' and the nought there would be the money to get her away. It just came and went—I never thought of it again. Then Davis went out to his lunch-eon, and I don't really remember what I did till I'd pushed the cheque through to the cashier under the rail. I remember his saying "Gold or notes?" Then I suppose I knew what I'd done. Anyway, when I got outside I wanted to chuck myself under a bus; I wanted to throw the money away; but it seemed I was in for it, so I thought at any rate I'd save her. Of course the tickets I took for the passage and the little I gave her's been wasted, and all, except what I was obliged to spend myself, I've restored. I keep thinking over and over however it was I came to do it, and how I can't have it all again to do differently!

FALDER is silent, twisting his hands before him.

FROME. How far is it from your office to the bank?

FALDER. Not more than fifty yards, sir.

FROME. From the time Davis went out to lunch to the time you cashed the cheque, how long do you say it must have been?

FALDER. It couldn't have been four minutes, sir, because I ran all the way.

FROME. During those four minutes you say you remember nothing?

FALDER. No, sir; only that I ran.

FROME. Not even adding the 'ty' and the nought?'

FALDER. No, sir. I don't really.

FROME sits down, and CLEAVER rises.

CLEAVER. But you remember running, do you?

FALDER. I was all out of breath when I got to the bank.

CLEAVER. And you don't remember altering the cheque?

FALDER. [Faintly] No, sir.

CLEAVER. Divested of the romantic glamour which my friend is casting over the case, is this anything but an ordinary forgery? Come.

FALDER. I was half frantic all that morning, sir.

CLEAVER. Now, now! You don't deny that the 'ty' and the nought were so like the rest of the handwriting as to thoroughly deceive the cashier?

FALDER. It was an accident.

CLEAVER. [Cheerfully] Queer sort of accident, wasn't it? On which day did you alter the counterfoil?

FALDER. [Hanging his head] On the Wednesday morning.

CLEAVER. Was that an accident too?

FALDER. [Faintly] No.

CLEAVER. To do that you had to watch your opportunity, I suppose?

FALDER. [Almost inaudibly] Yes.

CLEAVER. You don't suggest that you were suffering under great excitement when you did that?

FALDER. I was haunted.

CLEAVER. With the fear of being found out?

FALDER. [Very low] Yes.

THE JUDGE. Didn't it occur to you that the only thing for you to do was to confess to your employers, and restore the money?

FALDER. I was afraid. [There is silence]

CLEAVER. You desired, too, no doubt, to complete your design of taking this woman away?

FALDER. When I found I'd done a thing like that, to do it for nothing seemed so dreadful. I might just as well have chucked myself into the river.

CLEAVER. You knew that the clerk Davis was about to leave England —didn't it occur to you when you altered this cheque that suspicion would fall on him?

FALDER. It was all done in a moment. I thought of it afterwards.

CLEAVER. And that didn't lead you to avow what you'd done?

FALDER. [Sullenly] I meant to write when I got out there—I would have repaid the money.

THE JUDGE. But in the meantime your innocent fellow clerk might have been prosecuted.

FALDER. I knew he was a long way off, your lordship. I thought there'd be time. I didn't think they'd find it out so soon.

FROME. I might remind your lordship that as Mr. Walter How had the cheque-book in his pocket till after Davis had sailed, if the discovery had been made only one day later Falder himself would have left, and suspicion would have attached to him, and not to Davis, from the beginning.

THE JUDGE. The question is whether the prisoner knew that suspicion would light on himself, and not on Davis. [To FALDER sharply] Did you know that Mr. Walter How had the cheque-book till after Davis had sailed?

FALDER. I—I—thought—he——

THE JUDGE. Now speak the truth-yes or no!

FALDER. [Very low] No, my lord. I had no means of knowing.

THE JUDGE. That disposes of your point, Mr. Frome.

[FROME bows to the JUDGE]

CLEAVER. Has any aberration of this nature ever attacked you before?

FALDER. [Faintly] No, sir.

CLEAVER. You had recovered sufficiently to go back to your work that after-noon?

FALDER. Yes, I had to take the money back.

CLEAVER. You mean the nine pounds. Your wits were sufficiently keen for you to remember that? And you still persist in saying you don't remem-ber altering this cheque. [He sits down]

FALDER. If I hadn't been mad I should never have had the courage.

FROME. [Rising] Did you have your lunch before going back?

FALDER. I never ate a thing all day; and at night I couldn't sleep.

FROME.   Now, as to the four minutes that elapsed between Davis's going out
         and your cashing the cheque: do you say that you recollect nothing
         during those four minutes?

FALDER. [After a moment] I remember thinking of Mr. Cokeson's face.

FROME. Of Mr. Cokeson's face! Had that any connection with what you were
        doing?

FALDER. No, Sir.

FROME. Was that in the office, before you ran out?

FALDER. Yes, and while I was running.

FROME. And that lasted till the cashier said: "Will you have gold or notes?"

FALDER. Yes, and then I seemed to come to myself—and it was too late.

FROME. Thank you. That closes the evidence for the defence, my lord.

The JUDGE nods, and FALDER goes back to his seat in the dock.

FROME. [Gathering up notes] If it please your lordship—Gentlemen of the
        Jury,—My friend in cross-examination has shown a disposition to
        sneer at the defence which has been set up in this case, and I am free
        to admit that nothing I can say will move you, if the evidence has not
        already convinced you that the prisoner committed this act in a
        moment when to all practical intents and purposes he was not respon-
        sible for his actions; a moment of such mental and moral vacuity, aris-
        ing from the violent emotional agitation under which he had been
        suffering, as to amount to temporary madness. My friend has allud-
        ed to the "romantic glamour" with which I have sought to invest this
        case. Gentlemen, I have done nothing of the kind. I have merely
        shown you the background of "life"—that palpitating life which,
        believe me—whatever my friend may say—always lies behind the
        commission of a crime. Now gentlemen, we live in a highly, civilized

age, and the sight of brutal violence disturbs us in a very strange way, even when we have no personal interest in the matter. But when we see it inflicted on a woman whom we love—what then? Just think of what your own feelings would have been, each of you, at the prisoner's age; and then look at him. Well! he is hardly the comfortable, shall we say bucolic, person likely to contemplate with equanimity marks of gross violence on a woman to whom he was devotedly attached. Yes, gentlemen, look at him! He has not a strong face; but neither has he a vicious face. He is just the sort of man who would easily become the prey of his emotions. You have heard the description of his eyes. My friend may laugh at the word "funny"—I think it better describes the peculiar uncanny look of those who are strained to breaking-point than any other word which could have been used. I don't pretend, mind you, that his mental irresponsibility—was more than a flash of darkness, in which all sense of proportion became lost; but to contend, that, just as a man who destroys himself at such a moment may be, and often is, absolved from the stigma attaching to the crime of self-murder, so he may, and frequently does, commit other crimes while in this irresponsible condition, and that he may as justly be acquitted of criminal intent and treated as a patient. I admit that this is a plea which might well be abused. It is a matter for discretion. But here you have a case in which there is every reason to give the benefit of the doubt. You heard me ask the prisoner what he thought of during those four fatal minutes. What was his answer? "I thought of Mr. Cokeson's face!" Gentlemen, no man could invent an answer like that; it is absolutely stamped with truth. You have seen the great affection [legitimate or not] existing between him and this woman, who came here to give evidence for him at the risk of her life. It is impossible for you to doubt his distress on the morning when he committed this act. We well know what terrible havoc such distress can make in weak and highly nervous people. It was all the work of a moment. The rest has followed, as death follows a stab to the heart, or water drops if you hold up a jug to empty it. Believe me, gentlemen, there is nothing more tragic in life than the utter impossibility of changing what you have done. Once this cheque was altered and presented, the work of four minutes—four mad minutes —the rest has been silence. But in those four minutes the boy before you has slipped through a door, hardly opened, into that great cage which never again quite lets a man go—the cage of the Law. His further acts, his failure to confess, the alteration of the counterfoil, his preparations for flight, are all evidence—not of deliberate and guilty intention when he committed the prime act from which these subsequent acts arose; no—they are merely evidence of the weak character which is clearly enough his misfortune. But is a man to be lost because he is bred and born with a weak character? Gentlemen, men like the prisoner are destroyed daily under our law for want of that human insight which sees them as they are, patients, and not criminals. If the prisoner be found guilty, and treated as though he were a criminal type, he will, as all experience shows, in all probability become one. I beg you not to return a verdict that may thrust him back into prison and brand him for ever. Gentlemen, Justice is a machine that, when some one has once given it the starting push, rolls on of itself. Is this young man to be ground to pieces under this machine for an act which at the worst was one of weakness? Is he to become a member of the luckless crews that man those dark, ill-starred ships called prisons? Is that to be his voyage-from which so few return? Or is he to have another chance, to be still looked on as one who has gone a little astray, but who will come back? I urge you, gentlemen, do not ruin this young man! For, as a result of those four minutes, ruin, utter and irretrievable, stares him in the face. He can be saved now. Imprison him as a criminal, and I affirm to you that he will be lost. He has neither the face nor the manner of one who can survive that terrible ordeal. Weigh in the scales his criminality and the suffering he has undergone. The latter is ten times heavier already. He has lain in prison under this charge for more than two months. Is he likely ever to forget that? Imagine the anguish of his mind during that time. He has had his punishment, gentlemen, you may depend. The rolling of the chariot-wheels of Justice over this boy began when it was decided to prosecute him. We are now already at the second stage. If you permit it to go on to the third I would not give—that for him.

He holds up finger and thumb in the form of a circle, drops his hand, and sits dozen.

The jury stir, and consult each other's faces; then they turn towards the counsel for the Crown, who rises, and, fixing his eyes on a spot that seems to give him satisfaction, slides them every now and then towards the jury.

CLEAVER. May it please your lordship—[Rising on his toes] Gentlemen of the
           Jury,—The facts in this case are not disputed, and the defence, if my
           friend will allow me to say so, is so thin that I don't propose to waste
           the time of the Court by taking you over the evidence. The plea is

one of temporary insanity. Well, gentlemen, I daresay it is clearer to me than it is to you why this rather—what shall we call it?—bizarre defence has been set up. The alternative would have been to plead guilty. Now, gentlemen, if the prisoner had pleaded guilty my friend would have had to rely on a simple appeal to his lordship. Instead of that, he has gone into the byways and hedges and found this—er—peculiar plea, which has enabled him to show you the proverbial woman, to put her in the box—to give, in fact, a romantic glow to this affair. I compliment my friend; I think it highly ingenious of him. By these means, he has—to a certain extent—got round the Law. He has brought the whole story of motive and stress out in court, at first hand, in a way that he would not otherwise have been able to do. But when you have once grasped that fact, gentlemen, you have grasped everything. [With good-humoured contempt] For look at this plea of insanity; we can't put it lower than that. You have heard the woman. She has every reason to favour the prisoner, but what did she say? She said that the prisoner was not insane when she left him in the morning. If he were going out of his mind through distress, that was obviously the moment when insanity would have shown itself. You have heard the managing clerk, another witness for the defence. With some difficulty I elicited from him the admission that the prisoner, though jumpy [a word that he seemed to think you would understand, gentlemen, and I'm sure I hope you do], was not mad when the cheque was handed to Davis. I agree with my friend that it's unfortunate that we have not got Davis here, but the prisoner has told you the words with which Davis in turn handed him the cheque; he obviously, therefore, was not mad when he received it, or he would not have remembered those words. The cashier has told you that he was certainly in his senses when he cashed it. We have therefore the plea that a man who is sane at ten minutes past one, and sane at fifteen minutes past, may, for the purposes of avoiding the consequences of a crime, call himself insane between those points of time. Really, gentlemen, this is so peculiar a proposition that I am not disposed to weary you with further argument. You will form your own opinion of its value. My friend has adopted this way of saying a great deal to you—and very eloquently—on the score of youth, temptation, and the like. I might point out, however, that the offence with which the prisoner is charged is one of the most serious known to our law; and there are certain features in this case, such as the suspicion which he allowed to rest on his innocent fellow- clerk, and his relations with this married woman, which will render it difficult for you to attach too much importance to such pleading. I ask you, in short, gentlemen, for that verdict of guilty which, in the circumstances, I regard you as, unfortunately, bound to record.

Letting his eyes travel from the JUDGE and the jury to FROME, he sits down.

THE JUDGE. [Bending a little towards the jury, and speaking in a business-like voice] Gentlemen, you have heard the evidence, and the comments on it. My only business is to make clear to you the issues you have to try. The facts are admitted, so far as the alteration of this cheque and counterfoil by the prisoner. The defence set up is that he was not in a responsible condition when he committed the crime. Well, you have heard the prisoner's story, and the evidence of the other witnesses—so far as it bears on the point of insanity. If you think that what you have heard establishes the fact that the prisoner was insane at the time of the forgery, you will find him guilty, but insane. If, on the other hand, you conclude from what you have seen and heard that the prisoner was sane— and nothing short of insanity will count—you will find him guilty. In reviewing the testimony as to his mental condition you must bear in mind very carefully the evidence as to his demeanour and conduct both before and after the act of forgery—the evidence of the prisoner himself, of the woman, of the witness—er—COKESON, and—er—of the cashier. And in regard to that I especially direct your attention to the prisoner's admission that the idea of adding the 'ty' and the nought did come into his mind at the moment when the cheque was handed to him; and also to the alteration of the counterfoil, and to his subsequent conduct generally. The bearing of all this on the question of premeditation [and premeditation will imply sanity] is very obvious. You must not allow any considerations of age or temptation to weigh with you in the finding of your verdict. Before you can come to a verdict of guilty but insane you must be well and thoroughly convinced that the condition of his mind was such as would have qualified him at the moment for a lunatic asylum. [He pauses, then, seeing that the jury are doubtful whether to retire or no, adds:] You may retire, gentlemen, if you wish to do so.

The jury retire by a door behind the JUDGE. The JUDGE bends over his notes. FALDER, leaning from the dock, speaks excitedly to his solicitor, pointing dawn at RUTH. The solicitor in turn speaks to FROME.

FROME. [Rising] My lord. The prisoner is very anxious that I should ask you if your lordship would kindly request the reporters not to disclose the name of the woman witness in the Press reports of these proceedings. Your lordship will understand that the consequences might be extremely serious to her.

THE JUDGE. [Pointedly—with the suspicion of a smile] well, Mr. Frome, you deliberately took this course which involved bringing her here.

FROME. [With an ironic bow] If your lordship thinks I could have brought out the full facts in any other way?

THE JUDGE. H'm! Well.

FROME. There is very real danger to her, your lordship.

THE JUDGE. You see, I have to take your word for all that.

FROME. If your lordship would be so kind. I can assure your lordship that I am not exaggerating.

THE JUDGE. It goes very much against the grain with me that the name of a witness should ever be suppressed. [With a glance at FALDER, who is gripping and clasping his hands before him, and then at RUTH, who is sitting perfectly rigid with her eyes fixed on FALDER] I'll consider your application. It must depend. I have to remember that she may have come here to commit perjury on the prisoner's behalf.

FROME. Your lordship, I really——

THE JUDGE. Yes, yes—I don't suggest anything of the sort, Mr. Frome. Leave it at that for the moment.

As he finishes speaking, the jury return, and file back into the box.

CLERK of ASSIZE. Gentlemen, are you agreed on your verdict?

FOREMAN. We are.

CLERK of ASSIZE. Is it Guilty, or Guilty but insane?

FOREMAN. Guilty.

The JUDGE nods; then, gathering up his notes, sits looking at FALDER, who
stands motionless.

FROME. [Rising] If your lordship would allow me to address you in mitigation
        of sentence. I don't know if your lordship thinks I can add anything to
        what I have said to the jury on the score of the prisoner's youth, and the
        great stress under which he acted.

THE JUDGE. I don't think you can, Mr. Frome.

FROME. If your lordship says so—I do most earnestly beg your lordship to give
        the utmost weight to my plea. [He sits down.]

THE JUDGE. [To the CLERK] Call upon him.

THE CLERK. Prisoner at the bar, you stand convicted of felony. Have you any-
        thing to say for yourself, why the Court should not give you judg-
        ment according to law? [FALDER shakes his head]

THE JUDGE. William Falder, you have been given fair trial and found guilty,
        in my opinion rightly found guilty, of forgery. [He pauses; then,
        consulting his notes, goes on] The defence was set up that you
        were not responsible for your actions at the moment of commit-
        ting this crime. There is no, doubt, I think, that this was a device
        to bring out at first hand the nature of the temptation to which
        you succumbed. For throughout the trial your counsel was in
        reality making an appeal for mercy. The setting up of this
        defence of course enabled him to put in some evidence that
        might weigh in that direction. Whether he was well advised to so
        is another matter. He claimed that you should be treated rather
        as a patient than as a criminal. And this plea of his, which in the
        end amounted to a passionate appeal, he based in effect on an
        indictment of the march of Justice, which he practically accused
        of confirming and completing the process of criminality. Now,

in considering how far I should allow weight to his appeal; I have
a number of factors to take into account. I have to consider on
the one hand the grave nature of your offence, the deliberate way
in which you subsequently altered the counterfoil, the danger you
caused to an innocent man—and that, to my mind, is a very
grave point—and finally I have to consider the necessity of deter-
ring others from following your example. On the other hand, I
have to bear in mind that you are young, that you have hitherto
borne a good character, that you were, if I am to believe your evidence and that of your witnesses, in a state of some emotional
excitement when you committed this crime. I have every wish,
consistently with my duty—not only to you, but to the community—to treat you with leniency. And this brings me to what are
the determining factors in my mind in my consideration of your
case. You are a clerk in a lawyer's office—that is a very serious ele-
ment in this case; there can be no possible excuse made for you
on the ground that you were not fully conversant with the nature
of the crime you were committing, and the penalties that attach
to it. It is said, however, that you were carried away by your emotions. The story has been told here to-day of your relations with
this—er—Mrs. Honeywill; on that story both the defence and
the plea for mercy were in effect based. Now what is that story?
It is that you, a young man, and she, a young woman, unhappily married, had formed an attachment, which you both say—
with what truth I am unable to gauge- -had not yet resulted in
immoral relations, but which you both admit was about to result
in such relationship. Your counsel has made an attempt to palli-
ate this, on the ground that the woman is in what he describes, I
think, as "a hopeless position." As to that I can express no opinion. She is a married woman, and the fact is patent that you
committed this crime with the view of furthering an immoral
design. Now, however I might wish, I am not able to justify to
my conscience a plea for mercy which has a basis inimical to
morality. It is vitiated 'ab initio', and would, if successful, free you
for the completion of this immoral project. Your counsel has
made an attempt to trace your offence back to what he seems to
suggest is a defect in the marriage law; he has made an attempt
also to show that to punish you with further imprisonment
would be unjust. I do not follow him in these flights. The Law
is what it is—a majestic edifice, sheltering all of us, each stone of
which rests on another. I am concerned only with its administra-

tion. The crime you have committed is a very serious one. I cannot feel it in accordance with my duty to Society to exercise the powers I have in your favour. You will go to penal servitude for three years.

FALDER, who throughout the JUDGE'S speech has looked at him steadily, lets his head fall forward on his breast. RUTH starts up from her seat as he is taken out by the warders. There is a bustle in court.

THE JUDGE. [Speaking to the reporters] Gentlemen of the Press, I think that the name of the female witness should not be reported.

The reporters bow their acquiescence. THE JUDGE. [To RUTH, who is staring in the direction in which FALDER has disappeared] Do you understand, your name will not be mentioned?

COKESON. [Pulling her sleeve] The judge is speaking to you.

RUTH turns, stares at the JUDGE, and turns away.

THE JUDGE. I shall sit rather late to-day. Call the next case.

CLERK of ASSIZE. [To a warder] Put up John Booley.

To cries of "Witnesses in the case of Booley":

The curtain falls.

ACT III

SCENE I

A prison. A plainly furnished room, with two large barred windows, overlooking the prisoners' exercise yard, where men, in yellow clothes marked with arrows, and yellow brimless caps, are seen in single file at a distance of four yards from each other, walking rapidly on serpentine white lines marked on the concrete floor of the yard. Two warders in blue uniforms, with peaked caps and swords, are stationed amongst them. The room has distempered walls, a bookcase with numerous official-looking books, a cupboard between the windows, a plan of the prison on the wall, a writing-table covered with documents. It is Christmas Eve.

The GOVERNOR, a neat, grave-looking man, with a trim, fair moustache, the eyes of a theorist, and grizzled hair, receding from the temples, is standing close to this writing-table looking at a sort of rough saw made out of a piece of metal. The hand in which he holds it is gloved, for two fingers are missing. The chief warder, WOODER, a tall, thin, military- looking man of sixty, with grey moustache and melancholy, monkey-like eyes, stands very upright two paces from him.

THE GOVERNOR. [With a faint, abstracted smile] Queer-looking affair, Mr.
        Wooder! Where did you find it?

WOODER. In his mattress, sir. Haven't come across such a thing for two years
        now.

THE GOVERNOR. [With curiosity] Had he any set plan?

WOODER. He'd sawed his window-bar about that much. [He holds up his thumb and finger a quarter of an inch apart]

THE GOVERNOR. I'll see him this afternoon. What's his name? Moaney! An old hand, I think?

WOODER. Yes, sir-fourth spell of penal. You'd think an old lag like him would have had more sense by now. [With pitying contempt] Occupied his mind, he said. Breaking in and breaking out—that's all they think about.

THE GOVERNOR. Who's next him?

WOODER. O'Cleary, sir.

THE GOVERNOR. The Irishman.

WOODER. Next him again there's that young fellow, Falder—star class—and next him old Clipton.

THE GOVERNOR. Ah, yes! "The philosopher." I want to see him about his eyes.

WOODER. Curious thing, sir: they seem to know when there's one of these tries at escape going on. It makes them restive—there's a regular wave going through them just now.

THE GOVERNOR. [Meditatively] Odd things—those waves. [Turning to look at the prisoners exercising] Seem quiet enough out here!

WOODER. That Irishman, O'Cleary, began banging on his door this morning. Little thing like that's quite enough to upset the whole lot. They're just like dumb animals at times.

THE GOVERNOR. I've seen it with horses before thunder—it'll run right through cavalry lines.

The prison CHAPLAIN has entered. He is a dark-haired, ascetic man, in clerical undress, with a peculiarly steady, tight-lipped face and slow, cultured speech.

THE GOVERNOR. [Holding up the saw] Seen this, Miller?

THE CHAPLAIN. Useful-looking specimen.

THE GOVERNOR. Do for the Museum, eh! [He goes to the cupboard and opens it, displaying to view a number of quaint ropes, hooks, and metal tools with labels tied on them] That'll do, thanks, Mr. Wooder.

WOODER. [Saluting] Thank you, sir. [He goes out]

THE GOVERNOR. Account for the state of the men last day or two, Miller? Seems going through the whole place.

THE CHAPLAIN. No. I don't know of anything.

THE GOVERNOR. By the way, will you dine with us on Christmas Day?

THE CHAPLAIN. To-morrow. Thanks very much.

THE GOVERNOR. Worries me to feel the men discontented. [Gazing at the saw] Have to punish this poor devil. Can't help liking a man who tries to escape. [He places the saw in his pocket and locks the cupboard again]

THE CHAPLAIN. Extraordinary perverted will-power—some of them. Nothing to be done till it's broken.

THE GOVERNOR. And not much afterwards, I'm afraid. Ground too hard for golf?

WOODER comes in again.

WOODER. Visitor who's been seeing Q 3007 asks to speak to you, sir. I told him it wasn't usual.

THE GOVERNOR. What about?

WOODER. Shall I put him off, sir?

THE GOVERNOR. [Resignedly] No, no. Let's see him. Don't go, Miller.

WOODER motions to some one without, and as the visitor comes in withdraws.

The visitor is COKESON, who is attired in a thick overcoat to the knees, woollen gloves, arid carries a top hat.

COKESON. I'm sorry to trouble you. I've been talking to the young man.

THE GOVERNOR. We have a good many here.

COKESON. Name of Falder, forgery. [Producing a card, and handing it to the GOVERNOR] Firm of James and Walter How. Well known in the law.

THE GOVERNOR. [Receiving the card-with a faint smile] What do you want to see me about, sir?

COKESON. [Suddenly seeing the prisoners at exercise] Why! what a sight!

THE GOVERNOR. Yes, we have that privilege from here; my office is being done up. [Sitting down at his table] Now, please!

COKESON. [Dragging his eyes with difficulty from the window] I wanted to say a word to you; I shan't keep you long. [Confidentially] Fact is, I oughtn't to be here by rights. His sister came to me—he's got no father and mother—and she was in some distress. "My husband won't let me go and see him," she said; "says he's disgraced the family. And his other sister," she said, "is an invalid." And she asked me to come. Well, I take an interest in him. He was our junior— I go to the same chapel—and I didn't like to refuse. And what I wanted to tell you was, he seems lonely here.

THE GOVERNOR. Not unnaturally.

COKESON. I'm afraid it'll prey on my mind. I see a lot of them about working together.

THE GOVERNOR. Those are local prisoners. The convicts serve their three months here in separate confinement, sir.

COKESON. But we don't want to be unreasonable. He's quite downhearted. I wanted to ask you to let him run about with the others.

THE GOVERNOR. [With faint amusement] Ring the bell-would you, Miller? [To COKESON] You'd like to hear what the doctor says about him, perhaps.

THE CHAPLAIN. [Ringing the bell] You are not accustomed to prisons, it would seem, sir.

COKESON. No. But it's a pitiful sight. He's quite a young fellow. I said to him: "Before a month's up" I said, "you'll be out and about with the others; it'll be a nice change for you." "A month!" he said —like that! "Come!" I said, "we mustn't exaggerate. What's a month? Why, it's nothing!" "A day," he said, "shut up in your cell thinking and brooding as I do, it's longer than a year outside. I can't help it," he said; "I try—but I'm built that way, Mr. COKESON." And, he held his hand up to his face. I could see the tears trickling through his fingers. It wasn't nice.

THE CHAPLAIN. He's a young man with large, rather peculiar eyes, isn't he? Not Church of England, I think?

COKESON. No.

THE CHAPLAIN. I know.

THE GOVERNOR. [To WOODER, who has come in] Ask the doctor to be good enough to come here for a minute. [WOODER salutes, and goes out] Let's see, he's not married?

COKESON. No. [Confidentially] But there's a party he's very much attached to, not altogether com-il-fa. It's a sad story.

THE CHAPLAIN. If it wasn't for drink and women, sir, this prison might be closed.

COKESON. [Looking at the CHAPLAIN over his spectacles] Ye-es, but I wanted to tell you about that, special. He had hopes they'd have let her come and see him, but they haven't. Of course he asked me questions. I did my best, but I couldn't tell the poor young fellow a lie, with him in here—seemed like hitting him. But I'm afraid it's made him worse.

THE GOVERNOR. What was this news then?

COKESON. Like this. The woman had a nahsty, spiteful feller for a husband, and she'd left him. Fact is, she was going away with our young friend. It's not nice—but I've looked over it. Well, when he was put in here she said she'd earn her living apart, and wait for him to come out. That was a great consolation to him. But after a month she came to me—I don't know her personally—and she said: "I can't earn the children's living, let alone my own—I've got no friends. I'm obliged to keep out of everybody's way, else my husband'd get to know where I was. I'm very much reduced," she said. And she has lost flesh. "I'll have to go in the workhouse!" It's a painful story. I said to her: "No," I said, "not that! I've got a wife an' family, but sooner than you should do that I'll spare you a little myself." "Really," she said—she's a nice creature—" I don't like to take it from you. I think I'd better go back to my husband." Well, I know he's a nahsty, spiteful feller—drinks—but I didn't like to persuade her not to.

THE CHAPLAIN. Surely, no.

COKESON. Ye-es, but I'm sorry now; it's upset the poor young fellow dreadfully. And what I wanted to say was: He's got his three years to serve. I want things to be pleasant for him.

THE CHAPLAIN. [With a touch of impatience] The Law hardly shares your view, I'm afraid.

COKESON. But I can't help thinking that to shut him up there by himself'll turn him silly. And nobody wants that, I s'pose. I don't like to see a man cry.

THE CHAPLAIN. It's a very rare thing for them to give way like that.

COKESON. [Looking at him-in a tone of sudden dogged hostility] I keep dogs.

THE CHAPLAIN. Indeed?

COKESON. Ye-es. And I say this: I wouldn't shut one of them up all by himself, month after month, not if he'd bit me all over.

THE CHAPLAIN. Unfortunately, the criminal is not a dog; he has a sense of right and wrong.

COKESON. But that's not the way to make him feel it.

THE CHAPLAIN. Ah! there I'm afraid we must differ.

COKESON. It's the same with dogs. If you treat 'em with kindness they'll do anything for you; but to shut 'em up alone, it only makes 'em savage.

THE CHAPLAIN. Surely you should allow those who have had a little more experience than yourself to know what is best for prisoners.

COKESON. [Doggedly] I know this young feller, I've watched him for years. He's eurotic—got no stamina. His father died of consumption. I'm thinking of his future. If he's to be kept there shut up by himself, without a cat to keep him company, it'll do him harm. I said to him: "Where do you feel it?" "I can't tell you, Mr. COKESON," he said, "but sometimes I could beat my head against the wall." It's not nice.

During this speech the DOCTOR has entered. He is a medium-Sized, rather good-looking man, with a quick eye. He stands leaning against the window.

THE GOVERNOR. This gentleman thinks the separate is telling on Q 3007— Falder, young thin fellow, star class. What do you say, Doctor Clements?

THE DOCTOR. He doesn't like it, but it's not doing him any harm.

COKESON. But he's told me.

THE DOCTOR. Of course he'd say so, but we can always tell. He's lost no weight since he's been here.

COKESON. It's his state of mind I'm speaking of.

THE DOCTOR. His mind's all right so far. He's nervous, rather melancholy. I don't see signs of anything more. I'm watching him carefully.

COKESON. [Nonplussed] I'm glad to hear you say that.

THE CHAPLAIN. [More suavely] It's just at this period that we are able to make some impression on them, sir. I am speaking from my special standpoint.

COKESON. [Turning bewildered to the GOVERNOR] I don't want to be unpleasant, but having given him this news, I do feel it's awkward.

THE GOVERNOR. I'll make a point of seeing him to-day.

COKESON. I'm much obliged to you. I thought perhaps seeing him every day you wouldn't notice it.

THE GOVERNOR. [Rather sharply] If any sign of injury to his health shows itself his case will be reported at once. That's fully provided for. [He rises]

COKESON. [Following his own thoughts] Of course, what you don't see doesn't trouble you; but having seen him, I don't want to have him on my mind.

THE GOVERNOR. I think you may safely leave it to us, sir.

COKESON. [Mollified and apologetic] I thought you'd understand me. I'm a plain man—never set myself up against authority. [Expanding to the CHAPLAIN] Nothing personal meant. Good-morning.

As he goes out the three officials do not look at each other, but their faces wear peculiar expressions.

THE CHAPLAIN. Our friend seems to think that prison is a hospital.

COKESON. [Returning suddenly with an apologetic air] There's just one little thing. This woman—I suppose I mustn't ask you to let him see her. It'd be a rare treat for them both. He's thinking about her all the time. Of course she's not his wife. But he's quite safe in here. They're a pitiful couple. You couldn't make an exception?

THE GOVERNOR. [Wearily] As you say, my dear sir, I couldn't make an exception; he won't be allowed another visit of any sort till he goes to a convict prison.

COKESON. I see. [Rather coldly] Sorry to have troubled you. [He again goes out]

THE CHAPLAIN. [Shrugging his shoulders] The plain man indeed, poor fellow. Come and have some lunch, Clements?

He and the DOCTOR go out talking.

The GOVERNOR, with a sigh, sits down at his table and takes up a pen.

The curtain falls.

SCENE II

Part of the ground corridor of the prison. The walls are coloured with greenish distemper up to a stripe of deeper green about the height of a man's shoulder, and above this line are whitewashed. The floor is of blackened stones. Daylight is filtering through a heavily barred window at the end. The doors of four cells are visible. Each cell door has a little round peep-hole at the level of a man's eye, covered by a little round disc, which, raised upwards, affords a view o f the cell. On the wall, close to each cell door, hangs a little square board with the prisoner's name, number, and record.

Overhead can be seen the iron structures of the first-floor and second-floor corridors.

The WARDER INSTRUCTOR, a bearded man in blue uniform, with an apron, and some dangling keys, is just emerging from one of the cells.

INSTRUCTOR. [Speaking from the door into the cell] I'll have another bit for you when that's finished.

O'CLEARY. [Unseen—in an Irish voice] Little doubt o' that, sirr.

INSTRUCTOR. [Gossiping] Well, you'd rather have it than nothing, I s'pose.

O'CLEARY. An' that's the blessed truth.

Sounds are heard of a cell door being closed and locked, and of approaching foot-steps.

INSTRUCTOR. [In a sharp, changed voice] Look alive over it!

He shuts the cell door, and stands at attention.

The GOVERNOR comes walking down the corridor, followed by WOODER.

THE GOVERNOR. Anything to report?

INSTRUCTOR. [Saluting] Q 3007 [he points to a cell] is behind with his work, sir. He'll lose marks to-day.

The GOVERNOR nods and passes on to the end cell. The INSTRUCTOR goes away.

THE GOVERNOR. This is our maker of saws, isn't it?

He takes the saw from his pocket as WOODER throws open the door of the cell. The convict MOANEY is seen lying on his bed, athwart the cell, with his cap on. He springs up and stands in the middle of the cell. He is a raw-boned fellow, about fifty-six years old, with outstanding bat's ears and fierce, staring, steel-coloured eyes.

WOODER. Cap off! [MOANEY removes his cap] Out here! [MOANEY Comes to the door]

THE GOVERNOR. [Beckoning him out into the corridor, and holding up the saw—with the manner of an officer speaking to a private] Anything to say about this, my man? [MOANEY is silent] Come!

MOANEY. It passed the time.

THE GOVERNOR. [Pointing into the cell] Not enough to do, eh?

MOANEY. It don't occupy your mind.

THE GOVERNOR. [Tapping the saw] You might find a better way than this.

MOANEY. [Sullenly] Well! What way? I must keep my hand in against the time I get out. What's the good of anything else to me at my time of life? [With a gradual change to civility, as his tongue warms] Ye know that, sir. I'll be in again within a year or two, after I've done this lot. I don't want to disgrace meself when I'm out. You've got your pride keeping the prison smart; well, I've got mine. [Seeing that the GOVERNOR is listening with interest, he goes on, pointing to the saw] I must be doin' a little o' this. It's no harm to any one. I was five weeks makin' that saw—a bit of all right it is, too; now I'll get cells, I suppose, or seven days' bread and water. You can't help it, sir, I know that—I quite put meself in your place.

THE GOVERNOR. Now, look here, Moaney, if I pass it over will you give me your word not to try it on again? Think! [He goes into the cell, walks to the end of it, mounts the stool, and tries the window-bars]

THE GOVERNOR. [Returning] Well?

MOANEY. [Who has been reflecting] I've got another six weeks to do in here, alone. I can't do it and think o' nothing. I must have something to interest me. You've made me a sporting offer, sir, but I can't pass my word about it. I shouldn't like to deceive a gentleman. [Pointing into the cell] Another four hours' steady work would have done it.

THE GOVERNOR. Yes, and what then? Caught, brought back, punishment. Five weeks' hard work to make this, and cells at the end of it, while they put anew bar to your window. Is it worth it, Moaney?

MOANEY. [With a sort of fierceness] Yes, it is.

THE GOVERNOR. [Putting his hand to his brow] Oh, well! Two days' cells-bread and water.

MOANEY. Thank 'e, sir.

He turns quickly like an animal and slips into his cell.

The GOVERNOR looks after him and shakes his head as WOODER closes and locks the cell door.

THE GOVERNOR. Open Clipton's cell.

WOODER opens the door of CLIPTON'S cell. CLIPTON is sitting on a stool just inside the door, at work on a pair of trousers. He is a small, thick, oldish man, with an almost shaven head, and smouldering little dark eyes behind smoked spectacles. He gets up and stands motionless in the doorway, peering at his visitors.

THE GOVERNOR. [Beckoning] Come out here a minute, Clipton.

CLIPTON, with a sort of dreadful quietness, comes into the corridor, the needle and thread in his hand. The GOVERNOR signs to WOODER, who goes into the cell and inspects it carefully.

THE GOVERNOR. How are your eyes?

CLIFTON. I don't complain of them. I don't see the sun here. [He makes a
          stealthy movement, protruding his neck a little] There's just one
          thing, Mr. Governor, as you're speaking to me. I wish you'd ask the
          cove next door here to keep a bit quieter.

THE GOVERNOR. What's the matter? I don't want any tales, Clipton.

CLIPTON. He keeps me awake. I don't know who he is. [With contempt] One
          of this star class, I expect. Oughtn't to be here with us.

THE GOVERNOR. [Quietly] Quite right, Clipton. He'll be moved when
          there's a cell vacant.

CLIPTON. He knocks about like a wild beast in the early morning. I'm not used
          to it—stops me getting my sleep out. In the evening too. It's not
          fair, Mr. Governor, as you're speaking to me. Sleep's the comfort I've
          got here; I'm entitled to take it out full.

WOODER comes out of the cell, and instantly, as though extinguished, CLIP-TON moves with stealthy suddenness back into his cell.

WOODER. All right, sir.

THE GOVERNOR nods. The door is closed and locked.

THE GOVERNOR. Which is the man who banged on his door this morning?

WOODER. [Going towards O'CLEARY'S cell] This one, sir; O'Cleary.

He lifts the disc and glances through the peephole.

THE GOVERNOR. Open.

WOODER throws open the door. O'CLEARY, who is seated at a little table by the door as if listening, springs up and stands at attention jest inside the doorway. He is a broad-faced, middle-aged man, with a wide, thin, flexible mouth, and little holes under his high cheek-bones.

THE GOVERNOR. Where's the joke, O'Cleary?

O'CLEARY. The joke, your honour? I've not seen one for a long time.

THE GOVERNOR. Banging on your door?

O'CLEARY. Oh! that!

THE GOVERNOR. It's womanish.

O'CLEARY. An' it's that I'm becoming this two months past.

THE GOVERNOR. Anything to complain of?

O'CLEARY. NO, Sirr.

THE GOVERNOR. You're an old hand; you ought to know better.

O'CLEARY. Yes, I've been through it all.

THE GOVERNOR. You've got a youngster next door; you'll upset him.

O'CLEARY. It cam' over me, your honour. I can't always be the same steady man.

THE GOVERNOR. Work all right?

O'CLEARY. [Taking up a rush mat he is making] Oh! I can do it on me head. It's the miserablest stuff—don't take the brains of a mouse. [Working his mouth] It's here I feel it—the want of a little noise — a terrible little wud ease me.

THE GOVERNOR. You know as well as I do that if you were out in the shops you wouldn't be allowed to talk.

O'CLEARY. [With a look of profound meaning] Not with my mouth.

THE GOVERNOR. Well, then?

O'CLEARY. But it's the great conversation I'd have.

THE GOVERNOR. [With a smile] Well, no more conversation on your door.

O'CLEARY. No, sirr, I wud not have the little wit to repeat meself.

THE GOVERNOR. [Turning] Good-night.

O'CLEARY. Good-night, your honour.

He turns into his cell. The GOVERNOR shuts the door.

THE GOVERNOR. [Looking at the record card] Can't help liking the poor blackguard.

WOODER. He's an amiable man, sir.

THE GOVERNOR. [Pointing down the corridor] Ask the doctor to come here, Mr. Wooder.

WOODER salutes and goes away down the corridor.

The GOVERNOR goes to the door of FALDER'S cell. He raises his uninjured hand to uncover the peep-hole; but, without uncovering it, shakes his head and drops his hand; then, after scrutinising the record board, he opens the cell door. FALDER, who is standing against it, lurches forward.

THE GOVERNOR. [Beckoning him out] Now tell me: can't you settle down, Falder?

FALDER. [In a breathless voice] Yes, sir.

THE GOVERNOR. You know what I mean? It's no good running your head against a stone wall, is it?

FALDER. No, sir.

THE GOVERNOR. Well, come.

FALDER. I try, sir.

THE GOVERNOR. Can't you sleep?

FALDER. Very little. Between two o'clock and getting up's the worst time.

THE GOVERNOR. How's that?

FALDER. [His lips twitch with a sort of smile] I don't know, sir. I was always nervous. [Suddenly voluble] Everything seems to get such a size then. I feel I'll never get out as long as I live.

THE GOVERNOR. That's morbid, my lad. Pull yourself together.

FALDER. [With an equally sudden dogged resentment] Yes—I've got to.

THE GOVERNOR. Think of all these other fellows?

FALDER. They're used to it.

THE GOVERNOR. They all had to go through it once for the first time, just as you're doing now.

FALDER. Yes, sir, I shall get to be like them in time, I suppose.

THE GOVERNOR. [Rather taken aback] H'm! Well! That rests with you. Now come. Set your mind to it, like a good fellow. You're still quite young. A man can make himself what he likes.

FALDER. [Wistfully] Yes, sir.

THE GOVERNOR. Take a good hold of yourself. Do you read?

FALDER. I don't take the words in. [Hanging his head] I know it's no good; but I can't help thinking of what's going on outside. In my cell I can't see out at all. It's thick glass, sir.

THE GOVERNOR. You've had a visitor. Bad news?

FALDER. Yes.

THE GOVERNOR. You mustn't think about it.

FALDER. [Looking back at his cell] How can I help it, sir?

He suddenly becomes motionless as WOODER and the DOCTOR approach. The GOVERNOR motions to him to go back into his cell.

FALDER. [Quick and low] I'm quite right in my head, sir. [He goes back into his cell.]

THE GOVERNOR. [To the DOCTOR] Just go in and see him, Clements.

The DOCTOR goes into the cell. The GOVERNOR pushes the door to, nearly closing it, and walks towards the window.

WOODER. [Following] Sorry you should be troubled like this, sir. Very contented lot of men, on the whole.

THE GOVERNOR. [Shortly] You think so?

WOODER. Yes, sir. It's Christmas doing it, in my opinion.

THE GOVERNOR. [To himself] Queer, that!

WOODER. Beg pardon, sir?

THE GOVERNOR. Christmas!

He turns towards the window, leaving WOODER looking at him with a sort of pained anxiety.

WOODER. [Suddenly] Do you think we make show enough, sir? If you'd like us to have more holly?

THE GOVERNOR. Not at all, Mr. Wooder.

WOODER. Very good, sir.

The DOCTOR has come out of FALDER's Cell, and the GOVERNOR beckons to him.

THE GOVERNOR. Well?

THE DOCTOR. I can't make anything much of him. He's nervous, of course.

THE GOVERNOR. Is there any sort of case to report? Quite frankly, Doctor.

THE DOCTOR. Well, I don't think the separates doing him any good; but then I could say the same of a lot of them—they'd get on better in the shops, there's no doubt.

THE GOVERNOR. You mean you'd have to recommend others?

THE DOCTOR. A dozen at least. It's on his nerves. There's nothing tangible. That fellow there [pointing to O'CLEARY'S cell], for instance—feels it just as much, in his way. If I once get away from physical facts—I shan't know where I am. Conscientiously, sir, I don't know how to differentiate him. He hasn't lost weight. Nothing wrong with his eyes. His pulse is good. Talks all right.

THE GOVERNOR. It doesn't amount to melancholia?

THE DOCTOR. [Shaking his head] I can report on him if you like; but if I do I ought to report on others.

THE GOVERNOR. I see. [Looking towards FALDER'S cell] The poor devil must just stick it then.

As he says thin he looks absently at WOODER.

WOODER. Beg pardon, sir?

For answer the GOVERNOR stares at him, turns on his heel, and walks away. There is a sound as of beating on metal.

THE GOVERNOR. [Stopping] Mr. Wooder?

WOODER. Banging on his door, sir. I thought we should have more of that.

He hurries forward, passing the GOVERNOR, who follows closely.

The curtain falls.

<u>SCENE III</u>

FALDER's cell, a whitewashed space thirteen feet broad by seven deep, and nine feet high, with a rounded ceiling. The floor is of shiny blackened bricks. The barred window of opaque glass, with a ventilator, is high up in the middle of the end wall. In the middle of the opposite end wall is the narrow door. In a corner are the mattress and bedding rolled up [two blankets, two sheets, and a coverlet]. Above them is a quarter-circular wooden shelf, on which is a Bible and several little devotional books, piled in a symmetrical pyramid; there are also a black hair brush, tooth-brush, and a bit of soap. In another corner is the wooden frame of a bed, standing on end. There is a dark ventilator under the window, and another over the door. FALDER'S work [a shirt to which he is putting buttonholes] is hung to a nail on the wall over a small wooden table, on which the novel "Lorna Doone" lies open. Low down in the corner by the door is a thick glass screen, about a foot square, covering the gas-jet let into the wall. There is also a wooden stool, and a pair of shoes beneath it. Three bright round tins are set under the window.

In fast-failing daylight, FALDER, in his stockings, is seen standing motionless, with his head inclined towards the door, listening. He moves a little closer to the door, his stockinged feet making no noise. He stops at the door. He is trying harder and harder to hear something, any little thing that is going on outside. He springs suddenly upright—as if at a sound-and remains perfectly motionless. Then, with a heavy sigh, he moves to his work, and stands looking at it, with his head doom; he does a stitch or two, having the air of a man so lost in sadness that each stitch is, as it were, a coming to life. Then turning abruptly, he begins pacing the cell, moving his head, like an animal pacing its cage. He stops again at the door, listens, and, placing the palms of hip hands against it with his fingers spread out, leans his forehead against the iron. Turning from it, presently, he moves slowly back towards the window, tracing his way with his finger along the top line of the distemper that runs round the wall. He stops under the window, and, picking up the lid of one of the tins, peers into it. It has grown very nearly dark. Suddenly the lid falls out of his hand with a clatter—the only sound that has broken the silence—and he stands staring intently at the wall where the stuff of the shirt is hanging rather white in the darkness—he seems to be seeing somebody or something there. There is a sharp tap and click; the cell light behind the glass screen has been turned up. The cell is brightly lighted. FALDER is seen gasping for breath.

A sound from far away, as of distant, dull beating on thick metal, is suddenly audible. FALDER shrinks back, not able to bear this sudden clamour. But the sound grows, as though some great tumbril were rolling towards the cell. And gradually it seems to hypnotise him. He begins creeping inch by inch nearer to the door. The banging sound, travelling from cell to cell, draws closer and closer; FALDER'S hands are seen moving as if his spirit had already joined in this beating, and the sound swells till it seems to have entered the very cell. He suddenly raises his clenched fists. Panting violently, he flings himself at his door, and beats on it.

The curtain falls.

ACT IV

The scene is again COKESON'S room, at a few minutes to ten of a March morning, two years later. The doors are all open. SWEEDLE, now blessed with a sprouting moustache, is getting the offices ready. He arranges papers on COKESON'S table; then goes to a covered washstand, raises the lid, and looks at himself in the mirror. While he is gazing his full RUTH HONEYWILL comes in through the outer office and stands in the doorway. There seems a kind of exultation and excitement behind her habitual impassivity.

SWEEDLE. [Suddenly seeing her, and dropping the lid of the washstand with a bang] Hello! It's you!

RUTH. Yes.

SWEEDLE. There's only me here! They don't waste their time hurrying down in the morning. Why, it must be two years since we had the pleasure of seeing you. [Nervously] What have you been doing with yourself?

RUTH. [Sardonically] Living.

SWEEDLE. [Impressed] If you want to see him [he points to COKESON'S chair], he'll be here directly—never misses—not much. [Delicately] I hope our friend's back from the country. His time's been up these three months, if I remember. [RUTH nods] I was awful sorry about that. The governor made a mistake—if you ask me.

RUTH. He did.

SWEEDLE. He ought to have given him a chanst. And, I say, the judge ought to ha' let him go after that. They've forgot what human nature's like. Whereas we know. [RUTH gives him a honeyed smile]

SWEEDLE. They come down on you like a cartload of bricks, flatten you out, and when you don't swell up again they complain of it. I know 'em—seen a lot of that sort of thing in my time. [He shakes his head in the plenitude of wisdom] Why, only the other day the governor——

But COKESON has come in through the outer office; brisk with east wind, and decidedly greyer.

COKESON. [Drawing off his coat and gloves] Why! it's you! [Then motioning SWEEDLE out, and closing the door] Quite a stranger! Must be two years. D'you want to see me? I can give you a minute. Sit down! Family well?

RUTH. Yes. I'm not living where I was.

COKESON. [Eyeing her askance] I hope things are more comfortable at home.

RUTH. I couldn't stay with Honeywill, after all.

COKESON. You haven't done anything rash, I hope. I should be sorry if you'd done anything rash.

RUTH. I've kept the children with me.

COKESON. [Beginning to feel that things are not so jolly as ha had hoped] Well, I'm glad to have seen you. You've not heard from the young man, I suppose, since he came out?

RUTH. Yes, I ran across him yesterday.

COKESON. I hope he's well.

RUTH. [With sudden fierceness] He can't get anything to do. It's dreadful to
    see him. He's just skin and bone.

COKESON. [With genuine concern] Dear me! I'm sorry to hear that. [On his
    guard again] Didn't they find him a place when his time was up?

RUTH. He was only there three weeks. It got out.

COKESON. I'm sure I don't know what I can do for you. I don't like to be snub-
    by.

RUTH. I can't bear his being like that.

COKESON. [Scanning her not unprosperous figure] I know his relations aren't
    very forthy about him. Perhaps you can do something for him, till
    he finds his feet.

RUTH. Not now. I could have—but not now.

COKESON. I don't understand.

RUTH. [Proudly] I've seen him again—that's all over.

COKESON. [Staring at her—disturbed] I'm a family man—I don't want to hear
    anything unpleasant. Excuse me—I'm very busy.

RUTH. I'd have gone home to my people in the country long ago, but they've
    never got over me marrying Honeywill. I never was waywise, Mr.
    Cokeson, but I'm proud. I was only a girl, you see, when I married
    him. I thought the world of him, of course . . . he used to come trav-
    elling to our farm.

COKESON. [Regretfully] I did hope you'd have got on better, after you saw me.

RUTH. He used me worse than ever. He couldn't break my nerve, but I lost my
    health; and then he began knocking the children about. I couldn't
    stand that. I wouldn't go back now, if he were dying.

COKESON. [Who has risen and is shifting about as though dodging a stream
    of lava] We mustn't be violent, must we?

RUTH. [Smouldering] A man that can't behave better than that— [There is silence]

COKESON. [Fascinated in spite of himself] Then there you were! And what did you do then?

RUTH. [With a shrug] Tried the same as when I left him before..., making skirts... cheap things. It was the best I could get, but I never made more than ten shillings a week, buying my own cotton and working all day; I hardly ever got to bed till past twelve. I kept at it for nine months. [Fiercely] Well, I'm not fit for that; I wasn't made for it. I'd rather die.

COKESON. My dear woman! We mustn't talk like that.

RUTH. It was starvation for the children too—after what they'd always had. I soon got not to care. I used to be too tired. [She is silent]

COKESON. [With fearful curiosity] Why, what happened then?

RUTH. [With a laugh] My employer happened then—he's happened ever since.

COKESON. Dear! Oh dear! I never came across a thing like this.

RUTH. [Dully] He's treated me all right. But I've done with that. [Suddenly her lips begin to quiver, and she hides them with the back of her hand] I never thought I'd see him again, you see. It was just a chance I met him by Hyde Park. We went in there and sat down, and he told me all about himself. Oh! Mr. Cokeson, give him another chance.

COKESON. [Greatly disturbed] Then you've both lost your livings! What a horrible position!

RUTH. If he could only get here—where there's nothing to find out about him!

COKESON. We can't have anything derogative to the firm.

RUTH. I've no one else to go to.

COKESON. I'll speak to the partners, but I don't think they'll take him, under the circumstances. I don't really.

RUTH. He came with me; he's down there in the street. [She points to the window.]

COKESON. [On his dignity] He shouldn't have done that until he's sent for. [Then softening at the look on her face] We've got a vacancy, as it happens, but I can't promise anything.

RUTH. It would be the saving of him.

COKESON. Well, I'll do what I can, but I'm not sanguine. Now tell him that I don't want him till I see how things are. Leave your address? [Repeating her] 83 Mullingar Street? [He notes it on blotting-paper] Good-morning.

RUTH. Thank you.

She moves towards the door, turns as if to speak, but does not, and goes away.

COKESON. [Wiping his head and forehead with a large white cotton handkerchief] What a business! [Then looking amongst his papers, he sounds his bell. SWEEDLE answers it]

COKESON. Was that young Richards coming here to-day after the clerk's place?

SWEEDLE. Yes.

COKESON. Well, keep him in the air; I don't want to see him yet.

SWEEDLE. What shall I tell him, sir?

COKESON. [With asperity] invent something. Use your brains. Don't stump him off altogether.

SWEEDLE. Shall I tell him that we've got illness, sir?

COKESON. No! Nothing untrue. Say I'm not here to-day.

SWEEDLE. Yes, sir. Keep him hankering?

COKESON. Exactly. And look here. You remember Falder? I may be having him round to see me. Now, treat him like you'd have him treat you in a similar position.

SWEEDLE. I naturally should do.

COKESON. That's right. When a man's down never hit 'im. 'Tisn't necessary.
Give him a hand up. That's a metaphor I recommend to you in
life. It's sound policy.

SWEEDLE. Do you think the governors will take him on again, sir?

COKESON. Can't say anything about that. [At the sound of some one having
entered the outer office] Who's there?

SWEEDLE. [Going to the door and looking] It's Falder, sir.

COKESON. [Vexed] Dear me! That's very naughty of her. Tell him to call
again. I don't want——

He breaks off as FALDER comes in. FALDER is thin, pale, older, his eyes have
grown more restless. His clothes are very worn and loose.

SWEEDLE, nodding cheerfully, withdraws.

COKESON. Glad to see you. You're rather previous. [Trying to keep things
pleasant] Shake hands! She's striking while the iron's hot. [He
wipes his forehead] I don't blame her. She's anxious.

FALDER timidly takes COKESON's hand and glances towards the partners'
door.

COKESON. No—not yet! Sit down! [FALDER sits in the chair at the aide of
COKESON's table, on which he places his cap] Now you are here
I'd like you to give me a little account of yourself. [Looking at him
over his spectacles] How's your health?

FALDER. I'm alive, Mr. Cokeson.

COKESON. [Preoccupied] I'm glad to hear that. About this matter. I don't like
doing anything out of the ordinary; it's not my habit. I'm a plain
man, and I want everything smooth and straight. But I promised
your friend to speak to the partners, and I always keep my word.

FALDER. I just want a chance, Mr. Cokeson. I've paid for that job a thousand times and more. I have, sir. No one knows. They say I weighed more when I came out than when I went in. They couldn't weigh me here [he touches his head] or here [he touches—his heart, and gives a sort of laugh]. Till last night I'd have thought there was nothing in here at all.

COKESON. [Concerned] You've not got heart disease?

FALDER. Oh! they passed me sound enough.

COKESON. But they got you a place, didn't they?

FALSER. Yes; very good people, knew all about it—very kind to me. I thought I was going to get on first rate. But one day, all of a sudden, the other clerks got wind of it.... I couldn't stick it, Mr. COKESON, I couldn't, sir.

COKESON. Easy, my dear fellow, easy!

FALDER. I had one small job after that, but it didn't last.

COKESON. How was that?

FALDER. It's no good deceiving you, Mr. Cokeson. The fact is, I seem to be struggling against a thing that's all round me. I can't explain it: it's as if I was in a net; as fast as I cut it here, it grows up there. I didn't act as I ought to have, about references; but what are you to do? You must have them. And that made me afraid, and I left. In fact, I'm— I'm afraid all the time now.

He bows his head and leans dejectedly silent over the table.

COKESON. I feel for you—I do really. Aren't your sisters going to do anything for you?

FALDER. One's in consumption. And the other——

COKESON. Ye...es. She told me her husband wasn't quite pleased with you.

FALDER. When I went there—they were at supper—my sister wanted to give me a kiss—I know. But he just looked at her, and said: "What have you come for? "Well, I pocketed my pride and I said: "Aren't you going to give me your hand, Jim? Cis is, I know," I said. "Look here!" he said, "that's all very well, but we'd better come to an understanding. I've been expecting you, and I've made up my mind. I'll give you fifteen pounds to go to Canada with." "I see," I said-"good riddance! No, thanks; keep your fifteen pounds." Friendship's a queer thing when you've been where I have.

COKESON. I understand. Will you take the fifteen pound from me? [Flustered, as FALDER regards him with a queer smile] Quite without prejudice; I meant it kindly.

FALDER. I'm not allowed to leave the country.

COKESON. Oh! ye...es—ticket-of-leave? You aren't looking the thing.

FALDER. I've slept in the Park three nights this week. The dawns aren't all poetry there. But meeting her—I feel a different man this morning. I've often thought the being fond of hers the best thing about me; it's sacred, somehow—and yet it did for me. That's queer, isn't it?

COKESON. I'm sure we're all very sorry for you.

FALDER. That's what I've found, Mr. Cokeson. Awfully sorry for me. [With quiet bitterness] But it doesn't do to associate with criminals!

COKESON. Come, come, it's no use calling yourself names. That never did a man any good. Put a face on it.

FALDER. It's easy enough to put a face on it, sir, when you're independent. Try it when you're down like me. They talk about giving you your deserts. Well, I think I've had just a bit over.

COKESON. [Eyeing him askance over his spectacles] I hope they haven't made a Socialist of you.

FALDER is suddenly still, as if brooding over his past self; he utters a peculiar laugh.

COKESON. You must give them credit for the best intentions. Really you must. Nobody wishes you harm, I'm sure.

FALDER. I believe that, Mr. Cokeson. Nobody wishes you harm, but they down you all the same. This feeling—[He stares round him, as though at something closing in] It's crushing me. [With sudden impersonality] I know it is.

COKESON. [Horribly disturbed] There's nothing there! We must try and take it quiet. I'm sure I've often had you in my prayers. Now leave it to me. I'll use my gumption and take 'em when they're jolly. [As he speaks the two partners come in]

COKESON [Rather disconcerted, but trying to put them all at ease] I didn't expect you quite so soon. I've just been having a talk with this young man. I think you'll remember him.

JAMES. [With a grave, keen look] Quite well. How are you, Falder?

WALTER. [Holding out his hand almost timidly] Very glad to see you again, Falder.

FALDER. [Who has recovered his self-control, takes the hand] Thank you, sir.

COKESON. Just a word, Mr. James. [To FALDER, pointing to the clerks' office] You might go in there a minute. You know your way. Our junior won't be coming this morning. His wife's just had a little family.

FALDER, goes uncertainly out into the clerks' office.

COKESON. [Confidentially] I'm bound to tell you all about it. He's quite penitent. But there's a prejudice against him. And you're not seeing him to advantage this morning; he's under-nourished. It's very trying to go without your dinner.

JAMES. Is that so, COKESON?

COKESON. I wanted to ask you. He's had his lesson. Now we know all about him, and we want a clerk. There is a young fellow applying, but I'm keeping him in the air.

JAMES. A gaol-bird in the office, COKESON? I don't see it.

WALTER. "The rolling of the chariot-wheels of Justice!" I've never got that out of my head.

JAMES. I've nothing to reproach myself with in this affair. What's he been doing since he came out?

COKESON. He's had one or two places, but he hasn't kept them. He's sensitive—quite natural. Seems to fancy everybody's down on him.

JAMES. Bad sign. Don't like the fellow—never did from the first. "Weak character"'s written all over him.

WALTER. I think we owe him a leg up.

JAMES. He brought it all on himself.

WALTER. The doctrine of full responsibility doesn't quite hold in these days.

JAMES. [Rather grimly] You'll find it safer to hold it for all that, my boy.

WALTER. For oneself, yes—not for other people, thanks.

JAMES. Well! I don't want to be hard.

COKESON. I'm glad to hear you say that. He seems to see something [spreading his arms] round him. 'Tisn't healthy.

JAMES. What about that woman he was mixed up with? I saw some one uncommonly like her outside as we came in.

COKESON. That! Well, I can't keep anything from you. He has met her.

JAMES. Is she with her husband?

COKESON. No.

JAMES. Falder living with her, I suppose?

COKESON. [Desperately trying to retain the new-found jollity] I don't know that of my own knowledge. 'Tisn't my business.

JAMES. It's our business, if we're going to engage him, COKESON.

COKESON. [Reluctantly] I ought to tell you, perhaps. I've had the party here this morning.

JAMES. I thought so. [To WALTER] No, my dear boy, it won't do. Too shady altogether!

COKESON. The two things together make it very awkward for you—I see that.

WALTER. [Tentatively] I don't quite know what we have to do with his private life.

JAMES. No, no! He must make a clean sheet of it, or he can't come here.

WALTER. Poor devil!

COKESON. Will you—have him in? [And as JAMES nods] I think I can get him to see reason.

JAMES. [Grimly] You can leave that to me, COKESON.

WALTER. [To JAMES, in a low voice, while COKESON is summoning FALDER] His whole future may depend on what we do, dad.

FALDER comes in. He has pulled himself together, and presents a steady front.

JAMES. Now look here, Falder. My son and I want to give you another chance; but there are two things I must say to you. In the first place: It's no good coming here as a victim. If you've any notion that you've been unjustly treated—get rid of it. You can't play fast and loose with morality and hope to go scot-free. If Society didn't take care of itself, nobody would—the sooner you realise that the better.

FALDER. Yes, sir; but—may I say something?

JAMES. Well?

FALDER. I had a lot of time to think it over in prison. [He stops]

COKESON. [Encouraging him] I'm sure you did.

FALDER. There were all sorts there. And what I mean, sir, is, that if we'd been treated differently the first time, and put under somebody that could look after us a bit, and not put in prison, not a quarter of us would ever have got there.

JAMES. [Shaking his head] I'm afraid I've very grave doubts of that, Falder.

FALDER. [With a gleam of malice] Yes, sir, so I found.

JAMES. My good fellow, don't forget that you began it.

FALDER. I never wanted to do wrong.

JAMES. Perhaps not. But you did.

FALDER. [With all the bitterness of his past suffering] It's knocked me out of time. [Pulling himself up] That is, I mean, I'm not what I was.

JAMES. This isn't encouraging for us, Falder.

COKESON. He's putting it awkwardly, Mr. James.

FALDER. [Throwing over his caution from the intensity of his feeling] I mean it, Mr. Cokeson.

JAMES. Now, lay aside all those thoughts, Falder, and look to the future.

FALDER. [Almost eagerly] Yes, sir, but you don't understand what prison is. It's here it gets you.

He grips his chest.

COKESON. [In a whisper to James] I told you he wanted nourishment.

WALTER. Yes, but, my dear fellow, that'll pass away. Time's merciful.

FALDER. [With his face twitching] I hope so, sir.

JAMES. [Much more gently] Now, my boy, what you've got to do is to put all the past behind you and build yourself up a steady reputation. And that brings me to the second thing. This woman you were mixed up with you must give us your word, you know, to have done with that. There's no chance of your keeping straight if you're going to begin your future with such a relationship.

FALDER. [Looking from one to the other with a hunted expression] But sir . . . but sir . . . it's the one thing I looked forward to all that time. And she too . . . I couldn't find her before last night.

During this and what follows COKESON becomes more and more uneasy.

JAMES. This is painful, Falder. But you must see for yourself that it's impossible for a firm like this to close its eyes to everything. Give us this proof of your resolve to keep straight, and you can come back—not otherwise.

FALDER. [After staring at JAMES, suddenly stiffens himself] I couldn't give her up. I couldn't! Oh, sir!

I'm all she's got to look to. And I'm sure she's all I've got.

JAMES. I'm very sorry, Falder, but I must be firm. It's for the benefit of you both in the long run. No good can come of this connection. It was the cause of all your disaster.

FALDER. But sir, it means-having gone through all that-getting broken up—my nerves are in an awful state—for nothing. I did it for her.

JAMES. Come! If she's anything of a woman she'll see it for herself. She won't want to drag you down further. If there were a prospect of your being able to marry her—it might be another thing.

FALDER. It's not my fault, sir, that she couldn't get rid of him —she would have if she could. That's been the whole trouble from the beginning. [Looking suddenly at WALTER] . . . If anybody would help her! It's only money wants now, I'm sure.

COKESON. [Breaking in, as WALTER hesitates, and is about to speak] I don't think we need consider that—it's rather far-fetched.

FALDER. [To WALTER, appealing] He must have given her full cause since; she could prove that he drove her to leave him.

WALTER. I'm inclined to do what you say, Falder, if it can be managed.

FALDER. Oh, sir!

He goes to the window and looks down into the street.

COKESON. [Hurriedly] You don't take me, Mr. Walter. I have my reasons.

FALDER. [From the window] She's down there, sir. Will you see her? I can
          beckon to her from here.

WALTER hesitates, and looks from COKESON to JAMES.

JAMES. [With a sharp nod] Yes, let her come.

FALDER beckons from the window.

COKESON. [In a low fluster to JAMES and WALTER] No, Mr. James. She's
          not been quite what she ought to ha' been, while this young man's
          been away. She's lost her chance. We can't consult how to swindle
          the Law.

FALDER has come from the window. The three men look at him in a sort of
awed silence.

FALDER. [With instinctive apprehension of some change—looking from one to
          the other] There's been nothing between us, sir, to prevent it . . . .
          What I said at the trial was true. And last night we only just sat in
          the Park.

SWEEDLE comes in from the outer office.

COKESON. What is it?

SWEEDLE. Mrs. Honeywill. [There is silence]

JAMES. Show her in.

RUTH comes slowly in, and stands stoically with FALDER on one side and the
three men on the other. No one speaks. COKESON turns to his table, bending

over his papers as though the burden of the situation were forcing him back into his accustomed groove.

JAMES. [Sharply] Shut the door there. [SWEEDLE shuts the door] We've asked you to come up because there are certain facts to be faced in this matter. I understand you have only just met Falder again.

RUTH. Yes—only yesterday.

JAMES. He's told us about himself, and we're very sorry for him. I've promised to take him back here if he'll make a fresh start. [Looking steadily at RUTH] This is a matter that requires courage, ma'am.

RUTH, who is looking at FALDER, begins to twist her hands in front of her as though prescient of disaster.

FALDER. Mr. Walter How is good enough to say that he'll help us to get you a divorce.

RUTH flashes a startled glance at JAMES and WALTER.

JAMES. I don't think that's practicable, Falder.

FALDER. But, Sir——!

JAMES. [Steadily] Now, Mrs. Honeywill. You're fond of him.

RUTH. Yes, Sir; I love him.

She looks miserably at FALDER.

JAMES. Then you don't want to stand in his way, do you?

RUTH. [In a faint voice] I could take care of him.

JAMES. The best way you can take care of him will be to give him up.

FALDER. Nothing shall make me give you up. You can get a divorce. There's been nothing between us, has there?

RUTH. [Mournfully shaking her head-without looking at him] No.

FALDER. We'll keep apart till it's over, sir; if you'll only help us—we promise.

JAMES. [To RUTH] You see the thing plainly, don't you? You see what I mean?

RUTH. [Just above a whisper] Yes.

COKESON. [To himself] There's a dear woman.

JAMES. The situation is impossible.

RUTH. Must I, Sir?

JAMES. [Forcing himself to look at her] I put it to you, ma'am. His future is in your hands.

RUTH. [Miserably] I want to do the best for him.

JAMES. [A little huskily] That's right, that's right!

FALDER. I don't understand. You're not going to give me up—after all this? There's something—[Starting forward to JAMES] Sir, I swear solemnly there's been nothing between us.

JAMES. I believe you, Falder. Come, my lad, be as plucky as she is.

FALDER. Just now you were going to help us. [He starts at RUTH, who is standing absolutely still; his face and hands twitch and quiver as the truth dawns on him] What is it? You've not been

WALTER. Father!

JAMES. [Hurriedly] There, there! That'll do, that'll do! I'll give you your chance, Falder. Don't let me know what you do with yourselves, that's all.

FALDER. [As if he has not heard] Ruth?

RUTH looks at him; and FALDER covers his face with his hands. There is silence.

COKESON. [Suddenly] There's some one out there. [To RUTH] Go in here. You'll feel better by yourself for a minute.

He points to the clerks' room and moves towards the outer office. FALDER does not move. RUTH puts out her hand timidly. He shrinks back from the touch. She turns and goes miserably into the clerks' room. With a brusque movement he follows, seizing her by the shoulder just inside the doorway. COKESON shuts the door.

JAMES. [Pointing to the outer office] Get rid of that, whoever it is.

SWEEDLE. [Opening the office door, in a scared voice] Detective- Sergeant blister.

The detective enters, and closes the door behind him.

WISTER. Sorry to disturb you, sir. A clerk you had here, two years and a half ago: I arrested him in, this room.

JAMES. What about him?

WISTER. I thought perhaps I might get his whereabouts from you. [There is an awkward silence]

COKESON. [Pleasantly, coming to the rescue] We're not responsible for his movements; you know that.

JAMES. What do you want with him?

WISTER. He's failed to report himself this last four weeks.

WALTER. How d'you mean?

WISTER. Ticket-of-leave won't be up for another six months, sir.

WALTER. Has he to keep in touch with the police till then?

WISTER. We're bound to know where he sleeps every night. I dare say we shouldn't interfere, sir, even though he hasn't reported himself. But we've just heard there's a serious matter of obtaining employment with a forged reference. What with the two things together—we must have him.

Again there is silence. WALTER and COKESON steal glances at JAMES, who stands staring steadily at the detective.

COKESON. [Expansively] We're very busy at the moment. If you could make it convenient to call again we might be able to tell you then.

JAMES. [Decisively] I'm a servant of the Law, but I dislike peaching. In fact, I can't do such a thing. If you want him you must find him without us.

As he speaks his eye falls on FALDER'S cap, still lying on the table, and his face contracts.

WISTER. [Noting the gesture—quietly] Very good, sir. I ought to warn you that, having broken the terms of his licence, he's still a convict, and sheltering a convict.

JAMES. I shelter no one. But you mustn't come here and ask questions which it's not my business to answer.

WISTER. [Dryly] I won't trouble you further then, gentlemen.

COKESON. I'm sorry we couldn't give you the information. You quite understand, don't you? Good-morning!

WISTER turns to go, but instead of going to the door of the outer office he goes to the door of the clerks' room.

COKESON. The other door.... the other door!

WISTER opens the clerks' door. RUTHS's voice is heard: "Oh, do!" and FALDER,'S: "I can't !" There is a little pause; then, with sharp fright, RUTH says: "Who's that?"

WISTER has gone in.

The three men look aghast at the door.

WISTER [From within] Keep back, please!

He comes swiftly out with his arm twisted in FALDER'S. The latter gives a white, staring look at the three men.

WALTER. Let him go this time, for God's sake!

WISTER. I couldn't take the responsibility, sir.

FALDER. [With a queer, desperate laugh] Good!

Flinging a look back at RUTH, he throws up his head, and goes out through the outer office, half dragging WISTER after him.

WALTER. [With despair] That finishes him. It'll go on for ever now.

SWEEDLE can be seen staring through the outer door. There are sounds of footsteps descending the stone stairs; suddenly a dull thud, a faint "My God!" in WISTER's voice.

JAMES. What's that?

SWEEDLE dashes forward. The door swings to behind him. There is dead silence.

WALTER. [Starting forward to the inner room] The woman-she's fainting!

He and COKESON support the fainting RUTH from the doorway of the clerks' room.

COKESON. [Distracted] Here, my dear! There, there!

WALTER. Have you any brandy?

COKESON. I've got sherry.

WALTER. Get it, then. Quick!

He places RUTH in a chair—which JAMES has dragged forward.

COKESON. [With sherry] Here! It's good strong sherry. [They try to force the sherry between her lips.]

There is the sound of feet, and they stop to listen.

The outer door is reopened—WISTER and SWEEDLE are seen carrying some burden.

JAMES. [Hurrying forward] What is it?

They lay the burden doom in the outer office, out of sight, and all but RUTH cluster round it, speaking in hushed voices.

WISTER. He jumped—neck's broken.

WALTER. Good God!

WISTER. He must have been mad to think he could give me the slip like that. And what was it—just a few months!

WALTER. [Bitterly] Was that all?

JAMES. What a desperate thing! [Then, in a voice unlike his own] Run for a doctor—you! [SWEEDLE rushes from the outer office] An ambulance!

WISTER goes out. On RUTH's face an expression of fear and horror has been seen growing, as if she dared not turn towards the voices. She now rises and steals towards them.

WALTER. [Turning suddenly] Look!

The three men shrink back out of her way, one by one, into COKESON'S room. RUTH drops on her knees by the body.

RUTH. [In a whisper] What is it? He's not breathing. [She crouches over him] My dear! My pretty!

In the outer office doorway the figures of men am seen standing.

RUTH. [Leaping to her feet] No, no! No, no! He's dead!

[The figures of the men shrink back]

COKESON. [Stealing forward. In a hoarse voice] There, there, poor dear woman!

At the sound behind her RUTH faces round at him.

COKESON. No one'll touch him now! Never again! He's safe with gentle Jesus!

RUTH stands as though turned to stone in the doorway staring at COKESON,
who, bending humbly before her, holds out his hand as one would to a lost dog.

The curtain falls.

Third Series:

The Fugitive
The Pigeon
The Mob

THE FUGITIVE

A PLAY IN FOUR ACTS

PERSONS OF THE PLAY

GEORGE DEDMOND, a civilian
CLARE, his wife
GENERAL SIR CHARLES DEDMOND, K.C.B., his father.
LADY DEDMOND, his mother
REGINALD HUNTINGDON, Clare's brother
EDWARD FULLARTON, her friend
DOROTHY FULLARTON, her friend
PAYNTER, a manservant
BURNEY, a maid
TWISDEN, a solicitor
HAYWOOD, a tobacconist
MALISE, a writer
MRS. MILER, his caretaker
THE PORTER at his lodgings
A BOY messenger
ARNAUD, a waiter at "The Gascony"
MR. VARLEY, manager of "The Gascony"
TWO LADIES WITH LARGE HATS, A LADY AND GENTLEMAN, A
LANGUID LORD, HIS COMPANION, A YOUNG MAN, A BLOND
GENTLEMAN, A DARK GENTLEMAN.

ACT I. George Dedmond's Flat. Evening.

ACT II. The rooms of Malise. Morning.

ACT III.

    SCENE I. The rooms of Malice. Late afternoon.

SCENE II.   The rooms of Malise. Early Afternoon.

ACT IV. A small supper room at "The Gascony."

Between Acts I and II three nights elapse.

Between Acts II and Act III, Scene I, three months.

Between Act III, Scene I, and Act III, Scene II, three months.

Between Act III, Scene II, and Act IV, six months.

"With a hey-ho chivy
Hark forrard, hark forrard, tantivy!"

ACT I

The SCENE is the pretty drawing-room of a flat. There are two doors, one open into the hall, the other shut and curtained. Through a large bay window, the curtains of which are not yet drawn, the towers of Westminster can be seen darkening in a summer sunset; a grand piano stands across one corner. The man-servant PAYNTER, clean-shaven and discreet, is arranging two tables for Bridge.

BURNEY, the maid, a girl with one of those flowery Botticellian faces only met with in England, comes in through the curtained door, which she leaves open, disclosing the glimpse of a white wall. PAYNTER looks up at her; she shakes her head, with an expression of concern.

PAYNTER. Where's she gone?

BURNEY. Just walks about, I fancy.

PAYNTER. She and the Governor don't hit it! One of these days she'll flit— you'll see. I like her—she's a lady; but these thoroughbred 'uns— it's their skin and their mouths. They'll go till they drop if they like the job, and if they don't, it's nothing but jib—jib—jib. How was it down there before she married him?

BURNEY. Oh! Quiet, of course.

PAYNTER. Country homes—I know 'em. What's her father, the old Rector, like?

BURNEY. Oh! very steady old man. The mother dead long before I took the place.

PAYNTER. Not a penny, I suppose?

BURNEY. [Shaking her head] No; and seven of them.

PAYNTER. [At sound of the hall door] The Governor!

BURNEY withdraws through the curtained door.

GEORGE DEDMOND enters from the hall. He is in evening dress, opera hat, and overcoat; his face is broad, comely, glossily shaved, but with neat moustaches. His eyes, clear, small, and blue-grey, have little speculation. His hair is well brushed.

GEORGE. [Handing PAYNTER his coat and hat] Look here, Paynter! When I send up from the Club for my dress things, always put in a black waistcoat as well.

PAYNTER. I asked the mistress, sir.

GEORGE. In future—see?

PAYNTER. Yes, sir. [Signing towards the window] Shall I leave the sunset, sir?

But GEORGE has crossed to the curtained door; he opens it and says: "Clare!" Receiving no answer, he goes in. PAYNTER switches up the electric light. His face, turned towards the curtained door, is apprehensive.

GEORGE. [Re-entering] Where's Mrs. Dedmond?

PAYNTER. I hardly know, sir.

GEORGE. Dined in?

PAYNTER. She had a mere nothing at seven, sir.

GEORGE. Has she gone out, since?

PAYNTER. Yes, sir—that is, yes. The—er—mistress was not dressed at all. A little matter of fresh air, I think; sir.

GEORGE. What time did my mother say they'd be here for Bridge?

PAYNTER. Sir Charles and Lady Dedmond were coming at half-past nine; and Captain Huntingdon, too—Mr. and Mrs. Fullarton might be a bit late, sir.

GEORGE. It's that now. Your mistress said nothing?

PAYNTER. Not to me, sir.

GEORGE. Send Burney.

PAYNTER. Very good, sir. [He withdraws.]

GEORGE stares gloomily at the card tables. BURNEY comes in front the hall.

GEORGE. Did your mistress say anything before she went out?

BURNEY. Yes, sir.

GEORGE. Well?

BURNEY. I don't think she meant it, sir.

GEORGE. I don't want to know what you don't think, I want the fact.

BURNEY. Yes, sir. The mistress said: "I hope it'll be a pleasant evening, Burney!"

GEORGE. Oh!—Thanks.

BURNEY. I've put out the mistress's things, sir.

GEORGE. Ah!

BURNEY. Thank you, sir. [She withdraws.]

GEORGE. Damn!

He again goes to the curtained door, and passes through. PAYNTER, coming in from the hall, announces: "General Sir Charles and Lady Dedmond." SIR CHARLES is an upright, well- groomed, grey-moustached, red-faced man of sixty-seven, with a keen eye for molehills, and none at all for mountains. LADY DEDMOND has a firm, thin face, full of capability and decision, not without kindliness; and faintly weathered, as if she had faced many situations in many parts of the world. She is fifty five.

PAYNTER withdraws.

SIR CHARLES. Hullo! Where are they? H'm!

As he speaks, GEORGE re-enters.

LADY DEDMOND. [Kissing her son] Well, George. Where's Clare?

GEORGE. Afraid she's late.

LADY DEDMOND. Are we early?

GEORGE. As a matter of fact, she's not in.

LADY DEDMOND. Oh?

SIR CHARLES. H'm! Not—not had a rumpus?

GEORGE. Not particularly. [With the first real sign of feeling] What I can't stand is being made a fool of before other people. Ordinary friction one can put up with. But that——

SIR CHARLES. Gone out on purpose? What!

LADY DEDMOND. What was the trouble?

GEORGE. I told her this morning you were coming in to Bridge. Appears she'd asked that fellow Malise, for music.

LADY DEDMOND. Without letting you know?

GEORGE. I believe she did tell me.

LADY DEDMOND. But surely——

GEORGE. I don't want to discuss it. There's never anything in particular. We're all anyhow, as you know.

LADY DEDMOND. I see. [She looks shrewdly at her son] My dear, I should be rather careful about him, I think.

SIR CHARLES. Who's that?

LADY DEDMOND. That Mr. Malise.

SIR CHARLES. Oh! That chap!

GEORGE. Clare isn't that sort.

LADY DEDMOND. I know. But she catches up notions very easily. I think it's a great pity you ever came across him.

SIR CHARLES. Where did you pick him up?

GEORGE. Italy—this Spring—some place or other where they couldn't speak English.

SIR CHARLES. Um! That's the worst of travellin'.

LADY DEDMOND. I think you ought to have dropped him. These literary people—-[Quietly] From exchanging ideas to something else, isn't very far, George.

SIR CHARLES. We'll make him play Bridge. Do him good, if he's that sort of fellow.

LADY DEDMOND. Is anyone else coming?

GEORGE. Reggie Huntingdon, and the Fullartons.

LADY DEDMOND. [Softly] You know, my dear boy, I've been meaning to speak to you for a long time. It is such a pity you and Clare—What is it?

GEORGE. God knows! I try, and I believe she does.

SIR CHARLES. It's distressin'—for us, you know, my dear fellow— distressin'.

LADY DEDMOND. I know it's been going on for a long time.

GEORGE. Oh! leave it alone, mother.

LADY DEDMOND. But, George, I'm afraid this man has brought it to a point—put ideas into her head.

GEORGE.   You can't dislike him more than I do. But there's nothing one can object to.

LADY DEDMOND. Could Reggie Huntingdon do anything, now he's home? Brothers sometimes——

GEORGE. I can't bear my affairs being messed about——

LADY DEDMOND. Well! it would be better for you and Clare to be supposed to be out together, than for her to be out alone. Go quietly into the dining-room and wait for her.

SIR CHARLES. Good! Leave your mother to make up something. She'll do it!

LADY DEDMOND. That may be he. Quick!

[A bell sounds.]

GEORGE goes out into the hall, leaving the door open in his haste. LADY DEDMOND, following, calls "Paynter!" PAYNTER enters.

LADY DEDMOND. Don't say anything about your master and mistress being out. I'll explain.

PAYNTER. The master, my lady?

LADY DEDMOND. Yes, I know. But you needn't say so. Do you understand?

PAYNTER. [In polite dudgeon] Just so, my lady.

[He goes out.]

SIR CHARLES. By Jove! That fellow smells a rat!

LADY DEDMOND. Be careful, Charles!

SIR CHARLES. I should think so.

LADY DEDMOND. I shall simply say they're dining out, and that we're not to wait Bridge for them.

SIR CHARLES. [Listening] He's having a palaver with that man of George's.

PAYNTER, reappearing, announces: "Captain Huntingdon." SIR CHARLES and LADY DEDMOND turn to him with relief.

LADY DEDMOND. Ah! It's you, Reginald!

HUNTINGDON. [A tall, fair soldier, of thirty] How d'you do? How are you, sir? What's the matter with their man?

SHE CHARLES. What!

HUNTINGDON. I was going into the dining-room to get rid of my cigar; and he said: "Not in there, sir. The master's there, but my instructions are to the effect that he's not."

SHE CHARLES. I knew that fellow——

LADY DEDMOND. The fact is, Reginald, Clare's out, and George is waiting for her. It's so important people shouldn't——

HUNTINGDON. Rather!

They draw together, as people do, discussing the misfortunes of members of their families.

LADY DEDMOND. It's getting serious, Reginald. I don't know what's to become of them. You don't think the Rector—you don't think your father would speak to Clare?

HUNTINGDON. Afraid the Governor's hardly well enough. He takes anything of that sort to heart so—especially Clare.

SIR CHARLES. Can't you put in a word yourself?

HUNTINGDON. Don't know where the mischief lies.

SIR CHARLES. I'm sure George doesn't gallop her on the road. Very steady-goin' fellow, old George.

HUNTINGDON. Oh, yes; George is all right, sir.

LADY DEDMOND. They ought to have had children.

HUNTINGDON. Expect they're pretty glad now they haven't. I really don't know what to say, ma'am.

SIR CHARLES. Saving your presence, you know, Reginald, I've often noticed parsons' daughters grow up queer. Get too much morality and rice puddin'.

LADY DEDMOND. [With a clear look] Charles!

SIR CHARLES. What was she like when you were kids?

HUNTINGDON. Oh, all right. Could be rather a little devil, of course, when her monkey was up.

SIR CHARLES. I'm fond of her. Nothing she wants that she hasn't got, is there?

HUNTINGDON. Never heard her say so.

SIR CHARLES. [Dimly] I don't know whether old George is a bit too matter of fact for her. H'm?

[A short silence.]

LADY DEDMOND. There's a Mr. Malise coming here to-night. I forget if you know him.

HUNTINGDON. Yes. Rather a thorough-bred mongrel.

LADY DEDMOND. He's literary. [With hesitation] You—you don't think
    he—puts—er—ideas into her head?

HUNTINGDON. I asked Greyman, the novelist, about him; seems he's a bit of
    an Ishmaelite, even among those fellows. Can't see Clare—

LADY DEDMOND. No. Only, the great thing is that she shouldn't be encour-
    aged. Listen!—It is her-coming in. I can hear their voic-
    es. Gone to her room. What a blessing that man isn't here
    yet! [The door bell rings] Tt! There he is, I expect.

SIR CHARLES. What are we goin' to say?

HUNTINGDON. Say they're dining out, and we're not to wait Bridge for them.

SIR CHARLES. Good!

The door is opened, and PAYNTER announces "Mr. Kenneth Malise." MALISE
enters. He is a tall man, about thirty-five, with a strongly marked, dark, irregular, ironic face, and eyes which seem to have needles in their pupils. His thick hair
is rather untidy, and his dress clothes not too new.

LADY DEDMOND. How do you do? My son and daughter-in-law are so very
    sorry. They'll be here directly.

[MALISE bows with a queer, curly smile.]

SIR CHARLES. [Shaking hands] How d'you do, sir?

HUNTINGDON. We've met, I think.

He gives MALISE that peculiar smiling stare, which seems to warn the person
bowed to of the sort of person he is. MALISE'S eyes sparkle.

LADY DEDMOND. Clare will be so grieved. One of those invitations

MALISE. On the spur of the moment.

SIR CHARLES. You play Bridge, sir?

MALISE. Afraid not!

SIR CHARLES. Don't mean that? Then we shall have to wait for 'em.

LADY DEDMOND. I forget, Mr. Malise—you write, don't you?

MALISE. Such is my weakness.

LADY DEDMOND. Delightful profession.

SIR CHARLES. Doesn't tie you! What!

MALISE. Only by the head.

SIR CHARLES. I'm always thinkin' of writin' my experiences.

MALISE. Indeed!

[There is the sound of a door banged.]

SIR CHARLES. [Hastily] You smoke, Mr. MALISE?

MALISE. Too much.

SIR CHARLES. Ah! Must smoke when you think a lot.

MALISE. Or think when you smoke a lot.

SIR CHARLES. [Genially] Don't know that I find that.

LADY DEDMOND. [With her clear look at him] Charles!

The door is opened. CLARE DEDMOND in a cream-coloured evening frock comes in from the hall, followed by GEORGE. She is rather pale, of middle height, with a beautiful figure, wavy brown hair, full, smiling lips, and large grey mesmeric eyes, one of those women all vibration, iced over with a trained stoicism of voice and manner.

LADY DEDMOND. Well, my dear!

SIR CHARLES. Ah! George. Good dinner?

GEORGE. [Giving his hand to MALISE] How are you? Clare! Mr. MALISE!

CLARE. [Smiling-in a clear voice with the faintest possible lisp] Yes, we met on the door-mat. [Pause.]

SIR CHARLES. Deuce you did! [An awkward pause.]

LADY DEDMOND. [Acidly] Mr. Malise doesn't play Bridge, it appears. Afraid we shall be rather in the way of music.

SIR CHARLES. What! Aren't we goin' to get a game? [PAYNTER has entered with a tray.]

GEORGE. Paynter! Take that table into the dining room.

PAYNTER. [Putting down the tray on a table behind the door] Yes, sir.

MALISE. Let me give you a hand.

PAYNTER and MALISE carry one of the Bridge tables out, GEORGE making a half-hearted attempt to relieve MALISE.

SIR CHARLES. Very fine sunset!

Quite softly CLARE begins to laugh. All look at her first with surprise, then with offence, then almost with horror. GEORGE is about to go up to her, but HUNTINGDON heads him off.

HUNTINGDON. Bring the tray along, old man.

GEORGE takes up the tray, stops to look at CLARE, then allows HUNTING-DON to shepherd him out.

LADY DEDMOND. [Without looking at CLARE] Well, if we're going to play, Charles? [She jerks his sleeve.]

SIR CHARLES. What? [He marches out.]

LADY DEDMOND. [Meeting MALISE in the doorway] Now you will be able to have your music.

[She follows the GENERAL out]

[CLARE stands perfectly still, with her eyes closed.]

MALISE. Delicious!

CLARE. [In her level, clipped voice] Perfectly beastly of me! I'm so sorry. I simply can't help running amok to-night.

MALISE. Never apologize for being fey. It's much too rare.

CLARE. On the door-mat! And they'd whitewashed me so beautifully! Poor
dears! I wonder if I ought——[She looks towards the door.]

MALISE. Don't spoil it!

CLARE. I'd been walking up and down the Embankment for about three hours.
One does get desperate sometimes.

MALISE. Thank God for that!

CLARE. Only makes it worse afterwards. It seems so frightful to them, too.

MALISE. [Softly and suddenly, but with a difficulty in finding the right words]
Blessed be the respectable! May they dream of—me! And blessed be
all men of the world! May they perish of a surfeit of—good form!

CLARE. I like that. Oh, won't there be a row! [With a faint movement of her
shoulders] And the usual reconciliation.

MALISE. Mrs. Dedmond, there's a whole world outside yours. Why don't you
spread your wings?

CLARE. My dear father's a saint, and he's getting old and frail; and I've got a sister engaged; and three little sisters to whom I'm supposed to set a good
example. Then, I've no money, and I can't do anything for a living,
except serve in a shop. I shouldn't be free, either; so what's the good?
Besides, I oughtn't to have married if I wasn't going to be happy. You
see, I'm not a bit misunderstood or ill-treated. It's only——

MALISE. Prison. Break out!

CLARE. [Turning to the window] Did you see the sunset? That white cloud trying to fly up?

[She holds up her bare arms, with a motion of flight.]

MALISE. [Admiring her] Ah-h-h! [Then, as she drops her arms suddenly] Play me something.

CLARE. [Going to the piano] I'm awfully grateful to you. You don't make me feel just an attractive female. I wanted somebody like that. [Letting her hands rest on the notes] All the same, I'm glad not to be ugly.

MALISE. Thank God for beauty!

PAYNTER. [Opening the door] Mr. and Mrs. Fullarton.

MALISE. Who are they?

CLARE. [Rising] She's my chief pal. He was in the Navy.

She goes forward. MRS. FULLARTON is a rather tall woman, with dark hair and a quick eye. He, one of those clean-shaven naval men of good presence who have retired from the sea, but not from their susceptibility.

MRS. FULLARTON. [Kissing CLARE, and taking in both MALISE and her husband's look at CLARE] We've only come for a minute.

CLARE. They're playing Bridge in the dining-room. Mr. Malise doesn't play. Mr. Malise—Mrs. Fullarton, Mr. Fullarton.

[They greet.]

FULLARTON. Most awfully jolly dress, Mrs. Dedmond.

MRS. FULLARTON. Yes, lovely, Clare. [FULLARTON abases eyes which mechanically readjust themselves] We can't stay for Bridge, my dear; I just wanted to see you a minute, that's all. [Seeing HUNTINGDON coming in she speaks in a low voice to her husband] Edward, I want to speak to Clare. How d'you do, Captain Huntingdon?

MALISE. I'll say good-night.

He shakes hands with CLARE, bows to MRS. FULLARTON, and makes his way out. HUNTINGDON and FULLERTON foregather in the doorway.

MRS. FULLARTON. How are things, Clare? [CLARE just moves her shoulders] Have you done what I suggested? Your room?

CLARE. No.

MRS. FULLARTON. Why not?

CLARE. I don't want to torture him. If I strike—I'll go clean. I expect I shall strike.

MRS. FULLARTON. My dear! You'll have the whole world against you.

CLARE. Even you won't back me, Dolly?

MRS. FULLARTON. Of course I'll back you, all that's possible, but I can't invent things.

CLARE. You wouldn't let me come to you for a bit, till I could find my feet?

MRS. FULLARTON, taken aback, cannot refrain from her glance at FULLARTON automatically gazing at CLARE while he talks with HUNTINGDON.

MRS. FULLARTON. Of course—the only thing is that——

CLARE. [With a faint smile] It's all right, Dolly. I'm not coming.

MRS. FULLARTON. Oh! don't do anything desperate, Clare—you are so desperate sometimes. You ought to make terms—not tracks.

CLARE. Haggle? [She shakes her head] What have I got to make terms with? What he still wants is just what I hate giving.

MRS. FULLARTON. But, Clare——

CLARE. No, Dolly; even you don't understand. All day and every day —just as far apart as we can be—and still—Jolly, isn't it? If you've got a soul at all.

MRS. FULLARTON. It's awful, really.

CLARE. I suppose there are lots of women who feel as I do, and go on with it; only, you see, I happen to have something in me that—comes to an end. Can't endure beyond a certain time, ever.

She has taken a flower from her dress, and suddenly tears it to bits. It is the only sign of emotion she has given.

MRS. FULLARTON. [Watching] Look here, my child; this won't do. You must get a rest. Can't Reggie take you with him to India for a bit?

CLARE. [Shaking her head] Reggie lives on his pay.

MRS. FULLARTON. [With one of her quick looks] That was Mr. Malise, then?

FULLARTON. [Coming towards them] I say, Mrs. Dedmond, you wouldn't sing me that little song you sang the other night, [He hums] "If I might be the falling bee and kiss thee all the day"? Remember?

MRS. FULLARTON. "The falling dew," Edward. We simply must go, Clare. Good-night. [She kisses her.]

FULLARTON. [Taking half-cover between his wife and CLARE] It suits you down to the ground-that dress.

CLARE. Good-night.

HUNTINGDON sees them out. Left alone CLARE clenches her hands, moves swiftly across to the window, and stands looking out.

HUNTINGDON. [Returning] Look here, Clare!

CLARE. Well, Reggie?

HUNTINGDON. This is working up for a mess, old girl. You can't do this kind of thing with impunity. No man'll put up with it. If you've got anything against George, better tell me. [CLARE shakes her head] You ought to know I should stick by you. What is it? Come?

CLARE. Get married, and find out after a year that she's the wrong person; so wrong that you can't exchange a single real thought; that your blood runs cold when she kisses you—then you'll know.

HUNTINGDON. My dear old girl, I don't want to be a brute; but it's a bit difficult to believe in that, except in novels.

CLARE. Yes, incredible, when you haven't tried.

HUNTINGDON. I mean, you—you chose him yourself. No one forced you to marry him.

CLARE. It does seem monstrous, doesn't it?

HUNTINGDON. My dear child, do give us a reason.

CLARE. Look! [She points out at the night and the darkening towers] If George saw that for the first time he'd just say, "Ah, Westminster! Clock Tower! Can you see the time by it?" As if one cared where or what it was— beautiful like that! Apply that to every —every—everything.

HUNTINGDON. [Staring] George may be a bit prosaic. But, my dear old girl, if that's all——

CLARE. It's not all—it's nothing. I can't explain, Reggie—it's not reason, at all; it's—it's like being underground in a damp cell; it's like knowing you'll never get out. Nothing coming—never anything coming again-never anything.

HUNTINGDON. [Moved and puzzled] My dear old thing; you mustn't get into fantods like this. If it's like that, don't think about it.

CLARE. When every day and every night!—Oh! I know it's my fault for having married him, but that doesn't help.

HUNTINGDON. Look here! It's not as if George wasn't quite a decent chap. And it's no use blinking things; you are absolutely dependent on him. At home they've got every bit as much as they can do to keep going.

CLARE. I know.

HUNTINGDON. And you've got to think of the girls. Any trouble would be very beastly for them. And the poor old Governor would feel it awfully.

CLARE. If I didn't know all that, Reggie, I should have gone home long ago.

HUNTINGDON. Well, what's to be done? If my pay would run to it—but it simply won't.

CLARE. Thanks, old boy, of course not.

HUNTINGDON. Can't you try to see George's side of it a bit?

CLARE. I do. Oh! don't let's talk about it.

HUNTINGDON. Well, my child, there's just one thing you won't go sailing near the wind, will you? I mean, there are fellows always on the lookout.

CLARE. "That chap, Malise, you'd better avoid him!" Why?

HUNTINGDON. Well! I don't know him. He may be all right, but he's not our sort. And you're too pretty to go on the tack of the New Woman and that kind of thing—haven't been brought up to it.

CLARE. British home-made summer goods, light and attractive—don't wear long. [At the sound of voices in the hall] They seem 'to be going, Reggie.

[HUNTINGDON looks at her, vexed, unhappy.]

HUNTINGDON. Don't head for trouble, old girl. Take a pull. Bless you! Good-night.

CLARE kisses him, and when he has gone turns away from the door, holding herself in, refusing to give rein to some outburst of emotion. Suddenly she sits down at the untouched Bridge table, leaning her bare elbows on it and her chin on her hands, quite calm. GEORGE is coming in. PAYNTER follows him.

CLARE. Nothing more wanted, thank you, Paynter. You can go home, and the maids can go to bed.

PAYNTER. We are much obliged, ma'am.

CLARE. I ran over a dog, and had to get it seen to.

PAYNTER. Naturally, ma'am!

CLARE. Good-night.

PAYNTER. I couldn't get you a little anything, ma'am?

CLARE. No, thank you.

PAYNTER. No, ma'am. Good-night, ma'am.

[He withdraws.]

GEORGE. You needn't have gone out of your way to tell a lie that wouldn't deceive a guinea-pig. [Going up to her] Pleased with yourself tonight? [CLARE shakes her head] Before that fellow MALISE; as if our own people weren't enough!

CLARE. Is it worth while to rag me? I know I've behaved badly, but I couldn't help it, really!

GEORGE. Couldn't help behaving like a shop-girl? My God! You were brought up as well as I was.

CLARE. Alas!

GEORGE. To let everybody see that we don't get on—there's only one word for it—Disgusting!

CLARE. I know.

GEORGE. Then why do you do it? I've always kept my end up. Why in heaven's name do you behave in this crazy way?

CLARE. I'm sorry.

GEORGE. [With intense feeling] You like making a fool of me!

CLARE. No—Really! Only—I must break out sometimes.

GEORGE. There are things one does not do.

CLARE. I came in because I was sorry.

GEORGE. And at once began to do it again! It seems to me you delight in rows.

CLARE. You'd miss your—reconciliations.

GEORGE. For God's sake, Clare, drop cynicism!

CLARE. And truth?

GEORGE. You are my wife, I suppose.

CLARE. And they twain shall be one—spirit.

GEORGE. Don't talk wild nonsense!

[There is silence.]

CLARE. [Softly] I don't give satisfaction. Please give me notice!

GEORGE. Pish!

CLARE. Five years, and four of them like this! I'm sure we've served our time. Don't you really think we might get on better together—if I went away?

GEORGE. I've told you I won't stand a separation for no real reason, and have your name bandied about all over London. I have some primitive sense of honour.

CLARE. You mean your name, don't you?

GEORGE. Look here. Did that fellow Malise put all this into your head?

CLARE. No; my own evil nature.

GEORGE. I wish the deuce we'd never met him. Comes of picking up people
            you know nothing of. I distrust him—and his looks—and his infer-
            nal satiric way. He can't even 'dress decently. He's not—good form.

CLARE. [With a touch of rapture] Ah-h!

GEORGE. Why do you let him come? What d'you find interesting in him?

CLARE. A mind.

GEORGE. Deuced funny one! To have a mind—as you call it—it's not neces-
            sary to talk about Art and Literature.

CLARE. We don't.

GEORGE. Then what do you talk about—your minds? [CLARE looks at him]
            Will you answer a straight question? Is he falling in love with you?

CLARE. You had better ask him.

GEORGE. I tell you plainly, as a man of the world, I don't believe in the guide,
            philosopher and friend business.

CLARE. Thank you.

A silence. CLARE suddenly clasps her hands behind her head.

CLARE. Let me go! You'd be much happier with any other woman.

GEORGE. Clare!

CLARE. I believe—I'm sure I could earn my living. Quite serious.

GEORGE. Are you mad?

CLARE. It has been done.

GEORGE. It will never be done by you—understand that!

CLARE. It really is time we parted. I'd go clean out of your life. I don't want your support unless I'm giving you something for your money.

GEORGE. Once for all, I don't mean to allow you to make fools of us both.

CLARE. But if we are already! Look at us. We go on, and on. We're a spectacle!

GEORGE. That's not my opinion; nor the opinion of anyone, so long as you behave yourself.

CLARE. That is—behave as you think right.

GEORGE. Clare, you're pretty riling.

CLARE. I don't want to be horrid. But I am in earnest this time.

GEORGE. So am I.

[CLARE turns to the curtained door.]

GEORGE. Look here! I'm sorry. God knows I don't want to be a brute. I know you're not happy.

CLARE. And you—are you happy?

GEORGE. I don't say I am. But why can't we be?

CLARE. I see no reason, except that you are you, and I am I.

GEORGE. We can try.

CLARE. I HAVE—haven't you?

GEORGE. We used——

CLARE. I wonder!

GEORGE. You know we did.

CLARE. Too long ago—if ever.

GEORGE [Coming closer] I—still——

CLARE. [Making a barrier of her hand] You know that's only cupboard love.

GEORGE. We've got to face the facts.

CLARE. I thought I was.

GEORGE. The facts are that we're married—for better or worse, and certain things are expected of us. It's suicide for you, and folly for me, in my position, to ignore that. You have all you can reasonably want; and I don't—don't wish for any change. If you could bring anything against me—if I drank, or knocked about town, or expected too much of you. I'm not unreasonable in any way, that I can see.

CLARE. Well, I think we've talked enough.

[She again moves towards the curtained door.]

GEORGE. Look here, Clare; you don't mean you're expecting me to put up with the position of a man who's neither married nor unmarried? That's simple purgatory. You ought to know.

CLARE. Yes. I haven't yet, have I?

GEORGE. Don't go like that! Do you suppose we're the only couple who've found things aren't what they thought, and have to put up with each other and make the best of it.

CLARE. Not by thousands.

GEORGE. Well, why do you imagine they do it?

CLARE. I don't know.

GEORGE. From a common sense of decency.

CLARE. Very!

GEORGE. By Jove! You can be the most maddening thing in all the world! [Taking up a pack of cards, he lets them fall with a long slithering flutter] After behaving as you have this evening, you might try to make some amends, I should think.

CLARE moves her head from side to side, as if in sight of something she could not avoid. He puts his hand on her arm.

CLARE. No, no—no!

GEORGE. [Dropping his hand] Can't you make it up?

CLARE. I don't feel very Christian.

She opens the door, passes through, and closes it behind her. GEORGE steps quickly towards it, stops, and turns back into the room. He goes to the window and stands looking out; shuts it with a bang, and again contemplates the door. Moving forward, he rests his hand on the deserted card table, clutching its edge, and muttering. Then he crosses to the door into the hall and switches off the light. He opens the door to go out, then stands again irresolute in the darkness and heaves a heavy sigh. Suddenly he mutters: "No!" Crosses resolutely back to the curtained door, and opens it. In the gleam of light CLARE is standing, unhooking a necklet.

He goes in, shutting the door behind him with a thud.

CURTAIN.

ACT II

The scene is a large, whitewashed, disordered room, whose outer door opens on to a corridor and stairway. Doors on either side lead to other rooms. On the walls are unframed reproductions of fine pictures, secured with tintacks. An old wine-coloured armchair of low and comfortable appearance, near the centre of the room, is surrounded by a litter of manuscripts, books, ink, pens and newspapers, as though some one had already been up to his neck in labour, though by a grandfather's clock it is only eleven. On a smallish table close by, are sheets of paper, cigarette ends, and two claret bottles. There are many books on shelves, and on the floor, an overflowing pile, whereon rests a soft hat, and a black knobby stick. MALISE sits in his armchair, garbed in trousers, dressing-gown, and slippers, unshaved and uncollared, writing. He pauses, smiles, lights a cigarette, and tries the rhythm of the last sentence, holding up a sheet of quarto MS.

MALISE. "Not a word, not a whisper of Liberty from all those excellent frock-coated gentlemen—not a sign, not a grimace. Only the monumental silence of their profound deference before triumphant Tyranny."

While he speaks, a substantial woman, a little over middle-age, in old dark clothes and a black straw hat, enters from the corridor. She goes to a cupboard, brings out from it an apron and a Bissell broom. Her movements are slow and imperturbable, as if she had much time before her. Her face is broad and dark, with Chinese eyebrows.

MALISE. Wait, Mrs. Miller!

MRS. MILER. I'm gettin' be'ind'and, sir.

She comes and stands before him. MALISE writes.

MRS. MILER. There's a man 'angin' about below.

MALISE looks up; seeing that she has roused his attention, she stops. But as soon as he is about to write again, goes on.

MRS. MILER. I see him first yesterday afternoon. I'd just been out to get meself a pennyworth o' soda, an' as I come in I passed 'im on the second floor, lookin' at me with an air of suspicion. I thought to meself at the time, I thought: You're a'andy sort of 'ang-dog man.

MALISE. Well?

MRS. MILER. Well-peekin' down through the balusters, I see 'im lookin' at a photograft. That's a funny place, I thinks, to look at pictures— it's so dark there, ye 'ave to use yer eyesight. So I giv' a scrape with me 'eel [She illustrates] an' he pops it in his pocket, and puts up 'is 'and to knock at number three. I goes down an' I says: "You know there's no one lives there, don't yer?" "Ah!" 'e says with an air of innercence, "I wants the name of Smithers." "Oh!" I says, "try round the corner, number ten." "Ah!" 'e says tactful, "much obliged." "Yes," I says, "you'll find 'im in at this time o' day. Good evenin'!" And I thinks to meself [She closes one eye] Rats! There's a good many corners hereabouts.

MALISE. [With detached appreciation] Very good, Mrs. Miler.

MRS. MILER. So this mornin', there e' was again on the first floor with 'is 'and raised, pretendin' to knock at number two. "Oh! you're still lookin' for 'im?" I says, lettin' him see I was 'is grandmother. "Ah!" 'e says, affable, "you misdirected me; it's here I've got my business." "That's lucky," I says, "cos nobody lives there neither. Good mornin'!" And I come straight up. If you want to see 'im at work you've only to go downstairs, 'e'll be on the ground floor by now, pretendin' to knock at number one. Wonderful resource!

MALISE. What's he like, this gentleman?

MRS. MILER. Just like the men you see on the front page o' the daily papers.
Nasty, smooth-lookin' feller, with one o' them billycock hats you
can't abide.

MALISE. Isn't he a dun?

MRS. MILER. They don't be'ave like that; you ought to know, sir. He's after no
good. [Then, after a little pause] Ain't he to be put a stop to? If
I took me time I could get 'im, innercent-like, with a jug o' water.

[MALISE, smiling, shakes his head.]

MALISE. You can get on now; I'm going to shave.

He looks at the clock, and passes out into the inner room. MRS. MILER, gazes
round her, pins up her skirt, sits down in the armchair, takes off her hat and puts
it on the table, and slowly rolls up her sleeves; then with her hands on her knees
she rests. There is a soft knock on the door. She gets up leisurely and moves flat-
footed towards it. The door being opened CLARE is revealed.

CLARE. Is Mr. Malise in?

MRS. MILER. Yes. But 'e's dressin'.

CLARE. Oh.

MRS. MILER. Won't take 'im long. What name?

CLARE. Would you say—a lady.

MRS. MILER. It's against the rules. But if you'll sit down a moment I'll see what
I can do. [She brings forward a chair and rubs it with her apron.
Then goes to the door of the inner room and speaks through it]
A lady to see you. [Returning she removes some cigarette ends]
This is my hour. I shan't make much dust. [Noting CLARE's
eyebrows raised at the debris round the armchair] I'm particular
about not disturbin' things.

CLARE. I'm sure you are.

MRS. MILER. He likes 'is 'abits regular.

Making a perfunctory pass with the Bissell broom, she runs it to the cupboard, comes back to the table, takes up a bottle and holds it to the light; finding it empty, she turns it upside down and drops it into the wastepaper basket; then, holding up the other bottle, arid finding it not empty, she corks it and drops it into the fold of her skirt.

MRS. MILER. He takes his claret fresh-opened—not like these 'ere bawgwars.

CLARE. [Rising] I think I'll come back later.

MRS. MILER. Mr. Malise is not in my confidence. We keep each other to ourselves. Perhaps you'd like to read the paper; he has it fresh every
mornin'—the Westminister.

She plucks that journal from out of the armchair and hands it to CLARE, who sits doom again unhappily to brood. MRS. MILER makes a pass or two with a very dirty duster, then stands still. No longer hearing sounds, CLARE looks up.

MRS. MILER. I wouldn't interrupt yer with my workin,' but 'e likes things
clean. [At a sound from the inner room] That's 'im; 'e's cut
'isself! I'll just take 'im the tobaccer!

She lifts a green paper screw of tobacco from the debris round the armchair and taps on the door. It opens. CLARE moves restlessly across the room.

MRS. MILER. [Speaking into the room] The tobaccer. The lady's waitin'.

CLARE has stopped before a reproduction of Titian's picture "Sacred and Profane Love." MRS. MILER stands regarding her with a Chinese smile. MALISE enters, a thread of tobacco still hanging to his cheek.

MALISE. [Taking MRS. MILER's hat off the table and handing it to her] Do
the other room.

[Enigmatically she goes.]

MALISE. Jolly of you to come. Can I do anything?

CLARE. I want advice-badly.

MALISE. What! Spreading your wings?

CLARE. Yes.

MALISE. Ah! Proud to have given you that advice. When?

CLARE. The morning after you gave it me . . .

MALISE. Well?

CLARE. I went down to my people. I knew it would hurt my Dad frightfully, but somehow I thought I could make him see. No good. He was awfully sweet, only—he couldn't.

MALISE. [Softly] We English love liberty in those who don't belong to us. Yes.

CLARE. It was horrible. There were the children—and my old nurse. I could never live at home now. They'd think I was——. Impossible —utterly! I'd made up my mind to go back to my owner—And then— he came down himself. I couldn't d it. To be hauled back and begin all over again; I simply couldn't. I watched for a chance; and ran to the station, and came up to an hotel.

MALISE. Bravo!

CLARE. I don't know—no pluck this morning! You see, I've got to earn my living—no money; only a few things I can sell. All yesterday I was walking about, looking at the women. How does anyone ever get a chance?

MALISE. Sooner than you should hurt his dignity by working, your husband would pension you off.

CLARE. If I don't go back to him I couldn't take it.

MALISE. Good!

CLARE. I've thought of nursing, but it's a long training, and I do so hate watching pain. The fact is, I'm pretty hopeless; can't even do art work. I came to ask you about the stage.

MALISE. Have you ever acted? [CLARE shakes her head] You mightn't think so, but I've heard there's a prejudice in favour of training. There's Chorus—I don't recommend it. How about your brother?

CLARE. My brother's got nothing to spare, and he wants to get married; and he's going back to India in September. The only friend I should care to bother is Mrs. Fullarton, and she's—got a husband.

MALISE. I remember the gentleman.

CLARE. Besides, I should be besieged day and night to go back. I must lie doggo somehow.

MALISE. It makes my blood boil to think of women like you. God help all ladies without money.

CLARE. I expect I shall have to go back.

MALISE. No, no! We shall find something. Keep your soul alive at all costs. What! let him hang on to you till you're nothing but— emptiness and ache, till you lose even the power to ache. Sit in his drawing-room, pay calls, play Bridge, go out with him to dinners, return to—duty; and feel less and less, and be less and less, and so grow old and—die!

[The bell rings.]

MALISE. [Looking at the door in doubt] By the wayhe'd no means of tracing you?

[She shakes her head.]

[The bell rings again.]

MALISE. Was there a man on the stairs as you came up?

CLARE. Yes. Why?

MALISE. He's begun to haunt them, I'm told.

CLARE. Oh! But that would mean they thought I—oh! no!

MALISE. Confidence in me is not excessive.

CLARE. Spying!

MALISE. Will you go in there for a minute? Or shall we let them ring—or—
what? It may not be anything, of course.

CLARE. I'm not going to hide.

[The bell rings a third time.]

MALISE. [Opening the door of the inner room] Mrs. Miler, just see who it is;
and then go, for the present.

MRS. MILER comes out with her hat on, passes enigmatically to the door, and
opens it. A man's voice says: "Mr. Malise? Would you give him these cards?"

MRS. MILER. [Re-entering] The cards.

MALISE. Mr. Robert Twisden. Sir Charles and Lady Dedmond. [He looks at
CLARE.]

CLARE. [Her face scornful and unmoved] Let them come.

MALISE. [TO MRS. MILER] Show them in!

TWISDEN enters-a clean-shaved, shrewd-looking man, with a fighting underlip,
followed by SIR CHARLES and LADY DEDMOND. MRS. MILER goes.
There are no greetings.

TWISDEN. Mr. Malise? How do you do, Mrs. Dedmond? Had the pleasure
of meeting you at your wedding. [CLARE inclines her head] I am
Mr. George Dedmond's solicitor, sir. I wonder if you would be so
very kind as to let us have a few words with Mrs. Dedmond alone?

At a nod from CLARE, MALISE passes into the inner room, and shuts the door.
A silence.

SIR CHARLES. [Suddenly] What!

LADY DEDMOND. Mr. Twisden, will you——?

TWISDEN. [Uneasy] Mrs. Dedmond I must apologize, but you—you hardly gave us an alternative, did you? [He pauses for an answer, and, not getting one, goes on] Your disappearance has given your husband great anxiety. Really, my dear madam, you must forgive us for this—attempt to get into communication.

CLARE. Why did you spy, HERE?

SIR CHARLES. No, no! Nobody's spied on you. What!

TWISDEN. I'm afraid the answer is that we appear to have been justified. [At the expression on CLARE'S face he goes on hastily] Now, Mrs. Dedmond, I'm a lawyer and I know that appearances are misleading. Don't think I'm unfriendly; I wish you well. [CLARE raises her eyes. Moved by that look, which is exactly as if she had said: "I have no friends," he hurries on] What we want to say to you is this: Don't let this split go on! Don't commit yourself to what you'll bitterly regret. Just tell us what's the matter. I'm sure it can be put straight.

CLARE. I have nothing against my husband—it was quite unreasonable to leave him.

TWISDEN. Come, that's good.

CLARE. Unfortunately, there's something stronger than reason.

TWISDEN. I don't know it, Mrs. Dedmond.

CLARE. No?

TWISDEN. [Disconcerted] Are you—you oughtn't to take a step without advice, in your position.

CLARE. Nor with it?

TWISDEN. [Approaching her] Come, now; isn't there anything you feel you'd like to say—that might help to put matters straight?

CLARE. I don't think so, thank you.

LADY DEDMOND. You must see, Clare, that——

TWISDEN. In your position, Mrs. Dedmond—a beautiful young woman without money. I'm quite blunt. This is a hard world. Should be awfully sorry if anything goes wrong.

CLARE. And if I go back?

TWISDEN. Of two evils, if it be so—choose the least!

CLARE. I am twenty-six; he is thirty-two. We can't reasonably expect to die for fifty years.

LADY DESMOND. That's morbid, Clare.

TWISDEN. What's open to you if you don't go back? Come, what's your position? Neither fish, flesh, nor fowl; fair game for everybody. Believe me, Mrs. Dedmond, for a pretty woman to strike, as it appears you're doing, simply because the spirit of her marriage has taken flight, is madness. You must know that no one pays attention to anything but facts. If now—excuse me—you—you had a lover, [His eyes travel round the room and again rest on her] you would, at all events, have some ground under your feet, some sort of protection, but [He pauses] as you have not—you've none.

CLARE. Except what I make myself.

SIR CHARLES. Good God!

TWISDEN. Yes! Mrs. Dedmond! There's the bedrock difficulty. As you haven't money, you should never have been pretty. You're up against the world, and you'll get no mercy from it. We lawyers see too much of that. I'm putting it brutally, as a man of the world.

CLARE. Thank you. Do you think you quite grasp the alternative?

TWISDEN. [Taken aback] But, my dear young lady, there are two sides to every contract. After all, your husband's fulfilled his.

CLARE. So have I up till now. I shan't ask anything from him— nothing—do you understand?

LADY DEDMOND. But, my dear, you must live.

TWISDEN. Have you ever done any sort of work?

CLARE. Not yet.

TWISDEN. Any conception of the competition nowadays?

CLARE. I can try.

[TWISDEN, looking at her, shrugs his shoulders]

CLARE. [Her composure a little broken by that look] It's real to me—this—you see!

SIR CHARLES. But, my dear girl, what the devil's to become of George?

CLARE. He can do what he likes—it's nothing to me.

TWISDEN. Mrs. Dedmond, I say without hesitation you've no notion of what you're faced with, brought up to a sheltered life as you've been. Do realize that you stand at the parting of the ways, and one leads into the wilderness.

CLARE. Which?

TWISDEN. [Glancing at the door through which MALISE has gone] Of course, if you want to play at wild asses there are plenty who will help you.

SIR CHARLES. By Gad! Yes!

CLARE. I only want to breathe.

TWISDEN. Mrs. Dedmond, go back! You can now. It will be too late soon. There are lots of wolves about. [Again he looks at the door]

CLARE. But not where you think. You say I need advice. I came here for it.

TWISDEN. [With a curiously expressive shrug] In that case I don't know that I can usefully stay.

[He goes to the outer door.]

CLARE. Please don't have me followed when I leave here. Please!

LADY DEDMOND. George is outside, Clare.

CLARE. I don't wish to see him. By what right have you come here? [She goes
to the door through which MALISE has passed, opens it, and says]
Please come in, Mr. Malise.

[MALISE enters.]

TWISDEN. I am sorry. [Glancing at MALISE, he inclines his head] I am sorry.
Good morning. [He goes]

LADY DEDMOND. Mr. Malise, I'm sure, will see——

CLARE. Mr. Malise will stay here, please, in his own room.

[MALISE bows]

SIR CHARLES. My dear girl, 'pon my soul, you know, I can't grasp your line of
thought at all!

CLARE. No?

LADY DEDMOND. George is most willing to take up things just as they were
before you left.

CLARE. Ah!

LADY DEDMOND. Quite frankly—what is it you want?

CLARE. To be left alone. Quite frankly, he made a mistake to have me spied on.

LADY DEDMOND. But, my good girl, if you'd let us know where you were,
like a reasonable being. You can't possibly be left to yourself without money or position of any kind. Heaven
knows what you'd be driven to!

MALISE. [Softly] Delicious!

SIR CHARLES. You will be good enough to repeat that out loud, sir.

LADY DEDMOND. Charles! Clare, you must know this is all a fit of spleen;
your duty and your interest—marriage is sacred, Clare.

CLARE. Marriage! My marriage has become the—the reconciliation—of two
animals—one of them unwilling. That's all the sanctity there is about
it.

SIR CHARLES. What!

[She looks at MALISE]

LADY DEDMOND. You ought to be horribly ashamed. CLARE. Of the fact-
I am.

LADY DEDMOND. [Darting a glance at MALISE] If we are to talk this out,
it must be in private.

MALISE. [To CLARE] Do you wish me to go?

CLARE. No.

LADY DEDMOND. [At MALISE] I should have thought ordinary decent feeling—Good heavens, girl! Can't you see that you're being
played with?

CLARE. If you insinuate anything against Mr. Malise, you lie.

LADY DEDMOND. If you will do these things—come to a man's rooms——

CLARE. I came to Mr. Malise because he's the only person I know with imagination enough to see what my position is; I came to him a quarter of
an hour ago, for the first time, for definite advice, and you instantly
suspect him. That is disgusting.

LADY DEDMOND. [Frigidly] Is this the natural place for me to find my son's
wife?

CLARE. His woman.

LADY DEDMOND. Will you listen to Reginald?

CLARE. I have.

LADY DEDMOND. Haven't you any religious sense at all, Clare?

CLARE. None, if it's religion to live as we do.

LADY DEDMOND. It's terrible—this state of mind! It's really terrible!

CLARE breaks into the soft laugh of the other evening. As if galvanized by the sound, SIR CHARLES comes to life out of the transfixed bewilderment with which he has been listening.

SIR CHARLES. For God's sake don't laugh like that!

[CLARE Stops]

LADY DEDMOND. [With real feeling] For the sake of the simple right, Clare!

CLARE. Right? Whatever else is right—our life is not. [She puts her hand on her heart] I swear before God that I've tried and tried. I swear before God, that if I believed we could ever again love each other only a little tiny bit, I'd go back. I swear before God that I don't want to hurt any-body.

LADY DEDMOND. But you are hurting everybody. Do—do be reasonable!

CLARE. [Losing control] Can't you see that I'm fighting for all my life to come—not to be buried alive—not to be slowly smothered. Look at me! I'm not wax—I'm flesh and blood. And you want to prison me for ever—body and soul.

[They stare at her]

SIR CHARLES. [Suddenly] By Jove! I don't know, I don't know! What!

LADY DEDMOND. [To MALISE] If you have any decency left, sir, you will allow my son, at all events, to speak to his wife alone. [Beckoning to her husband] We'll wait below.

SIR CHARLES. I—I want to speak. [To CLARE] My dear, if you feel like this, I can only say—as a—as a gentleman——

LADY DEDMOND. Charles!

SIR CHARLES. Let me alone! I can only say that—damme, I don't know that I can say anything!

He looks at her very grieved, then turns and marches out, followed by LADY DEDMOND, whose voice is heard without, answered by his: "What!" In the doorway, as they pass, GEORGE is standing; he comes in.

GEORGE. [Going up to CLARE, who has recovered all her self-control] Will you come outside and speak to me?

CLARE. No.

GEORGE glances at MALISE, who is leaning against the wall with folded arms.

GEORGE. [In a low voice] Clare!

CLARE. Well!

GEORGE. You try me pretty high, don't you, forcing me to come here, and speak before this fellow? Most men would think the worst, finding you like this.

CLARE. You need not have come—or thought at all.

GEORGE. Did you imagine I was going to let you vanish without an effort—

CLARE. To save me?

GEORGE. For God's sake be just! I've come here to say certain things. If you force me to say them before him—on your head be it! Will you appoint somewhere else?

CLARE. No.

GEORGE. Why not?

CLARE. I know all those "certain things." "You must come back. It is your duty. You have no money. Your friends won't help you. You can't earn your living. You are making a scandal." You might even say for the moment: "Your room shall be respected."

GEORGE. Well, it's true and you've no answer.

CLARE. Oh! [Suddenly] Our life's a lie. It's stupid; it's disgusting. I'm tired of it! Please leave me alone!

GEORGE. You rather miss the point, I'm afraid. I didn't come here to tell you what you know perfectly well when you're sane. I came here to say this: Anyone in her senses could see the game your friend here is playing. It wouldn't take a baby in. If you think that a gentleman like that [His stare travels round the dishevelled room till it rests on MALISE] champions a pretty woman for nothing, you make a fairly bad mistake.

CLARE. Take care.

But MALISE, after one convulsive movement of his hands, has again become rigid.

GEORGE. I don't pretend to be subtle or that kind of thing; but I have ordinary common sense. I don't attempt to be superior to plain facts——

CLARE. [Under her breath] Facts!

GEORGE. Oh! for goodness' sake drop that hifalutin' tone. It doesn't suit you. Look here! If you like to go abroad with one of your young sisters until the autumn, I'll let the flat and go to the Club.

CLARE. Put the fire out with a penny hose. [Slowly] I am not coming back to you, George. The farce is over.

GEORGE. [Taken aback for a moment by the finality of her tone, suddenly fronts MALISE] Then there is something between you and this fellow.

MALISE. [Dangerously, but without moving] I beg your pardon!

CLARE. There—is—nothing.

GEORGE. [Looking from one to the other] At all events, I won't—I won't see a woman who once—[CLARE makes a sudden effacing movement with her hands] I won't see her go to certain ruin without lifting a finger.

CLARE. That is noble.

GEORGE. [With intensity] I don't know that you deserve anything of me. But on my honour, as a gentleman, I came here this morning for your sake, to warn you of what you're doing. [He turns suddenly on MALISE] And I tell this precious friend of yours plainly what I think of him, and that I'm not going to play into his hands.

[MALISE, without stirring from the wall, looks at CLARE, and his lips move.]

CLARE. [Shakes her head at him—then to GEORGE] Will you go, please?

GEORGE. I will go when you do.

MALISE. A man of the world should know better than that.

GEORGE. Are you coming?

MALISE. That is inconceivable.

GEORGE. I'm not speaking to you, sir.

MALISE. You are right. Your words and mine will never kiss each other.

GEORGE. Will you come? [CLARE shakes her head]

GEORGE. [With fury] D'you mean to stay in this pigsty with that rhapsodical swine?

MALISE. [Transformed] By God, if you don't go, I'll kill you.

GEORGE. [As suddenly calm] That remains to be seen.

MALISE. [With most deadly quietness] Yes, I will kill you.

He goes stealthily along the wall, takes up from where it lies on the pile of books the great black knobby stick, and stealthily approaches GEORGE, his face quite fiendish.

CLARE. [With a swift movement, grasping the stick] Please.

MALISE resigns the stick, and the two men, perfectly still, glare at each other. CLARE, letting the stick fall, puts her foot on it. Then slowly she takes off her hat and lays it on the table.

CLARE. Now will you go! [There is silence]

GEORGE. [Staring at her hat] You mad little fool! Understand this; if you've not returned home by three o'clock I'll divorce you, and you may roll in the gutter with this high-souled friend of yours. And mind this, you sir—I won't spare you—by God! Your pocket shall suffer. That's the only thing that touches fellows like you.

Turning, he goes out, and slams the door. CLARE and MALISE remain face to face. Her lips have begun to quiver.

CLARE. Horrible!

She turns away, shuddering, and sits down on the edge of the armchair, covering her eyes with the backs of her hands. MALISE picks up the stick, and fingers it lovingly. Then putting it down, he moves so that he can see her face. She is sitting quite still, staring straight before her.

MALISE. Nothing could be better.

CLARE. I don't know what to do! I don't know what to do!

MALISE. Thank the stars for your good fortune.

CLARE. He means to have revenge on you! And it's all my fault.

MALISE. Let him. Let him go for his divorce. Get rid of him. Have done with him—somehow.

She gets up and stands with face averted. Then swiftly turning to him.

CLARE. If I must bring you harm—let me pay you back! I can't bear it otherwise! Make some use of me, if you don't mind!

MALISE. My God!

[She puts up her face to be kissed, shutting her eyes.]

MALISE. You poor——

He clasps and kisses her, then, drawing back, looks in her face. She has not moved, her eyes are still closed; but she is shivering; her lips are tightly pressed together; her hands twitching.

MALISE. [Very quietly] No, no! This is not the house of a "gentleman."

CLARE. [Letting her head fall, and almost in a whisper] I'm sorry.

MALISE. I understand.

CLARE. I don't feel. And without—I can't, can't.

MALISE. [Bitterly] Quite right. You've had enough of that.

There is a long silence. Without looking at him she takes up her hat, and puts it on.

MALISE. Not going?

[CLARE nods]

MALISE. You don't trust me?

CLARE. I do! But I can't take when I'm not giving.

MALISE. I beg—I beg you! What does it matter? Use me! Get free somehow.

CLARE. Mr. Malise, I know what I ought to be to you, if I let you in for all this. I know what you want—or will want. Of course—why not?

MALISE. I give you my solemn word——

CLARE. No! if I can't be that to you—it's not real. And I can't. It isn't to be man-
    ufactured, is it?

MALISE. It is not.

CLARE. To make use of you in such a way! No.

[She moves towards the door]

MALISE. Where are you going?

CLARE does not answer. She is breathing rapidly. There is a change in her, a sort
of excitement beneath her calmness.

MALISE. Not back to him? [CLARE shakes her head] Thank God! But where?
    To your people again?

CLARE. No.

MALISE. Nothing—desperate?

CLARE. Oh! no.

MALISE. Then what—tell me—come!

CLARE. I don't know. Women manage somehow.

MALISE. But you—poor dainty thing!

CLARE. It's all right! Don't be unhappy! Please!

MALISE. [Seizing her arm] D'you imagine they'll let you off, out there—you
    with your face? Come, trust me trust me! You must!

CLARE. [Holding out her hand] Good-bye!

MALISE. [Not taking that hand] This great damned world, and—you! Listen!
    [The sound of the traffic far down below is audible in the stillness]
    Into that! alone—helpless—without money. The men who work

with you; the men you make friends of—d'you think they'll let you be? The men in the streets, staring at you, stopping you—pudgy, bull-necked brutes; devils with hard eyes; senile swine; and the "chivalrous" men, like me, who don't mean you harm, but can't help seeing you're made for love! Or suppose you don't take covert but struggle on in the open. Society! The respectable! The pious! Even those who love you! Will they let you be? Hue and cry! The hunt was joined the moment you broke away! It will never let up! Covert to covert—till they've run you down, and you're back in the cart, and God pity you!

CLARE. Well, I'll die running!

MALISE. No, no! Let me shelter you! Let me!

CLARE. [Shaking her head and smiling] I'm going to seek my fortune. Wish me luck!

MALISE. I can't let you go.

CLARE. You must.

He looks into her face; then, realizing that she means it, suddenly bends down to her fingers, and puts his lips to them.

MALISE. Good luck, then! Good luck!

He releases her hand. Just touching his bent head with her other hand, CLARE turns and goes. MALISE remains with bowed head, listening to the sound of her receding footsteps. They die away. He raises himself, and strikes out into the air with his clenched fist.

CURTAIN.

ACT III

MALISE'S sitting-room. An afternoon, three months later. On the table are an open bottle of claret, his hat, and some tea- things. Down in the hearth is a kettle on a lighted spirit- stand. Near the door stands HAYWOOD, a short, round-faced man, with a tobacco-coloured moustache; MALISE, by the table, is contemplating a piece of blue paper.

HAYWOOD. Sorry to press an old customer, sir, but a year and an 'alf without any return on your money——

MALISE. Your tobacco is too good, Mr. Haywood. I wish I could see my way to smoking another.

HAYWOOD. Well, sir—that's a funny remedy.

With a knock on the half-opened door, a Boy appears.

MALISE. Yes. What is it?

BOY. Your copy for "The Watchfire," please, sir.

MALISE. [Motioning him out] Yes. Wait!

The Boy withdraws. MALISE goes up to the pile of books, turns them over, and takes up some volumes.

MALISE.   This is a very fine unexpurgated translation of Boccaccio's "Decameron," Mr. Haywood illustrated. I should say you would get more than the amount of your bill for them.

HAYWOOD. [Shaking his head] Them books worth three pound seven!

MALISE. It's scarce, and highly improper. Will you take them in discharge?

HAYWOOD. [Torn between emotions] Well, I 'ardly know what to say— No, Sir, I don't think I'd like to 'ave to do with that.

MALISE. You could read them first, you know?

HAYWOOD. [Dubiously] I've got my wife at 'ome.

MALISE. You could both read them.

HAYWOOD. [Brought to his bearings] No, Sir, I couldn't.

MALISE. Very well; I'll sell them myself, and you shall have the result.

HAYWOOD. Well, thank you, sir. I'm sure I didn't want to trouble you.

MALISE. Not at all, Mr. Haywood. It's for me to apologize.

HAYWOOD. So long as I give satisfaction.

MALISE. [Holding the door for him] Certainly. Good evening.

HAYWOOD. Good evenin', sir; no offence, I hope.

MALISE. On the contrary.

Doubtfully HAYWOOD goes. And MALISE stands scratching his head; then slipping the bill into one of the volumes to remind him, he replaces them at the top of the pile. The Boy again advances into the doorway.

MALISE. Yes, now for you.

He goes to the table and takes some sheets of MS. from an old portfolio. But the door is again timidly pushed open, and HAYWOOD reappears.

MALISE. Yes, Mr. Haywood?

HAYWOOD. About that little matter, sir. If—if it's any convenience to you—
I've—thought of a place where I could——

MALISE. Read them? You'll enjoy them thoroughly.

HAYWOOD. No, sir, no! Where I can dispose of them.

MALISE. [Holding out the volumes] It might be as well. [HAYWOOD takes
the books gingerly] I congratulate you, Mr. Haywood; it's a classic.

HAYWOOD. Oh, indeed—yes, sir. In the event of there being any——

MALISE. Anything over? Carry it to my credit. Your bill—[He hands over the
blue paper] Send me the receipt. Good evening!

HAYWOOD, nonplussed, and trying to hide the books in an evening paper,
fumbles out. "Good evenin', sir!" and departs. MALISE again
takes up the sheets of MS. and cons a sentence over to himself,
gazing blankly at the stolid BOY.

MALISE. "Man of the world—good form your god! Poor buttoned-up philosopher" [the Boy shifts his feet] "inbred to the point of cretinism, and
founded to the bone on fear of ridicule [the Boy breathes heavily]—
you are the slave of facts!"

[There is a knock on the door]

MALISE. Who is it?

The door is pushed open, and REGINALD HUNTINGDON stands there.

HUNTINGDON. I apologize, sir; can I come in a minute?

[MALISE bows with ironical hostility]

HUNTINGDON. I don't know if you remember me—Clare Dedmond's brother.

MALISE. I remember you.

[He motions to the stolid Boy to go outside again]

HUNTINGDON. I've come to you, sir, as a gentleman——

MALISE. Some mistake. There is one, I believe, on the first floor.

HUNTINGDON. It's about my sister.

MALISE. D—n you! Don't you know that I've been shadowed these last three months? Ask your detectives for any information you want.

HUNTINGDON. We know that you haven't seen her, or even known where she is.

MALISE. Indeed! You've found that out? Brilliant!

HUNTINGDON. We know it from my sister.

MALISE. Oh! So you've tracked her down?

HUNTINGDON. Mrs. Fullarton came across her yesterday in one of those big shops—selling gloves.

MALISE. Mrs. Fullarton the lady with the husband. Well! you've got her. Clap her back into prison.

HUNTINGDON. We have not got her. She left at once, and we don't know where she's gone.

MALISE. Bravo!

HUNTINGDON. [Taking hold of his bit] Look here, Mr. Malise, in a way I share your feeling, but I'm fond of my sister, and it's damnable to have to go back to India knowing she must be all adrift, without protection, going through God knows what! Mrs. Fullarton says she's looking awfully pale and down.

MALISE. [Struggling between resentment and sympathy] Why do you come to me?

HUNTINGDON. We thought——

MALISE. Who?

HUNTINGDON. My—my father and myself.

MALISE. Go on.

HUNTINGDON. We thought there was just a chance that, having lost that job,
    she might come to you again for advice. If she does, it would
    be really generous of you if you'd put my father in touch with
    her. He's getting old, and he feels this very much. [He hands
    MALISE a card] This is his address.

MALISE. [Twisting the card] Let there be no mistake, sir; I do nothing that will
    help give her back to her husband. She's out to save her soul alive, and
    I don't join the hue and cry that's after her. On the contrary—if I had
    the power. If your father wants to shelter her, that's another matter.
    But she'd her own ideas about that.

HUNTINGDON. Perhaps you don't realize how unfit my sister is for rough and
    tumble. She's not one of this new sort of woman. She's
    always been looked after, and had things done for her. Pluck
    she's got, but that's all, and she's bound to come to grief.

MALISE. Very likely—the first birds do. But if she drops half-way it's better
    than if she'd never flown. Your sister, sir, is trying the wings of her
    spirit, out of the old slave market. For women as for men, there's
    more than one kind of dishonour, Captain Huntingdon, and worse
    things than being dead, as you may know in your profession.

HUNTINGDON. Admitted—but——

MALISE. We each have our own views as to what they are. But they all come
    to—death of our spirits, for the sake of our carcases. Anything more?

HUNTINGDON. My leave's up. I sail to-morrow. If you do see my sister I
    trust you to give her my love and say I begged she would see
    my father.

MALISE. If I have the chance—yes.

He makes a gesture of salute, to which HUNTINGDON responds. Then the latter turns and goes out.

MALISE. Poor fugitive! Where are you running now?

He stands at the window, through which the evening sunlight is powdering the room with smoky gold. The stolid Boy has again come in. MALISE stares at him, then goes back to the table, takes up the MS., and booms it at him; he receives the charge, breathing hard.

MALISE. "Man of the world—product of a material age; incapable of perceiving reality in motions of the spirit; having 'no use,' as you would say, for 'sentimental nonsense'; accustomed to believe yourself the national spine—your position is unassailable. You will remain the idol of the country—arbiter of law, parson in mufti, darling of the playwright and the novelist—God bless you!—while waters lap these shores."

He places the sheets of MS. in an envelope, and hands them to the Boy.

MALISE. You're going straight back to "The Watchfire"?

BOY. [Stolidly] Yes, sir.

MALISE. [Staring at him] You're a masterpiece. D'you know that?

BOY. No, sir.

MALISE. Get out, then.

He lifts the portfolio from the table, and takes it into the inner room. The Boy, putting his thumb stolidly to his nose, turns to go. In the doorway he shies violently at the figure of CLARE, standing there in a dark-coloured dress, skids past her and goes. CLARE comes into the gleam of sunlight, her white face alive with emotion or excitement. She looks round her, smiles, sighs; goes swiftly to the door, closes it, and comes back to the table. There she stands, fingering the papers on the table, smoothing MALISE's hat wistfully, eagerly, waiting.

MALISE. [Returning] You!

CLARE. [With a faint smile] Not very glorious, is it?

He goes towards her, and checks himself, then slews the armchair round.

MALISE. Come! Sit down, sit down! [CLARE, heaving a long sigh, sinks down
          into the chair] Tea's nearly ready.

He places a cushion for her, and prepares tea; she looks up at him softly, but as he
finishes and turns to her, she drops that glance.

CLARE. Do you think me an awful coward for coming? [She has taken a little
          plain cigarette case from her dress] Would you mind if I smoked?

MALISE shakes his head, then draws back from her again, as if afraid to be too
close. And again, unseen, she looks at him.

MALISE. So you've lost your job?

CLARE. How did you——?

MALISE. Your brother. You only just missed him. [CLARE starts up] They had
          an idea you'd come. He's sailing to-morrow—he wants you to see your
          father.

CLARE. Is father ill?

MALI$E. Anxious about you.

CLARE. I've written to him every week. [Excited] They're still hunting me!

MALISE. [Touching her shoulder gently] It's all right—all right.

She sinks again into the chair, and again he withdraws. And once more she gives
him that soft eager look, and once more averts it as he turns to her.

CLARE. My nerves have gone funny lately. It's being always on one's guard, and
          stuffy air, and feeling people look and talk about you, and dislike your
          being there.

MALISE. Yes; that wants pluck.

CLARE. [Shaking her head] I curl up all the time. The only thing I know for certain is, that I shall never go back to him. The more I've hated what I've been doing, the more sure I've been. I might come to anything— but not that.

MALISE. Had a very bad time?

CLARE. [Nodding] I'm spoilt. It's a curse to be a lady when you have to earn your living. It's not really been so hard, I suppose; I've been selling things, and living about twice as well as most shop girls.

MALISE. Were they decent to you?

CLARE. Lots of the girls are really nice. But somehow they don't want me, can't help thinking I've got airs or something; and in here [She touches her breast] I don't want them!

MALISE. I know.

CLARE. Mrs. Fullarton and I used to belong to a society for helping reduced gentlewomen to get work. I know now what they want: enough money not to work—that's all! [Suddenly looking up at him] Don't think me worse than I am-please! It's working under people; it's having to do it, being driven. I have tried, I've not been altogether a coward, really! But every morning getting there the same time; every day the same stale "dinner," as they call it; every evening the same "Good evening, Miss Clare," "Good evening, Miss Simpson," "Good evening, Miss Hart," "Good evening, Miss Clare." And the same walk home, or the same 'bus; and the same men that you mustn't look at, for fear they'll follow you. [She rises] Oh! and the feeling-always, always—that there's no sun, or life, or hope, or anything. It was just like being ill, the way I've wanted to ride and dance and get out into the country. [Her excitement dies away into the old clipped composure, and she sits down again] Don't think too badly of me—it really is pretty ghastly!

MALISE. [Gruffly] H'm! Why a shop?

CLARE. References. I didn't want to tell more lies than I could help; a married woman on strike can't tell the truth, you know. And I can't typewrite or do shorthand yet. And chorus—I thought—you wouldn't like.

MALISE. I? What have I——? [He checks himself] Have men been brutes?

CLARE. [Stealing a look at him] One followed me a lot. He caught hold of my
    arm one evening. I just took this out [She draws out her hatpin and
    holds it like a dagger, her lip drawn back as the lips of a dog going to
    bite] and said: "Will you leave me alone, please?" And he did. It was
    rather nice. And there was one quite decent little man in the shop—I
    was sorry for him—such a humble little man!

MALISE. Poor devil—it's hard not to wish for the moon.

At the tone of his voice CLARE looks up at him; his face is turned away.

CLARE. [Softly] How have you been? Working very hard?

MALISE. As hard as God will let me.

CLARE. [Stealing another look] Have you any typewriting I could do? I could
    learn, and I've still got a brooch I could sell. Which is the best kind?

MALISE. I had a catalogue of them somewhere.

He goes into the inner room. The moment he is gone, CLARE stands up, her
hands pressed to her cheeks as if she felt them flaming. Then, with hands clasped,
she stands waiting. He comes back with the old portfolio.

MALISE. Can you typewrite where you are?

CLARE. I have to find a new room anyway. I'm changing—to be safe. [She takes
    a luggage ticket from her glove] I took my things to Charing Cross—
    only a bag and one trunk. [Then, with that queer expression on her
    face which prefaces her desperations] You don't want me now, I sup-
    pose.

MALISE. What?

CLARE. [Hardly above a whisper] Because—if you still wanted me— I do—
    now.

[Etext editors note: In the 1924 revision, 11 years after this 1913 edition: "I do—
now" is changed to "I could—now"— a significant change in meaning. D.W.]

MALISE. [Staring hard into her face that is quivering and smiling] You mean it? You do? You care——?

CLARE. I've thought of you—so much! But only—if you're sure.

He clasps her and kisses her closed eyes; and so they stand for a moment, till the sound of a latchkey in the door sends them apart.

MALISE. It's the housekeeper. Give me that ticket; I'll send for your things.

Obediently she gives him the ticket, smiles, and goes quietly into the inner room. MRS. MILER has entered; her face, more Chinese than ever, shows no sign of having seen.

MALISE. That lady will stay here, Mrs. Miler. Kindly go with this ticket to the cloak-room at Charing Cross station, and bring back her luggage in a cab. Have you money?

MRS. MILER. 'Arf a crown. [She takes the ticket—then impassively] In case you don't know—there's two o' them men about the stairs now.

The moment she is gone MALISE makes a gesture of maniacal fury. He steals on tiptoe to the outer door, and listens. Then, placing his hand on the knob, he turns it without noise, and wrenches back the door. Transfigured in the last sunlight streaming down the corridor are two men, close together, listening and consulting secretly. They start back.

MALISE. [With strange, almost noiseless ferocity] You've run her to earth; your job's done. Kennel up, hounds! [And in their faces he slams the door]

CURTAIN.

SCENE II

SCENE II—The same, early on a winter afternoon, three months later. The room has now a certain daintiness. There are curtains over the doors, a couch, under the window, all the books are arranged on shelves. In small vases, over the fire-place, are a few violets and chrysanthemums. MALISE sits huddled in his arm-chair drawn close to the fore, paper on knee, pen in hand. He looks rather grey and drawn, and round his chair is the usual litter. At the table, now nearer to the window, CLARE sits working a typewriter. She finishes a line, puts sheets of paper together, makes a note on a card—adds some figures, and marks the total.

CLARE. Kenneth, when this is paid, I shall have made two pound seventeen in the three months, and saved you about three pounds. One hundred and seventeen shillings at tenpence a thousand is one hundred and forty thousand words at fourteen hundred words an hour. It's only just over an hour a day. Can't you get me more?

MALISE lifts the hand that holds his pen and lets it fall again. CLARE puts the cover on the typewriter, and straps it.

CLARE. I'm quite packed. Shall I pack for you? [He nods] Can't we have more than three days at the sea? [He shakes his head. Going up to him] You did sleep last night.

MALISE. Yes, I slept.

CLARE. Bad head? [MALISE nods] By this time the day after to- morrow the case will be heard and done with. You're not worrying for me? Except for my poor old Dad, I don't care a bit.

MALISE heaves himself out of the chair, and begins pacing up and down.

CLARE. Kenneth, do you understand why he doesn't claim damages, after what he said that day-here? [Looking suddenly at him] It is true that he doesn't?

MALISE. It is not.

CLARE. But you told me yourself

MALISE. I lied.

CLARE. Why?

MALISE. [Shrugging] No use lying any longer—you'd know it tomorrow.

CLARE. How much am I valued at?

MALISE. Two thousand. [Grimly] He'll settle it on you. [He laughs] Masterly!
By one stroke, destroys his enemy, avenges his "honour," and gilds his
name with generosity!

CLARE. Will you have to pay?

MALISE. Stones yield no blood.

CLARE. Can't you borrow?

MALISE. I couldn't even get the costs.

CLARE. Will they make you bankrupt, then? [MALISE nods] But that doesn't
mean that you won't have your income, does it? [MALISE laughs]
What is your income, Kenneth? [He is silent] A hundred and fifty
from "The Watchfire," I know. What else?

MALISE. Out of five books I have made the sum of forty pounds.

CLARE. What else? Tell me.

MALISE. Fifty to a hundred pounds a year. Leave me to gnaw my way out,
child.

CLARE stands looking at him in distress, then goes quickly into the room behind
her. MALISE takes up his paper and pen. The paper is quite blank.

MALISE. [Feeling his head] Full of smoke.

He drops paper and pen, and crossing to the room on the left goes in. CLARE
re-enters with a small leather box. She puts it down on her typing table as
MALISE returns followed by MRS. MILER, wearing her hat, and carrying His
overcoat.

MRS. MILER. Put your coat on. It's a bitter wind.

[He puts on the coat]

CLARE. Where are you going?

MALISE. To "The Watchfire."

The door closes behind him, and MRS. MILER goes up to CLARE holding out
a little blue bottle with a red label, nearly full.

MRS. MILER. You know he's takin' this [She makes a little motion towards her
        mouth] to make 'im sleep?

CLARE. [Reading the label] Where was it?

MRS. MILER. In the bathroom chest o' drawers, where 'e keeps 'is odds and
        ends. I was lookin' for 'is garters.

CLARE. Give it to me!

MRS. MILER. He took it once before. He must get his sleep.

CLARE. Give it to me!

MRS. MILER resigns it, CLARE takes the cork out, smells, then tastes it from
her finger. MRS. MILER, twisting her apron in her hands, speaks.

MILS. MILER. I've 'ad it on my mind a long time to speak to yer. Your comin'
        'ere's not done 'im a bit o' good.

CLARE. Don't!

MRS. MILER. I don't want to, but what with the worry o' this 'ere divorce suit,
        an' you bein' a lady an' 'im havin' to be so careful of yer, and
        tryin' to save, not smokin' all day like 'e used, an' not gettin' 'is
        two bottles of claret regular; an' losin' his sleep, an' takin' that
        stuff for it; and now this 'ere last business. I've seen 'im some-
        times holdin' 'is 'ead as if it was comin' off. [Seeing CLARE
        wince, she goes on with a sort of compassion in her Chinese
        face] I can see yer fond of him; an' I've nothin' against yer you
        don't trouble me a bit; but I've been with 'im eight years—we're
        used to each other, and I can't bear to see 'im not 'imself, really
        I can't.

She gives a sudden sniff. Then her emotion passes, leaving her as Chinese as ever.

CLARE. This last business—what do you mean by that?

MRS. MILER. If 'e a'n't told yer, I don't know that I've any call to.

CLARE. Please.

MRS. MILER. [Her hands twisting very fast] Well, it's to do with this 'ere "Watchfire." One of the men that sees to the writin' of it 'e's an old friend of Mr. Malise, 'e come 'ere this mornin' when you was out. I was doin' my work in there [She points to the room on the right] an' the door open, so I 'earl 'em. Now you've 'ung them curtains, you can't 'elp it.

CLARE. Yes?

MRS. MILER. It's about your divorce case. This 'ere "Watchfire," ye see, belongs to some fellers that won't 'ave their men gettin' into the papers. So this 'ere friend of Mr. Malise—very nice 'e spoke about it: "If it comes into Court," 'e says, "you'll 'ave to go," 'e says. "These beggars, these dogs, these dogs," 'e says, "they'll 'oof you out," 'e says. An' I could tell by the sound of his voice, 'e meant it—proper upset 'e was. So that's that!

CLARE. It's inhuman!

MRS. MILER. That's what I thinks; but it don't 'elp, do it? "'Tain't the circulation," 'e says, "it's the principle," 'e says; and then 'e starts in swearin' horrible. 'E's a very nice man. And Mr. Malise, 'e says: "Well, that about does for me!" 'e says.

CLARE. Thank you, Mrs. Miler—I'm glad to know.

MRS. MILER. Yes; I don't know as I ought to 'ave told you. [Desperately uncomfortable] You see, I don't take notice of Mr. MALISE, but I know 'im very well. 'E's a good 'arted gentleman, very funny, that'll do things to help others, and what's more, keep on doin' 'em, when they hurt 'im; very obstinate 'e is. Now, when you first come 'ere, three months ago, I says to meself: "He'll enjoy this 'ere for a bit, but she's too much of a lady for 'im." What 'e wants about 'im permanent is a woman that thinks an' talks about all them things he talks about. And sometimes I fancy 'e don't want nothin' permanent about 'im at all.

CLARE. Don't!

MRS. MILER. [With another sudden sniff] Gawd knows I don't want to upset ye. You're situated very hard; an' women's got no business to 'urt one another—that's what I thinks.

CLARE. Will you go out and do something for me? [MRS. MILER nods]

[CLARE takes up the sheaf of papers and from the leather box a note and an emerald pendant]

Take this with the note to that address—it's quite close. He'll give you thirty pounds for it. Please pay these bills and bring me back the receipts, and what's over.

MRS. MILER. [Taking the pendant and note] It's a pretty thing.

CLARE. Yes. It was my mother's.

MRS. MILER. It's a pity to part with it; ain't you got another?

CLARE. Nothing more, Mrs. Miler, not even a wedding ring.

MRS. MILER. [Without expression] You make my 'eart ache sometimes.

[She wraps pendant and note into her handkerchief and goes out to the door.]

MRS. MILER. [From the door] There's a lady and gentleman out here. Mrs. Fuller—wants you, not Mr. Malise.

CLARE. Mrs. Fullarton? [MRS. MILER nods] Ask them to come in.

MRS. MILER opens the door wide, says "Come in," and goes. MRS. FULLARTON is accompanied not by FULLARTON, but by the lawyer, TWISDON. They come in.

MRS. FULLARTON. Clare! My dear! How are you after all this time?

CLARE. [Her eyes fixed on TWISDEN] Yes?

MRS. FULLARTON. [Disconcerted by the strange greeting] I brought Mr. Twisden to tell you something. May I stay?

CLARE. Yes. [She points to the chair at the same table: MRS. FULLARTON sits down] Now!

[TWISDEN comes forward]

TWISDEN. As you're not defending this case, Mrs. Dedmond, there is nobody but yourself for me to apply to.

CLARE. Please tell me quickly, what you've come for.

TWISDEN. [Bowing slightly] I am instructed by Mr. Dedmond to say that if you will leave your present companion and undertake not to see him again, he will withdraw the suit and settle three hundred a year on you. [At CLARE's movement of abhorrence] Don't misunderstand me, please—it is not—it could hardly be, a request that you should go back. Mr. Dedmond is not prepared to receive you again. The proposal—forgive my saying so—remarkably Quixotic—is made to save the scandal to his family and your own. It binds you to nothing but the abandonment of your present companion, with certain conditions of the same nature as to the future. In other words, it assures you a position—so long as you live quietly by yourself.

CLARE. I see. Will you please thank Mr. Dedmond, and say that I refuse?

MRS. FULLARTON. Clare, Clare! For God's sake don't be desperate.

[CLARE, deathly still, just looks at her]

TWISDEN. Mrs. Dedmond, I am bound to put the position to you in its naked brutality. You know there's a claim for damages?

CLARE. I have just learnt it.

TWISDEN. You realize what the result of this suit must be: You will be left dependent on an undischarged bankrupt. To put it another way, you'll be a stone round the neck of a drowning man.

CLARE. You are cowards.

MRS. FULLARTON. Clare, Clare! [To TWISDEN] She doesn't mean it; please
be patient.

CLARE. I do mean it. You ruin him because of me. You get him down, and
kick him to intimidate me.

MRS. FULLARTON. My dear girl! Mr. Twisden is not personally concerned.
How can you?

CLARE. If I were dying, and it would save me, I wouldn't take a penny from my
husband.

TWISDEN. Nothing could be more bitter than those words. Do you really wish
me to take them back to him?

CLARE. Yes. [She turns from them to the fire]

MRS. FULLARTON. [In a low voice to TWISDEN] Please leave me alone with
her, don't say anything to Mr. Dedmond yet.

TWISDEN. Mrs. De a coward, I still do that. For God's sake, think—before it's
too late.

CLARE. [Putting out her hand blindly] I'm sorry I called you a coward. It's the
whole thing, I meant.

TWISDEN. Never mind that. Think!

With the curious little movement of one who sees something he does not like to
see, he goes. CLARE is leaning her forehead against the mantel-shelf, seemingly
unconscious that she is not alone. MRS. FULLARTON approaches quietly till
she can see CLARE'S face.

MRS. FULLARTON. My dear sweet thing, don't be cross with met [CLARE
turns from her. It is all the time as if she were trying to get
away from words and people to something going on within herself] How can I help wanting to see you saved from
all this ghastliness?

CLARE. Please don't, Dolly! Let me be!

MRS. FULLARTON. I must speak, Clare! I do think you're hard on George. It's generous of him to offer to withdraw the suit— considering. You do owe it to us to try and spare your father and your sisters and—and all of us who care for you.

CLARE. [Facing her] You say George is generous! If he wanted to be that he'd never have claimed these damages. It's revenge he wants—I heard him here. You think I've done him an injury. So I did—when I married him. I don't know what I shall come to, Dolly, but I shan't fall so low as to take money from him. That's as certain as that I shall die.

MRS. FULLARTON. Do you know, Clare, I think it's awful about you! You're too fine, and not fine enough, to put up with things; you're too sensitive to take help, and you're not strong enough to do without it. It's simply tragic. At any rate, you might go home to your people.

CLARE. After this!

MRS. FULLARTON. To us, then?

CLARE. "If I could be the falling bee, and kiss thee all the day!" No, Dolly!

MRS. FULLARTON turns from her ashamed and baffled, but her quick eyes take in the room, trying to seize on some new point of attack.

MRS. FULLARTON. You can't be—you aren't-happy, here?

CLARE. Aren't I?

MRS. FULLARTON. Oh! Clare! Save yourself—and all of us!

CLARE. [Very still] You see, I love him.

MRS. FULLARTON. You used to say you'd never love; did not want it— would never want it.

CLARE. Did I? How funny!

MRS. FULLARTON. Oh! my dear! Don't look like that, or you'll make me cry.

CLARE. One doesn't always know the future, does one? [Desperately] I love
          him! I love him!

MRS. FULLARTON. [Suddenly] If you love him, what will it be like for you,
          knowing you've ruined him?

CLARE. Go away! Go away!

MRS. FULLARTON. Love!—you said!

CLARE. [Quivering at that stab-suddenly] I must—I will keep him. He's all I've
          got.

MRS. FULLARTON. Can you—can you keep him?

CLARE. Go!

MRS. FULLARTON. I'm going. But, men are hard to keep, even when you've
          not been the ruin of them. You know whether the love
          this man gives you is really love. If not—God help you!
          [She turns at the door, and says mournfully] Good-bye,
          my child! If you can——

Then goes. CLARE, almost in a whisper, repeats the words: "Love! you said!"
At the sound of a latchkey she runs as if to escape into the bedroom, but changes
her mind and stands blotted against the curtain of the door. MALISE enters. For
a moment he does not see her standing there against the curtain that is much the
same colour as her dress. His face is that of a man in the grip of a rage that he
feels to be impotent. Then, seeing her, he pulls himself together, walks to his armchair, and sits down there in his hat and coat.

CLARE. Well? "The Watchfire?" You may as well tell me.

MALISE. Nothing to tell you, child.

At that touch of tenderness she goes up to his chair and kneels down beside it.
Mechanically MALISE takes off his hat.

CLARE. Then you are to lose that, too? [MALISE stares at her] I know about it—never mind how.

MALISE. Sanctimonious dogs!

CLARE. [Very low] There are other things to be got, aren't there?

MALISE. Thick as blackberries. I just go out and cry, "MALISE, unsuccessful author, too honest journalist, freethinker, co- respondent, bankrupt," and they tumble!

CLARE. [Quietly] Kenneth, do you care for me? [MALISE stares at her] Am I anything to you but just prettiness?

MALISE. Now, now! This isn't the time to brood! Rouse up and fight.

CLARE. Yes.

MALISE. We're not going to let them down us, are we? [She rubs her cheek against his hand, that still rests on her shoulder] Life on sufferance, breath at the pleasure of the enemy! And some day in the fullness of his mercy to be made a present of the right to eat and drink and breathe again. [His gesture sums up the rage within him] Fine! [He puts his hat on and rises] That's the last groan they get from me.

CLASS. Are you going out again? [He nods] Where?

MALISE. Blackberrying! Our train's not till six.

He goes into the bedroom. CLARE gets up and stands by the fire, looking round in a dazed way. She puts her hand up and mechanically gathers together the violets in the little vase. Suddenly she twists them to a buttonhole, and sinks down into the armchair, which he must pass. There she sits, the violets in her hand. MALISE comes out and crosses towards the outer door. She puts the violets up to him. He stares at them, shrugs his shoulders, and passes on. For just a moment CLARE sits motionless.

CLARE. [Quietly] Give me a kiss!

He turns and kisses her. But his lips, after that kiss, have the furtive bitterness one sees on the lips of those who have done what does not suit their mood. He goes

out. She is left motionless by the armchair, her throat working. Then, feverishly, she goes to the little table, seizes a sheet of paper, and writes. Looking up suddenly she sees that MRS. MILER has let herself in with her latchkey.

MRS. MILER. I've settled the baker, the milk, the washin' an' the groceries—this
            'ere's what's left.

She counts down a five-pound note, four sovereigns, and two shillings on to the
little table. CLARE folds the letter into an envelope, then takes up the five-
pound note and puts it into her dress.

CLARE. [Pointing to the money on the table] Take your wages; and give him
       this when he comes in. I'm going away.

MRS. MILER. Without him? When'll you be comin' back?

CLARE. [Rising] I shan't be coming back. [Gazing at MRS. MILER'S hands,
       which are plaiting at her dress] I'm leaving Mr. Malise, and shan't see
       him again. And the suit against us will be withdrawn—the divorce
       suit—you understand?

MRS. MILER. [Her face all broken up] I never meant to say anything to yer.

CLARE. It's not you. I can see for myself. Don't make it harder; help me. Get
       a cab.

MRS. MILER. [Disturbed to the heart] The porter's outside, cleanin' the landin'
            winder.

CLARE. Tell him to come for my trunk. It is packed. [She goes into the bed-
       room]

MRS. MILER. [Opening the door-desolately] Come 'ere!

[The PORTER appears in shirt-sleeves at the door]

MRS. MILER. The lady wants a cab. Wait and carry 'er trunk down.

CLARE comes from the bedroom in her hat and coat.

MRS. MILER. [TO the PORTER] Now.

They go into the bedroom to get the trunk. CLARE picks up from the floor the bunch of violets, her fingers play with it as if they did not quite know what it was; and she stands by the armchair very still, while MRS. MILER and the PORTER pass her with trunk and bag. And even after the PORTER has shouldered the trunk outside, and marched away, and MRS. MILER has come back into the room, CLARE still stands there.

MRS. MILER. [Pointing to the typewriter] D'you want this 'ere, too?

CLARE. Yes.

MRS. MILER carries it out. Then, from the doorway, gazing at CLARE taking her last look, she sobs, suddenly. At sound of that sob CLARE throws up her head.

CLARE. Don't! It's all right. Good-bye!

She walks out and away, not looking back. MRS. MILER chokes her sobbing into the black stuff of her thick old jacket.

CURTAIN

ACT IV

Supper-time in a small room at "The Gascony" on Derby Day. Through the windows of a broad corridor, out of which the door opens, is seen the dark blue of a summer night. The walls are of apricot-gold; the carpets, curtains, lamp-shades, and gilded chairs, of red; the wood-work and screens white; the palms in gilded tubs. A doorway that has no door leads to another small room. One little table behind a screen, and one little table in the open, are set for two persons each. On a service-table, above which hangs a speaking-tube, are some dishes of hors d'ouvres, a basket of peaches, two bottles of champagne in ice- pails, and a small barrel of oysters in a gilded tub. ARNAUD, the waiter, slim, dark, quick, his face seamed with a quiet, soft irony, is opening oysters and listening to the robust joy of a distant supper-party, where a man is playing the last bars of: "Do ye ken John Peel" on a horn. As the sound dies away, he murmurs: "Tres Joli!" and opens another oyster. Two Ladies with bare shoulders and large hats pass down the corridor. Their talk is faintly wafted in: "Well, I never like Derby night! The boys do get so bobbish!" "That horn—vulgar, I call it!"

ARNAUD'S eyebrows rise, the corners of his mouth droop. A Lady with bare shoulders, and crimson roses in her hair, comes along the corridor, and stops for a second at the window, for a man to join her. They come through into the room. ARNAUD has sprung to attention, but with: "Let's go in here, shall we?" they pass through into the further room. The MANAGER, a gentleman with neat moustaches, and buttoned into a frock-coat, has appeared, brisk, noiseless, his eyes everywhere; he inspects the peaches.

MANAGER. Four shillin' apiece to-night, see?

ARNAUD. Yes, Sare.

From the inner room a young man and his partner have come in. She is dark, almost Spanish-looking; he fair, languid, pale, clean-shaved, slackly smiling, with half-closed eyes-one of those who are bred and dissipated to the point of having lost all save the capacity for hiding their emotions. He speaks in a——

LANGUID VOICE. Awful row they're kickin' up in there, Mr. Varley. A fellow
     with a horn.

MANAGER. [Blandly] Gaddesdon Hunt, my lord—always have their supper
     with us, Derby night. Quiet corner here, my lord. Arnaud!

ARNAUD is already at the table, between screen and palm. And, there ensconced, the couple take their seats. Seeing them safely landed, the MANAG-ER, brisk and noiseless, moves away. In the corridor a lady in black, with a cloak falling open, seems uncertain whether to come in. She advances into the door-way. It is CLARE.

ARNAUD. [Pointing to the other table as he flies with dishes] Nice table,
     Madame.

CLARE moves to the corner of it. An artist in observation of his clients, ARNAUD takes in her face—very pale under her wavy, simply-dressed hair; shad-owy beneath the eyes; not powdered; her lips not reddened; without a single orna-ment; takes in her black dress, finely cut, her arms and neck beautifully white, and at her breast three gardenias. And as he nears her, she lifts her eyes. It is very much the look of something lost, appealing for guidance.

ARNAUD. Madame is waiting for some one? [She shakes her head] Then
     Madame will be veree well here—veree well. I take Madame's cloak?

He takes the cloak gently and lays it on the back of the chair fronting the room, that she may put it round her when she wishes. She sits down.

LANGUID VOICE. [From the corner] Waiter!

ARNAUD. Milord!

LANGUID VOICE. The Roederer.

ARNAUD. At once, Milord.

CLARE sits tracing a pattern with her finger on the cloth, her eyes lowered. Once she raises them, and follows ARNAUD's dark rapid figure.

ARNAUD. [Returning] Madame feels the 'eat? [He scans her with increased curiosity] You wish something, Madame?

CLARE. [Again giving him that look] Must I order?

ARNAUD. Non, Madame, it is not necessary. A glass of water. [He pours it out] I have not the pleasure of knowing Madame's face.

CLARE. [Faintly smiling] No.

ARNAUD. Madame will find it veree good 'ere, veree quiet.   .

LANGUID VOICE. Waiter!

ARNAUD. Pardon! [He goes]

The bare-necked ladies with large hats again pass down the corridor outside, and again their voices are wafted in: "Tottie! Not she! Oh! my goodness, she has got a pride on her!" "Bobbie'll never stick it!" "Look here, dear——" Galvanized by those sounds, CLARE has caught her cloak and half-risen; they die away and she subsides.

ARNAUD. [Back at her table, with a quaint shrug towards the corridor] It is not rowdy here, Madame, as a rule—not as in some places. To-night a little noise. Madame is fond of flowers? [He whisks out, and returns almost at once with a bowl of carnations from some table in the next room] These smell good!

CLARE. You are very kind.

ARNAUD. [With courtesy] Not at all, Madame; a pleasure. [He bows]

A young man, tall, thin, hard, straight, with close-cropped, sandyish hair and moustache, a face tanned very red, and one of those small, long, lean heads that only grow in Britain; clad in a thin dark overcoat thrown open, an opera hat pushed back, a white waistcoat round his lean middle, he comes in from the corridor. He looks round, glances at CLARE, passes her table towards the further room, stops in the doorway, and looks back at her. Her eyes have just been lifted, and are at once cast down again. The young man wavers, catches ARNAUD's eye, jerks his head to summon him, and passes into the further room. ARNAUD takes up the vase that has been superseded, and follows him out. And CLARE sits alone in silence, broken by the murmurs of the languid lord and his partner, behind the screen. She is breathing as if she had been running hard. She lifts her eyes. The tall young man, divested of hat and coat, is standing by her table, holding out his hand with a sort of bashful hardiness.

YOUNG MAN. How d'you do? Didn't recognize you at first. So sorry- awfully rude of me.

CLARE'S eyes seem to fly from him, to appeal to him, to resign herself all at once. Something in the YOUNG MAN responds. He drops his hand.

CLARE. [Faintly] How d'you do?

YOUNG MAN. [Stammering] You—you been down there to-day?

CLARE. Where?

YOUNG MAN. [With a smile] The Derby. What? Don't you generally go down? [He touches the other chair] May I?

CLARE. [Almost in a whisper] Yes.

As he sits down, ARNAUD returns and stands before them.

ARNAUD. The plovers' eggs veree good to-night, Sare. Veree good, Madame. A peach or two, after. Veree good peaches. The Roederer, Sare— not bad at all. Madame likes it frappe, but not too cold—yes?

[He is away again to his service-table.]

YOUNG MAN. [Burying his face in the carnations] I say—these are jolly, aren't they? They do you pretty well here.

CLARE. Do they?

YOUNG MAN. You've never been here? [CLARE shakes her head] By Jove! I
            thought I didn't know your face. [CLARE looks full at him.
            Again something moves in the YOUNG MAN, and he stam-
            mers] I mean—not——

CLARE. It doesn't matter.

YOUNG MAN. [Respectfully] Of course, if I—if you were waiting for anybody,
            or anything—I——

[He half rises]

CLARE. It's all right, thank you.

The YOUNG MAN sits down again, uncomfortable, nonplussed. There is
silence, broken by the inaudible words of the languid lord, and the distant mer-
riment of the supper-party. ARNAUD brings the plovers' eggs.

YOUNG MAN. The wine, quick.

ARNAUD. At once, Sare.

YOUNG MAN. [Abruptly] Don't you ever go racing, then?

CLARE. No.

[ARNAUD pours out champagne]

YOUNG MAN. I remember awfully well my first day. It was pretty thick—lost
            every blessed bob, and my watch and chain, playin' three cards
            on the way home.

CLARE. Everything has a beginning, hasn't it?

[She drinks. The YOUNG MAN stares at her]

YOUNG MAN. [Floundering in these waters deeper than he had bargained for]
            I say—about things having beginnings—did you mean any-
            thing?

[CLARE nods]

YOUNG MAN. What! D'you mean it's really the first——?

CLARE nods. The champagne has flicked her courage.

YOUNG MAN. By George! [He leans back] I've often wondered.

ARNAUD. [Again filling the glasses] Monsieur finds——

YOUNG MAN. [Abruptly] It's all right.

He drains his glass, then sits bolt upright. Chivalry and the camaraderie of class have begun to stir in him.

YOUNG MAN. Of course I can see that you're not—I mean, that you're a—a
        lady. [CLARE smiles] And I say, you know—if you have to—
        because you're in a hole—I should feel a cad. Let me lend
        you——?

CLARE. [Holding up her glass] 'Le vin est tire, il faut le boire'!

She drinks. The French words, which he does not too well understand, completing his conviction that she is a lady, he remains quite silent, frowning. As CLARE held up her glass, two gentlemen have entered. The first is blond, of good height and a comely insolence. His crisp, fair hair, and fair brushed-up moustache are just going grey; an eyeglass is fixed in one of two eyes that lord it over every woman they see; his face is broad, and coloured with air and wine. His companion is a tall, thin, dark bird of the night, with sly, roving eyes, and hollow cheeks. They stand looking round, then pass into the further room; but in passing, they have stared unreservedly at CLARE.

YOUNG MAN. [Seeing her wince] Look here! I'm afraid you must feel me
        rather a brute, you know.

CLARE. No, I don't; really.

YOUNG MAN. Are you absolute stoney? [CLARE nods] But [Looking at her
        frock and cloak] you're so awfully well——

CLARE. I had the sense to keep them.

YOUNG MAN. [More and more disturbed] I say, you know—I wish you'd let
        me lend you something. I had quite a good day down there.

CLARE. [Again tracing her pattern on the cloth—then looking up at him full]
        I can't take, for nothing.

YOUNG MAN. By Jove! I don't know-really, I don't—this makes me feel pret-
        ty rotten. I mean, it's your being a lady.

CLARE. [Smiling] That's not your fault, is it? You see, I've been beaten all along
        the line. And I really don't care what happens to me. [She has that
        peculiar fey look on her face now] I really don't; except that I don't take
        charity. It's lucky for me it's you, and not some——

The supper-party is getting still more boisterous, and there comes a long view hol-
loa, and a blast of the horn.

YOUNG MAN. But I say, what about your people? You must have people of
        some sort.

He is fast becoming fascinated, for her cheeks have begun to flush and her eyes to
shine.

CLARE. Oh, yes; I've had people, and a husband, and—everything—— And
        here I am! Queer, isn't it? [She touches her glass] This is going to my
        head! Do you mind? I sha'n't sing songs and get up and dance, and I
        won't cry, I promise you!

YOUNG MAN. [Between fascination and chivalry] By George! One simply
        can't believe in this happening to a lady.

CLARE. Have you got sisters? [Breaking into her soft laughter] My brother's in
        India. I sha'n't meet him, anyway.

YOUNG MAN. No, but—I say-are you really quite cut off from everybody?
        [CLARE nods] Something rather awful must have happened?

She smiles. The two gentlemen have returned. The blond one is again staring
fixedly at CLARE. This time she looks back at him, flaming; and, with a little
laugh, he passes with his friend into the corridor.

CLARE. Who are those two?

YOUNG MAN. Don't know—not been much about town yet. I'm just back from India myself. You said your brother was there; what's his regiment?

CLARE. [Shaking her head] You're not going to find out my name. I haven't got one—nothing.

She leans her bare elbows on the table, and her face on her hands.

CLARE. First of June! This day last year I broke covert—I've been running ever since.

YOUNG MAN. I don't understand a bit. You—must have had a—a—some one——

But there is such a change in her face, such rigidity of her whole body, that he stops and averts his eyes. When he looks again she is drinking. She puts the glass down, and gives a little laugh.

YOUNG MAN. [With a sort of awe] Anyway it must have been like riding at a pretty stiff fence, for you to come here to-night.

CLARE. Yes. What's the other side?

The YOUNG MAN puts out his hand and touches her arm. It is meant for sympathy, but she takes it for attraction.

CLARE. [Shaking her head] Not yet please! I'm enjoying this. May I have a cigarette?

[He takes out his case, and gives her one]

CLARE. [Letting the smoke slowly forth] Yes, I'm enjoying it. Had a pretty poor time lately; not enough to eat, sometimes.

YOUNG MAN. Not really! How damnable! I say—do have something more substantial.

CLARE gives a sudden gasp, as if going off into hysterical laughter, but she stifles it, and shakes her head.

YOUNG MAN. A peach?

[ARNAUD brings peaches to the table]

CLARE. [Smiling] Thank you.

[He fills their glasses and retreats]

CLARE. [Raising her glass] Eat and drink, for tomorrow we—Listen!

From the supper-party comes the sound of an abortive chorus: "With a hey ho, chivy, hark forrard, hark forrard, tantivy!" Jarring out into a discordant whoop, it sinks.

CLARE. "This day a stag must die." Jolly old song!

YOUNG MAN. Rowdy lot! [Suddenly] I say—I admire your pluck.

CLARE. [Shaking her head] Haven't kept my end up. Lots of women do! You see: I'm too fine, and not fine enough! My best friend said that. Too fine, and not fine enough. [She laughs] I couldn't be a saint and martyr, and I wouldn't be a soulless doll. Neither one thing nor the other—that's the tragedy.

YOUNG MAN. You must have had awful luck!

CLARE. I did try. [Fiercely] But what's the good—when there's nothing before you?—Do I look ill?

YOUNG MAN. No; simply awfully pretty.

CLARE. [With a laugh] A man once said to me: "As you haven't money, you should never have been pretty!" But, you see, it is some good. If I hadn't been, I couldn't have risked coming here, could I? Don't you think it was rather sporting of me to buy these [She touches the gardenias] with the last shilling over from my cab fare?

YOUNG MAN. Did you really? D—d sporting!

CLARE. It's no use doing things by halves, is it? I'm—in for it— wish me luck! [She drinks, and puts her glass down with a smile] In for it—deep! [She flings up her hands above her smiling face] Down, down, till they're just above water, and then—down, down, down, and —all over! Are you sorry now you came and spoke to me?

YOUNG MAN. By Jove, no! It may be caddish, but I'm not.

CLARE. Thank God for beauty! I hope I shall die pretty! Do you think I shall do well?

YOUNG MAN. I say—don't talk like that!

CLARE. I want to know. Do you?

YOUNG MAN. Well, then—yes, I do.

CLARE. That's splendid. Those poor women in the streets would give their eyes, wouldn't they?—that have to go up and down, up and down! Do you think I—shall——

The YOUNG MAN, half-rising, puts his hand on her arm.

YOUNG MAN. I think you're getting much too excited. You look all— Won't you eat your peach? [She shakes her head] Do! Have something else, then—some grapes, or something?

CLARE. No, thanks.

[She has become quite calm again]

YOUNG MAN. Well, then, what d'you think? It's awfully hot in here, isn't it? Wouldn't it be jollier drivin'? Shall we—shall we make a move?

CLARE. Yes.

The YOUNG MAN turns to look for the waiter, but ARNAUD is not in the room. He gets up.

YOUNG MAN. [Feverishly] D—-n that waiter! Wait half a minute, if you don't mind, while I pay the bill.

As he goes out into the corridor, the two gentlemen re-appear. CLARE is sitting motionless, looking straight before her.

DARK ONE. A fiver you don't get her to!

BLOND ONE. Done!

He advances to her table with his inimitable insolence, and taking the cigar from his mouth, bends his stare on her, and says: "Charmed to see you lookin' so well! Will you have supper with me here to-morrow night?" Startled out of her reverie, CLARE looks up. She sees those eyes, she sees beyond him the eyes of his companion-sly, malevolent, amused-watching; and she just sits gazing, without a word. At that regard, so clear, the BLOND ONE does not wince. But rather suddenly he says: "That's arranged then. Half-past eleven. So good of you. Good-night!" He replaces his cigar and strolls back to his companion, and in a low voice says: "Pay up!" Then at a languid "Hullo, Charles!" they turn to greet the two in their nook behind the screen. CLARE has not moved, nor changed the direction of her gaze. Suddenly she thrusts her hand into the, pocket of the cloak that hangs behind her, and brings out the little blue bottle which, six months ago, she took from MALISE. She pulls out the cork and pours the whole contents into her champagne. She lifts the glass, holds it before her—smiling, as if to call a toast, puts it to her lips and drinks. Still smiling, she sets the empty glass down, and lays the gardenia flowers against her face. Slowly she droops back in her chair, the drowsy smile still on her lips; the gardenias drop into her lap; her arms relax, her head falls forward on her breast. And the voices behind the screen talk on, and the sounds of joy from the supper-party wax and wane.

The waiter, ARNAUD, returning from the corridor, passes to his service-table with a tall, beribboned basket of fruit. Putting it down, he goes towards the table behind the screen, and sees. He runs up to CLARE.

ARNAUD. Madame! Madame! [He listens for her breathing; then suddenly
          catching sight of the little bottle, smells at it] Bon Dieu!

[At that queer sound they come from behind the screen—all four, and look. The dark night bird says: "Hallo; fainted!" ARNAUD holds out the bottle.]

LANGUID LORD. [Taking it, and smelling] Good God! [The woman bends
               over CLARE, and lifts her hands; ARNAUD rushes to his
               service-table, and speaks into his tube]

ARNAUD. The boss. Quick! [Looking up he sees the YOUNG MAN, returning] 'Monsieur, elle a fui! Elle est morte'!

LANGUID LORD. [To the YOUNG MAN standing there aghast] What's this? Friend of yours?

YOUNG MAN. My God! She was a lady. That's all I know about her.

LANGUID LORD. A lady!

[The blond and dark gentlemen have slipped from the room; and out of the supper-party's distant laughter comes suddenly a long, shrill: "Gone away!" And the sound of the horn playing the seven last notes of the old song: "This day a stag must die!" From the last note of all the sound flies up to an octave higher, sweet and thin, like a spirit passing, till it is drowned once more in laughter. The YOUNG MAN has covered his eyes with his hands; ARNAUD is crossing himself fervently; the LANGUID LORD stands gazing, with one of the dropped gardenias twisted in his fingers; and the woman, bending over CLARE, kisses her forehead.]

CURTAIN.

THE PIGEON

A FANTASY IN THREE ACTS

PERSONS OF THE PLAY

CHRISTOPHER WELLWYN, an artist
ANN, his daughter
GUINEVERE MEGAN, a flower-seller
RORY MEGAN, her husband
FERRAND, an alien
TIMSON, once a cabman
EDWARD BERTLEY, a Canon
ALFRED CALWAY, a Professor
SIR THOMAS HOXTON, a Justice of the Peace
Also a police constable, three humble-men, and some curious persons

The action passes in Wellwyn's Studio, and the street outside.

ACT I. Christmas Eve.

ACT II. New Year's Day.

ACT III. The First of April.

ACT I

It is the night of Christmas Eve, the SCENE is a Studio, flush with the street, having a skylight darkened by a fall of snow. There is no one in the room, the walls of which are whitewashed, above a floor of bare dark boards. A fire is cheerfully burning. On a model's platform stands an easel and canvas. There are busts and pictures; a screen, a little stool, two arm. chairs, and a long old-fashioned settle under the window. A door in one wall leads to the house, a door in the opposite wall to the model's dressing-room, and the street door is in the centre of the wall between. On a low table a Russian samovar is hissing, and beside it on a tray stands a teapot, with glasses, lemon, sugar, and a decanter of rum. Through a huge uncurtained window close to the street door the snowy lamplit street can be seen, and beyond it the river and a night of stars.

The sound of a latchkey turned in the lock of the street door, and ANN WELL-WYN enters, a girl of seventeen, with hair tied in a ribbon and covered by a scarf. Leaving the door open, she turns up the electric light and goes to the fire. She throws of her scarf and long red cloak. She is dressed in a high evening frock of some soft white material. Her movements are quick and substantial. Her face, full of no nonsense, is decided and sincere, with deep-set eyes, and a capable, well-shaped forehead. Shredding of her gloves she warms her hands.

In the doorway appear the figures of two men. The first is rather short and slight, with a soft short beard, bright soft eyes, and a crumply face. Under his squash hat his hair is rather plentiful and rather grey. He wears an old brown ulster and woollen gloves, and is puffing at a hand-made cigarette. He is ANN'S father, WELLWYN, the artist. His companion is a well-wrapped clergyman of medium height and stoutish build, with a pleasant, rosy face, rather shining eyes, and rather chubby clean-shaped lips; in appearance, indeed, a grown-up boy. He is the Vicar of the parish—CANON BERTLEY.

BERTLEY. My dear Wellwyn, the whole question of reform is full of difficulty. When you have two men like Professor Calway and Sir Thomas Hoxton taking diametrically opposite points of view, as we've seen to-night, I confess, I——

WELLWYN. Come in, Vicar, and have some grog.

BERTLEY. Not to-night, thanks! Christmas tomorrow! Great temptation, though, this room! Goodnight, Wellwyn; good-night, Ann!

ANN. [Coming from the fire towards the tea-table.] Good-night, Canon Bertley.

[He goes out, and WELLWYN, shutting the door after him, approaches the fire.]

ANN. [Sitting on the little stool, with her back to the fire, and making tea.] Daddy!

WELLWYN. My dear?

ANN. You say you liked Professor Calway's lecture. Is it going to do you any good, that's the question?

WELLWYN. I—I hope so, Ann.

ANN. I took you on purpose. Your charity's getting simply awful. Those two this morning cleared out all my housekeeping money.

WELLWYN. Um! Um! I quite understand your feeling.

ANN. They both had your card, so I couldn't refuse—didn't know what you'd said to them. Why don't you make it a rule never to give your card to anyone except really decent people, and—picture dealers, of course.

WELLWYN. My dear, I have—often.

ANN. Then why don't you keep it? It's a frightful habit. You are naughty, Daddy. One of these days you'll get yourself into most fearful complications.

WELLWYN. My dear, when they—when they look at you?

ANN. You know the house wants all sorts of things. Why do you speak to them at all?

WELLWYN. I don't—they speak to me.

[He takes of his ulster and hangs it over the back of an arm-chair.]

ANN. They see you coming. Anybody can see you coming, Daddy. That's why you ought to be so careful. I shall make you wear a hard hat. Those squashy hats of yours are hopelessly inefficient.

WELLWYN. [Gazing at his hat.] Calway wears one.

ANN. As if anyone would beg of Professor Calway.

WELLWYN. Well-perhaps not. You know, Ann, I admire that fellow. Wonderful power of-of-theory! How a man can be so absolutely tidy in his mind! It's most exciting.

ANN. Has any one begged of you to-day?

WELLWYN. [Doubtfully.] No—no.

ANN. [After a long, severe look.] Will you have rum in your tea?

WELLWYN. [Crestfallen.] Yes, my dear—a good deal.

ANN. [Pouring out the rum, and handing him the glass.] Well, who was it?

WELLWYN. He didn't beg of me. [Losing himself in recollection.] Interesting old creature, Ann—real type. Old cabman.

ANN. Where?

WELLWYN. Just on the Embankment.

ANN. Of course! Daddy, you know the Embankment ones are always rotters.

WELLWYN. Yes, my dear; but this wasn't.

ANN. Did you give him your card?

WELLWYN. I—I—don't

ANN. Did you, Daddy?

WELLWYN. I'm rather afraid I may have!

ANN. May have! It's simply immoral.

WELLWYN. Well, the old fellow was so awfully human, Ann. Besides, I didn't
      give him any money—hadn't got any.

ANN. Look here, Daddy! Did you ever ask anybody for anything? You know
      you never did, you'd starve first. So would anybody decent. Then, why
      won't you see that people who beg are rotters?

WELLWYN. But, my dear, we're not all the same. They wouldn't do it if it was-
      n't natural to them. One likes to be friendly. What's the use of
      being alive if one isn't?

ANN. Daddy, you're hopeless.

WELLWYN. But, look here, Ann, the whole thing's so jolly complicated.
      According to Calway, we're to give the State all we can spare, to
      make the undeserving deserving. He's a Professor; he ought to
      know. But old Hoxton's always dinning it into me that we ought to
      support private organisations for helping the deserving, and damn
      the undeserving. Well, that's just the opposite. And he's a J.P.
      Tremendous experience. And the Vicar seems to be for a little bit
      of both. Well, what the devil——? My trouble is, whichever I'm
      with, he always converts me. [Ruefully.] And there's no fun in any
      of them.

ANN. [Rising.] Oh! Daddy, you are so—don't you know that you're the despair
      of all social reformers? [She envelops him.] There's a tear in the left knee
      of your trousers. You're not to wear them again.

WELLWYN. Am I likely to?

ANN. I shouldn't be a bit surprised if it isn't your only pair. D'you know what I live in terror of?

[WELLWYN gives her a queer and apprehensive look.]

ANN. That you'll take them off some day, and give them away in the street. Have you got any money? [She feels in his coat, and he his trousers—they find nothing.] Do you know that your pockets are one enormous hole?

WELLWYN. No!

ANN. Spiritually.

WELLWYN. Oh! Ah! H'm!

ANN. [Severely.] Now, look here, Daddy! [She takes him by his lapels.] Don't imagine that it isn't the most disgusting luxury on your part to go on giving away things as you do! You know what you really are, I suppose—a sickly sentimentalist!

WELLWYN. [Breaking away from her, disturbed.] It isn't sentiment. It's simply that they seem to me so—so—jolly. If I'm to give up feeling sort of—nice in here [he touches his chest] about people—it doesn't matter who they are—then I don't know what I'm to do. I shall have to sit with my head in a bag.

ANN. I think you ought to.

WELLWYN. I suppose they see I like them—then they tell me things. After that, of course you can't help doing what you can.

ANN. Well, if you will love them up!

WELLWYN. My dear, I don't want to. It isn't them especially—why, I feel it even with old Calway sometimes. It's only Providence that he does-n't want anything of me—except to make me like himself—con-found him!

ANN. [Moving towards the door into the house—impressively.] What you don't
    see is that other people aren't a bit like you.

WELLWYN. Well, thank God!

ANN. It's so old-fashioned too! I'm going to bed—I just leave you to your con-
    science.

WELLWYN. Oh!

ANN. [Opening the door-severely.] Good-night—[with a certain weakening]
    you old—Daddy!

[She jumps at him, gives him a hug, and goes out.]

[WELLWYN stands perfectly still. He first gazes up at the skylight, then down
at the floor. Slowly he begins to shake his head, and mutter, as he moves towards
the fire.]

WELLWYN. Bad lot. . . . Low type—no backbone, no stability!

[There comes a fluttering knock on the outer door. As the sound slowly enters
his consciousness, he begins to wince, as though he knew, but would not admit
its significance. Then he sits down, covering his ears. The knocking does not
cease. WELLWYN drops first one, then both hands, rises, and begins to sidle
towards the door. The knocking becomes louder.]

WELLWYN. Ah dear! Tt! Tt! Tt!

[After a look in the direction of ANN's disappearance, he opens the street door a
very little way. By the light of the lamp there can be seen a young girl in dark
clothes, huddled in a shawl to which the snow is clinging. She has on her arm a
basket covered with a bit of sacking.]

WELLWYN. I can't, you know; it's impossible.

[The girl says nothing, but looks at him with dark eyes.]

WELLWYN. [Wincing.] Let's see—I don't know you—do I?

[The girl, speaking in a soft, hoarse voice, with a faint accent of reproach: "Mrs.
Megan—you give me this——" She holds out a dirty visiting card.]

WELLWYN. [Recoiling from the card.] Oh! Did I? Ah! When?

MRS. MEGAN. You 'ad some vi'lets off of me larst spring. You give me 'arf a
        crown.

[A smile tries to visit her face.]

WELLWYN. [Looking stealthily round.] Ah! Well, come in—just for a
        minute—it's very cold—and tell us what it is.

[She comes in stolidly, a Sphinx-like figure, with her pretty tragic little face.]

WELLWYN. I don't remember you. [Looking closer.] Yes, I do. Only— you
        weren't the same-were you?

MRS. MEGAN. [Dully.] I seen trouble since.

WELLWYN. Trouble! Have some tea?

[He looks anxiously at the door into the house, then goes quickly to the table, and
pours out a glass of tea, putting rum into it.]

WELLWYN. [Handing her the tea.] Keeps the cold out! Drink it off!

[MRS. MEGAN drinks it of, chokes a little, and almost immediately seems to get
a size larger. WELLWYN watches her with his head held on one side, and a smile
broadening on his face.]

WELLWYN. Cure for all evils, um?

MRS. MEGAN. It warms you. [She smiles.]

WELLWYN. [Smiling back, and catching himself out.] Well! You know, I
        oughtn't.

MRS. MEGAN. [Conscious of the disruption of his personality, and withdraw-
        ing into her tragic abyss.] I wouldn't 'a come, but you told me
        if I wanted an 'and——

WELLWYN. [Gradually losing himself in his own nature.] Let me see—corner
        of Flight Street, wasn't it?

MRS. MEGAN. [With faint eagerness.] Yes, sir, an' I told you about me vi'lets—
it was a luvly spring-day.

WELLWYN. Beautiful! Beautiful! Birds singing, and the trees, &c.! We had
quite a talk. You had a baby with you.

MRS. MEGAN. Yes. I got married since then.

WELLWYN. Oh! Ah! Yes! [Cheerfully.] And how's the baby?

MRS. MEGAN. [Turning to stone.] I lost her.

WELLWYN. Oh! poor—- Um!

MRS. MEGAN. [Impassive.] You said something abaht makin' a picture of me.
[With faint eagerness.] So I thought I might come, in case
you'd forgotten.

WELLWYN. [Looking at, her intently.] Things going badly?

MRS. MEGAN. [Stripping the sacking off her basket.] I keep 'em covered up,
but the cold gets to 'em. Thruppence—that's all I've took.

WELLWYN. Ho! Tt! Tt! [He looks into the basket.] Christmas, too!

MRS. MEGAN. They're dead.

WELLWYN. [Drawing in his breath.] Got a good husband?

MRS. MEGAN. He plays cards.

WELLWYN. Oh, Lord! And what are you doing out—with a cold like that?
[He taps his chest.]

MRS. MEGAN. We was sold up this morning—he's gone off with 'is mates.
Haven't took enough yet for a night's lodgin'.

WELLWYN. [Correcting a spasmodic dive into his pockets.] But who buys
flowers at this time of night?

[MRS. MEGAN looks at him, and faintly smiles.]

WELLWYN. [Rumpling his hair.] Saints above us! Here! Come to the fire!

[She follows him to the fire. He shuts the street door.]

WELLWYN. Are your feet wet? [She nods.] Well, sit down here, and take them
off. That's right.

[She sits on the stool. And after a slow look up at him, which has in it a deeper
knowledge than belongs of right to her years, begins taking off her shoes and
stockings. WELLWYN goes to the door into the house, opens it, and listens with
a sort of stealthy casualness. He returns whistling, but not out loud. The girl has
finished taking off her stockings, and turned her bare toes to the flames. She shuf-
fles them back under her skirt.]

WELLWYN. How old are you, my child?

MRS. MEGAN. Nineteen, come Candlemas.

WELLWYN. And what's your name?

MRS. MEGAN. Guinevere.

WELLWYN. What? Welsh?

MRS. MEGAN. Yes—from Battersea.

WELLWYN. And your husband?

MRS. MEGAN. No. Irish, 'e is. Notting Dale, 'e comes from.

WELLWYN. Roman Catholic?

MRS. MEGAN. Yes. My 'usband's an atheist as well.

WELLWYN. I see. [Abstractedly.] How jolly! And how old is he—this young
man of yours?

MRS. MEGAN. 'E'll be twenty soon.

WELLWYN. Babes in the wood! Does he treat you badly?

MRS. MEGAN. No.

WELLWYN. Nor drink?

MRS. MEGAN. No. He's not a bad one. Only he gets playin' cards then 'e'll fly the kite.

WELLWYN. I see. And when he's not flying it, what does he do?

MRS. MEGAN. [Touching her basket.] Same as me. Other jobs tires 'im.

WELLWYN. That's very nice! [He checks himself.] Well, what am I to do with you?

MRS. MEGAN. Of course, I could get me night's lodging if I like to do—the same as some of them.

WELLWYN. No! no! Never, my child! Never!

MRS. MEGAN. It's easy that way.

WELLWYN. Heavens! But your husband! Um?

MRS. MEGAN. [With stoical vindictiveness.] He's after one I know of.

WELLWYN. Tt! What a pickle!

MRS. MEGAN. I'll 'ave to walk about the streets.

WELLWYN. [To himself.] Now how can I?

[MRS. MEGAN looks up and smiles at him, as if she had already discovered that he is peculiar.]

WELLWYN. You see, the fact is, I mustn't give you anything—because —well, for one thing I haven't got it. There are other reasons, but that's the—real one. But, now, there's a little room where my models dress. I wonder if you could sleep there. Come, and see.

[The Girl gets up lingeringly, loth to leave the warmth. She takes up her wet stockings.]

MRS. MEGAN. Shall I put them on again?

WELLWYN. No, no; there's a nice warm pair of slippers. [Seeing the steam ris-
        ing from her.] Why, you're wet all over. Here, wait a little!

[He crosses to the door into the house, and after stealthy listening, steps through. The Girl, like a cat, steals back to the warmth of the fire. WELLWYN returns with a candle, a canary-coloured bath gown, and two blankets.]

WELLWYN. Now then! [He precedes her towards the door of the model's
        room.] Hsssh! [He opens the door and holds up the candle to
        show her the room.] Will it do? There's a couch. You'll find some
        washing things. Make yourself quite at home. See!

[The Girl, perfectly dumb, passes through with her basket—and her shoes and stockings. WELLWYN hands her the candle, blankets, and bath gown.]

WELLWYN. Have a good sleep, child! Forget that you're alive! [He closes the
        door, mournfully.] Done it again! [He goes to the table, cuts a
        large slice of cake, knocks on the door, and hands it in.] Chow-
        chow! [Then, as he walks away, he sights the opposite door.]
        Well—damn it, what could I have done? Not a farthing on me!
        [He goes to the street door to shut it, but first opens it wide to con-
        firm himself in his hospitality.] Night like this!

[A sputter of snow is blown in his face. A voice says: "Monsieur, pardon!" WELLWYN recoils spasmodically. A figure moves from the lamp-post to the doorway. He is seen to be young and to have ragged clothes. He speaks again: "You do not remember me, Monsieur? My name is Ferrand—it was in Paris, in the Champs-Elysees—by the fountain . . . . When you came to the door, Monsieur—I am not made of iron . . . . Tenez, here is your card I have never lost it." He holds out to WELLWYN an old and dirty wing card. As inch by inch he has advanced into the doorway, the light from within falls on him, a tall gaunt young pagan with fair hair and reddish golden stubble of beard, a long ironical nose a little to one side, and large, grey, rather prominent eyes. There is a certain grace in his figure and movements; his clothes are nearly dropping off him.]

WELLWYN. [Yielding to a pleasant memory.] Ah! yes. By the fountain. I was
        sitting there, and you came and ate a roll, and drank the water.

FERRAND. [With faint eagerness.] My breakfast. I was in poverty— veree bad off. You gave me ten francs. I thought I had a little the right [WELLWYN makes a movement of disconcertion] seeing you said that if I came to England——

WELLWYN. Um! And so you've come?

FERRAND. It was time that I consolidated my fortunes, Monsieur.

WELLWYN. And you—have——

[He stops embarrassed. FERRAND. [Shrugging his ragged shoulders.] One is not yet Rothschild.

WELLWYN. [Sympathetically.] No. [Yielding to memory.] We talked philosophy.

FERRAND. I have not yet changed my opinion. We other vagabonds, we are exploited by the bourgeois. This is always my idea, Monsieur.

WELLWYN. Yes—not quite the general view, perhaps! Well—— [Heartily.] Come in! Very glad to see you again.

FERRAND. [Brushing his arms over his eyes.] Pardon, Monsieur—your goodness—I am a little weak. [He opens his coat, and shows a belt drawn very tight over his ragged shirt.] I tighten him one hole for each meal, during two days now. That gives you courage.

WELLWYN. [With cooing sounds, pouring out tea, and adding rum.] Have some of this. It'll buck you up. [He watches the young man drink.]

FERRAND. [Becoming a size larger.] Sometimes I think that I will never succeed to dominate my life, Monsieur—though I have no vices, except that I guard always the aspiration to achieve success. But I will not roll myself under the machine of existence to gain a nothing every day. I must find with what to fly a little.

WELLWYN. [Delicately.] Yes; yes—I remember, you found it difficult to stay long in any particular—yes.

FERRAND. [Proudly.] In one little corner? No—Monsieur—never! That is not in my character. I must see life.

WELLWYN. Quite, quite! Have some cake?

[He cuts cake.]

FERRAND. In your country they say you cannot eat the cake and have it. But one must always try, Monsieur; one must never be content. [Refusing the cake.] 'Grand merci', but for the moment I have no stomach—I have lost my stomach now for two days. If I could smoke, Monsieur! [He makes the gesture of smoking.]

WELLWYN. Rather! [Handing his tobacco pouch.] Roll yourself one.

FERRAND. [Rapidly rolling a cigarette.] If I had not found you, Monsieur—I would have been a little hole in the river to-night— I was so discouraged. [He inhales and puffs a long luxurious whif of smoke. Very bitterly.] Life! [He disperses the puff of smoke with his finger, and stares before him.] And to think that in a few minutes HE will be born! Monsieur! [He gazes intently at WELLWYN.] The world would reproach you for your goodness to me.

WELLWYN. [Looking uneasily at the door into the house.] You think so? Ah!

FERRAND. Monsieur, if HE himself were on earth now, there would be a little heap of gentlemen writing to the journals every day to call Him sloppee sentimentalist! And what is veree funny, these gentlemen they would all be most strong Christians. [He regards WELLWYN deeply.] But that will not trouble you, Monsieur; I saw well from the first that you are no Christian. You have so kind a face.

WELLWYN. Oh! Indeed!

FERRAND. You have not enough the Pharisee in your character. You do not judge, and you are judged.

[He stretches his limbs as if in pain.]

WELLWYN. Are you in pain?

FERRAND. I 'ave a little the rheumatism.

WELLWYN. Wet through, of course! [Glancing towards the house.] Wait a bit!
I wonder if you'd like these trousers; they've—er—they're not
quite——

[He passes through the door into the house. FERRAND stands at the fire, with
his limbs spread as it were to embrace it, smoking with abandonment. WELL-
WYN returns stealthily, dressed in a Jaeger dressing-gown, and bearing a pair of
drawers, his trousers, a pair of slippers, and a sweater.]

WELLWYN. [Speaking in a low voice, for the door is still open.] Can you make
these do for the moment?

FERRAND. 'Je vous remercie', Monsieur. [Pointing to the screen.] May I retire?

WELLWYN. Yes, yes.

[FERRAND goes behind the screen. WELLWYN closes the door into the house,
then goes to the window to draw the curtains. He suddenly recoils and stands
petrified with doubt.]

WELLWYN. Good Lord!

[There is the sound of tapping on glass. Against the window-pane is pressed the
face of a man. WELLWYN motions to him to go away. He does not go, but con-
tinues tapping. WELLWYN opens the door. There enters a square old man, with
a red, pendulous jawed, shaking face under a snow besprinkled bowler hat. He is
holding out a visiting card with tremulous hand.]

WELLWYN. Who's that? Who are you?

TIMSON. [In a thick, hoarse, shaking voice.] 'Appy to see you, sir; we 'ad a talk
this morning. Timson—I give you me name. You invited of me, if ye remember.

WELLWYN. It's a little late, really.

TIMSON. Well, ye see, I never expected to 'ave to call on yer. I was 'itched up
all right when I spoke to yer this mornin', but bein' Christmas,
things 'ave took a turn with me to-day. [He speaks with increasing

thickness.] I'm reg'lar disgusted—not got the price of a bed abaht me. Thought you wouldn't like me to be delicate—not at my age.

WELLWYN. [With a mechanical and distracted dive of his hands into his pockets.] The fact is, it so happens I haven't a copper on me.

TIMSON. [Evidently taking this for professional refusal.] Wouldn't arsk you if I could 'elp it. 'Ad to do with 'orses all me life. It's this 'ere cold I'm frightened of. I'm afraid I'll go to sleep.

WELLWYN. Well, really, I——

TIMSON. To be froze to death—I mean—it's awkward.

WELLWYN. [Puzzled and unhappy.] Well—come in a moment, and let's—think it out. Have some tea!

[He pours out the remains of the tea, and finding there is not very much, adds rum rather liberally. TIMSON, who walks a little wide at the knees, steadying his gait, has followed.]

TIMSON. [Receiving the drink.] Yer 'ealth. 'Ere's—soberiety! [He applies the drink to his lips with shaking hand. Agreeably surprised.] Blimey! Thish yer tea's foreign, ain't it?

FERRAND. [Reappearing from behind the screen in his new clothes of which the trousers stop too soon.] With a needle, Monsieur, I would soon have with what to make face against the world.

WELLWYN. Too short! Ah!

[He goes to the dais on which stands ANN's workbasket, and takes from it a needle and cotton.]

[While he is so engaged FERRAND is sizing up old TIMSON, as one dog will another. The old man, glass in hand, seems to have lapsed into coma.]

FERRAND. [Indicating TIMSON] Monsieur!

[He makes the gesture of one drinking, and shakes his head.]

WELLWYN. [Handing him the needle and cotton.] Um! Afraid so!

[They approach TIMSON, who takes no notice.]

FERRAND. [Gently.] It is an old cabby, is it not, Monsieur? 'Ceux sont tous des buveurs'.

WELLWYN. [Concerned at the old man's stupefaction.] Now, my old friend, sit down a moment. [They manoeuvre TIMSON to the settle.] Will you smoke?

TIMSON. [In a drowsy voice.] Thank 'ee-smoke pipe of 'baccer. Old 'orse—standin' abaht in th' cold.

[He relapses into coma.]

FERRAND. [With a click of his tongue.] 'Il est parti'.

WELLWYN. [Doubtfully.] He hasn't really left a horse outside, do you think?

FERRAND. Non, non, Monsieur—no 'orse. He is dreaming. I know very well that state of him—that catches you sometimes. It is the warmth sudden on the stomach. He will speak no more sense to-night. At the most, drink, and fly a little in his past.

WELLWYN. Poor old buffer!

FERRAND. Touching, is it not, Monsieur? There are many brave gents among the old cabbies—they have philosophy—that comes from 'orses, and from sitting still.

WELLWYN. [Touching TIMSON's shoulder.] Drenched!

FERRAND. That will do 'im no 'arm, Monsieur-no 'arm at all. He is well wet inside, remember—it is Christmas to-morrow. Put him a rug, if you will, he will soon steam.

[WELLWYN takes up ANN's long red cloak, and wraps it round the old man.]

TIMSON. [Faintly roused.] Tha's right. Put—the rug on th' old 'orse.

[He makes a strange noise, and works his head and tongue.]

WELLWYN. [Alarmed.] What's the matter with him?

FERRAND. It is nothing, Monsieur; for the moment he thinks 'imself a 'orse. 'Il joue "cache-cache,"' 'ide and seek, with what you call— 'is bitt.

WELLWYN. But what's to be done with him? One can't turn him out in this state.

FERRAND. If you wish to leave him 'ere, Monsieur, have no fear. I charge myself with him.

WELLWYN. Oh! [Dubiously.] You—er—I really don't know, I—hadn't con-templated—You think you could manage if I—if I went to bed?

FERRAND. But certainly, Monsieur.

WELLWYN. [Still dubiously.] You—you're sure you've everything you want?

FERRAND. [Bowing.] 'Mais oui, Monsieur'.

WELLWYN. I don't know what I can do by staying.

FERRAND. There is nothing you can do, Monsieur. Have confidence in me.

WELLWYN. Well-keep the fire up quietly—very quietly. You'd better take this coat of mine, too. You'll find it precious cold, I expect, about three o'clock. [He hands FERRAND his Ulster.]

FERRAND. [Taking it.] I shall sleep in praying for you, Monsieur.

WELLWYN. Ah! Yes! Thanks! Well-good-night! By the way, I shall be down rather early. Have to think of my household a bit, you know.

FERRAND. 'Tres bien, Monsieur'. I comprehend. One must well be regular in this life.

WELLWYN. [With a start.] Lord! [He looks at the door of the model's room.] I'd forgotten——

FERRAND. Can I undertake anything, Monsieur?

WELLWYN. No, no! [He goes to the electric light switch by the outer door.]
You won't want this, will you?

FERRAND. 'Merci, Monsieur'.

[WELLWYN switches off the light.]

FERRAND. 'Bon soir, Monsieur'!

WELLWYN. The devil! Er—good-night!

[He hesitates, rumples his hair, and passes rather suddenly away.]

FERRAND. [To himself.] Poor pigeon! [Looking long at old TIMSON]
'Espece de type anglais!'

[He sits down in the firelight, curls up a foot on his knee, and taking out a knife,
rips the stitching of a turned-up end of trouser, pinches the cloth double, and puts
in the preliminary stitch of a new hem—all with the swiftness of one well- accustomed. Then, as if hearing a sound behind him, he gets up quickly and slips
behind the screen. MRS. MEGAN, attracted by the cessation of voices, has
opened the door, and is creeping from the model's room towards the fire. She has
almost reached it before she takes in the torpid crimson figure of old TIMSON.
She halts and puts her hand to her chest—a queer figure in the firelight, garbed
in the canary-coloured bath gown and rabbit's- wool slippers, her black matted
hair straggling down on her neck. Having quite digested the fact that the old man
is in a sort of stupor, MRS. MEGAN goes close to the fire, and sits on the little
stool, smiling sideways at old TIMSON. FERRAND, coming quietly up behind,
examines her from above, drooping his long nose as if enquiring with it as to her
condition in life; then he steps back a yard or two.]

FERRAND. [Gently.] 'Pardon, Ma'moiselle'.

MRS. MEGAN. [Springing to her feet.] Oh!

FERRAND. All right, all right! We are brave gents!

TIMSON. [Faintly roused.] 'Old up, there!

FERRAND. Trust in me, Ma'moiselle!

[MRS. MEGAN responds by drawing away.]

FERRAND. [Gently.] We must be good comrades. This asylum—it is better
                than a doss-'ouse.

[He pushes the stool over towards her, and seats himself. Somewhat reassured,
MRS. MEGAN again sits down.]

MRS. MEGAN. You frightened me.

TIMSON. [Unexpectedly-in a drowsy tone.] Purple foreigners!

FERRAND. Pay no attention, Ma'moiselle. He is a philosopher.

MRS. MEGAN. Oh! I thought 'e was boozed.

[They both look at TIMSON]

FERRAND. It is the same-veree 'armless.

MRS. MEGAN. What's that he's got on 'im?

FERRAND. It is a coronation robe. Have no fear, Ma'moiselle. Veree docile
                potentate.

MRS. MEGAN. I wouldn't be afraid of him. [Challenging FERRAND.] I'm
                afraid o' you.

FERRAND. It is because you do not know me, Ma'moiselle. You are wrong, it
                is always the unknown you should love.

MRS. MEGAN. I don't like the way you-speaks to me.

FERRAND. Ah! You are a Princess in disguise?

MRS. MEGAN. No fear!

FERRAND. No? What is it then you do to make face against the necessities of
                life? A living?

MRS. MEGAN. Sells flowers.

FERRAND. [Rolling his eyes.] It is not a career.

MRS. MEGAN. [With a touch of devilry.] You don't know what I do.

FERRAND. Ma'moiselle, whatever you do is charming.

[MRS. MEGAN looks at him, and slowly smiles.]

MRS. MEGAN. You're a foreigner.

FERRAND. It is true.

MRS. MEGAN. What do you do for a livin'?

FERRAND. I am an interpreter.

MRS. MEGAN. You ain't very busy, are you?

FERRAND. [With dignity.] At present I am resting.

MRS. MEGAN. [Looking at him and smiling.] How did you and 'im come
            here?

FERRAND. Ma'moiselle, we would ask you the same question.

MRS. MEGAN. The gentleman let me. 'E's funny.

FERRAND. 'C'est un ange' [At MRS. MEGAN's blank stare he interprets.] An
          angel!

MRS. MEGAN. Me luck's out-that's why I come.

FERRAND. [Rising.] Ah! Ma'moiselle! Luck! There is the little God who dom-
          inates us all. Look at this old! [He points to TIMSON.] He is fin-
          ished. In his day that old would be doing good business. He could
          afford himself—[He maker a sign of drinking.]—Then come the
          motor cars. All goes—he has nothing left, only 'is 'abits of a
          'cocher'! Luck!

TIMSON. [With a vague gesture—drowsily.] Kick the foreign beggars out.

FERRAND. A real Englishman . . . . And look at me! My father was mer-
chant of ostrich feathers in Brussels. If I had been content to go in
his business, I would 'ave been rich. But I was born to roll—
"rolling stone" to voyage is stronger than myself. Luck! . . And
you, Ma'moiselle, shall I tell your fortune? [He looks in her face.]
You were born for 'la joie de vivre'—to drink the wines of life. 'Et
vous voila'! Luck!

[Though she does not in the least understand what he has said, her expression
changes to a sort of glee.]

FERRAND. Yes. You were born loving pleasure. Is it not? You see, you cannot
say, No. All of us, we have our fates. Give me your hand. [He kneels down and
takes her hand.] In each of us there is that against which we cannot struggle. Yes,
yes!

[He holds her hand, and turns it over between his own. MRS. MEGAN remains
stolid, half fascinated, half-reluctant.]

TIMSON. [Flickering into consciousness.] Be'ave yourselves! Yer crimson
canary birds!

[MRS. MEGAN would withdraw her hand, but cannot.]

FERRAND. Pay no attention, Ma'moiselle. He is a Puritan.

[TIMSON relapses into comatosity, upsetting his glass, which falls with a crash.]

MRS. MEGAN. Let go my hand, please!

FERRAND. [Relinquishing it, and staring into the fore gravely.] There is one
thing I have never done—'urt a woman—that is hardly in my
character. [Then, drawing a little closer, he looks into her face.]
Tell me, Ma'moiselle, what is it you think of all day long?

MRS. MEGAN. I dunno—lots, I thinks of.

FERRAND. Shall I tell you? [Her eyes remain fixed on his, the strangeness of
him preventing her from telling him to "get along." He goes on in

his ironic voice.] It is of the streets—the lights— the faces—it is of all which moves, and is warm—it is of colour—it is [he brings his face quite close to hers] of Love. That is for you what the road is for me. That is for you what the rum is for that old—[He jerks his thumb back at TIMSON. Then bending swiftly forward to the girl.] See! I kiss you—Ah!

[He draws her forward off the stool. There is a little struggle, then she resigns her lips. The little stool, overturned, falls with a clatter. They spring up, and move apart. The door opens and ANN enters from the house in a blue dressing-gown, with her hair loose, and a candle held high above her head. Taking in the strange half-circle round the stove, she recoils. Then, standing her ground, calls in a voice sharpened by fright: "Daddy—Daddy!"]

TIMSON. [Stirring uneasily, and struggling to his feet.] All right! I'm comin'!

FERRAND. Have no fear, Madame!

[In the silence that follows, a clock begins loudly striking twelve. ANN remains, as if carved in atone, her eyes fastened on the strangers. There is the sound of someone falling downstairs, and WELLWYN appears, also holding a candle above his head.]

ANN. Look!

WELLWYN. Yes, yes, my dear! It—it happened.

ANN. [With a sort of groan.] Oh! Daddy!

[In the renewed silence, the church clock ceases to chime.]

FERRAND. [Softly, in his ironic voice.] HE is come, Monsieur! 'Appy Christmas! Bon Noel!

[There is a sudden chime of bells. The Stage is blotted dark.]

Curtain.

ACT II

It is four o'clock in the afternoon of New Year's Day. On the raised dais MRS. MEGAN is standing, in her rags; with bare feet and ankles, her dark hair as if blown about, her lips parted, holding out a dishevelled bunch of violets. Before his easel, WELLWYN is painting her. Behind him, at a table between the cupboard and the door to the model's room, TIMSON is washing brushes, with the movements of one employed upon relief works. The samovar is hissing on the table by the stove, the tea things are set out.

WELLWYN. Open your mouth.

[MRS. MEGAN opens her mouth.]

ANN. [In hat and coat, entering from the house.] Daddy!

[WELLWYN goes to her; and, released from restraint, MRS. MEGAN looks round at TIMSON and grimaces.]

WELLWYN. Well, my dear?

[They speak in low voices.]

ANN. [Holding out a note.] This note from Canon Bentley. He's going to bring her husband here this afternoon. [She looks at MRS. MEGAN.]

WELLWYN. Oh! [He also looks at MRS. MEGAN.]

ANN. And I met Sir Thomas Hoxton at church this morning, and spoke to him
          about Timson.

WELLWYN. Um!

[They look at TIMSON. Then ANN goes back to the door, and WELLWYN
follows her.]

ANN. [Turning.] I'm going round now, Daddy, to ask Professor Calway what
          we're to do with that Ferrand.

WELLWYN. Oh! One each! I wonder if they'll like it.

ANN. They'll have to lump it.

[She goes out into the house.]

WELLWYN. [Back at his easel.] You can shut your mouth now.

[MRS. MEGAN shuts her mouth, but opens it immediately to smile.]

WELLWYN. [Spasmodically.] Ah! Now that's what I want. [He dabs furious-
          ly at the canvas. Then standing back, runs his hands through his
          hair and turns a painter's glance towards the skylight.]   Dash!
          Light's gone! Off you get, child—don't tempt me!

[MRS. MEGAN descends. Passing towards the door of the model's room she
stops, and stealthily looks at the picture.]

TIMSON. Ah! Would yer!

WELLWYN. [Wheeling round.] Want to have a look? Well—come on!

[He takes her by the arm, and they stand before the canvas. After a stolid
moment, she giggles.]

WELLWYN. Oh! You think so?

MRS. MEGAN.   [Who has lost her hoarseness.] It's not like my picture that I had on the pier.

WELLWYN. No-it wouldn't be.

MRS. MEGAN. [Timidly.] If I had an 'at on, I'd look better.

WELLWYN. With feathers?

MRS. MEGAN. Yes.

WELLWYN. Well, you can't! I don't like hats, and I don't like feathers.

[MRS. MEGAN timidly tugs his sleeve. TIMSON, screened as he thinks by the picture, has drawn from his bulky pocket a bottle and is taking a stealthy swig.]

WELLWYN. [To MRS. MEGAN, affecting not to notice.] How much do I owe you?

MRS. MEGAN. [A little surprised.] You paid me for to-day-all 'cept a penny.

WELLWYN. Well! Here it is. [He gives her a coin.] Go and get your feet on!

MRS. MEGAN. You've give me 'arf a crown.

WELLWYN. Cut away now!

[MRS. MEGAN, smiling at the coin, goes towards the model's room. She looks back at WELLWYN, as if to draw his eyes to her, but he is gazing at the picture; then, catching old TIMSON'S sour glance, she grimaces at him, kicking up her feet with a little squeal. But when WELLWYN turns to the sound, she is demurely passing through the doorway.]

TIMSON.   [In his voice of dubious sobriety.] I've finished these yer brushes, sir. It's not a man's work. I've been thinkin' if you'd keep an 'orse, I could give yer satisfaction.

WELLWYN. Would the horse, Timson?

TIMSON.   [Looking him up and down.] I knows of one that would just suit yer. Reel 'orse, you'd like 'im.

WELLWYN. [Shaking his head.] Afraid not, Timson! Awfully sorry, though, to have nothing better for you than this, at present.

TIMSON. [Faintly waving the brushes.] Of course, if you can't afford it, I don't press you—it's only that I feel I'm not doing meself justice. [Confidentially.] There's just one thing, sir; I can't bear to see a gen'leman imposed on. That foreigner—'e's not the sort to 'ave about the place. Talk? Oh! ah! But 'e'll never do any good with 'imself. He's a alien.

WELLWYN. Terrible misfortune to a fellow, Timson.

TIMSON. Don't you believe it, sir; it's his fault I says to the young lady yester-day: Miss Ann, your father's a gen'leman [with a sudden accent of hoarse sincerity], and so you are—I don't mind sayin' it—but, I said, he's too easy-goin'.

WELLWYN. Indeed!

TIMSON. Well, see that girl now! [He shakes his head.] I never did believe in goin' behind a person's back—I'm an Englishman—but [lowering his voice] she's a bad hat, sir. Why, look at the street she comes from!

WELLWYN. Oh! you know it.

TIMSON. Lived there meself larst three years. See the difference a few days' corn's made in her. She's that saucy you can't touch 'er head.

WELLWYN. Is there any necessity, Timson?

TIMSON. Artful too. Full o' vice, I call'er. Where's 'er 'usband?

WELLWYN. [Gravely.] Come, Timson! You wouldn't like her to——

TIMSON. [With dignity, so that the bottle in his pocket is plainly visible.] I'm a man as always beared inspection.

WELLWYN. [With a well-directed smile.] So I see.

TIMSON. [Curving himself round the bottle.] It's not for me to say nothing—but I can tell a gen'leman as quick as ever I can tell an 'orse.

WELLWYN. [Painting.] I find it safest to assume that every man is a gentleman, and every woman a lady. Saves no end of self-contempt. Give me the little brush.

TIMSON. [Handing him the brush—after a considerable introspective pause.] Would yer like me to stay and wash it for yer again? [With great resolution.] I will—I'll do it for you—never grudged workin' for a gen'leman.

WELLWYN. [With sincerity.] Thank you, Timson—very good of you, I'm sure. [He hands him back the brush.] Just lend us a hand with this. [Assisted by TIMSON he pushes back the dais.] Let's see! What do I owe you?

TIMSON. [Reluctantly.] It so 'appens, you advanced me to-day's yesterday.

WELLWYN. Then I suppose you want to-morrow's?

TIMSON. Well, I 'ad to spend it, lookin' for a permanent job. When you've got to do with 'orses, you can't neglect the publics, or you might as well be dead.

WELLWYN. Quite so!

TIMSON. It mounts up in the course o' the year.

WELLWYN. It would. [Passing him a coin.] This is for an exceptional purpose—Timson—see. Not——

TIMSON. [Touching his forehead.] Certainly, sir. I quite understand. I'm not that sort, as I think I've proved to yer, comin' here regular day after day, all the week. There's one thing, I ought to warn you perhaps—I might 'ave to give this job up any day.

[He makes a faint demonstration with the little brush, then puts it, absent-mindedly, into his pocket.]

WELLWYN. [Gravely.] I'd never stand in the way of your bettering yourself, Timson. And, by the way, my daughter spoke to a friend about you to-day. I think something may come of it.

TIMSON. Oh! Oh! She did! Well, it might do me a bit o' good. [He makes
    for the outer door, but stops.] That foreigner! 'E sticks in my gizzard.
    It's not as if there wasn't plenty o' pigeons for 'im to pluck in 'is own
    Gawd-forsaken country. Reg-lar jay, that's what I calls 'im. I could
    tell yer something——

[He has opened the door, and suddenly sees that FERRAND himself is standing
there. Sticking out his lower lip, TIMSON gives a roll of his jaw and lurches
forth into the street. Owing to a slight miscalculation, his face and raised arms
are plainly visible through the window, as he fortifies himself from his battle
against the cold. FERRAND, having closed the door, stands with his thumb acting as pointer towards this spectacle. He is now remarkably dressed in an artist's
squashy green hat, a frock coat too small for him, a bright blue tie of knitted silk,
the grey trousers that were torn, well-worn brown boots, and a tan waistcoat.]

WELLWYN. What luck to-day?

FERRAND. [With a shrug.] Again I have beaten all London, Monsieur- -not
    one bite. [Contemplating himself.] I think perhaps, that, for the
    bourgeoisie, there is a little too much colour in my costume.

WELLWYN. [Contemplating him.] Let's see—I believe I've an old top hat
    somewhere.

FERRAND. Ah! Monsieur, 'merci', but that I could not. It is scarcely in my
    character.

WELLWYN. True!

FERRAND. I have been to merchants of wine, of tabac, to hotels, to Leicester
    Square. I have been to a Society for spreading Christian knowl-
    edge—I thought there I would have a chance perhaps as inter-
    preter. 'Toujours meme chose', we regret, we have no situation for
    you—same thing everywhere. It seems there is nothing doing in
    this town.

WELLWYN. I've noticed, there never is.

FERRAND. I was thinking, Monsieur, that in aviation there might be a career
    for me—but it seems one must be trained.

WELLWYN. Afraid so, Ferrand.

FERRAND. [Approaching the picture.] Ah! You are always working at this. You will have something of very good there, Monsieur. You wish to fix the type of wild savage existing ever amongst our high civilisation. 'C'est tres chic ça'! [WELLWYN manifests the quiet delight of an English artist actually understood.] In the figures of these good citizens, to whom she offers her flower, you would give the idea of all the cage doors open to catch and make tame the wild bird, that will surely die within. 'Tres gentil'! Believe me, Monsieur, you have there the greatest comedy of life! How anxious are the tame birds to do the wild birds good. [His voice changes.] For the wild birds it is not funny. There is in some human souls, Monsieur, what cannot be made tame.

WELLWYN. I believe you, Ferrand.

[The face of a young man appears at the window, unseen. Suddenly ANN opens the door leading to the house.]

ANN. Daddy—I want you.

WELLWYN. [To FERRAND.] Excuse me a minute!

[He goes to his daughter, and they pass out. FERRAND remains at the picture. MRS. MEGAN dressed in some of ANN's discarded garments, has come out of the model's room. She steals up behind FERRAND like a cat, reaches an arm up, and curls it round his mouth. He turns, and tries to seize her; she disingenuously slips away. He follows. The chase circles the tea table. He catches her, lifts her up, swings round with her, so that her feet fly out; kisses her bent-back face, and sets her down. She stands there smiling. The face at the window darkens.]

FERRAND. La Valse!

[He takes her with both hands by the waist, she puts her hands against his shoulders to push him of—and suddenly they are whirling. As they whirl, they bob together once or twice, and kiss. Then, with a warning motion towards the door, she wrenches herself free, and stops beside the picture, trying desperately to appear demure. WELLWYN and ANN have entered. The face has vanished.]

FERRAND. [Pointing to the picture.]   One does not comprehend all this, Monsieur, without well studying.   I was in train to interpret for Ma'moiselle the chiaroscuro.

WELLWYN. [With a queer look.] Don't take it too seriously, Ferrand.

FERRAND. It is a masterpiece.

WELLWYN. My daughter's just spoken to a friend, Professor Calway. He'd like to meet you. Could you come back a little later?

FERRAND. Certainly, Ma'moiselle. That will be an opening for me, I trust. [He goes to the street door.]

ANN. [Paying no attention to him.] Mrs. Megan, will you too come back in half an hour?

FERRAND. 'Tres bien, Ma'moiselle'! I will see that she does. We will take a little promenade together. That will do us good.

[He motions towards the door; MRS. MEGAN, all eyes, follows him out.]

ANN. Oh! Daddy, they are rotters. Couldn't you see they were having the most high jinks?

WELLWYN. [At his picture.] I seemed to have noticed something.

ANN. [Preparing for tea.] They were kissing.

WELLWYN. Tt! Tt!

ANN. They're hopeless, all three—especially her. Wish I hadn't given her my clothes now.

WELLWYN. [Absorbed.] Something of wild-savage.

ANN. Thank goodness it's the Vicar's business to see that married people live together in his parish.

WELLWYN. Oh! [Dubiously.] The Megans are Roman Catholic-Atheists, Ann.

ANN. [With heat.] Then they're all the more bound. [WELLWYN gives a sudden and alarmed whistle.]

ANN. What's the matter?

WELLWYN. Didn't you say you spoke to Sir Thomas, too. Suppose he comes in while the Professor's here. They're cat and dog.

ANN. [Blankly.] Oh! [As WELLWYN strikes a match.] The samovar is lighted. [Taking up the nearly empty decanter of rum and going to the cupboard.] It's all right. He won't.

WELLWYN. We'll hope not.

[He turns back to his picture.]

ANN. [At the cupboard.] Daddy!

WELLWYN. Hi!

ANN. There were three bottles.

WELLWYN. Oh!

ANN. Well! Now there aren't any.

WELLWYN. [Abstracted.] That'll be Timson.

ANN. [With real horror.] But it's awful!

WELLWYN. It is, my dear.

ANN. In seven days. To say nothing of the stealing.

WELLWYN. [Vexed.] I blame myself-very much. Ought to have kept it locked up.

ANN. You ought to keep him locked up!

[There is heard a mild but authoritative knock.]

WELLWYN. Here's the Vicar!

ANN. What are you going to do about the rum?

WELLWYN. [Opening the door to CANON BERTLEY.] Come in, Vicar!
Happy New Year!

BERTLEY. Same to you! Ah! Ann! I've got into touch with her young husband—he's coming round.

ANN. [Still a little out of her plate.] Thank Go—-Moses!

BERTLEY. [Faintly surprised.] From what I hear he's not really a bad youth.
Afraid he bets on horses. The great thing, WELLWYN, with those
poor fellows is to put your finger on the weak spot.

ANN. [To herself-gloomily.] That's not difficult. What would you do, Canon
Bertley, with a man who's been drinking father's rum?

BERTLEY. Remove the temptation, of course.

WELLWYN. He's done that.

BERTLEY. Ah! Then—[WELLWYN and ANN hang on his words] then I
should—er

ANN. [Abruptly.] Remove him.

BERTLEY. Before I say that, Ann, I must certainly see the individual.

WELLWYN. [Pointing to the window.] There he is!

[In the failing light TIMSON'S face is indeed to be seen pressed against the window pane.]

ANN. Daddy, I do wish you'd have thick glass put in. It's so disgusting to be
spied at! [WELLWYN going quickly to the door, has opened it.] What
do you want? [TIMSON enters with dignity. He is fuddled.]

TIMSON. [Slowly.] Arskin' yer pardon-thought it me duty to come back-found
thish yer little brishel on me. [He produces the little paint brush.]

ANN. [In a deadly voice.] Nothing else?

[TIMSON accords her a glassy stare.]

WELLWYN. [Taking the brush hastily.] That'll do, Timson, thanks!

TIMSON. As I am 'ere, can I do anything for yer?

ANN. Yes, you can sweep out that little room. [She points to the model's room.] There's a broom in there.

TIMSON. [Disagreeably surprised.] Certainly; never make bones about a little extra—never 'ave in all me life. Do it at onsh, I will. [He moves across to the model's room at that peculiar broad gait so perfectly adjusted to his habits.] You quite understand me —couldn't bear to 'ave anything on me that wasn't mine.

[He passes out.]

ANN. Old fraud!

WELLWYN. "In" and "on." Mark my words, he'll restore the—bottles.

BERTLEY. But, my dear WELLWYN, that is stealing.

WELLWYN. We all have our discrepancies, Vicar.

ANN. Daddy! Discrepancies!

WELLWYN. Well, Ann, my theory is that as regards solids Timson's an Individualist, but as regards liquids he's a Socialist . . . or 'vice versa', according to taste.

BERTLEY. No, no, we mustn't joke about it. [Gravely.] I do think he should be spoken to.

WELLWYN. Yes, but not by me.

BERTLEY. Surely you're the proper person.

WELLWYN. [Shaking his head.] It was my rum, Vicar. Look so personal.

[There sound a number of little tat-tat knocks.]

WELLWYN. Isn't that the Professor's knock?

[While Ann sits down to make tea, he goes to the door and opens it. There, dressed in an ulster, stands a thin, clean-shaved man, with a little hollow sucked into either cheek, who, taking off a grey squash hat, discloses a majestically bald forehead, which completely dominates all that comes below it.]

WELLWYN. Come in, Professor! So awfully good of you! You know Canon
            Bentley, I think?

CALWAY. Ah! How d'you do?

WELLWYN. Your opinion will be invaluable, Professor.

ANN. Tea, Professor Calway?

[They have assembled round the tea table.]

CALWAY. Thank you; no tea; milk.

WELLWYN. Rum?

[He pours rum into CALWAY's milk.]

CALWAY. A little-thanks! [Turning to ANN.] You were going to show me some
one you're trying to rescue, or something, I think.

ANN. Oh! Yes. He'll be here directly—simply perfect rotter.

CALWAY. [Smiling.] Really! Ah! I think you said he was a congenital?

WELLWYN. [With great interest.] What!

ANN. [Low.] Daddy! [To CALWAY.] Yes; I—I think that's what you call him.

CALWAY. Not old?

ANN. No; and quite healthy—a vagabond.

CALWAY. [Sipping.] I see! Yes. Is it, do you think chronic unemployment with a vagrant tendency? Or would it be nearer the mark to say: Vagrancy——

WELLWYN. Pure! Oh! pure! Professor. Awfully human.

CALWAY. [With a smile of knowledge.] Quite! And—er——

ANN. [Breaking in.] Before he comes, there's another——

BERTLEY. [Blandly.] Yes, when you came in, we were discussing what should be done with a man who drinks rum—[CALWAY pauses in the act of drinking]—that doesn't belong to him.

CALWAY. Really! Dipsomaniac?

BERTLEY. Well—perhaps you could tell us—drink certainly changing thine to mine. The Professor could see him, WELLWYN?

ANN. [Rising.] Yes, do come and look at him, Professor CALWAY. He's in there.

[She points towards the model's room. CALWAY smiles deprecatingly.]

ANN. No, really; we needn't open the door. You can see him through the glass. He's more than half——

CALWAY. Well, I hardly——

ANN. Oh! Do! Come on, Professor CALWAY! We must know what to do with him. [CALWAY rises.] You can stand on a chair. It's all science.

[She draws CALWAY to the model's room, which is lighted by a glass panel in the top of the high door. CANON BERTLEY also rises and stands watching. WELLWYN hovers, torn between respect for science and dislike of espionage.]

ANN. [Drawing up a chair.] Come on!

CALWAY. Do you seriously wish me to?

ANN. Rather! It's quite safe; he can't see you.

CALWAY. But he might come out.

[ANN puts her back against the door. CALWAY mounts the chair dubiously, and raises his head cautiously, bending it more and more downwards.]

ANN. Well?

CALWAY. He appears to be——-sitting on the floor.

WELLWYN. Yes, that's all right!

[BERTLEY covers his lips.]

CALWAY. [To ANN—descending.] By the look of his face, as far as one can see it, I should say there was a leaning towards mania. I know the treatment.

[There come three loud knocks on the door. WELLWYN and ANN exchange a glance of consternation.]

ANN. Who's that?

WELLWYN. It sounds like Sir Thomas.

CALWAY. Sir Thomas Hoxton?

WELLWYN. [Nodding.] Awfully sorry, Professor. You see, we——

CALWAY. Not at all. Only, I must decline to be involved in argument with him, please.

BERTLEY. He has experience. We might get his opinion, don't you think?

CALWAY. On a point of reform? A J.P.!

BERTLEY. [Deprecating.] My dear Sir—we needn't take it.

[The three knocks resound with extraordinary fury.]

ANN. You'd better open the door, Daddy.

[WELLWYN opens the door. SIR, THOMAS HOXTON is disclosed in a fur overcoat and top hat. His square, well-coloured face is remarkable for a massive jaw, dominating all that comes above it. His Voice is resolute.]

HOXTON. Afraid I didn't make myself heard.

WELLWYN. So good of you to come, Sir Thomas. Canon Bertley! [They greet.] Professor CALWAY you know, I think.

HOXTON. [Ominously.] I do.

[They almost greet. An awkward pause.]

ANN. [Blurting it out.] That old cabman I told you of's been drinking father's rum.

BERTLEY. We were just discussing what's to be done with him, Sir Thomas. One wants to do the very best, of course. The question of reform is always delicate.

CALWAY. I beg your pardon. There is no question here.

HOXTON. [Abruptly.] Oh! Is he in the house?

ANN. In there.

HOXTON. Works for you, eh?

WELLWYN. Er—yes.

HOXTON. Let's have a look at him!

[An embarrassed pause.]

BERTLEY. Well—the fact is, Sir Thomas——

CALWAY. When last under observation——

ANN. He was sitting on the floor.

WELLWYN. I don't want the old fellow to feel he's being made a show of. Disgusting to be spied at, Ann.

ANN. You can't, Daddy! He's drunk.

HOXTON. Never mind, Miss WELLWYN. Hundreds of these fellows before me in my time. [At CALWAY.] The only thing is a sharp lesson!

CALWAY. I disagree. I've seen the man; what he requires is steady control, and the bobbins treatment.

[WELLWYN approaches them with fearful interest.]

HOXTON. Not a bit of it! He wants one for his knob! Brace 'em up! It's the only thing.

BERTLEY. Personally, I think that if he were spoken to seriously

CALWAY. I cannot walk arm in arm with a crab!

HOXTON. [Approaching CALWAY.] I beg your pardon?

CALWAY. [Moving back a little.] You're moving backwards, Sir Thomas. I've told you before, convinced reactionaryism, in these days——

[There comes a single knock on the street door.]

BERTLEY. [Looking at his watch.] D'you know, I'm rather afraid this may be our young husband, WELLWYN. I told him half-past four.

WELLWYN. Oh! Ah! Yes. [Going towards the two reformers.] Shall we go into the house, Professor, and settle the question quietly while the Vicar sees a young man?

CALWAY. [Pale with uncompleted statement, and gravitating insensibly in the direction indicated.] The merest sense of continuity—a simple instinct for order——

HOXTON. [Following.] The only way to get order, sir, is to bring the disorderly up with a round turn. [CALWAY turns to him in the doorway.] You people without practical experience——

CALWAY. If you'll listen to me a minute.

HOXTON. I can show you in a mo——

[They vanish through the door.]

WELLWYN. I was afraid of it.

BERTLEY. The two points of view. Pleasant to see such keenness. I may want you, WELLWYN. And Ann perhaps had better not be present.

WELLWYN. [Relieved.] Quite so! My dear!

[ANN goes reluctantly. WELLWYN opens the street door. The lamp outside has just been lighted, and, by its gleam, is seen the figure of RORY MEGAN, thin, pale, youthful. ANN turning at the door into the house gives him a long, inquisitive look, then goes.]

WELLWYN. Is that Megan?

MEGAN. Yus.

WELLWYN. Come in.

[MEGAN comes in. There follows an awkward silence, during which WELLWYN turns up the light, then goes to the tea table and pours out a glass of tea and rum.]

BERTLEY. [Kindly.] Now, my boy, how is it that you and your wife are living apart like this?

MEGAN. I dunno.

BERTLEY. Well, if you don't, none of us are very likely to, are we?

MEGAN. That's what I thought, as I was comin' along.

WELLWYN. [Twinkling.] Have some tea, Megan? [Handing him the glass.] What d'you think of her picture? 'Tisn't quite finished.

MEGAN. [After scrutiny.] I seen her look like it—once.

WELLWYN. Good! When was that?

MEGAN. [Stoically.] When she 'ad the measles.

[He drinks.]

WELLWYN. [Ruminating.] I see—yes. I quite see feverish!

BERTLEY. My dear WELLWYN, let me—[To, MEGAN.] Now, I hope you're
          willing to come together again, and to maintain her?

MEGAN. If she'll maintain me.

BERTLEY. Oh! but—I see, you mean you're in the same line of business?

MEGAN. Yus.

BERTLEY. And lean on each other. Quite so!

MEGAN. I leans on 'er mostly—with 'er looks.

BERTLEY. Indeed! Very interesting—that!

MEGAN. Yus. Sometimes she'll take 'arf a crown off of a toff. [He looks at
        WELLWYN.]

WELLWYN. [Twinkling.] I apologise to you, Megan.

MEGAN. [With a faint smile.] I could do with a bit more of it.

BERTLEY. [Dubiously.] Yes! Yes! Now, my boy, I've heard you bet on horses.

MEGAN. No, I don't.

BERTLEY. Play cards, then? Come! Don't be afraid to acknowledge it.

MEGAN. When I'm 'ard up—yus.

BERTLEY. But don't you know that's ruination?

MEGAN. Depends. Sometimes I wins a lot.

BERTLEY. You know that's not at all what I mean. Come, promise me to give it up.

MEGAN. I dunno abaht that.

BERTLEY. Now, there's a good fellow. Make a big effort and throw the habit off!

MEGAN. Comes over me—same as it might over you.

BERTLEY. Over me! How do you mean, my boy?

MEGAN. [With a look up.] To tork!

[WELLWYN, turning to the picture, makes a funny little noise.]

BERTLEY. [Maintaining his good humour.] A hit! But you forget, you know, to talk's my business. It's not yours to gamble.

MEGAN. You try sellin' flowers. If that ain't a—gamble

BERTLEY. I'm afraid we're wandering a little from the point. Husband and wife should be together. You were brought up to that. Your father and mother——

MEGAN. Never was.

WELLWYN. [Turning from the picture.] The question is, Megan: Will you take your wife home? She's a good little soul.

MEGAN. She never let me know it.

[There is a feeble knock on the door.]

WELLWYN. Well, now come. Here she is!

[He points to the door, and stands regarding MEGAN with his friendly smile.]

MEGAN. [With a gleam of responsiveness.] I might, perhaps, to please you, sir.

BERTLEY. [Appropriating the gesture.] Capital, I thought we should get on in
          time.

MEGAN. Yus.

[WELLWYN opens the door. MRS. MEGAN and FERRAND are revealed.
They are about to enter, but catching sight of MEGAN, hesitate.]

BERTLEY. Come in! Come in!

[MRS. MEGAN enters stolidly. FERRAND, following, stands apart with an air
of extreme detachment. MEGAN, after a quick glance at them both, remains
unmoved. No one has noticed that the door of the model's room has been
opened, and that the unsteady figure of old TIMSON is standing there.]

BERTLEY. [A little awkward in the presence of FERRAND—to the MEGANS.]
          This begins a new chapter. We won't improve the occasion. No
          need.

[MEGAN, turning towards his wife, makes her a gesture as if to say: "Here! let's
get out of this!"]

BENTLEY. Yes, yes, you'll like to get home at once—I know. [He holds up his
          hand mechanically.]

TIMSON. I forbids the banns.

BERTLEY, [Startled.] Gracious!

TIMSON. [Extremely unsteady.] Just cause and impejiment. There 'e stands.
          [He points to FERRAND.] The crimson foreigner! The mockin'
          jay!

WELLWYN. Timson!

TIMSON. You're a gen'leman—I'm aweer o' that but I must speak the truth—
          [he waves his hand] an' shame the devil!

BERTLEY. Is this the rum—?

TIMSON. [Struck by the word.] I'm a teetotaler.

WELLWYN. Timson, Timson!

TIMSON. Seein' as there's ladies present, I won't be conspicuous. [Moving away, and making for the door, he strikes against the dais, and mounts upon it.] But what I do say, is: He's no better than 'er and she's worse.

BERTLEY. This is distressing.

FERRAND. [Calmly.] On my honour, Monsieur!

[TIMSON growls.]

WELLWYN. Now, now, Timson!

TIMSON. That's all right. You're a gen'leman, an' I'm a gen'leman, but he ain't an' she ain't.

WELLWYN. We shall not believe you.

BERTLEY. No, no; we shall not believe you.

TIMSON. [Heavily.] Very well, you doubts my word. Will it make any difference, Guv'nor, if I speaks the truth?

BERTLEY. No, certainly not—that is—of course, it will.

TIMSON. Well, then, I see 'em plainer than I see [pointing at BERTLEY] the two of you.

WELLWYN. Be quiet, Timson!

BERTLEY. Not even her husband believes you.

MEGAN. [Suddenly.] Don't I!

WELLWYN. Come, Megan, you can see the old fellow's in Paradise.

BERTLEY. Do you credit such a—such an object?

[He points at TIMSON, who seems falling asleep.]

MEGAN. Naow!

[Unseen by anybody, ANN has returned.]

BERTLEY. Well, then, my boy?

MEGAN. I seen 'em meself.

BERTLEY. Gracious! But just now you were will——

MEGAN. [Sardonically.] There wasn't nothing against me honour, then. Now you've took it away between you, cumin' aht with it like this. I don't want no more of 'er, and I'll want a good deal more of 'im; as 'e'll soon find.

[He jerks his chin at FERRAND, turns slowly on his heel, and goes out into the street.]

[There follows a profound silence.]

ANN. What did I say, Daddy? Utter! All three.

[Suddenly alive to her presence, they all turn.]

TIMSON. [Waking up and looking round him.] Well, p'raps I'd better go.

[Assisted by WELLWYN he lurches gingerly off the dais towards the door, which WELLWYN holds open for him.]

TIMSON. [Mechanically.] Where to, sir?

[Receiving no answer he passes out, touching his hat; and the door is closed.]

WELLWYN. Ann!

[ANN goes back whence she came.]

[BERTLEY, steadily regarding MRS. MEGAN, who has put her arm up in front of her face, beckons to FERRAND, and the young man comes gravely forward.]

BERTLEY. Young people, this is very dreadful. [MRS. MEGAN lowers her arm a little, and looks at him over it.] Very sad!

MRS. MEGAN. [Dropping her arm.] Megan's no better than what I am.

BERTLEY. Come, come! Here's your home broken up! [MRS. MEGAN Smiles. Shaking his head gravely.] Surely-surely-you mustn't smile. [MRS. MEGAN becomes tragic.] That's better. Now, what is to be done?

FERRAND. Believe me, Monsieur, I greatly regret.

BERTLEY. I'm glad to hear it.

FERRAND. If I had foreseen this disaster.

BERTLEY. Is that your only reason for regret?

FERRAND. [With a little bow.] Any reason that you wish, Monsieur. I will do my possible.

MRS. MEGAN. I could get an unfurnished room if [she slides her eyes round at WELLWYN] I 'ad the money to furnish it.

BERTLEY. But suppose I can induce your husband to forgive you, and take you back?

MRS. MEGAN. [Shaking her head.] 'E'd 'it me.

BERTLEY. I said to forgive.

MRS. MEGAN. That wouldn't make no difference. [With a flash at BERTLEY.] An' I ain't forgiven him!

BERTLEY. That is sinful.

MRS. MEGAN. I'm a Catholic.

BERTLEY. My good child, what difference does that make?

FERRAND. Monsieur, if I might interpret for her.

[BERTLEY silences him with a gesture. MRS. MEGAN.]

[Sliding her eyes towards WELLWYN.] If I 'ad the money to buy some fresh stock.]

BERTLEY. Yes; yes; never mind the money. What I want to find in you both, is repentance.

MRS. MEGAN. [With a flash up at him.] I can't get me livin' off of repentin'.

BERTLEY. Now, now! Never say what you know to be wrong.

FERRAND. Monsieur, her soul is very simple.

BERTLEY. [Severely.] I do not know, sir, that we shall get any great assistance from your views. In fact, one thing is clear to me, she must discontinue your acquaintanceship at once.

FERRAND. Certainly, Monsieur. We have no serious intentions.

BERTLEY. All the more shame to you, then!

FERRAND. Monsieur, I see perfectly your point of view. It is very natural. [He bows and is silent.]

MRS. MEGAN. I don't want'im hurt'cos o' me. Megan'll get his mates to belt him—bein' foreign like he is.

BERTLEY. Yes, never mind that. It's you I'm thinking of.

MRS. MEGAN. I'd sooner they'd hit me.

WELLWYN. [Suddenly.] Well said, my child!

MRS. MEGAN. 'Twasn't his fault.

FERRAND. [Without irony—to WELLWYN.] I cannot accept that Monsieur. The blame—it is all mine.

ANN. [Entering suddenly from the house.] Daddy, they're having an awful——!

[The voices of PROFESSOR CALWAY and SIR THOMAS HOXTON are distinctly heard.]

CALWAY. The question is a much wider one, Sir Thomas.

HOXTON. As wide as you like, you'll never——

[WELLWYN pushes ANN back into the house and closes the door behind her. The voices are still faintly heard arguing on the threshold.]

BERTLEY. Let me go in here a minute, Wellyn. I must finish speaking to her. [He motions MRS. MEGAN towards the model's room.] We can't leave the matter thus.

FERRAND. [Suavely.] Do you desire my company, Monsieur?

[BERTLEY, with a prohibitive gesture of his hand, shepherds the reluctant MRS. MEGAN into the model's room.]

WELLWYN. [Sorrowfully.] You shouldn't have done this, Ferrand. It wasn't the square thing.

FERRAND. [With dignity.] Monsieur, I feel that I am in the wrong. It was stronger than me.

[As he speaks, SIR THOMAS HOXTON and PROFESSOR CALWAY enter from the house. In the dim light, and the full cry of argument, they do not notice the figures at the fire. SIR THOMAS HOXTON leads towards the street door.]

HOXTON. No, Sir, I repeat, if the country once commits itself to your views of reform, it's as good as doomed.

CALWAY. I seem to have heard that before, Sir Thomas. And let me say at once that your hitty-missy cart-load of bricks regime——

HOXTON. Is a deuced sight better, sir, than your grand-motherly methods. What the old fellow wants is a shock! With all this socialistic molly-coddling, you're losing sight of the individual.

CALWAY. [Swiftly.] You, sir, with your "devil take the hindmost," have never even seen him.

[SIR THOMAS HOXTON, throwing back a gesture of disgust, steps out into the night, and falls heavily PROFESSOR CALWAY, hastening to his rescue, falls more heavily still.]

[TIMSON, momentarily roused from slumber on the doorstep, sits up.]

HOXTON. [Struggling to his knees.] Damnation!

CALWAY. [Sitting.] How simultaneous!

[WELLWYN and FERRAND approach hastily.]

FERRAND. [Pointing to TIMSON.] Monsieur, it was true, it seems. They had lost sight of the individual.

[A Policeman has appeared under the street lamp. He picks up HOXTON'S hat.]

CONSTABLE. Anything wrong, sir?

HOXTON. [Recovering his feet.] Wrong? Great Scott! Constable! Why do you let things lie about in the street like this? Look here, Wellyn!

[They all scrutinize TIMSON.]

WELLWYN. It's only the old fellow whose reform you were discussing.

HOXTON. How did he come here?

CONSTABLE. Drunk, sir. [Ascertaining TIMSON to be in the street.] Just off the premises, by good luck. Come along, father.

TIMSON. [Assisted to his feet-drowsily.] Cert'nly, by no means; take my arm.

[They move from the doorway. HOXTON and CALWAY re-enter, and go towards the fire.]

ANN. [Entering from the house.] What's happened?

CALWAY. Might we have a brush?

HOXTON. [Testily.] Let it dry!

[He moves to the fire and stands before it. PROFESSOR CALWAY following stands a little behind him. ANN returning begins to brush the PROFESSOR's sleeve.]

WELLWYN. [Turning from the door, where he has stood looking after the receding TIMSON.] Poor old Timson!

FERRAND. [Softly.] Must be philosopher, Monsieur! They will but run him in a little.

[From the model's room MRS. MEGAN has come out, shepherded by CANON BERTLEY.]

BERTLEY. Let's see, your Christian name is——.

MRS. MEGAN. Guinevere.

BERTLEY. Oh! Ah! Ah! Ann, take Gui—take our little friend into the study a minute: I am going to put her into service. We shall make a new woman of her, yet.

ANN. [Handing CANON BERTLEY the brush, and turning to MRS. MEGAN.] Come on!

[She leads into the house, and MRS. MEGAN follows Stolidly.]

BERTLEY. [Brushing CALWAY'S back.] Have you fallen?

CALWAY. Yes.

BERTLEY. Dear me! How was that?

HOXTON. That old ruffian drunk on the doorstep. Hope they'll give him a sharp dose! These rag-tags!

[He looks round, and his angry eyes light by chance on FERRAND.]

FERRAND. [With his eyes on HOXTON—softly.] Monsieur, something tells me it is time I took the road again.

WELLWYN. [Fumbling out a sovereign.] Take this, then!

FERRAND. [Refusing the coin.] Non, Monsieur. To abuse 'ospitality is not in
          my character.

BERTLEY. We must not despair of anyone.

HOXTON. Who talked of despairing? Treat him, as I say, and you'll see!

CALWAY. The interest of the State——

HOXTON. The interest of the individual citizen sir——

BERTLEY. Come! A little of both, a little of both!

[They resume their brushing.]

FERRAND. You are now debarrassed of us three, Monsieur. I leave you
          instead—these sirs. [He points.] 'Au revoir, Monsieur'! [Motioning
          towards the fire.] 'Appy New Year!

[He slips quietly out. WELLWYN, turning, contemplates the three reformers.
They are all now brushing away, scratching each other's backs, and gravely hissing. As he approaches them, they speak with a certain unanimity.]

HOXTON. My theory——!

CALWAY. My theory——!

BERTLEY. My theory——!

[They stop surprised. WELLWYN makes a gesture of discomfort, as they speak
again with still more unanimity.]

HOXTON. My——! CALWAY. My——! BERTLEY. My——!

[They stop in greater surprise. The stage is blotted dark.]

Curtain.

ACT III

It is the first of April—a white spring day of gleams and driving showers. The street door of WELLWYN's studio stands wide open, and, past it, in the street, the wind is whirling bits of straw and paper bags. Through the door can be seen the butt end of a stationary furniture van with its flap let down. To this van three humble-men in shirt sleeves and aprons, are carrying out the contents of the studio. The hissing samovar, the tea-pot, the sugar, and the nearly empty decanter of rum stand on the low round table in the fast-being-gutted room. WELLWYN in his ulster and soft hat, is squatting on the little stool in front of the blazing fire, staring into it, and smoking a hand-made cigarette. He has a moulting air. Behind him the humble-men pass, embracing busts and other articles of vertu.

CHIEF H'MAN. [Stopping, and standing in the attitude of expectation.] We've about pinched this little lot, sir. Shall we take the—reservoir?

[He indicates the samovar.]

WELLWYN. Ah! [Abstractedly feeling in his pockets, and finding coins.] Thanks—thanks—heavy work, I'm afraid.

H'MAN. [Receiving the coins—a little surprised and a good deal pleased.] Thank'ee, sir. Much obliged, I'm sure. We'll 'ave to come back for this. [He gives the dais a vigorous push with his foot.] Not a fixture, as I understand. Perhaps you'd like us to leave these 'ere for a bit. [He indicates the tea things.]

WELLWYN. Ah! do.

[The humble-men go out. There is the sound of horses being started, and the butt end of the van disappears. WELLWYN stays on his stool, smoking and brooding over the fare. The open doorway is darkened by a figure. CANON BERTLEY is standing there.]

BERTLEY. WELLWYN! [WELLWYN turns and rises.] It's ages since I saw you. No idea you were moving. This is very dreadful.

WELLWYN.   Yes, Ann found this—too exposed. That tall house in Flight
                Street—we're going there. Seventh floor.

BERTLEY. Lift?

[WELLWYN shakes his head.]

BERTLEY. Dear me! No lift? Fine view, no doubt. [WELLWYN nods.] You'll
                be greatly missed.

WELLWYN. So Ann thinks. Vicar, what's become of that little flower-seller I
                was painting at Christmas? You took her into service.

BERTLEY. Not we—exactly! Some dear friends of ours. Painful subject!

WELLWYN. Oh!

BERTLEY. Yes. She got the footman into trouble.

WELLWYN. Did she, now?

BERTLEY. Disappointing. I consulted with CALWAY, and he advised me to try
                a certain institution. We got her safely in—excellent place; but, d'you
                know, she broke out three weeks ago. And since— I've heard [he
                holds his hands up] hopeless, I'm afraid—quite!

WELLWYN. I thought I saw her last night. You can't tell me her address, I sup-
                pose?

BERTLEY. [Shaking his head.] The husband too has quite passed out of my ken.
                He betted on horses, you remember. I'm sometimes tempted to

believe there's nothing for some of these poor folk but to pray for death.

[ANN has entered from the house. Her hair hangs from under a knitted cap. She wears a white wool jersey, and a loose silk scarf.]

BERTLEY. Ah! Ann. I was telling your father of that poor little Mrs. Megan.

ANN. Is she dead?

BERTLEY. Worse I fear. By the way—what became of her accomplice?

ANN. We haven't seen him since. [She looks searchingly at WELLWYN.] At least—have you—Daddy?

WELLWYN. [Rather hurt.] No, my dear; I have not.

BERTLEY. And the—old gentleman who drank the rum?

ANN. He got fourteen days. It was the fifth time.

BERTLEY. Dear me!

ANN. When he came out he got more drunk than ever. Rather a score for Professor Calway, wasn't it?

BERTLEY. I remember. He and Sir Thomas took a kindly interest in the old fellow.

ANN. Yes, they fell over him. The Professor got him into an Institution.

BERTLEY. Indeed!

ANN. He was perfectly sober all the time he was there.

WELLWYN. My dear, they only allow them milk.

ANN. Well, anyway, he was reformed.

WELLWYN. Ye-yes!

ANN. [Terribly.] Daddy! You've been seeing him!

WELLWYN. [With dignity.] My dear, I have not.

ANN. How do you know, then?

WELLWYN. Came across Sir Thomas on the Embankment yesterday; told me old Timso—had been had up again for sitting down in front of a brewer's dray.

ANN. Why?

WELLWYN. Well, you see, as soon as he came out of the what d'you call 'em, he got drunk for a week, and it left him in low spirits.

BERTLEY. Do you mean he deliberately sat down, with the intention—of—er?

WELLWYN. Said he was tired of life, but they didn't believe him.

ANN. Rather a score for Sir Thomas! I suppose he'd told the Professor? What did he say?

WELLWYN. Well, the Professor said [with a quick glance at BERTLEY] he felt there was nothing for some of these poor devils but a lethal chamber.

BERTLEY. [Shocked.] Did he really!

[He has not yet caught WELLWYN' s glance.]

WELLWYN. And Sir Thomas agreed. Historic occasion. And you, Vicar H'm!

[BERTLEY winces.]

ANN. [To herself.] Well, there isn't.

BERTLEY. And yet! Some good in the old fellow, no doubt, if one could put one's finger on it. [Preparing to go.] You'll let us know, then, when you're settled. What was the address? [WELLWYN takes out and hands him a card.] Ah! yes. Good-bye, Ann. Good-bye, Wellyn. [The wind blows his hat along the street.] What a wind! [He goes, pursuing.]

ANN. [Who has eyed the card askance.] Daddy, have you told those other two where we're going?

WELLWYN. Which other two, my dear?

ANN. The Professor and Sir Thomas.

WELLWYN. Well, Ann, naturally I——

ANN. [Jumping on to the dais with disgust.] Oh, dear! When I'm trying to get you away from all this atmosphere. I don't so much mind the Vicar knowing, because he's got a weak heart——

[She jumps off again.]

WELLWYN. [To himself.] Seventh floor! I felt there was something.

ANN. [Preparing to go.] I'm going round now. But you must stay here till the van comes back. And don't forget you tipped the men after the first load.

WELLWYN. Oh! Yes, yes. [Uneasily.] Good sorts they look, those fellows!

ANN. [Scrutinising him.] What have you done?

WELLWYN. Nothing, my dear, really——!

ANN. What?

WELLWYN. I—I rather think I may have tipped them twice.

ANN. [Drily.] Daddy! If it is the first of April, it's not necessary to make a fool of oneself. That's the last time you ever do these ridiculous things. [WELLWYN eyes her askance.] I'm going to see that you spend your money on yourself. You needn't look at me like that! I mean to. As soon as I've got you away from here, and all—these——

WELLWYN. Don't rub it in, Ann!

ANN. [Giving him a sudden hug—then going to the door—with a sort of triumph.] Deeds, not words, Daddy!

[She goes out, and the wind catching her scarf blows it out beneath her firm young chin. WELLWYN returning to the fire, stands brooding, and gazing at his extinct cigarette.]

WELLWYN. [To himself.] Bad lot—low type! No method! No theory!

[In the open doorway appear FERRAND and MRS. MEGAN. They stand, unseen, looking at him. FERRAND is more ragged, if possible, than on Christmas Eve. His chin and cheeks are clothed in a reddish golden beard. MRS. MEGAN's dress is not so woe-begone, but her face is white, her eyes dark-circled. They whisper. She slips back into the shadow of the doorway. WELLWYN turns at the sound, and stares at FERRAND in amazement.]

FERRAND. [Advancing.] Enchanted to see you, Monsieur. [He looks round the empty room.] You are leaving?

WELLWYN. [Nodding—then taking the young man's hand.] How goes it?

FERRAND. [Displaying himself, simply.] As you see, Monsieur. I have done of my best. It still flies from me.

WELLWYN. [Sadly—as if against his will.] Ferrand, it will always fly.

[The young foreigner shivers suddenly from head to foot; then controls himself with a great effort.]

FERRAND. Don't say that, Monsieur! It is too much the echo of my heart.

WELLWYN. Forgive me! I didn't mean to pain you.

FERRAND. [Drawing nearer the fire.] That old cabby, Monsieur, you remember—they tell me, he nearly succeeded to gain happiness the other day.

[WELLWYN nods.]

FERRAND. And those Sirs, so interested in him, with their theories? He has worn them out? [WELLWYN nods.] That goes without saying. And now they wish for him the lethal chamber.

WELLWYN. [Startled.] How did you know that?

[There is silence.]

FERRAND. [Staring into the fire.] Monsieur, while I was on the road this time I fell ill of a fever. It seemed to me in my illness that I saw the truth—how I was wasting in this world—I would never be good for any one—nor any one for me—all would go by, and I never of it— fame, and fortune, and peace, even the necessities of life, ever mocking me.

[He draws closer to the fire, spreading his fingers to the flame. And while he is speaking, through the doorway MRS. MEGAN creeps in to listen.]

FERRAND. [Speaking on into the fire.] And I saw, Monsieur, so plain, that I should be vagabond all my days, and my days short, I dying in the end the death of a dog. I saw it all in my fever— clear as that flame—there was nothing for us others, but the herb of death. [WELLWYN takes his arm and presses it.] And so, Monsieur, I wished to die. I told no one of my fever. I lay out on the ground— it was verree cold. But they would not let me die on the roads of their parishes—they took me to an Institution, Monsieur, I looked in their eyes while I lay there, and I saw more clear than the blue heaven that they thought it best that I should die, although they would not let me. Then Monsieur, naturally my spirit rose, and I said: "So much the worse for you. I will live a little more." One is made like that! Life is sweet, Monsieur.

WELLWYN. Yes, Ferrand; Life is sweet.

FERRAND. That little girl you had here, Monsieur [WELLWYN nods.] in her too there is something of wild-savage. She must have joy of life. I have seen her since I came back. She has embraced the life of joy. It is not quite the same thing. [He lowers his voice.] She is lost, Monsieur, as a stone that sinks in water. I can see, if she cannot. [As WELLWYN makes a movement of distress.] Oh! I am not to blame for that, Monsieur. It had well begun before I knew her.

WELLWYN. Yes, yes—I was afraid of it, at the time.

[MRS. MEGAN turns silently, and slips away.]

FEERRAND. I do my best for her, Monsieur, but look at me! Besides, I am not good for her—it is not good for simple souls to be with those who see things clear. For the great part of mankind, to see anything—is fatal.

WELLWYN. Even for you, it seems.

FERRAND. No, Monsieur. To be so near to death has done me good; I shall not lack courage any more till the wind blows on my grave. Since I saw you, Monsieur, I have been in three Institutions. They are palaces. One may eat upon the floor—though it is true—for Kings—they eat too much of skilly there. One little thing they lack—those palaces. It is understanding of the 'uman heart. In them tame birds pluck wild birds naked.

WELLWYN. They mean well.

FERRAND. Ah! Monsieur, I am loafer, waster—what you like—for all that [bitterly] poverty is my only crime. If I were rich, should I not be simply veree original, 'ighly respected, with soul above commerce, travelling to see the world? And that young girl, would she not be "that charming ladee," "veree chic, you know!" And the old Tims—good old-fashioned gentleman—drinking his liquor well. Eh! bien—what are we now? Dark beasts, despised by all. That is life, Monsieur. [He stares into the fire.]

WELLWYN. We're our own enemies, Ferrand. I can afford it—you can't. Quite true!

FERRAND. [Earnestly.] Monsieur, do you know this? You are the sole being that can do us good—we hopeless ones.

WELLWYN. [Shaking his head.] Not a bit of it; I'm hopeless too.

FERRAND. [Eagerly.] Monsieur, it is just that. You understand. When we are with you we feel something—here—[he touches his heart.] If I had one prayer to make, it would be, Good God, give me to understand! Those sirs, with their theories, they can clean our skins and chain our 'abits—that soothes for them the aesthetic sense; it gives them too their good little importance. But our spirits they cannot touch, for they nevare understand. Without that, Monsieur, all is dry as a parched skin of orange.

WELLWYN. Don't be so bitter. Think of all the work they do!

FERRAND. Monsieur, of their industry I say nothing. They do a good work while they attend with their theories to the sick and the tame old, and the good unfortunate deserving. Above all to the little children. But, Monsieur, when all is done, there are always us hopeless ones. What can they do with me, Monsieur, with that girl, or with that old man? Ah! Monsieur, we, too, 'ave our qualities, we others—it wants you courage to undertake a career like mine, or like that young girl's. We wild ones—we know a thousand times more of life than ever will those sirs. They waste their time trying to make rooks white. Be kind to us if you will, or let us alone like Mees Ann, but do not try to change our skins. Leave us to live, or leave us to die when we like in the free air. If you do not wish of us, you have but to shut your pockets and—your doors—we shall die the faster.

WELLWYN. [With agitation.] But that, you know—we can't do—now can we?

FERRAND. If you cannot, how is it our fault? The harm we do to others—is it so much? If I am criminal, dangerous—shut me up! I would not pity myself—nevare. But we in whom something moves— like that flame, Monsieur, that cannot keep still—we others—we are not many—that must have motion in our lives, do not let them make us prisoners, with their theories, because we are not like them—it is life itself they would enclose! [He draws up his tattered figure, then bending over the fire again.] I ask your pardon; I am talking. If I could smoke, Monsieur!

[WELLWYN hands him a tobacco pouch; and he rolls a cigarette with his yellow-Stained fingers.]

FERRAND. The good God made me so that I would rather walk a whole month of nights, hungry, with the stars, than sit one single day making round business on an office stool! It is not to my advantage. I cannot help it that I am a vagabond. What would you have? It is stronger than me. [He looks suddenly at WELLWYN.] Monsieur, I say to you things I have never said.

WELLWYN. [Quietly.] Go on, go on. [There is silence.]

FERRAND. [Suddenly.] Monsieur! Are you really English? The English are so
          civilised.

WELLWYN. And am I not?

FERRAND. You treat me like a brother.

[WELLWYN has turned towards the street door at a sound of feet, and the clamour of voices.]

TIMSON. [From the street.] Take her in 'ere. I knows 'im.

[Through the open doorway come a POLICE CONSTABLE and a LOAFER,
bearing between them the limp white faced form of MRS. MEGAN, hatless and
with drowned hair, enveloped in the policeman's waterproof. Some curious persons bring up the rear, jostling in the doorway, among whom is TIMSON carrying in his hands the policeman's dripping waterproof leg pieces.]

FERRAND. [Starting forward.] Monsieur, it is that little girl!

WELLWYN. What's happened? Constable! What's happened!

[The CONSTABLE and LOAFER have laid the body down on the dais; with
WELLWYN and FERRAND they stand bending over her.]

CONSTABLE. 'Tempted sooicide, sir; but she hadn't been in the water 'arf a
minute when I got hold of her. [He bends lower.] Can't understand her collapsin'
like this.

WELLWYN. [Feeling her heart.] I don't feel anything.

FERRAND. [In a voice sharpened by emotion.] Let me try, Monsieur.

CONSTABLE. [Touching his arm.] You keep off, my lad.

WELLWYN. No, constable—let him. He's her friend.

CONSTABLE. [Releasing FERRAND—to the LOAFER.] Here you! Cut off
          for a doctor-sharp now! [He pushes back the curious persons.]
          Now then, stand away there, please—we can't have you round
          the body. Keep back—Clear out, now!

[He slowly moves them back, and at last shepherds them through the door and shuts it on them, TIMSON being last.]

FERRAND. The rum!

[WELLWYN fetches the decanter. With the little there is left FERRAND chafes the girl's hands and forehead, and pours some between her lips. But there is no response from the inert body.]

FERRAND. Her soul is still away, Monsieur!

[WELLWYN, seizing the decanter, pours into it tea and boiling water.]

CONSTABLE. It's never drownin', sir—her head was hardly under; I was on to her like knife.

FERRAND. [Rubbing her feet.] She has not yet her philosophy, Monsieur; at the beginning they often try. If she is dead! [In a voice of awed rapture.] What fortune!

CONSTABLE. [With puzzled sadness.] True enough, sir—that! We'd just begun to know 'er. If she 'as been taken—her best friends couldn't wish 'er better.

WELLWYN. [Applying the decanter to her dips.] Poor little thing! I'll try this hot tea.

FERRAND. [Whispering.] 'La mort—le grand ami!'

WELLWYN. Look! Look at her! She's coming round!

[A faint tremor passes over MRS. MEGAN's body. He again applies the hot drink to her mouth. She stirs and gulps.]

CONSTABLE. [With intense relief.] That's brave! Good lass! She'll pick up now, sir.

[Then, seeing that TIMSON and the curious persons have again opened the door, he drives them out, and stands with his back against it. MRS. MEGAN comes to herself.]

WELLWYN. [Sitting on the dais and supporting her—as if to a child.] There
   you are, my dear. There, there—better now! That's right. Drink a little
   more of this tea.

[MRS. MEGAN drinks from the decanter.]

FERRAND. [Rising.] Bring her to the fire, Monsieur.

[They take her to the fire and seat her on the little stool. From the moment of her
restored animation FERRAND has resumed his air of cynical detachment, and
now stands apart with arms folded, watching.]

WELLWYN. Feeling better, my child?

MRS. MEGAN. Yes.

WELLWYN. That's good. That's good. Now, how was it? Um?

MRS. MEGAN. I dunno. [She shivers.] I was standin' here just now when you
   was talkin', and when I heard 'im, it cam' over me to do it—
   like.

WELLWYN. Ah, yes I know.

MRS. MEGAN. I didn't seem no good to meself nor any one. But when I got
   in the water, I didn't want to any more. It was cold in there.

WELLWYN. Have you been having such a bad time of it?

MRS. MEGAN. Yes. And listenin' to him upset me. [She signs with her head
   at FERRAND.] I feel better now I've been in the water. [She
   smiles and shivers.]

WELLWYN. There, there! Shivery? Like to walk up and down a little?

[They begin walking together up and down.]

WELLWYN. Beastly when your head goes under?

MRS. MEGAN. Yes. It frightened me. I thought I wouldn't come up again.

WELLWYN. I know—sort of world without end, wasn't it? What did you think of, um?

MRS. MEGAN. I wished I 'adn't jumped—an' I thought of my baby— that died—and—[in a rather surprised voice] and I thought of d-dancin'.

[Her mouth quivers, her face puckers, she gives a choke and a little sob.]

WELLWYN. [Stopping and stroking her.] There, there—there!

[For a moment her face is buried in his sleeve, then she recovers herself.]

MRS. MEGAN. Then 'e got hold o' me, an' pulled me out.

WELLWYN. Ah! what a comfort—um?

MRS. MEGAN. Yes. The water got into me mouth.

[They walk again.] I wouldn't have gone to do it but for him. [She looks towards FERRAND.] His talk made me feel all funny, as if people wanted me to.

WELLWYN. My dear child! Don't think such things! As if anyone would——!

MRS. MEGAN. [Stolidly.] I thought they did. They used to look at me so sometimes, where I was before I ran away—I couldn't stop there, you know.

WELLWYN. Too cooped-up?

MRS. MEGAN. Yes. No life at all, it wasn't—not after sellin' flowers, I'd rather be doin' what I am.

WELLWYN. Ah! Well-it's all over, now! How d'you feel—eh? Better?

MRS. MEGAN. Yes. I feels all right now.

[She sits up again on the little stool before the fire.]

WELLWYN. No shivers, and no aches; quite comfy?

MRS. MEGAN. Yes.

WELLWYN. That's a blessing. All well, now, Constable—thank you!

CONSTABLE. [Who has remained discreetly apart at the door-cordially.] First
              rate, sir! That's capital! [He approaches and scrutinises MRS.
              MEGAN.] Right as rain, eh, my girl?

MRS. MEGAN. [Shrinking a little.] Yes.

CONSTABLE. That's fine. Then I think perhaps, for 'er sake, sir, the sooner we
              move on and get her a change o' clothin', the better.

WELLWYN. Oh! don't bother about that—I'll send round for my daughter—
              we'll manage for her here.

CONSTABLE. Very kind of you, I'm sure, sir. But [with embarrassment] she
              seems all right. She'll get every attention at the station.

WELLWYN. But I assure you, we don't mind at all; we'll take the greatest care
              of her.

CONSTABLE. [Still more embarrassed.] Well, sir, of course, I'm thinkin' of—
              I'm afraid I can't depart from the usual course.

WELLWYN. [Sharply.] What! But-oh! No! No! That'll be all right, Constable!
              That'll be all right! I assure you.

CONSTABLE. [With more decision.] I'll have to charge her, sir.

WELLWYN. Good God! You don't mean to say the poor little thing has got to
              be——

CONSTABLE. [Consulting with him.] Well, sir, we can't get over the facts, can
              we? There it is! You know what sooicide amounts to— it's an
              awkward job.

WELLWYN. [Calming himself with an effort.] But look here, Constable, as a
              reasonable man—This poor wretched little girl—you know what
              that life means better than anyone! Why! It's to her credit to try
              and jump out of it!

[The CONSTABLE shakes his head.]

WELLWYN.   You said yourself her best friends couldn't wish her better!
                [Dropping his voice still more.] Everybody feels it! The Vicar was
                here a few minutes ago saying the very same thing—the Vicar,
                Constable! [The CONSTABLE shakes his head.] Ah! now, look
                here, I know something of her. Nothing can be done with her. We
                all admit it. Don't you see? Well, then hang it—you needn't go
                and make fools of us all by——

FERRAND. Monsieur, it is the first of April.

CONSTABLE. [With a sharp glance at him.] Can't neglect me duty, sir; that's
                impossible.

WELLWYN.   Look here! She—slipped. She's been telling me. Come,
                Constable, there's a good fellow. May be the making of her, this.

CONSTABLE. I quite appreciate your good 'eart, sir, an' you make it very 'ard
                for me—but, come now! I put it to you as a gentleman, would
                you go back on yer duty if you was me?

[WELLWYN raises his hat, and plunges his fingers through and through his hair.]

WELLWYN. Well! God in heaven! Of all the d——d topsy—turvy—! Not a soul
                in the world wants her alive—and now she's to be prosecuted for
                trying to be where everyone wishes her.

CONSTABLE. Come, sir, come! Be a man!

[Throughout all this MRS. MEGAN has sat stolidly before the fire, but as FER-
RAND suddenly steps forward she looks up at him.]

FERRAND. Do not grieve, Monsieur! This will give her courage. There is noth-
                ing that gives more courage than to see the irony of things. [He
                touches MRS. MEGAN'S shoulder.] Go, my child; it will do you
                good.

[MRS. MEGAN rises, and looks at him dazedly.]

CONSTABLE. [Coming forward, and taking her by the hand.] That's my good
          lass. Come along! We won't hurt you.

MRS. MEGAN. I don't want to go. They'll stare at me.

CONSTABLE. [Comforting.] Not they! I'll see to that.

WELLWYN. [Very upset.] Take her in a cab, Constable, if you must- -for God's
          sake! [He pulls out a shilling.] Here!

CONSTABLE. [Taking the shilling.] I will, sir, certainly. Don't think I want
          to——

WELLWYN. No, no, I know. You're a good sort.

CONSTABLE. [Comfortable.] Don't you take on, sir. It's her first try; they
          won't be hard on 'er. Like as not only bind 'er over in her own
          recogs. not to do it again. Come, my dear.

MRS. MEGAN. [Trying to free herself from the policeman's cloak.] I want to
          take this off. It looks so funny.

[As she speaks the door is opened by ANN; behind whom is dimly seen the form
of old TIMSON, still heading the curious persons.]

ANN. [Looking from one to the other in amazement.] What is it? What's hap-
          pened? Daddy!

FERRAND. [Out of the silence.] It is nothing, Ma'moiselle! She has failed to
          drown herself. They run her in a little.

WELLWYN. Lend her your jacket, my dear; she'll catch her death.

[ANN, feeling MRS. MEGAN's arm, strips of her jacket, and helps her into it
without a word.]

CONSTABLE. [Donning his cloak.] Thank you. Miss—very good of you, I'm
          sure.

MRS. MEGAN. [Mazed.] It's warm!

[She gives them all a last half-smiling look, and Passes with the CONSTABLE through the doorway.]

FERRAND. That makes the third of us, Monsieur. We are not in luck. To wish us dead, it seems, is easier than to let us die.

[He looks at ANN, who is standing with her eyes fixed on her father. WELL-WYN has taken from his pocket a visiting card.]

WELLWYN. [To FERRAND.] Here quick; take this, run after her! When they've done with her tell her to come to us.

FERRAND. [Taking the card, and reading the address.] "No. 7, Haven House, Flight Street!" Rely on me, Monsieur—I will bring her myself to call on you. 'Au revoir, mon bon Monsieur'!

[He bends over WELLWYN's hand; then, with a bow to ANN goes out; his tattered figure can be seen through the window, passing in the wind. WELLWYN turns back to the fire. The figure of TIMSON advances into the doorway, no longer holding in either hand a waterproof leg-piece.]

TIMSON. [In a croaky voice.] Sir!

WELLWYN. What—you, Timson?

TIMSON. On me larst legs, sir. 'Ere! You can see 'em for yerself! Shawn't trouble yer long....

WELLWYN. [After a long and desperate stare.] Not now—TIMSON not now! Take this! [He takes out another card, and hands it to TIMSON] Some other time.

TIMSON. [Taking the card.] Yer new address! You are a gen'leman. [He lurches slowly away.]

[ANN shuts the street door and sets her back against it. The rumble of the approaching van is heard outside. It ceases.]

ANN. [In a fateful voice.] Daddy! [They stare at each other.] Do you know what you've done? Given your card to those six rotters.

WELLWYN. [With a blank stare.] Six?

ANN. [Staring round the naked room.] What was the good of this?

WELLWYN. [Following her eyes——very gravely.] Ann! It is stronger than me.

[Without a word ANN opens the door, and walks straight out. With a heavy sigh, WELLWYN sinks down on the little stool before the fire. The three humble-men come in.]

CHIEF HUMBLE-MAN. [In an attitude of expectation.] This is the larst of it, sir.

WELLWYN. Oh! Ah! yes!

[He gives them money; then something seems to strike him, and he exhibits certain signs of vexation. Suddenly he recovers, looks from one to the other, and then at the tea things. A faint smile comes on his face.]

WELLWYN. You can finish the decanter.

[He goes out in haste.]

CHIEF HUMBLE-MAN. [Clinking the coins.] Third time of arskin'! April fool! Not 'arf! Good old pigeon!

SECOND HUMBLE-MAN. 'Uman being, I call 'im.

CHIEF HUMBLE-MAN. [Taking the three glasses from the last packing-case, and pouring very equally into them.] That's right. Tell you wot, I'd never 'a touched this unless 'e'd told me to, I wouldn't—not with 'im.

SECOND HUMBLE-MAN. Ditto to that! This is a bit of orl right! [Raising his glass.] Good luck!

THIRD HUMBLE-MAN. Same 'ere!

[Simultaneously they place their lips smartly against the liquor, and at once let fall their faces and their glasses.]

CHIEF HUMBLE-MAN. [With great solemnity.] Crikey! Bill! Tea! .....'E's got
                us!

[The stage is blotted dark.]

Curtain.

THE MOB

A PLAY IN FOUR ACTS

PERSONS OF THE PLAY

STEPHEN MORE, Member of Parliament
KATHERINE, his wife
OLIVE, their little daughter
THE DEAN OF STOUR, Katherine's uncle
GENERAL SIR JOHN JULIAN, her father
CAPTAIN HUBERT JULIAN, her brother
HELEN, his wife
EDWARD MENDIP, editor of "The Parthenon"
ALAN STEEL, More's secretary
JAMES HOME, architect
CHARLES SHELDER, Solicitor   A deputation of More's
MARK WACE, bookseller   constituents
WILLIAM BANNING, manufacturer
NURSE WREFORD
WREFORD (her son), Hubert's orderly
HIS SWEETHEART
THE FOOTMAN HENRY
A DOORKEEPER
SOME BLACK-COATED GENTLEMEN
A STUDENT
A GIRL

A MOB

ACT III.
> SCENE I. An alley at the back of a suburban theatre.
> SCENE II. Katherine's bedroom.

ACT IV.   The dining-room of More's house, late afternoon.

AFTERMATH. The corner of a square, at dawn.

Between ACTS I and II some days elapse.
Between ACTS II and III three months.
Between ACT III SCENE I and ACT III SCENE II no time.
Between ACTS III and IV a few hours.
Between ACTS IV and AFTERMATH an indefinite period.

ACT I

It is half-past nine of a July evening. In a dining-room lighted by sconces, and apparelled in wall-paper, carpet, and curtains of deep vivid blue, the large French windows between two columns are open on to a wide terrace, beyond which are seen trees in darkness, and distant shapes of lighted houses. On one side is a bay window, over which curtains are partly drawn. Opposite to this window is a door leading into the hall. At an oval rosewood table, set with silver, flowers, fruit, and wine, six people are seated after dinner. Back to the bay window is STEPHEN MORE, the host, a man of forty, with a fine-cut face, a rather charming smile, and the eyes of an idealist; to his right, SIR, JOHN JULIAN, an old soldier, with thin brown features, and grey moustaches; to SIR JOHN's right, his brother, the DEAN OF STOUR, a tall, dark, ascetic-looking Churchman: to his right KATHERINE is leaning forward, her elbows on the table, and her chin on her hands, staring across at her husband; to her right sits EDWARD MENDIP, a pale man of forty-five, very bald, with a fine forehead, and on his clear-cut lips a smile that shows his teeth; between him and MORE is HELEN JULIAN, a pretty dark-haired young woman, absorbed in thoughts of her own. The voices are tuned to the pitch of heated discussion, as the curtain rises.

THE DEAN. I disagree with you, Stephen; absolutely, entirely disagree.

MORE. I can't help it.

MENDIP. Remember a certain war, Stephen! Were your chivalrous notions any good, then? And, what was winked at in an obscure young Member is anathema for an Under Secretary of State. You can't afford——

MORE. To follow my conscience? That's new, Mendip.

MENDIP. Idealism can be out of place, my friend.

THE DEAN. The Government is dealing here with a wild lawless race, on whom I must say I think sentiment is rather wasted.

MORE. God made them, Dean.

MENDIP. I have my doubts.

THE DEAN. They have proved themselves faithless. We have the right to chastise.

MORE. If I hit a little man in the eye, and he hits me back, have I the right to chastise him?

SIR JOHN. We didn't begin this business.

MORE. What! With our missionaries and our trading?

THE DEAN. It is news indeed that the work of civilization may be justifiably met by murder. Have you forgotten Glaive and Morlinson?

SIR JOHN. Yes. And that poor fellow Groome and his wife?

MORE. They went into a wild country, against the feeling of the tribes, on their own business. What has the nation to do with the mishaps of gamblers?

SIR JOHN. We can't stand by and see our own flesh and blood ill-treated!

THE DEAN. Does our rule bring blessing—or does it not, Stephen?

MORE. Sometimes; but with all my soul I deny the fantastic superstition that our rule can benefit a people like this, a nation of one race, as different from ourselves as dark from light—in colour, religion, every mortal thing. We can only pervert their natural instincts.

THE DEAN. That to me is an unintelligible point of view.

MENDIP. Go into that philosophy of yours a little deeper, Stephen— it spells stagnation. There are no fixed stars on this earth. Nations can't let each other alone.

MORE. Big ones could let little ones alone.

MENDIP. If they could there'd be no big ones. My dear fellow, we know little nations are your hobby, but surely office should have toned you down.

SIR JOHN. I've served my country fifty years, and I say she is not in the wrong.

MORE. I hope to serve her fifty, Sir John, and I say she is.

MENDIP. There are moments when such things can't be said, More.

MORE. They'll be said by me to-night, Mendip.

MENDIP. In the House?

[MORE nods.]

KATHERINE. Stephen!

MENDIP. Mrs. More, you mustn't let him. It's madness.

MORE. [Rising] You can tell people that to-morrow, Mendip. Give it a leader in 'The Parthenon'.

MENDIP. Political lunacy! No man in your position has a right to fly out like this at the eleventh hour.

MORE. I've made no secret of my feelings all along. I'm against this war, and against the annexation we all know it will lead to.

MENDIP. My dear fellow! Don't be so Quixotic! We shall have war within the next twenty-four hours, and nothing you can do will stop it.

HELEN. Oh! No!

MENDIP. I'm afraid so, Mrs. Hubert.

SIR JOHN. Not a doubt of it, Helen.

MENDIP. [TO MORE] And you mean to charge the windmill?

[MORE nods.]

MENDIP. 'C'est magnifique'!

MORE. I'm not out for advertisement.

MENDIP. You will get it!

MORE. Must speak the truth sometimes, even at that risk.

SIR JOHN. It is not the truth.

MENDIP. The greater the truth the greater the libel, and the greater the resentment of the person libelled.

THE DEAN. [Trying to bring matters to a blander level] My dear Stephen, even
if you were right—which I deny—about the initial merits, there
surely comes a point where the individual conscience must resign
it self to the country's feeling. This has become a question of
national honour.

SIR JOHN. Well said, James!

MORE. Nations are bad judges of their honour, Dean.

THE DEAN. I shall not follow you there.

MORE. No. It's an awkward word.

KATHERINE. [Stopping THE DEAN] Uncle James! Please!

[MORE looks at her intently.]

SIR JOHN. So you're going to put yourself at the head of the cranks, ruin your
career, and make me ashamed that you're my son-in-law?

MORE. Is a man only to hold beliefs when they're popular? You've stood up to be shot at often enough, Sir John.

SIR JOHN. Never by my country! Your speech will be in all the foreign press-trust 'em for seizing on anything against us. A show-up before other countries——!

MORE. You admit the show-up?

SIR JOHN. I do not, sir.

THE DEAN. The position has become impossible. The state of things out there must be put an end to once for all! Come, Katherine, back us up!

MORE. My country, right or wrong! Guilty—still my country!

MENDIP. That begs the question.

[KATHERINE rises. THE DEAN, too, stands up.]

THE DEAN. [In a low voice] 'Quem Deus volt perdere'——!

SIR JOHN. Unpatriotic!

MORE. I'll have no truck with tyranny.

KATHERINE. Father doesn't admit tyranny. Nor do any of us, Stephen.

HUBERT JULIAN, a tall Soldier-like man, has come in.

HELEN. Hubert!

[She gets up and goes to him, and they talk together near the door.]

SIR JOHN. What in God's name is your idea? We've forborne long enough, in all conscience.

MORE. Sir John, we great Powers have got to change our ways in dealing with weaker nations. The very dogs can give us lessons— watch a big dog with a little one.

MENDIP. No, no, these things are not so simple as all that.

MORE. There's no reason in the world, Mendip, why the rules of chivalry should
not apply to nations at least as well as to——dogs.

MENDIP. My dear friend, are you to become that hapless kind of outcast, a
champion of lost causes?

MORE. This cause is not lost.

MENDIP. Right or wrong, as lost as ever was cause in all this world. There was
never a time when the word "patriotism" stirred mob sentiment as it
does now. 'Ware "Mob," Stephen——'ware "Mob"!

MORE. Because general sentiment's against me, I—a public man—am to deny
my faith? The point is not whether I'm right or wrong, Mendip, but
whether I'm to sneak out of my conviction because it's unpopular.

THE DEAN. I'm afraid I must go. [To KATHERINE] Good-night, my dear!
Ah! Hubert! [He greets HUBERT] Mr. Mendip, I go your way.
Can I drop you?

MENDIP. Thank you. Good-night, Mrs. More. Stop him! It's perdition.

[He and THE DEAN go out. KATHERINE puts her arm in HELEN'S, and
takes her out of the room. HUBERT remains standing by the door]

SIR JOHN. I knew your views were extreme in many ways, Stephen, but I never
thought the husband of my daughter would be a Peace-at-any-
price man!

MORE. I am not! But I prefer to fight some one my own size.

SIR JOHN. Well! I can only hope to God you'll come to your senses before you
commit the folly of this speech. I must get back to the War Office.
Good-night, Hubert.

HUBERT. Good-night, Father.

[SIR JOHN goes out. HUBERT stands motionless, dejected.]

HUBERT. We've got our orders.

MORE. What? When d'you sail?

HUBERT. At once.

MORE. Poor Helen!

HUBERT. Not married a year; pretty bad luck! [MORE touches his arm in sympathy] Well! We've got to put feelings in our pockets. Look here, Stephen—don't make that speech! Think of Katherine—with the Dad at the War Office, and me going out, and Ralph and old George out there already! You can't trust your tongue when you're hot about a thing.

MORE. I must speak, Hubert.

HUBERT. No, no! Bottle yourself up for to-night. The next few hours 'll see it begin. [MORE turns from him] If you don't care whether you mess up your own career—don't tear Katherine in two!

MORE. You're not shirking your duty because of your wife.

HUBERT. Well! You're riding for a fall, and a godless mucker it'll be. This'll be no picnic. We shall get some nasty knocks out there. Wait and see the feeling here when we've had a force or two cut up in those mountains. It's awful country. Those fellows have got modern arms, and are jolly good fighters. Do drop it, Stephen!

MORE. Must risk something, sometimes, Hubert—even in my profession!

[As he speaks, KATHERINE comes in.]

HUBERT. But it's hopeless, my dear chap—absolutely.

[MORE turns to the window, HUBERT to his sister—then with a gesture towards MORE, as though to leave the matter to her, he goes out.]

KATHERINE. Stephen! Are you really going to speak? [He nods] I ask you not.

MORE. You know my feeling.

KATHERINE. But it's our own country. We can't stand apart from it. You won't stop anything—only make people hate you. I can't bear that.

MORE. I tell you, Kit, some one must raise a voice. Two or three reverses—certain to come—and the whole country will go wild. And one more little nation will cease to live.

KATHERINE. If you believe in your country, you must believe that the more land and power she has, the better for the world.

MORE. Is that your faith?

KATHERINE. Yes.

MORE. I respect it; I even understand it; but—I can't hold it.

KATHERINE. But, Stephen, your speech will be a rallying cry to all the cranks, and every one who has a spite against the country. They'll make you their figurehead. [MORE smiles] They will. Your chance of the Cabinet will go—you may even have to resign your seat.

MORE. Dogs will bark. These things soon blow over.

KATHERINE. No, no! If you once begin a thing, you always go on; and what earthly good?

MORE. History won't say: "And this they did without a single protest from their public men!"

KATHERINE. There are plenty who——

MORE. Poets?

KATHERINE. Do you remember that day on our honeymoon, going up Ben Lawers? You were lying on your face in the heather; you said it was like kissing a loved woman. There was a lark singing—you said that was the voice of one's worship. The hills were very blue; that's why we had blue here, because it was the best dress of our country. You do love her.

MORE. Love her!

KATHERINE. You'd have done this for me—then.

MORE. Would you have asked me—then, Kit?

KATHERINE. Yes. The country's our country! Oh! Stephen, think what it'll
      be like for me—with Hubert and the other boys out there. And
      poor Helen, and Father! I beg you not to make this speech.

MORE. Kit! This isn't fair. Do you want me to feel myself a cur?

KATHERINE. [Breathless] I—I—almost feel you'll be a cur to do it [She looks
      at him, frightened by her own words. Then, as the footman
      HENRY has come in to clear the table—very low] I ask you not!

[He does not answer, and she goes out.]

MORE [To the servant] Later, please, Henry, later!

The servant retires. MORE still stands looking down at the dining-table; then
putting his hand to his throat, as if to free it from the grip of his collar, he pours
out a glass of water, and drinks it of. In the street, outside the bay window, two
street musicians, a harp and a violin, have taken up their stand, and after some
twangs and scrapes, break into music. MORE goes towards the sound, and draws
aside one curtain. After a moment, he returns to the table, and takes up the notes
of the speech. He is in an agony of indecision.

MORE. A cur!

He seems about to tear his notes across. Then, changing his mind, turns them
over and over, muttering. His voice gradually grows louder, till he is declaiming
to the empty room the peroration of his speech.

MORE. . . . We have arrogated to our land the title Champion of Freedom,
      Foe of Oppression. Is that indeed a bygone glory? Is it not worth some
      sacrifice of our pettier dignity, to avoid laying another stone upon its
      grave; to avoid placing before the searchlight eyes of History the spec-
      tacle of yet one more piece of national cynicism? We are about to force
      our will and our dominion on a race that has always been free, that

loves its country, and its independence, as much as ever we love ours. I cannot sit silent to-night and see this begin. As we are tender of our own land, so we should be of the lands of others. I love my country. It is because I love my country that I raise my voice. Warlike in spirit these people may be—but they have no chance against ourselves. And war on such, however agreeable to the blind moment, is odious to the future. The great heart of mankind ever beats in sense and sympathy with the weaker. It is against this great heart of mankind that we are going. In the name of Justice and Civilization we pursue this policy; but by Justice we shall hereafter be judged, and by Civilization—condemned.

While he is speaking, a little figure has flown along the terrace outside, in the direction of the music, but has stopped at the sound of his voice, and stands in the open window, listening—a dark-haired, dark-eyed child, in a blue dressing-gown caught up in her hand. The street musicians, having reached the end of a tune, are silent.

In the intensity of MORES feeling, a wine-glass, gripped too strongly, breaks and falls in pieces onto a finger-bowl. The child starts forward into the room.

MORE. Olive!

OLIVE. Who were you speaking to, Daddy?

MORE. [Staring at her] The wind, sweetheart!

OLIVE. There isn't any!

MORE. What blew you down, then?

OLIVE. [Mysteriously] The music. Did the wind break the wine-glass, or did it come in two in your hand?

MORE. Now my sprite! Upstairs again, before Nurse catches you. Fly! Fly!

OLIVE. Oh! no, Daddy! [With confidential fervour] It feels like things to-night!

MORE. You're right there!

OLIVE. [Pulling him down to her, and whispering] I must get back again in secret. H'sh!

She suddenly runs and wraps herself into one of the curtains of the bay window. A young man enters, with a note in his hand.

MORE. Hello, Steel!

[The street musicians have again begun to play.]

STEEL. From Sir John—by special messenger from the War Office.

MORE. [Reading the note] "The ball is opened."

He stands brooding over the note, and STEEL looks at him anxiously. He is a dark, sallow, thin-faced young man, with the eyes of one who can attach himself to people, and suffer with them.

STEEL. I'm glad it's begun, sir. It would have been an awful pity to have made that speech.

MORE. You too, Steel!

STEEL. I mean, if it's actually started——

MORE. [Tearing tie note across] Yes. Keep that to yourself.

STEEL. Do you want me any more?

MORE takes from his breast pocket some papers, and pitches them down on the bureau.

MORE. Answer these.

STEEL. [Going to the bureau] Fetherby was simply sickening. [He begins to write. Struggle has begun again in MORE] Not the faintest recognition that there are two sides to it.

MORE gives him a quick look, goes quietly to the dining-table and picks up his sheaf of notes. Hiding them with his sleeve, he goes back to the window, where he again stands hesitating.

STEEL. Chief gem: [Imitating] "We must show Impudence at last that Dignity is not asleep!"

MORE. [Moving out on to the terrace] Nice quiet night!

STEEL. This to the Cottage Hospital—shall I say you will preside?

MORE. No.

STEEL writes; then looking up and seeing that MORE is no longer there, he goes to the window, looks to right and left, returns to the bureau, and is about to sit down again when a thought seems to strike him with consternation. He goes again to the window. Then snatching up his hat, he passes hurriedly out along the terrace. As he vanishes, KATHERINE comes in from the hall. After looking out on to the terrace she goes to the bay window; stands there listening; then comes restlessly back into the room. OLIVE, creeping quietly from behind the curtain, clasps her round the waist.

KATHERINE. O my darling! How you startled me! What are you doing down here, you wicked little sinner!

OLIVE. I explained all that to Daddy. We needn't go into it again, need we?

KATHERINE. Where is Daddy?

OLIVE. Gone.

KATHERINE. When?

OLIVE. Oh! only just, and Mr. Steel went after him like a rabbit. [The music stops] They haven't been paid, you know.

KATHERINE. Now, go up at once. I can't think how you got down here.

OLIVE. I can. [Wheedling] If you pay them, Mummy, they're sure to play another.

KATHERINE. Well, give them that! One more only.

She gives OLIVE a coin, who runs with it to the bay window, opens the aide casement, and calls to the musicians.

OLIVE. Catch, please! And would you play just one more?

She returns from the window, and seeing her mother lost in thought, rubs herself against her.

OLIVE. Have you got an ache?

KATHARINE. Right through me, darling!

OLIVE. Oh!

[The musicians strike up a dance.]

OLIVE. Oh! Mummy! I must just dance!

She kicks off her lisle blue shoes, and begins dancing. While she is capering HUBERT comes in from the hall. He stands watching his little niece for a minute, and KATHERINE looks at him.

HUBERT. Stephen gone!

KATHERINE. Yes—stop, Olive!

OLIVE. Are you good at my sort of dancing, Uncle?

HUBERT. Yes, chick—awfully!

KATHERINE. Now, Olive!

The musicians have suddenly broken off in the middle of a bar. From the street comes the noise of distant shouting.

OLIVE. Listen, Uncle! Isn't it a particular noise?

HUBERT and KATHERINE listen with all their might, and OLIVE stares at their faces. HUBERT goes to the window. The sound comes nearer. The shouted words are faintly heard: "Pyper—— war——our force crosses frontier—sharp fightin'——pyper."

KATHERINE. [Breathless] Yes! It is.

The street cry is heard again in two distant voices coming from different directions: "War—pyper—sharp fightin' on the frontier—pyper."

KATHERINE. Shut out those ghouls!

As HUBERT closes the window, NURSE WREFORD comes in from the hall. She is an elderly woman endowed with a motherly grimness. She fixes OLIVE with her eye, then suddenly becomes conscious of the street cry.

NURSE. Oh! don't say it's begun.

[HUBERT comes from the window.]

NURSE. Is the regiment to go, Mr. Hubert?

HUBERT. Yes, Nanny.

NURSE. Oh, dear! My boy!

KATHERINE. [Signing to where OLIVE stands with wide eyes] Nurse!

HUBERT. I'll look after him, Nurse.

NURSE. And him keepin' company. And you not married a year. Ah! Mr. Hubert, now do 'ee take care; you and him's both so rash.

HUBERT. Not I, Nurse!

NURSE looks long into his face, then lifts her finger, and beckons OLIVE.

OLIVE. [Perceiving new sensations before her, goes quietly] Good- night, Uncle! Nanny, d'you know why I was obliged to come down? [In a fervent whisper] It's a secret!

[As she passes with NURSE out into the hall, her voice is heard saying, "Do tell me all about the war."]

HUBERT. [Smothering emotion under a blunt manner] We sail on Friday, Kit. Be good to Helen, old girl.

KATHERINE. Oh! I wish——! Why—can't—women—fight?

HUBERT. Yes, it's bad for you, with Stephen taking it like this. But he'll come round now it's once begun.

KATHERINE shakes her head, then goes suddenly up to him, and throws her arms round his neck. It is as if all the feeling pent up in her were finding vent in this hug.

The door from the hall is opened, and SIR JOHN'S voice is heard outside: "All right, I'll find her."

KATHERINE. Father!

[SIR JOHN comes in.]

SIR JOHN. Stephen get my note? I sent it over the moment I got to the War Office.

KATHERINE. I expect so. [Seeing the torn note on the table] Yes.

SIR JOHN. They're shouting the news now. Thank God, I stopped that crazy speech of his in time.

KATHERINE. Have you stopped it?

SIR JOHN. What! He wouldn't be such a sublime donkey?

KATHERINE. I think that is just what he might be. [Going to the window] We shall know soon.

[SIR JOHN, after staring at her, goes up to HUBERT.]

SIR JOHN. Keep a good heart, my boy. The country's first. [They exchange a hand-squeeze.]

KATHERINE backs away from the window. STEEL has appeared there from the terrace, breathless from running.

STEEL. Mr. More back?

KATHERINE. No. Has he spoken?

STEEL. Yes.

KATHERINE. Against?

STEEL. Yes.

SIR JOHN. What? After!

SIR, JOHN stands rigid, then turns and marches straight out into the hall. At a sign from KATHERINE, HUBERT follows him.

KATHERINE. Yes, Mr. Steel?

STEEL. [Still breathless and agitated] We were here—he slipped away from me somehow. He must have gone straight down to the House. I ran over, but when I got in under the Gallery he was speaking already. They expected something—I never heard it so still there. He gripped them from the first word—deadly—every syllable. It got some of those fellows. But all the time, under the silence you could feel a—sort of—of—current going round. And then Sherratt—I think it was—began it, and you saw the anger rising in them; but he kept them down—his quietness! The feeling! I've never seen anything like it there.

Then there was a whisper all over the House that fighting had begun. And the whole thing broke out—regular riot—as if they could have killed him. Some one tried to drag him down by the coat-tails, but he shook him off, and went on. Then he stopped dead and walked out, and the noise dropped like a stone. The whole thing didn't last five minutes. It was fine, Mrs. More; like—like lava; he was the only cool person there. I wouldn't have missed it for anything—it was grand!

MORE has appeared on the terrace, behind STEEL.

KATHERINE. Good-night, Mr. Steel.

STEEL. [Startled] Oh!—Good-night!

He goes out into the hall. KATHERINE picks up OLIVE'S shoes, and stands clasping them to her breast. MORE comes in.

KATHERINE. You've cleared your conscience, then! I didn't think you'd hurt me so.

MORE does not answer, still living in the scene he has gone through, and KATHERINE goes a little nearer to him.

KATHERINE. I'm with the country, heart and soul, Stephen. I warn you.

While they stand in silence, facing each other, the footman, HENRY, enters from the hall.

FOOTMAN. These notes, sir, from the House of Commons.

KATHERINE. [Taking them] You can have the room directly.

[The FOOTMAN goes out.]

MORE. Open them!

KATHERINE opens one after the other, and lets them fall on the table.

MORE. Well?

KATHERINE. What you might expect. Three of your best friends. It's begun.

MORE. 'Ware Mob! [He gives a laugh] I must write to the Chief.

KATHERINE makes an impulsive movement towards him; then quietly goes to the bureau, sits down and takes up a pen.

KATHERINE. Let me make the rough draft. [She waits] Yes?

MORE. [Dictating]

"July 15th.

"DEAR SIR CHARLES, After my speech to-night, embodying my most unalterable convictions [KATHERINE turns and looks up at him, but he is staring straight before him, and with a little movement of despair she goes on writing] I have no alternative but to place the resignation of my Under-Secretaryship in your hands. My view, my faith in this matter may be wrong—but I am surely right to keep the flag of my faith flying. I imagine I need not enlarge on the reasons——"

THE CURTAIN FALLS.

ACT. II

Before noon a few days later. The open windows of the dining- room let in the sunlight. On the table a number of newspapers are littered. HELEN is sitting there, staring straight before her. A newspaper boy runs by outside calling out his wares. At the sound she gets up anti goes out on to the terrace. HUBERT enters from the hall. He goes at once to the terrace, and draws HELEN into the room.

HELEN. Is it true—what they're shouting?

HUBERT. Yes. Worse than we thought. They got our men all crumpled up in the Pass—guns helpless. Ghastly beginning.

HELEN. Oh, Hubert!

HUBERT. My dearest girl!

HELEN puts her face up to his. He kisses her. Then she turns quickly into the bay window. The door from the hall has been opened, and the footman, HENRY, comes in, preceding WREFORD and his sweetheart.

HENRY. Just wait here, will you, while I let Mrs. More know. [Catching sight of HUBERT] Beg pardon, sir!

HUBERT. All right, Henry. [Off-hand] Ah! Wreford! [The FOOTMAN with-
draws] So you've brought her round. That's good! My sister'll look
after her—don't you worry! Got everything packed? Three o'clock
sharp.

WREFORD. [A broad faced soldier, dressed in khaki with a certain look of dry
humour, now dimmed-speaking with a West Country burr] That's
right, zurr; all's ready.

HELEN has come out of the window, and is quietly looking at WREFORD and
the girl standing there so awkwardly.

HELEN. [Quietly] Take care of him, Wreford.

HUBERT. We'll take care of each other, won't we, Wreford?

HELEN. How long have you been engaged?

THE GIRL. [A pretty, indeterminate young woman] Six months. [She sobs suddenly.]

HELEN. Ah! He'll soon be safe back.

WREFORD. I'll owe 'em for this. [In a lacy voice to her] Don't 'ee now! Don't
'ee!

HELEN. No! Don't cry, please!

She stands struggling with her own lips, then goes out on to the terrace,
HUBERT following. WREFORD and his girl remain where they were, strange
and awkward, she muffling her sobs.

WREFORD. Don't 'ee go on like that, Nance; I'll 'ave to take you 'ome. That's
silly, now we've a-come. I might be dead and buried by the fuss
you're makin'. You've a-drove the lady away. See!

She regains control of herself as the door is opened and KATHERINE appears,
accompanied by OLIVE, who regards WREFORD with awe and curiosity, and
by NURSE, whose eyes are red, but whose manner is composed.

KATHERINE. My brother told me; so glad you've brought her.

WREFORD. Ye—as, M'. She feels me goin', a bit.

KATHERINE. Yes, yes! Still, it's for the country, isn't it?

THE GIRL. That's what Wreford keeps tellin' me. He've got to go—so it's no use upsettin' 'im. And of course I keep tellin' him I shall be all right.

NURSE. [Whose eyes never leave her son's face] And so you will.

THE GIRL. Wreford thought it'd comfort him to know you were interested in me. 'E's so 'ot-headed I'm sure somethin'll come to 'im.

KATHERINE. We've all got some one going. Are you coming to the docks? We must send them off in good spirits, you know.

OLIVE. Perhaps he'll get a medal.

KATHERINE. Olive!

NURSE. You wouldn't like for him to be hanging back, one of them anti-patriot, stop-the-war ones.

KATHERINE. [Quickly] Let me see—I have your address. [Holding out her hand to WREFORD] We'll look after her.

OLIVE. [In a loud whisper] Shall I lend him my toffee?

KATHERINE. If you like, dear. [To WREFORD] Now take care of my brother and yourself, and we'll take care of her.

WREFORD. Ye—as, M'.

He then looks rather wretchedly at his girl, as if the interview had not done so much for him as he had hoped. She drops a little curtsey. WREFORD salutes.

OLIVE. [Who has taken from the bureau a packet, places it in his hand] It's very nourishing!

WREFORD. Thank you, miss.

Then, nudging each other, and entangled in their feelings and the conventions, they pass out, shepherded by NURSE.

KATHERINE. Poor things!

OLIVE. What is an anti-patriot, stop-the-war one, Mummy?

KATHERINE. [Taking up a newspaper] Just a stupid name, dear—don't chatter!

OLIVE. But tell me just one weeny thing!

KATHERINE. Well?

OLIVE. Is Daddy one?

KATHERINE. Olive! How much do you know about this war?

OLIVE. They won't obey us properly. So we have to beat them, and take away their country. We shall, shan't we?

KATHERINE. Yes. But Daddy doesn't want us to; he doesn't think it fair, and he's been saying so. People are very angry with him.

OLIVE. Why isn't it fair? I suppose we're littler than them.

KATHERINE. No.

OLIVE. Oh! in history we always are. And we always win. That's why I like history. Which are you for, Mummy—us or them?

KATHERINE. Us.

OLIVE. Then I shall have to be. It's a pity we're not on the same side as Daddy. [KATHERINE shudders] Will they hurt him for not taking our side?

KATHERINE. I expect they will, Olive.

OLIVE. Then we shall have to be extra nice to him.

KATHERINE. If we can.

OLIVE. I can; I feel like it.

HELEN and HUBERT have returned along the terrace. Seeing KATHERINE and the child, HELEN passes on, but HUBERT comes in at the French window.

OLIVE. [Catching sight of him-softly] Is Uncle Hubert going to the front to-day? [KATHERINE nods] But not grandfather?

KATHERINE. No, dear.

OLIVE. That's lucky for them, isn't it?

HUBERT comes in. The presence of the child give him self- control.

HUBERT. Well, old girl, it's good-bye. [To OLIVE] What shall I bring you back, chick?

OLIVE. Are there shops at the front? I thought it was dangerous.

HUBERT. Not a bit.

OLIVE. [Disillusioned] Oh!

KATHERINE. Now, darling, give Uncle a good hug.

[Under cover of OLIVE's hug, KATHERINE repairs her courage.]

KATHERINE. The Dad and I'll be with you all in spirit. Good-bye, old boy!

They do not dare to kiss, and HUBERT goes out very stiff and straight, in the doorway passing STEEL, of whom he takes no notice. STEEL hesitates, and would go away.

KATHERINE. Come in, Mr. Steel.

STEEL. The deputation from Toulmin ought to be here, Mrs. More. It's twelve.

OLIVE. [Having made a little ball of newspaper-slyly] Mr. Steel, catch!

[She throws, and STEEL catches it in silence.]

KATHERINE. Go upstairs, won't you, darling?

OLIVE. Mayn't I read in the window, Mummy? Then I shall see if any soldiers
pass.

KATHERINE. No. You can go out on the terrace a little, and then you must go
up.

[OLIVE goes reluctantly out on to the terrace.]

STEEL. Awful news this morning of that Pass! And have you seen these?
[Reading from the newspaper] "We will have no truck with the jargon
of the degenerate who vilifies his country at such a moment. The
Member for Toulmin has earned for himself the contempt of all virile
patriots." [He takes up a second journal] "There is a certain type of
public man who, even at his own expense, cannot resist the itch to
advertise himself. We would, at moments of national crisis, muzzle
such persons, as we muzzle dogs that we suspect of incipient rabies . .
. ." They're in full cry after him!

KATHERINE. I mind much more all the creatures who are always flinging mud
at the country making him their hero suddenly! You know what's
in his mind?

STEEL. Oh! We must get him to give up that idea of lecturing everywhere
against the war, Mrs. More; we simply must.

KATHERINE. [Listening] The deputation's come. Go and fetch him, Mr. Steel.
He'll be in his room, at the House.

[STEEL goes out, and KATHERINE Stands at bay. In a moment he opens the
door again, to usher in the deputation; then retires. The four gentlemen have
entered as if conscious of grave issues. The first and most picturesque is JAMES
HOME, a thin, tall, grey-bearded man, with plentiful hair, contradictious eyebrows, and the half-shy, half-bold manners, alternately rude and over polite, of
one not accustomed to Society, yet secretly much taken with himself. He is
dressed in rough tweeds, with a red silk tie slung through a ring, and is closely followed by MARK WACE, a waxy, round-faced man of middle-age, with sleek dark
hair, traces of whisker, and a smooth way of continually rubbing his hands together, as if selling something to an esteemed customer. He is rather stout, wears dark

clothes, with a large gold chain. Following him comes CHARLES SHELDER, a lawyer of fifty, with a bald egg-shaped head, and gold pince-nez. He has little side whiskers, a leathery, yellowish skin, a rather kind but watchful and dubious face, and when he speaks seems to have a plum in his mouth, which arises from the preponderance of his shaven upper lip. Last of the deputation comes WILLIAM BANNING, an energetic-looking, square-shouldered, self-made country-man, between fifty and sixty, with grey moustaches, ruddy face, and lively brown eyes.]

KATHERINE. How do you do, Mr. Home?

HOME. [Bowing rather extravagantly over her hand, as if to show his independence of women's influence] Mrs. More! We hardly expected— This is an honour.

WACE. How do you do, Ma'am?

KATHERINE. And you, Mr. Wace?

WACE. Thank you, Ma'am, well indeed!

SHELDER. How d'you do, Mrs. More?

KATHERINE. Very well, thank you, Mr. Shelder.

BANNING. [Speaking with a rather broad country accent] This is but a poor occasion, Ma'am.

KATHERINE. Yes, Mr. Banning. Do sit down, gentlemen.

Seeing that they will not settle down while she is standing, she sits at the table. They gradually take their seats. Each member of the deputation in his own way is severely hanging back from any mention of the subject in hand; and KATHERINE as intent on drawing them to it.

KATHERINE. My husband will be here in two minutes. He's only over at the House.

SHELDER. [Who is of higher standing and education than the others] Charming position—this, Mrs. More! So near the—er—Centre of— Gravity um?

KATHERINE. I read the account of your second meeting at Toulmin.

BANNING. It's bad, Mrs. More—bad. There's no disguising it. That speech was moon-summer madness—Ah! it was! Take a lot of explaining away. Why did you let him, now? Why did you? Not your views, I'm sure!

[He looks at her, but for answer she only compresses her lips.]

BANNING. I tell you what hit me—what's hit the whole constituency— and that's his knowing we were over the frontier, fighting already, when he made it.

KATHERINE. What difference does it make if he did know?

HOME. Hitting below the belt—I should have thought—you'll pardon me!

BANNING. Till war's begun, Mrs. More, you're entitled to say what you like, no doubt—but after! That's going against your country. Ah! his speech was strong, you know—his speech was strong.

KATHERINE. He had made up his mind to speak. It was just an accident the news coming then.

[A silence.]

BANNING. Well, that's true, I suppose. What we really want is to make sure he won't break out again.

HOME. Very high-minded, his views of course—but, some consideration for the common herd. You'll pardon me!

SHELDER. We've come with the friendliest feelings, Mrs. More—but, you know, it won't do, this sort of thing!

WACE. We shall be able to smooth him down. Oh! surely.

BANNING. We'd be best perhaps not to mention about his knowing that fighting had begun.

[As he speaks, MORE enters through the French windows. They all rise.]

MORE. Good-morning, gentlemen.

[He comes down to the table, but does not offer to shake hands.]

BANNING. Well, Mr. More? You've made a woeful mistake, sir; I tell you to
your face.

MORE. As everybody else does, Banning. Sit down again, please.

[They gradually resume their seats, and MORE sits in KATHERINE's chair. She
alone remains standing leaning against the corner of the bay window, watching
their faces.]

BANNING. You've seen the morning's telegrams? I tell you, Mr. More—another reverse like that, and the flood will sweep you clean away. And
I'll not blame it. It's only flesh and blood.

MORE, Allow for the flesh and blood in me, too, please. When I spoke the other
night it was not without a certain feeling here. [He touches his heart.]

BANNING. But your attitude's so sudden—you'd not been going that length
when you were down with us in May.

MORE. Do me the justice to remember that even then I was against our policy.
It cost me three weeks' hard struggle to make up my mind to that
speech. One comes slowly to these things, Banning.

SHELDER. Case of conscience?

MORE. Such things have happened, Shelder, even in politics.

SHELDER. You see, our ideals are naturally low—how different from yours!

[MORE smiles.]

KATHERINE, who has drawn near her husband, moves back again, as if relieved
at this gleam of geniality. WACE rubs his hands.

BANNING. There's one thing you forget, sir. We send you to Parliament, rep-
resenting us; but you couldn't find six men in the whole constituency that would have bidden you to make that speech.

MORE. I'm sorry; but I can't help my convictions, Banning.

SHELDER. What was it the prophet was without in his own country?

BANNING. Ah! but we're not funning, Mr. More. I've never known feeling run
so high. The sentiment of both meetings was dead against you.
We've had showers of letters to headquarters. Some from very good
men—very warm friends of yours.

SHELDER. Come now! It's not too late. Let's go back and tell them you won't
do it again.

MORE. Muzzling order?

BANNING. [Bluntly] That's about it.

MORE. Give up my principles to save my Parliamentary skin. Then, indeed,
they might call me a degenerate! [He touches the newspapers on the
table.]

KATHERINE makes an abrupt and painful movement, then remains as still as
before, leaning against the corner of the window-seat.

BANNING. Well, Well! I know. But we don't ask you to take your words
back—we only want discretion in the future.

MORE. Conspiracy of silence! And have it said that a mob of newspapers have
hounded me to it.

BANNING. They won't say that of you.

SHELDER. My dear More, aren't you rather dropping to our level? With your
principles you ought not to care two straws what people say.

MORE. But I do. I can't betray the dignity and courage of public men. If popular opinion is to control the utterances of her politicians, then good-
bye indeed to this country!

BANNING. Come now! I won't say that your views weren't sound enough
before the fighting began. I've never liked our policy out there. But

our blood's being spilled; and that makes all the difference. I don't suppose they'd want me exactly, but I'd be ready to go myself. We'd all of us be ready. And we can't have the man that represents us talking wild, until we've licked these fellows. That's it in a nutshell.

MORE. I understand your feeling, Banning. I tender you my resignation. I can't and won't hold on where I'm not wanted.

BANNING. No, no, no! Don't do that! [His accent broader and broader] You've 'ad your say, and there it is. Coom now! You've been our Member nine years, in rain and shine.

SHELDER. We want to keep you, More. Come! Give us your promise- that's a good man!

MORE. I don't make cheap promises. You ask too much.

[There is silence, and they all look at MORE.]

SHELDER. There are very excellent reasons for the Government's policy.

MORE. There are always excellent reasons for having your way with the weak.

SHELDER. My dear More, how can you get up any enthusiasm for those cattle-lifting ruffians?

MORE. Better lift cattle than lift freedom.

SHELDER. Well, all we'll ask is that you shouldn't go about the country, saying so.

MORE. But that is just what I must do.

[Again they all look at MORE in consternation.]

HOME. Not down our way, you'll pardon me.

WACE. Really—really, sir——

SHELDER. The time of crusades is past, More.

MORE. Is it?

BANNING. Ah! no, but we don't want to part with you, Mr. More. It's a bitter thing, this, after three elections. Look at the 'uman side of it! To speak ill of your country when there's been a disaster like this terrible business in the Pass. There's your own wife. I see her brother's regiment's to start this very afternoon. Come now—how must she feel?

MORE breaks away to the bay window. The DEPUTATION exchange glances.

MORE. [Turning] To try to muzzle me like this—is going too far.

BANNING. We just want to put you out of temptation.

MORE. I've held my seat with you in all weathers for nine years. You've all been bricks to me. My heart's in my work, Banning; I'm not eager to undergo political eclipse at forty.

SHELDER. Just so—we don't want to see you in that quandary.

BANNING. It'd be no friendliness to give you a wrong impression of the state of feeling. Silence—till the bitterness is overpast; there's naught else for it, Mr. More, while you feel as you do. That tongue of yours! Come! You owe us something. You're a big man; it's the big view you ought to take.

MORE. I am trying to.

HOME. And what precisely is your view—you'll pardon my asking?

MORE. [Turning on him] Mr. Home a great country such as ours—is trustee for the highest sentiments of mankind. Do these few outrages justify us in stealing the freedom of this little people?

BANNING. Steal—their freedom! That's rather running before the hounds.

MORE. Ah, Banning! now we come to it. In your hearts you're none of you for that—neither by force nor fraud. And yet you all know that we've gone in there to stay, as we've gone into other lands—as all we big Powers go into other lands, when they're little and weak. The Prime Minister's words the other night were these: "If we are forced to spend this blood and money now, we must never again be forced." What does that mean but swallowing this country?

SHELDER. Well, and quite frankly, it'd be no bad thing.

HOME. We don't want their wretched country—we're forced.

MORE. We are not forced.

SHELDER. My dear More, what is civilization but the logical, inevitable swallowing up of the lower by the higher types of man? And what else will it be here?

MORE. We shall not agree there, Shelder; and we might argue it all day. But the point is, not whether you or I are right—the point is: What is a man who holds a faith with all his heart to do? Please tell me.

[There is a silence.]

BANNING. [Simply] I was just thinkin' of those poor fellows in the Pass.

MORE. I can see them, as well as you, Banning. But, imagine! Up in our own country—the Black Valley—twelve hundred foreign devils dead and dying—the crows busy over them—in our own country, our own valley—ours—ours—violated. Would you care about "the poor fellows" in that Pass?—Invading, stealing dogs! Kill them—kill them! You would, and I would, too!

The passion of those words touches and grips as no arguments could; and they are silent.

MORE. Well! What's the difference out there? I'm not so inhuman as not to want to see this disaster in the Pass wiped out. But once that's done, in spite of my affection for you; my ambitions, and they're not few; [Very low] in spite of my own wife's feeling, I must be free to raise my voice against this war.

BANNING. [Speaking slowly, consulting the others, as it were, with his eyes] Mr. More, there's no man I respect more than yourself. I can't tell what they'll say down there when we go back; but I, for one, don't feel it in me to take a hand in pressing you farther against your faith.

SHELDER. We don't deny that—that you have a case of sorts.

WACE. No—surely.

SHELDER. A—man should be free, I suppose, to hold his own opinions.

MORE. Thank you, Shelder.

BANNING. Well! well! We must take you as you are; but it's a rare pity; there'll be a lot of trouble——

His eyes light on Honk who is leaning forward with hand raised to his ear, listening. Very faint, from far in the distance, there is heard a skirling sound. All become conscious of it, all listen.

HOME. [Suddenly] Bagpipes!

The figure of OLIVE flies past the window, out on the terrace. KATHERINE turns, as if to follow her.

SHELDER. Highlanders!

[He rises. KATHERINE goes quickly out on to the terrace. One by one they all follow to the window. One by one go out on to the terrace, till MORE is left alone. He turns to the bay window. The music is swelling, coming nearer. MORE leaves the window—his face distorted by the strafe of his emotions. He paces the room, taking, in some sort, the rhythm of the march.]

[Slowly the music dies away in the distance to a drum-tap and the tramp of a company. MORE stops at the table, covering his eyes with his hands.]

[The DEPUTATION troop back across the terrace, and come in at the French windows. Their faces and manners have quite changed. KATHERINE follows them as far as the window.]

HOME. [In a strange, almost threatening voice] It won't do, Mr. More. Give us your word, to hold your peace!

SHELDER. Come! More.

WACE. Yes, indeed—indeed!

BANNING. We must have it.

MORE. [Without lifting his head] I—I——

The drum-tap of a regiment marching is heard.

BANNING. Can you hear that go by, man—when your country's just been
            struck?

Now comes the scale and mutter of a following crowd.

MORE. I give you——

Then, sharp and clear above all other sounds, the words: "Give the beggars hell,
boys!" "Wipe your feet on their dirty country!" "Don't leave 'em a gory acre!
"And a burst of hoarse cheering.

MORE. [Flinging up his head] That's reality! By Heaven! No!

KATHERINE. Oh!

SHELDER. In that case, we'll go.

BANNING. You mean it? You lose us, then!

[MORE bows.]

HOME. Good riddance! [Venomously—his eyes darting between MORE and
KATHERINE] Go and stump the country! Find out what they think of you!
You'll pardon me!

One by one, without a word, only BANNING looking back, they pass out into
the hall. MORE sits down at the table before the pile of newspapers. KATHER-
INE, in the window, never moves. OLIVE comes along the terrace to her mother.

OLIVE. They were nice ones! Such a lot of dirty people following, and some
            quite clean, Mummy. [Conscious from her mother's face that some-

thing is very wrong, she looks at her father, and then steals up to his side] Uncle Hubert's gone, Daddy; and Auntie Helen's crying. And—look at Mummy!

[MORE raises his head and looks.]

OLIVE. Do be on our side! Do!

She rubs her cheek against his. Feeling that he does not rub his cheek against hers, OLIVE stands away, and looks from him to her mother in wonder.

THE CURTAIN FALLS

ACT III

SCENE I

A cobble-stoned alley, without pavement, behind a suburban theatre. The tall, blind, dingy-yellowish wall of the building is plastered with the tattered remnants of old entertainment bills, and the words: "To Let," and with several torn, and one still virgin placard, containing this announcement: "Stop-the- War Meeting, October 1st. Addresses by STEPHEN MORE, Esq., and others." The alley is plentifully strewn with refuse and scraps of paper. Three stone steps, inset, lead to the stage door. It is a dark night, and a street lamp close to the wall throws all the light there is. A faint, confused murmur, as of distant hooting is heard. Suddenly a boy comes running, then two rough girls hurry past in the direction of the sound; and the alley is again deserted. The stage door opens, and a door-keeper, poking his head out, looks up and down. He withdraws, but in a second reappears, preceding three black-coated gentlemen.

DOORKEEPER. It's all clear. You can get away down here, gentlemen. Keep to the left, then sharp to the right, round the corner.

THE THREE. [Dusting themselves, and settling their ties] Thanks, very much! Thanks!

FIRST BLACK-COATED GENTLEMAN. Where's More? Isn't he coming?

They are joined by a fourth black-coated GENTLEMAN.

FOURTH BLACK-COATED GENTLEMAN. Just behind. [TO the DOOR-KEEPER] Thanks.

They hurry away. The DOORKEEPER retires. Another boy runs past. Then the door opens again. STEEL and MORE come out.

MORE stands hesitating on the steps; then turns as if to go back.

STEEL. Come along, sir, come!

MORE. It sticks in my gizzard, Steel.

STEEL. [Running his arm through MORE'S, and almost dragging him down the steps] You owe it to the theatre people. [MORE still hesitates] We might be penned in there another hour; you told Mrs. More half- past ten; it'll only make her anxious. And she hasn't seen you for six weeks.

MORE. All right; don't dislocate my arm.

They move down the steps, and away to the left, as a boy comes running down the alley. Sighting MORE, he stops dead, spins round, and crying shrilly: "'Ere 'e is! That's 'im! 'Ere 'e is!" he bolts back in the direction whence he came.

STEEL. Quick, Sir, quick!

MORE. That is the end of the limit, as the foreign ambassador remarked.

STEEL. [Pulling him back towards the door] Well! come inside again, anyway!

A number of men and boys, and a few young girls, are trooping quickly from the left. A motley crew, out for excitement; loafers, artisans, navvies; girls, rough or dubious. All in the mood of hunters, and having tasted blood. They gather round the steps displaying the momentary irresolution and curiosity that follows on a new development of any chase. MORE, on the bottom step, turns and eyes them.

A GIRL. [At the edge] Which is 'im! The old 'un or the young?

[MORE turns, and mounts the remaining steps.]

TALL YOUTH. [With lank black hair under a bowler hat] You blasted traitor!

MORE faces round at the volley of jeering that follows; the chorus of booing swells, then gradually dies, as if they realized that they were spoiling their own sport.

A ROUGH GIRL. Don't frighten the poor feller!

[A girl beside her utters a shrill laugh.]

STEEL. [Tugging at MORE's arm] Come along, sir.

MORE. [Shaking his arm free—to the crowd] Well, what do you want?

A VOICE. Speech.

MORE. Indeed! That's new.

ROUGH VOICE. [At the back of the crowd] Look at his white liver. You can see it in his face.

A BIG NAVY. [In front] Shut it! Give 'im a chanst!

TALL YOUTH. Silence for the blasted traitor?

A youth plays the concertina; there is laughter, then an abrupt silence.

MORE. You shall have it in a nutshell!

A SHOPBOY. [Flinging a walnut-shell which strikes MORE on the shoulder] Here y'are!

MORE. Go home, and think! If foreigners invaded us, wouldn't you be fighting tooth and nail like those tribesmen, out there?

TALL YOUTH. Treacherous dogs! Why don't they come out in the open?

MORE. They fight the best way they can.

[A burst of hooting is led by a soldier in khaki on the outskirt.]

MORE. My friend there in khaki led that hooting. I've never said a word against our soldiers. It's the Government I condemn for putting them to this, and the Press for hounding on the Government, and all of you for being led by the nose to do what none of you would do, left to yourselves.

The TALL YOUTH leads a somewhat unspontaneous burst of execration.

MORE. I say not one of you would go for a weaker man.

VOICES IN THE CROWD.

ROUGH VOICE. Tork sense!

GIRL'S VOICE. He's gittin' at you!

TALL YOUTH'S VOICE. Shiny skunk!

A NAVVY. [Suddenly shouldering forward] Look 'ere, Mister! Don't you come gaflin' to those who've got mates out there, or it'll be the worse for you-you go 'ome!

COCKNEY VOICE. And git your wife to put cottonwool in yer ears.

[A spurt of laughter.]

A FRIENDLY VOICE. [From the outskirts] Shame! there! Bravo, More! Keep it up!

[A scuffle drowns this cry.]

MORE. [With vehemence] Stop that! Stop that! You——!

TALL YOUTH. Traitor!

AN ARTISAN. Who black-legged?

MIDDLE-AGED MAN. Ought to be shot-backin' his country's enemies!

MORE. Those tribesmen are defending their homes.

TWO VOICES. Hear! hear!

[They are hustled into silence.]

TALL YOUTH. Wind-bag!

MORE. [With sudden passion] Defending their homes! Not mobbing unarmed
men!

[STEEL again pulls at his arm.]

ROUGH. Shut it, or we'll do you in!

MORE. [Recovering his coolness] Ah! Do me in by all means! You'd deal such
a blow at cowardly mobs as wouldn't be forgotten in your time.

STEEL. For God's sake, sir!

MORE. [Shaking off his touch] Well!

There is an ugly rush, checked by the fall of the foremost figures, thrown too suddenly against the bottom step. The crowd recoils.

There is a momentary lull, and MORE stares steadily down at them.

COCKNEY VOICE. Don't 'e speak well! What eloquence!

Two or three nutshells and a piece of orange-peel strike MORE across the face.
He takes no notice.

ROUGH VOICE. That's it! Give 'im some encouragement.

The jeering laughter is changed to anger by the contemptuous smile on MORE'S
face.

A TALL YOUTH. Traitor!

A VOICE. Don't stand there like a stuck pig.

A ROUGH. Let's 'ave 'im dahn off that!

Under cover of the applause that greets this, he strikes MORE across the legs with a belt. STEEL starts forward. MORE, flinging out his arm, turns him back, and resumes his tranquil staring at the crowd, in whom the sense of being foiled by this silence is fast turning to rage.

THE CROWD. Speak up, or get down! Get off! Get away, there—or we'll make
             you! Go on!

[MORE remains immovable.]

A YOUTH. [In a lull of disconcertion] I'll make 'im speak! See!

He darts forward and spits, defiling MORES hand. MORE jerks it up as if it had been stung, then stands as still as ever. A spurt of laughter dies into a shiver of repugnance at the action. The shame is fanned again to fury by the sight of MORES scornful face.

TALL YOUTH. [Out of murmuring] Shift! or you'll get it!

A VOICE. Enough of your ugly mug!

A ROUGH. Give 'im one!

Two flung stones strike MORE. He staggers and nearly falls, then rights himself.

A GIRL'S VOICE. Shame!

FRIENDLY VOICE. Bravo, More! Stick to it!

A ROUGH. Give 'im another!

A VOICE. No!

A GIRL'S VOICE. Let 'im alone! Come on, Billy, this ain't no fun!

Still looking up at MORE, the whole crowd falls into an uneasy silence, broken only by the shuffling of feet. Then the BIG NAVVY in the front rank turns and elbows his way out to the edge of the crowd.

THE NAVVY. Let 'im be!

With half-sullen and half-shamefaced acquiescence the crowd breaks up and drifts back whence it came, till the alley is nearly empty.

MORE. [As if coming to, out of a trance-wiping his hand and dusting his coat] Well, Steel!

And followed by STEEL, he descends the steps and moves away. Two policemen pass glancing up at the broken glass. One of them stops and makes a note.

THE CURTAIN FALLS.

<u>SCENE II</u>

The window-end of KATHERINE'S bedroom, panelled in cream-coloured wood. The light from four candles is falling on KATHERINE, who is sitting before the silver mirror of an old oak dressing-table, brushing her hair. A door, on the left, stands ajar. An oak chair against the wall close to a recessed window is all the other furniture. Through this window the blue night is seen, where a mist is rolled out flat amongst trees, so that only dark clumps of boughs show here and there, beneath a moonlit sky. As the curtain rises, KATHERINE, with brush arrested, is listening. She begins again brushing her hair, then stops, and taking a packet of letters from a drawer of her dressing-table, reads. Through the just open door behind her comes the voice of OLIVE.

OLIVE. Mummy! I'm awake!

But KATHERINE goes on reading; and OLIVE steals into the room in her night-gown.

OLIVE. [At KATHERINE'S elbow—examining her watch on its stand] It's fourteen minutes to eleven.

KATHERINE. Olive, Olive!

OLIVE. I just wanted to see the time. I never can go to sleep if I try—it's quite helpless, you know. Is there a victory yet? [KATHERINE, shakes her head] Oh! I prayed extra special for one in the evening papers. [Straying round her mother] Hasn't Daddy come?

KATHERINE. Not yet.

OLIVE. Are you waiting for him? [Burying her face in her mother's hair] Your hair is nice, Mummy. It's particular to-night.

KATHERINE lets fall her brush, and looks at her almost in alarm.

OLIVE. How long has Daddy been away?

KATHERINE. Six weeks.

OLIVE. It seems about a hundred years, doesn't it? Has he been making speeches all the time?

KATHERINE. Yes.

OLIVE. To-night, too?

KATHERINE. Yes.

OLIVE. The night that man was here whose head's too bald for anything—oh! Mummy, you know—the one who cleans his teeth so termendously— I heard Daddy making a speech to the wind. It broke a wine-glass. His speeches must be good ones, mustn't they!

KATHERINE. Very.

OLIVE. It felt funny; you couldn't see any wind, you know.

KATHERINE. Talking to the wind is an expression, Olive.

OLIVE. Does Daddy often?

KATHERINE. Yes, nowadays.

OLIVE. What does it mean?

KATHERINE. Speaking to people who won't listen.

OLIVE. What do they do, then?

KATHERINE. Just a few people go to hear him, and then a great crowd comes and breaks in; or they wait for him outside, and throw things, and hoot.

OLIVE. Poor Daddy! Is it people on our side who throw things?

KATHERINE. Yes, but only rough people.

OLIVE. Why does he go on doing it? I shouldn't.

KATHERINE. He thinks it is his duty.

OLIVE. To your neighbour, or only to God?

KATHERINE. To both.

OLIVE. Oh! Are those his letters?

KATHERINE. Yes.

OLIVE. [Reading from the letter] "My dear Heart." Does he always call you his dear heart, Mummy? It's rather jolly, isn't it? "I shall be home about half-past ten to-morrow night. For a few hours the fires of p-u-r-g-a-t-or-y will cease to burn—" What are the fires of p-u-r-g-a-t-o-r-y?

KATHERINE. [Putting away the letters] Come, Olive!

OLIVE. But what are they?

KATHERINE. Daddy means that he's been very unhappy.

OLIVE. Have you, too?

KATHERINE. Yes.

OLIVE. [Cheerfully] So have I. May I open the window?

KATHERINE. No; you'll let the mist in.

OLIVE. Isn't it a funny mist-all flat!

KATHERINE. Now, come along, frog!

OLIVE. [Making time] Mummy, when is Uncle Hubert coming back?

KATHERINE. We don't know, dear.

OLIVE. I suppose Auntie Helen'll stay with us till he does.

KATHERINE. Yes.

OLIVE. That's something, isn't it?

KATHERINE. [Picking her up] Now then!

OLIVE. [Deliciously limp] Had I better put in the duty to your neighbour if there isn't a victory soon? [As they pass through the door] You're tickling under my knee! [Little gurgles of pleasure follow. Then silence. Then a drowsy voice] I must keep awake for Daddy.

KATHERINE comes back. She is about to leave the door a little open, when she hears a knock on the other door. It is opened a few inches, and NURSE'S voice says: "Can I come in, Ma'am?" The NURSE comes in.

KATHERINE. [Shutting OLIVE's door, and going up to her] What is it, Nurse?

NURSE. [Speaking in a low voice] I've been meaning to—I'll never do it in the daytime. I'm giving you notice.

KATHERINE. Nurse! You too!

She looks towards OLIVE'S room with dismay. The NURSE smudges a slow tear away from her cheek.

NURSE. I want to go right away at once.

KATHERINE. Leave Olive! That is the sins of the fathers with a vengeance.

NURSE. I've had another letter from my son. No, Miss Katherine, while the master goes on upholdin' these murderin' outlandish creatures, I can't live in this house, not now he's coming back.

KATHERINE. But, Nurse——!

NURSE. It's not like them [With an ineffable gesture] downstairs, because I'm frightened of the mob, or of the window's bein' broke again, or mind what the boys in the street say. I should think not— no! It's my heart. I'm sore night and day thinkin' of my son, and him lying out there at night without a rag of dry clothing, and water that the bullocks won't drink, and maggots in the meat; and every day one of his friends laid out stark and cold, and one day—'imself perhaps. If anything were to 'appen to him. I'd never forgive meself—here. Ah! Miss Katherine, I wonder how you bear it—bad news comin' every day—And Sir John's face so sad—And all the time the master speaking against us, as it might be Jonah 'imself.

KATHERINE. But, Nurse, how can you leave us, you?

NURSE. [Smudging at her cheeks] There's that tells me it's encouragin' something to happen, if I stay here; and Mr. More coming back to-night. You can't serve God and Mammon, the Bible says.

KATHERINE. Don't you know what it's costing him?

NURSE. Ah! Cost him his seat, and his reputation; and more than that it'll cost him, to go against the country.

KATHERINE. He's following his conscience.

NURSE. And others must follow theirs, too. No, Miss Katherine, for you to let him—you, with your three brothers out there, and your father fair wasting away with grief. Sufferin' too as you've been these three months past. What'll you feel if anything happens to my three young gentlemen out there, to my dear Mr. Hubert that I nursed myself, when your precious mother couldn't? What would she have said —with you in the camp of his enemies?

KATHERINE. Nurse, Nurse!

NURSE. In my paper they say he's encouraging these heathens and makin' the foreigners talk about us; and every day longer the war lasts, there's our blood on this house.

KATHERINE. [Turning away] Nurse, I can't—I won't listen.

NURSE. [Looking at her intently] Ah! You'll move him to leave off! I see your heart, my dear. But if you don't, then go I must!

She nods her head gravely, goes to the door of OLIVE'S room, opens it gently, stands looking for a-moment, then with the words "My Lamb!" she goes in noiselessly and closes the door.

KATHERINE turns back to her glass, puts back her hair, and smooths her lips and eyes. The door from the corridor is opened, and HELEN's voice says: "Kit! You're not in bed?"

KATHERINE. No.

HELEN too is in a wrapper, with a piece of lace thrown over her head. Her face is scared and miserable, and she runs into KATHERINE's arms.

KATHERINE. My dear, what is it?

HELEN. I've seen—a vision!

KATHERINE. Hssh! You'll wake Olive!

HELEN. [Staring before her] I'd just fallen asleep, and I saw a plain that seemed to run into the sky—like—that fog. And on it there were—dark things. One grew into a body without a head, and a gun by its side. And one was a man sitting huddled up, nursing a wounded leg. He had the face of Hubert's servant, Wreford. And then I saw—Hubert. His face was all dark and thin; and he had—a wound, an awful wound here [She touches her breast]. The blood was running from it, and he kept trying to stop it—oh! Kit—by kissing it [She pauses, stifled by emotion]. Then I heard Wreford laugh, and say vultures didn't touch live bodies. And there came a voice, from somewhere, calling out: "Oh! God! I'm dying!" And Wreford began to swear at it, and I heard Hubert say: "Don't, Wreford; let the poor fellow be!" But the voice went on and on, moaning and crying out: "I'll lie here all night dying—and then I'll die!" And Wreford dragged himself along the ground; his face all devilish, like a man who's going to kill.

KATHERINE. My dear! HOW ghastly!

HELEN. Still that voice went on, and I saw Wreford take up the dead man's gun. Then Hubert got upon his feet, and went tottering along, so feebly, so dreadfully—but before he could reach and stop him, Wreford fired at the man who was crying. And Hubert called out: "You brute!" and fell right down. And when Wreford saw him lying there, he began to moan and sob, but Hubert never stirred. Then it all got black again—and I could see a dark woman—thing creeping, first to the man without a head; then to Wreford; then to Hubert, and it touched him, and sprang away. And it cried out: "A-ai-ah!" [Pointing out at the mist] Look! Out there! The dark things!

KATHERINE. [Putting her arms round her] Yes, dear, yes! You must have been looking at the mist.

HELEN. [Strangely calm] He's dead!

KATHERINE. It was only a dream.

HELEN. You didn't hear that cry. [She listens] That's Stephen. Forgive me, Kit; I oughtn't to have upset you, but I couldn't help coming.

She goes out, KATHERINE, into whom her emotion seems to have passed, turns feverishly to the window, throws it open and leans out. MORE comes in.

MORE. Kit!

Catching sight of her figure in the window, he goes quickly to her.

KATHERINE. Ah! [She has mastered her emotion.]

MORE. Let me look at you!

He draws her from the window to the candle-light, and looks long at her.

MORE. What have you done to your hair?

KATHERINE. Nothing.

MORE. It's wonderful to-night.

[He takes it greedily and buries his face in it.]

KATHERINE. [Drawing her hair away] Well?

MORE. At last!

KATHERINE. [Pointing to OLIVE's room] Hssh!

MORE. How is she?

KATHERINE. All right.

MORE. And you?

[KATHERINE shrugs her shoulders.]

MORE. Six weeks!

KATHERINE. Why have you come?

MORE. Why!

KATHERINE. You begin again the day after tomorrow. Was it worth while?

MORE. Kit!

KATHERINE. It makes it harder for me, that's all.

MORE. [Staring at her] What's come to you?

KATHERINE. Six weeks is a long time to sit and read about your meetings.

MORE. Put that away to-night. [He touches her] This is what travellers feel
       when they come out of the desert to-water.

KATHERINE. [Suddenly noticing the cut on his forehead] Your forehead! It's
            cut.

MORE. It's nothing.

KATHERINE. Oh! Let me bathe it!

MORE. No, dear! It's all right.

KATHERINE. [Turning away] Helen has just been telling me a dream she's had
          of Hubert's death.

MORE. Poor child!

KATHERINE. Dream bad dreams, and wait, and hide oneself—there's been
          nothing else to do. Nothing, Stephen—nothing!

MORE. Hide? Because of me?

[KATHERINE nods.]

MORE. [With a movement of distress] I see. I thought from your letters you
          were coming to feel——. Kit! You look so lovely!

[Suddenly he sees that she is crying, and goes quickly to her.]

MORE. My dear, don't cry! God knows I don't want to make things worse for
          you. I'll go away.

She draws away from him a little, and after looking long at her, he sits down at
the dressing-table and begins turning over the brushes and articles of toilet, trying to find words.

MORE. Never look forward. After the time I've had—I thought— tonight—it
would be summer—I thought it would be you—and everything!

While he is speaking KATHERINE has stolen closer. She suddenly drops on her
knees by his side and wraps his hand in her hair. He turns and clasps her.

MORE. Kit!

KATHERINE. Ah! yes! But-to-morrow it begins again. Oh! Stephen! How
          long—how long am I to be torn in two? [Drawing back in his
          arms] I can't—can't bear it.

MORE. My darling!

KATHERINE. Give it up! For my sake! Give it up! [Pressing closer to him] It shall be me—and everything——

MORE. God!

KATHERINE. It shall be—if—if——

MORE. [Aghast] You're not making terms? Bargaining? For God's sake, Kit!

KATHERINE. For God's sake, Stephen!

MORE. You!—of all people—you!

KATHERINE. Stephen!

[For a moment MORE yields utterly, then shrinks back.]

MORE. A bargain! It's selling my soul!

He struggles out of her arms, gets up, and stands without speaking, staring at her, and wiping the sweat from his forehead. KATHERINE remains some seconds on her knees, gazing up at him, not realizing. Then her head droops; she too gets up and stands apart, with her wrapper drawn close round her. It is as if a cold and deadly shame had come to them both. Quite suddenly MORE turns, and, without looking back, feebly makes his way out of the room. When he is gone KATHERINE drops on her knees and remains there motionless, huddled in her hair.

THE CURTAIN FALLS

ACT IV

It is between lights, the following day, in the dining-room of MORE's house. The windows are closed, but curtains are not drawn. STEEL is seated at the bureau, writing a letter from MORE's dictation.

STEEL. [Reading over the letter] "No doubt we shall have trouble. But, if the town authorities at the last minute forbid the use of the hall, we'll hold the meeting in the open. Let bills be got out, and an audience will collect in any case."

MORE. They will.

STEEL. "Yours truly"; I've signed for you.

[MORE nods.]

STEEL. [Blotting and enveloping the letter] You know the servants have all given notice—except Henry.

MORE. Poor Henry!

STEEL. It's partly nerves, of course—the windows have been broken twice—but it's partly——

MORE.   Patriotism.   Quite! they'll do the next smashing themselves. That reminds me—to-morrow you begin holiday, Steel.

STEEL.   Oh, no!

MORE.   My dear fellow—yes. Last night ended your sulphur cure. Truly sorry ever to have let you in for it.

STEEL.   Some one must do the work. You're half dead as it is.

MORE.   There's lots of kick in me.

STEEL.   Give it up, sir. The odds are too great. It isn't worth it.

MORE.   To fight to a finish; knowing you must be beaten—is anything better worth it?

STEEL.   Well, then, I'm not going.

MORE.   This is my private hell, Steel; you don't roast in it any longer. Believe me, it's a great comfort to hurt no one but yourself.

STEEL.   I can't leave you, sir.

MORE.   My dear boy, you're a brick—but we've got off by a miracle so far, and I can't have the responsibility of you any longer. Hand me over that correspondence about to-morrow's meeting.

STEEL takes some papers from his pocket, but does not hand them.

MORE.   Come! [He stretches out his hand for the papers. As STEEL still draws back, he says more sharply] Give them to me, Steel! [STEEL hands them over] Now, that ends it, d'you see?

They stand looking at each other; then STEEL, very much upset, turns and goes out of the room. MORE, who has watched him with a sorry smile, puts the papers into a dispatch-case. As he is closing the bureau, the footman HENRY enters, announcing: "Mr. Mendip, sir." MENDIP comes in, and the FOOT-MAN withdraws. MORE turns to his visitor, but does not hold out his hand.

MENDIP.   [Taking MORE'S hand] Give me credit for a little philosophy, my friend. Mrs. More told me you'd be back to-day. Have you heard?

MORE. What?

MENDIP. There's been a victory.

MORE. Thank God!

MENDIP. Ah! So you actually are flesh and blood.

MORE. Yes!

MENDIP. Take off the martyr's shirt, Stephen. You're only flouting human
nature.

MORE. So—even you defend the mob!

MENDIP. My dear fellow, you're up against the strongest common instinct in the
world. What do you expect? That the man in the street should be a
Quixote? That his love of country should express itself in philosoph-
ic altruism? What on earth do you expect? Men are very simple creatures; and Mob is just conglomerate essence of simple men.

MORE. Conglomerate excrescence. Mud of street and market-place gathered in
a torrent—This blind howling "patriotism"—what each man feels in
here? [He touches his breast] No!

MENDIP. You think men go beyond instinct—they don't. All they know is that
something's hurting that image of themselves that they call country.
They just feel something big and religious, and go it blind.

MORE. This used to be the country of free speech. It used to be the country
where a man was expected to hold to his faith.

MENDIP. There are limits to human nature, Stephen.

MORE. Let no man stand to his guns in face of popular attack. Still your advice,
is it?

MENDIP. My advice is: Get out of town at once. The torrent you speak of will
be let loose the moment this news is out. Come, my dear fellow, don't
stay here!

MORE. Thanks! I'll see that Katherine and Olive go.

MENDIP. Go with them! If your cause is lost, that's no reason why you should be.

MORE. There's the comfort of not running away. And—I want comfort.

MENDIP. This is bad, Stephen; bad, foolish—foolish. Well! I'm going to the House. This way?

MORE. Down the steps, and through the gate. Good-bye?

KATHERINE has come in followed by NURSE, hatted and cloaked, with a small bag in her hand. KATHERINE takes from the bureau a cheque which she hands to the NURSE. MORE comes in from the terrace.

MORE. You're wise to go, Nurse.

NURSE. You've treated my poor dear badly, sir. Where's your heart?

MORE. In full use.

NURSE. On those heathens. Don't your own hearth and home come first? Your wife, that was born in time of war, with her own father fighting, and her grandfather killed for his country. A bitter thing, to have the windows of her house broken, and be pointed at by the boys in the street.

[MORE stands silent under this attack, looking at his wife.]

KATHERINE. Nurse!

NURSE. It's unnatural, sir—what you're doing! To think more of those savages than of your own wife! Look at her! Did you ever see her look like that? Take care, sir, before it's too late!

MORE. Enough, please!

NURSE stands for a moment doubtful; looks long at KATHERINE; then goes.

MORE. [Quietly] There has been a victory.

[He goes out. KATHERINE is breathing fast, listening to the distant hum and stir rising in the street. She runs to the window as the footman, HENRY, entering, says: "Sir John Julian, Ma'am!" SIR JOHN comes in, a newspaper in his hand.]

KATHERINE. At last! A victory!

SIR JOHN. Thank God! [He hands her the paper.]

KATHERINE. Oh, Dad!

[She tears the paper open, and feverishly reads.]

KATHERINE. At last!

The distant hum in the street is rising steadily. But SIR JOHN, after the one exultant moment when he handed her the paper, stares dumbly at the floor.

KATHERINE. [Suddenly conscious of his gravity] Father!

SIR JOHN. There is other news.

KATHERINE. One of the boys? Hubert?

[SIR JOHN bows his head.]

KATHERINE. Killed?

[SIR JOHN again bows his head.]

KATHERINE. The dream! [She covers her face] Poor Helen!

They stand for a few seconds silent, then SIR JOHN raises his head, and putting up a hand, touches her wet cheek.

SIR JOHN. [Huskily] Whom the gods love——

KATHERINE. Hubert!

SIR JOHN. And hulks like me go on living!

KATHERINE. Dear Dad!

SIR JOHN. But we shall drive the ruffians now! We shall break them. Stephen back?

KATHERINE. Last night.

SIR JOHN. Has he finished his blasphemous speech-making at last? [KATHER-INE shakes her head] Not?

[Then, seeing that KATHERINE is quivering with emotion, he ` strokes her hand.]

SIR JOHN. My dear! Death is in many houses!

KATHERINE. I must go to Helen. Tell Stephen, Father. I can't.

SIR JOHN. If you wish, child.

[She goes out, leaving SIR JOHN to his grave, puzzled grief, and in a few seconds MORE comes in.]

MORE. Yes, Sir John. You wanted me?

SIR JOHN. Hubert is killed.

MORE. Hubert!

SIR JOHN. By these—whom you uphold. Katherine asked me to let you know. She's gone to Helen. I understand you only came back last night from your——No word I can use would give what I feel about that. I don't know how things stand now between you and Katherine; but I tell you this, Stephen: you've tried her these last two months beyond what any woman ought to bear!

[MORE makes a gesture of pain.]

SIR JOHN. When you chose your course——

MORE. Chose!

SIR JOHN. You placed yourself in opposition to every feeling in her. You knew this might come. It may come again with another of my sons

MORE. I would willingly change places with any one of them.

SIR JOHN. Yes—I can believe in your unhappiness. I cannot conceive of greater misery than to be arrayed against your country. If I could have Hubert back, I would not have him at such a price—no, nor all my sons. 'Pro patri mori'—My boy, at all events, is happy!

MORE. Yes!

SIR JOHN. Yet you can go on doing what you are! What devil of pride has got into you, Stephen?

MORE. Do you imagine I think myself better than the humblest private fighting out there? Not for a minute.

SIR JOHN. I don't understand you. I always thought you devoted to Katherine.

MORE. Sir John, you believe that country comes before wife and child?

SIR JOHN. I do.

MORE. So do I.

SIR JOHN. [Bewildered] Whatever my country does or leaves undone, I no more presume to judge her than I presume to judge my God. [With all the exaltation of the suffering he has undergone for her] My country!

MORE. I would give all I have—for that creed.

SIR JOHN. [Puzzled] Stephen, I've never looked on you as a crank; I always believed you sane and honest. But this is—visionary mania.

MORE. Vision of what might be.

SIR JOHN. Why can't you be content with what the grandest nation— the grandest men on earth—have found good enough for them? I've known them, I've seen what they could suffer, for our country.

MORE. Sir John, imagine what the last two months have been to me! To see people turn away in the street—old friends pass me as if I were a wall! To dread the post! To go to bed every night with the sound of hooting in my ears! To know that my name is never referred to without contempt——

SIR JOHN. You have your new friends. Plenty of them, I understand.

MORE. Does that make up for being spat at as I was last night? Your battles are fool's play to it.

The stir and rustle of the crowd in the street grows louder. SIR JOHN turns his head towards it.

SIR JOHN. You've heard there's been a victory. Do you carry your unnatural feeling so far as to be sorry for that? [MORE shakes his head] That's something! For God's sake, Stephen, stop before it's gone past mending. Don't ruin your life with Katherine. Hubert was her favourite brother; you are backing those who killed him. Think what that means to her! Drop this—mad Quixotism—idealism—whatever you call it. Take Katherine away. Leave the country till the thing's over—this country of yours that you're opposing, and—and— traducing. Take her away! Come! What good are you doing? What earthly good? Come, my boy! Before you're utterly undone.

MORE. Sir John! Our men are dying out there for, the faith that's in them! I believe my faith the higher, the better for mankind—Am I to slink away? Since I began this campaign I've found hundreds who've thanked me for taking this stand. They look on me now as their leader. Am I to desert them? When you led your forlorn hope— did you ask yourself what good you were doing, or, whether you'd come through alive? It's my forlorn hope not to betray those who are following me; and not to help let die a fire—a fire that's sacred— not only now in this country, but in all countries, for all time.

SIR JOHN. [After a long stare] I give you credit for believing what you say. But let me tell you whatever that fire you talk of—I'm too old-fashioned to grasp—one fire you are letting die—your wife's love. By God! This crew of your new friends, this crew of cranks and jays, if they can make up to you for the loss of her love—of your career, of all those who used to like and respect you—so much the better for you. But if you find yourself bankrupt of affection— alone as the last man on earth; if this business ends in your utter ruin and destruction—as it must—I shall not pity—I cannot pity you. Good-night!

He marches to the door, opens it, and goes out. MORE is left standing perfectly still. The stir and murmur of the street is growing all the time, and slowly forces itself on his consciousness. He goes to the bay window and looks out; then rings the bell. It is not answered, and, after turning up the lights, he rings again. KATHERINE comes in. She is wearing a black hat, and black outdoor coat. She speaks coldly without looking up.

KATHERINE. You rang!

MORE. For them to shut this room up.

KATHERINE. The servants have gone out. They're afraid of the house being set on fire.

MORE. I see.

KATHERINE. They have not your ideals to sustain them. [MORE winces] I am going with Helen and Olive to Father's.

MORE. [Trying to take in the exact sense of her words] Good! You prefer that to an hotel? [KATHERINE nods. Gently] Will you let me say, Kit, how terribly I feel for you—Hubert's——

KATHERINE. Don't. I ought to have made what I meant plainer. I am not coming back.

MORE. Not? Not while the house——

KATHERINE. Not—at all.

MORE. Kit!

KATHERINE. I warned you from the first. You've gone too far!

MORE. [Terribly moved] Do you understand what this means? After ten years—and all—our love!

KATHERINE. Was it love? How could you ever have loved one so unheroic as myself!

MORE. This is madness, Kit—Kit!

KATHERINE. Last night I was ready. You couldn't. If you couldn't then, you never can. You are very exalted, Stephen. I don't like living—I won't live, with one whose equal I am not. This has been coming ever since you made that speech. I told you that night what the end would be.

MORE. [Trying to put his arms round her] Don't be so terribly cruel!

KATHERINE. No! Let's have the truth! People so wide apart don't love! Let me go!

MORE. In God's name, how can I help the difference in our faiths?

KATHERINE. Last night you used the word—bargain. Quite right. I meant to buy you. I meant to kill your faith. You showed me what I was doing. I don't like to be shown up as a driver of bargains, Stephen.

MORE. God knows—I never meant——

KATHERINE. If I'm not yours in spirit—I don't choose to be your— mistress.

MORE, as if lashed by a whip, has thrown up his hands in an attitude of defence.

KATHERINE. Yes, that's cruel! It shows the heights you live on. I won't drag you down.

MORE. For God's sake, put your pride away, and see! I'm fighting for the faith that's in me. What else can a man do? What else? Ah! Kit! Do see!

KATHERINE. I'm strangled here! Doing nothing—sitting silent—when my brothers are fighting, and being killed. I shall try to go out nursing. Helen will come with me. I have my faith, too; my poor common love of country. I can't stay here with you. I spent last night on the floor—thinking—and I know!

MORE. And Olive?

KATHERINE. I shall leave her at Father's, with Nurse; unless you forbid me to
          take her. You can.

MORE. [Icily] That I shall not do—you know very well. You are free to go, and
          to take her.

KATHERINE. [Very low] Thank you! [Suddenly she turns to him, and draws
          his eyes on her. Without a sound, she puts her whole strength
          into that look] Stephen! Give it up! Come down to me!

The festive sounds from the street grow louder. There can be heard the blowing
of whistles, and bladders, and all the sounds of joy.

MORE. And drown in—that?

KATHERINE turns swiftly to the door. There she stands and again looks at him.
Her face is mysterious, from the conflicting currents of her emotions.

MORE. So—you're going?

KATHERINE. [In a whisper] Yes.

She bends her head, opens the door, and goes. MORE starts forward as if to follow her, but OLIVE has appeared in the doorway. She has on a straight little
white coat and a round white cap.

OLIVE. Aren't you coming with us, Daddy?

[MORE shakes his head.]

OLIVE. Why not?

MORE. Never mind, my dicky bird.

OLIVE. The motor'll have to go very slow. There are such a lot of people in the
          street. Are you staying to stop them setting the house on fire? [MORE
          nods] May I stay a little, too? [MORE shakes his head] Why?

MORE. [Putting his hand on her head] Go along, my pretty!

OLIVE. Oh! love me up, Daddy!

[MORE takes and loves her up]

OLIVE. Oo-o!

MORE. Trot, my soul!

[She goes, looks back at him, turns suddenly, and vanishes.]

MORE follows her to the door, but stops there. Then, as full realization begins to dawn on him, he runs to the bay window, craning his head to catch sight of the front door. There is the sound of a vehicle starting, and the continual hooting of its horn as it makes its way among the crowd. He turns from the window.

MORE. Alone as the last man on earth!

[Suddenly a voice rises clear out of the hurly-burly in the street.]

VOICE. There 'e is! That's 'im! More! Traitor! More!

A shower of nutshells, orange-peel, and harmless missiles begins to rattle against the glass of the window. Many voices take up the groaning: "More! Traitor! Black-leg! More!" And through the window can be seen waving flags and lighted Chinese lanterns, swinging high on long bamboos. The din of execration swells. MORE stands unheeding, still gazing after the cab. Then, with a sharp crack, a flung stone crashes through one of the panes. It is followed by a hoarse shout of laughter, and a hearty groan. A second stone crashes through the glass. MORE turns for a moment, with a contemptuous look, towards the street, and the flare of the Chinese lanterns lights up his face. Then, as if forgetting all about the din outside, he moves back into the room, looks round him, and lets his head droop. The din rises louder and louder; a third stone crashes through. MORE raises his head again, and, clasping his hands, looks straight before him. The footman, HENRY, entering, hastens to the French windows.

MORE. Ah! Henry, I thought you'd gone.

FOOTMAN. I came back, sir.

MORE. Good fellow!

FOOTMAN. They're trying to force the terrace gate, sir. They've no business coming on to private property—no matter what!

In the surging entrance of the mob the footman, HENRY, who shows fight, is overwhelmed, hustled out into the crowd on the terrace, and no more seen. The MOB is a mixed crowd of revellers of both sexes, medical students, clerks, shop men and girls, and a Boy Scout or two. Many have exchanged hats—Some wear masks, or false noses, some carry feathers or tin whistles. Some, with bamboos and Chinese lanterns, swing them up outside on the terrace. The medley of noises is very great. Such ringleaders as exist in the confusion are a GROUP OF STU-DENTS, the chief of whom, conspicuous because unadorned, is an athletic, hat-less young man with a projecting underjaw, and heavy coal-black moustache, who seems with the swing of his huge arms and shoulders to sway the currents of motion. When the first surge of noise and movement subsides, he calls out: "To him, boys! Chair the hero!" THE STUDENTS rush at the impassive MORE, swing him roughly on to their shoulders and bear him round the room. When they have twice circled the table to the music of their confused singing, groans and whistling, THE CHIEF OF THE STUDENTS calls out: "Put him down!" Obediently they set him down on the table which has been forced into the bay window, and stand gaping up at him.

CHIEF STUDENT. Speech! Speech!

[The noise ebbs, and MORE looks round him.]

CHIEF STUDENT. Now then, you, sir.

MORE. [In a quiet voice] Very well. You are here by the law that governs the action of all mobs—the law of Force. By that law, you can do what you like to this body of mine.

A VOICE. And we will, too.

MORE. I don't doubt it. But before that, I've a word to say.

A VOICE. You've always that.

[ANOTHER VOICE raises a donkey's braying.]

MORE. You—Mob—are the most contemptible thing under the sun. When you walk the street—God goes in.

CHIEF STUDENT. Be careful, you—sir.

VOICES. Down him! Down with the beggar!

MORE. [Above the murmurs] My fine friends, I'm not afraid of you. You've forced your way into my house, and you've asked me to speak. Put up with the truth for once! [His words rush out] You are the thing that pelts the weak; kicks women; howls down free speech. This to-day, and that to-morrow. Brain—you have none. Spirit—not the ghost of it! If you're not meanness, there's no such thing. If you're not cowardice, there is no cowardice [Above the growing fierceness of the hubbub] Patriotism—there are two kinds—that of our soldiers, and this of mine. You have neither!

CHIEF STUDENT. [Checking a dangerous rush] Hold on! Hold on! [To MORE] Swear to utter no more blasphemy against your country: Swear it!

CROWD. Ah! Ay! Ah!

MORE. My country is not yours. Mine is that great country which shall never take toll from the weakness of others. [Above the groaning] Ah! you can break my head and my windows; but don't think that you can break my faith. You could never break or shake it, if you were a million to one.

A girl with dark eyes and hair all wild, leaps out from the crowd and shakes her fist at him.

GIRL. You're friends with them that killed my lad! [MORE smiles down at her, and she swiftly plucks the knife from the belt of a Boy Scout beside her] Smile, you—cur!

A violent rush and heave from behind flings MORE forward on to the steel. He reels, staggers back, and falls down amongst the crowd. A scream, a sway, a rush, a hubbub of cries. The CHIEF STUDENT shouts above the riot: "Steady!" Another: "My God! He's got it!"

CHIEF STUDENT. Give him air!

The crowd falls back, and two STUDENTS, bending over MORE, lift his arms and head, but they fall like lead. Desperately they test him for life.

CHIEF STUDENT. By the Lord, it's over!

Then begins a scared swaying out towards the window. Some one turns out the lights, and in the darkness the crowd fast melts away. The body of MORE lies in the gleam from a single Chinese lantern. Muttering the words: "Poor devil! He kept his end up anyway!" the CHIEF STUDENT picks from the floor a little abandoned Union Jack and lays it on MORE's breast. Then he, too, turns, and rushes out.

And the body of MORE lies in the streak of light; and flee noises in the street continue to rise.

THE CURTAIN FALLS, BUT RISES AGAIN ALMOST AT ONCE.

AFTERMATH

A late Spring dawn is just breaking. Against trees in leaf and blossom, with the houses of a London Square beyond, suffused by the spreading glow, is seen a dark life-size statue on a granite pedestal. In front is the broad, dust-dim pavement. The light grows till the central words around the pedestal can be clearly read:

ERECTED To the Memory of STEPHEN MORE "Faithful to his ideal"

High above, the face of MORE looks straight before him with a faint smile. On one shoulder and on his bare head two sparrows have perched, and from the gardens, behind, comes the twittering and singing of birds.

THE CURTAIN FALLS.

2099623R00366

Printed in Great Britain
by Amazon.co.uk, Ltd.,
Marston Gate.